THE SUPREME COURT
IN A FREE SOCIETY

Alpheus Thomas Mason and William M. Beaney
PRINCETON UNIVERSITY

THE SUPREME COURT
IN A FREE SOCIETY

W · W · NORTON & COMPANY · INC · New York

SBN 393 09777 3

LIBRARY OF CONGRESS CATALOG CARD NO. 67–28498

PRINTED IN THE UNITED STATES OF AMERICA

2 3 4 5 6 7 8 9 0

CONTENTS

PREFACE

This book discusses the Supreme Court against a background of history and theory, portraying the Judiciary as a *participant* in the political process. Each chapter is organized around a basic topic; each is alert to forces and factors that inevitably affect judicial decision. The Court's relation to administrative action and the increasing importance of statutory interpretation are taken into account. Highlighted are certain critical periods—1803, 1857, 1895, 1937, 1954—during which the Court's role has been hotly debated and illuminated.

American constitutional law is not a closed system. It bristles with alternatives. The Judiciary, hardly less than other branches of the government, is a forum wherein great public issues are explored, debated, decided, but never finally resolved. Though the decisions now stirring protest find strong support in the Constitution and in our heritage, few would be so rash as to contend that the Warren Court has now entered upon an era in which it will lead and instruct public opinion rather than merely follow it. In the judicial process, as elsewhere, everything turns on men.

Demonstrated throughout this book is the Court's high-minded effort to achieve free government—"to temper together," as Burke put it, "the opposite elements of liberty and restraint in one consistent work." This quest requires "a sagacious, powerful, and combining mind."

"Our Courts have occasionally misused their great power of judicial review," as Chief Justice Warren has said, "but never to the point of justifying forfeiture."

A.T.M.
W.M.B.

Princeton, New Jersey

I

THE COURT IS
THE CONSTITUTION

THE CONSTITUTION OF 1787 AND
its twenty-two amendments can be read in about half an hour. One
could memorize the written document word for word, as many
school children did a generation ago, and still know little or nothing
of its meaning or implications. The reason is that the formal body
of rules known as *constitutional law* consists primarily of decisions
and opinions of the United States Supreme Court—that is, the gloss
or veneer the Justices have spread on the formal document itself.
"The gloss, not the text, is the thing."

Yet the historian Charles Warren cautions us not to forget that,
"however the Court may interpret the provisions of the Constitution, it is still the Constitution which is law and not the decisions
of the Court." The Constitution itself, Justice Frankfurter declares,
is the "ultimate touchstone of constitutionality." Against all such
reminders stands Charles Evans Hughes's blunt assertion of 1907,
"The Constitution is what the Judges say it is." "The Supreme
Court," Professor Frankfurter used to tell his law students, "*is* the
Constitution."

GRANTING AND LIMITING POWER

"What is the Constitution?" Justice Paterson inquired in a Supreme Court opinion of 1795. "It is the form of government," he answered, "delineated by the mighty hand of the people, in which certain first principles of fundamental law are established." To all the agencies of government, the Constitution stands in the relationship of creator to creatures. "The theory of our governments, state and national," Justice Miller commented in 1875, "is opposed to the deposit of unlimited power anywhere." There is, Woodrow Wilson remarked, "no sovereign government in America."

The intricate design of our basic law is in response to the problem James Madison posed in *The Federalist*, No. 51: "In framing a government which is to be administered by men over men, the great difficulty lies in this: you must first enable the government to control the governed; and in the next place oblige it to control itself." The Constitution both grants and limits power. Article I lists the powers of Congress; Article II invests executive authority in the President; Article III confers the judicial power of the United States on one Supreme Court and on such other courts as Congress may establish. Article I, Section 9, restrains national power; Article I, Section 10, restricts the states. But the Constitution itself provides no *definition* of either powers or limitations.

In ways both obvious and subtle, the Constitution appears to be an instrument of rights and of limitations, rather than of powers. Certain things Congress is expressly forbidden to do. It may not pass an *ex post facto* law or a bill of attainder; it may not tax exports from any state; and it may not—except in great emergencies—suspend the writ of habeas corpus. The Bill of Rights (Amendments I through VIII) contains a long list of things the national government is powerless to do. The state governments are similarly circumscribed. They may not enact *ex post facto* laws, coin money, emit bills of credit, or enter into any treaty or alliance with a foreign state.

The framers of the Constitution sought in other ways to control the governors. Separation of powers and federalism, the "due process" clauses of the Constitution, and the doctrine of judicial review manifest the framers' determination to oblige the government to restrain itself. None of these limiting principles is spelled out; they are either implicit in the organization and structure of the Constitution, or, as with judicial review, deducible from its general provisions.

The separation of powers principle in our law divides and limits authority even as it confers it. Congress is endowed with legislative power; it may not, therefore (except as a result of a specific grant or by implication), exercise executive or judicial power. The same restrictions apply to the other major branches of the national government: the terms *judicial power* and *executive power*, like *legislative power*, have a technical meaning. In the exercise of their respective functions neither Congress, President, nor Judiciary may, under the principle of separation of powers, invade fields allocated to the other branches of government. Instead of requiring that the departments be kept *absolutely* separate and distinct, however, the Constitution blends and mingles their functions. Congress is granted legislative power, but the grant is not exclusive. Lawmaking is shared by the President in his exercise of the veto. The appointing authority is vested in the President; but the Senate must give its advice and consent to certain appointments.

Federalism, the second great limiting principle, means a constitutional system in which two authorities, each having a complete governmental system, exist in the same territory and act on the same people. In its American manifestation, federalism is a complicated arrangement whereby the national government exercises certain enumerated powers, all others being "reserved to the States respectively, or to the people." Each government is supreme within its own sphere; neither is supreme within the sphere of the other. Thus federalism, like separation of powers and checks and balances, is a means of compelling government to control itself.

Madison describes this system of intricate controls as a "compound republic." "The power surrendered by the people is first divided between two distinct governments (the national government and the states) and then the portion allotted to each subdivided among distinct and separate departments. Hence a double security arises to the rights of the people. The different governments will control

each other, at the same time that each will be controlled by itself."
Just how such controls were to be enforced, the Father of the
Constitution did not say.

Not only is each government, national and state, bound to restrain
itself lest the operations of one encroach upon the domain of the
other, but each must heed the injunction that "no person" may be
deprived of life, liberty, or property "without due process of law."
The Fifth Amendment limits national authority in this respect; the
Fourteenth Amendment controls the states. Applying standards
drawn from the vague "due process" formula, the courts constitute
the ultimate safeguard of individual privilege and governmental
prerogative alike. As to all these relations—those of the various
organs of the national government to each other, of the states and
national government, and of both these authorities to individual
rights—the judiciary is, in the words of Woodrow Wilson, "the
balance-wheel of our entire system."

Madison and Hamilton used a more positive label to describe
the role of courts in American society. They referred to them as
"guardians." "The want of a Judiciary," observed Hamilton in
Federalist, No. 22, "was the circumstance which crown[ed] the
defects of the [Articles] of Confederation." There ought to be,
he had remarked on the floor of the Philadelphia Convention, "a
principle in government capable of resisting the popular current."
"When occasions present themselves," he wrote in *Federalist*, No.
71, "in which the interests of the people are at variance with their
inclinations, it is the duty of the persons whom they have appointed
to be the guardians of those interests to withstand the temporary
delusion, in order to give them time and opportunity for more
cool and sedate reflection."

In piloting the bill of rights through the first Congress, Madison
explained:

> The prescriptions in favor of liberty ought to be levelled against
> that quarter where the greatest danger lies, namely, that which
> possesses the highest prerogative of power. But this is not found in
> either the Executive or Legislative departments of Government,
> but in the body of the people, operating by the majority against
> the minority. . . . If they [the bill of rights] are incorporated into
> the Constitution, independent tribunals of justice will consider
> themselves in a peculiar manner the guardians of those rights; they
> will be an impenetrable bulwark against every assumption of power

in the Legislative or Executive; they will be naturally led to resist every encroachment upon rights, expressly stipulated for in the Constitution by the declaration of rights.

Hamilton's famous essay, *Federalist, No. 78*, is more than an apologia of judicial review; it is also a demonstration of how the Court could be counted on to safeguard individual rights against the excesses of popular power. "In a monarchy," he reasoned, "[the Judiciary] is an excellent barrier to the despotism of the prince; in a republic, it is a no less excellent barrier to the encroachments and oppressions of the representative body." The Judiciary is necessary "to guard the constitution and rights of the individuals, from the effects of those ill-humours which the arts of designing men, or the influence of particular conjunctures, sometimes disseminate among the people themselves, and which though they speedily give place to better information, and more deliberate reflection, have a tendency, in the meantime, to occasion dangerous innovations in the government and serious oppressions of the minor part in the community."

The founding fathers, being distrustful of popular power and alert to the necessity of safeguarding individual rights against "interested and overbearing majorities," established *free government*. Those entrusted with the management of public affairs must, of course, be governed by "the deliberate sense of the community," but "unqualified complaisance to every sudden breeze of passion, or every transient impulse" was not considered either necessary or desirable. Unrestrained majority rule, a political system absolutely dependent on society, was rejected as not providing adequate security for individual liberties, rights, and privileges. Government must be dependent on the people, but the government itself ought to possess the independence necessary to guard the "liberties of a great community."

Americans, unlike most freedom-loving people, have not been content to rely on political checks. "A dependence on the people," Madison held, "is, no doubt, the primary control on the government; but experience has taught mankind the necessity of auxiliary precautions." Government is kept within bounds, not only by the electoral process, but also by separation of powers, federalism, "due process of law," and (as an adjunct to all these) the well-nigh unique device of judicial review.

The Founding Fathers made the Constitution "the supreme law of the land" but they left open the question of who was to sustain this supremacy. They did not say precisely whether this responsibility lay with the men who make the law, those who execute it, or the judges who interpret it. That the Constitution itself does not settle this matter is all the more extraordinary in light of the discussion in the Philadelphia Convention of 1787. At one point it was proposed that each House of Congress might, when in doubt, call upon the judges for an opinion as to the validity of national legislation. Madison said that a "law violating a constitution established by the people themselves would be considered by the judges as null and void."

More than once delegates suggested and urged with much persistence that Supreme Court Justices be joined with the Executive in a council of revision, and empowered to veto congressional legislation. Certain delegates objected to this proposal, contending that the Justices would have this power anyway in cases properly before them. Any such provision would be objectionable as giving the Court a double check. It would compromise "the impartiality of the Court by making them go on record before they were called in due course, to give . . . their exposition of the laws, which involved a power of deciding on their constitutionality." Other members of the Convention expressly denied that the Justices would sit in judgment as to acts of Congress. Judicial review, Elbridge Gerry objected, would have the effect of "making statesmen of judges, setting them up as guardians of the rights of the people." He would have preferred reliance on the Representatives of the people as the guardians of their rights and interests.

In the end the power of judicial review was not expressly granted, leading Professor Edward S. Corwin to conclude that "judicial review [of acts of Congress] was rested by the framers of the Constitution upon certain general principles which in their estimation made a specific provision for it unnecessary." Professor William W. Crosskey, on the other hand, queries the contention that general judicial review was a widely accepted or favored institution in 1787. "Judicial review," he writes, "was not meant to be provided generally in the Constitution, as to acts of Congress, though it was meant to be provided generally as to the acts of the states, and a limited right likewise was intended to be given to the Court, even as against Congress, to preserve its own judiciary prerogatives intact."

Whatever the reason for leaving the matter unresolved, Hamilton upheld the doctrine of judicial review. It is the duty of the Court, he wrote in *Federalist*, No. 78, "to declare all acts contrary to the manifest tenor of the Constitution void." Specific limitations on legislative power could be preserved in no other way "than through the medium of courts of justice." The Constitution is fundamental *law*, and in deciding "cases" and "controversies" judges must ascertain the meaning of law, whether contained in the Constitution or in a legislative act. "If there should happen to be an irreconcilable variance between the two," Hamilton argued, "that which has the superior obligation and validity ought, of course, to be preferred; or, in other words, the Constitution ought to be preferred to the statute, the intention of the people to the intention of their agents." The import of Hamilton's argument is that the Court will invoke this power only where the legislative act is *clearly* contrary to a specific clause of the Constitution.

Hamilton was at special pains to square the Court's protective function with that other requisite of "free government"—the principle of popular participation, i.e., the notion that legitimate power is derived from the people and must ultimately reflect their will. Judicial review, he suggested, does not "suppose a superiority of the judicial to the legislative power. It only supposes that the power of the people is superior to both; and that where the will of the legislature declared in statutes, stands in opposition to that of the people declared in the Constitution, the judges ought to be governed by the latter, rather than the former." Since the Court merely discovers and declares the "will of the people," there was no possibility of placing it above Congress. "The judiciary," Hamilton asserted, "is beyond comparison the weakest of the three departments of power. . . . [It] has no influence over either the sword or the purse; no direction either of the strength or the wealth of the society; and can take no active resolution whatever. It may truly be said to have; neither FORCE nor WILL, but merely judgment."

It remained for Chief Justice Marshall to spell out Hamilton's ideas and give them official gloss. "It is emphatically the province and duty of the judicial department to say what the law is," the Chief Justice ruled in *Marbury* v. *Madison*.

This case (1 Cranch 137, 1803) arose from the refusal of Madison, Jefferson's Secretary of State, to deliver the commissions appointing Marbury and three others to the office of Justice of the Peace in the District of Columbia. Claiming that these minor appointments, made at the very end of President Adams' administration, had been completed and that Jefferson was wrongfully withholding the documents authenticating their right to office, Marbury asked the Supreme Court to issue a writ of mandamus ordering Madison to deliver the commission.

Marshall's strategy was masterful. He set aside the act of Congress on which Marbury based his action, but condemned Jefferson's order advising the Secretary of State to withhold the commission. Marbury, though entitled to his office, could not obtain from the Supreme Court the remedy he sought, because Section 13 of the Judiciary Act of 1789, authorizing the Court to issue original writs of mandamus, exceeded the power of Congress. Comparing the section of the 1789 Judiciary Act in dispute with the relevant provisions of the Constitution, Marshall concluded that "the authority given to the Supreme Court by the act establishing the judicial courts of the United States, to issue writs of mandamus to public officers, appears not to be warranted by the Constitution."

The judicial process, as Marshall revealed it, is quite simple. The Chief Justice put the Constitution beside the law to determine whether they squared with each other. He "discovered" that they did not, so the act had to be disregarded.

Anyone reading this historic opinion would be inclined to believe that the decision was routine. For John Marshall the inquiry whether an act of Congress, contrary to the Constitution, can nevertheless be law was "deeply interesting," but not "intricate." The problem was easily resolved because certain fundamental principles to which Americans were accustomed had been confirmed by the Constitution itself. The people have an "original right" to establish a government, the right to set up a political system of their own choice. This recognition of the people as the source of legitimate authority goes back to John Locke and to the Declaration of Independence. Jefferson asserted the people's right to "alter or abolish" government and "to institute new government, laying its foundation on such principles and organizing its power in such form, as to them seem most likely to effect their safety and happiness." On this proposition, Marshall declared "the whole American fabric" had been erected.

This "original right," this "very great exertion" organizes a government and assigns to the different departments their respective powers. The Constitution is written that these limits may not be mistaken or forgotten. From the fact of a written Constitution Marshall makes deductions of major importance. The _written_ Constitution underscores the difference between paramount, fundamental law and ordinary acts of legislation. This distinction is "essentially attached to a written Constitution." Without it written Constitutions would become "absurd attempts, on the part of the people, to limit a power, in its nature, illimitable." The conclusion is that judicial review is the necessary and inevitable corollary of a written Constitution, an instrument of government "designed to be permanent." Marshall repeats this several times. To concede to Congress the power to determine the limits of its own power would be to give to the legislature a "practical and real omnipotence." There is no middle ground; either the Constitution is supreme or it is not. Herein the Chief Justice echoed the Massachusetts circular letter of 1768: ". . . in all free states the Constitution is fixed, and as the supreme legislature derives its power and authority from the Constitution, it cannot overleap the bounds of it, without destroying its own foundation."

But if it be true that authority in Congress to determine the scope of its own power would give it omnipotence, why does it not follow that any other agency of government enjoying such power, including the Court, would achieve a similar preeminence? At this point Marshall's argument, based on accepted political principles, is fused with reasoning grounded in specific provisions of the Constitution. Without so characterizing it, Marshall invokes separation of powers as the keystone of judicial review. The Constitution is law; it is supreme law. Article VI, Paragraph 2 says so. Article III, Section 1 provides that "THE JUDICIAL POWER OF THE UNITED STATES SHALL BE VESTED IN ONE SUPREME COURT AND IN SUCH INFERIOR COURTS AS THE CONGRESS MAY FROM TIME TO TIME ORDAIN AND ESTABLISH." Judicial power is the power to interpret law and decide cases. It follows that in cases properly before it, the Court is duty bound to uphold the Constitution and ignore any act of Congress in conflict with it. In other words, judicial review is an incidental power derived from the Court's constitutionally granted authority to interpret law and decide cases. It is a necessary means of insuring the Constitution's supremacy and permanence.

> If two laws conflict with each other [Marshall reasoned], the courts must decide on the operation of each. So, if a law be in opposition to the Constitution; if both the law and the Constitution apply to a particular case, so that the Court must either decide that case, conformably to the law, disregarding the Constitution; or conformably to the Constitution, disregarding the law; the Court must determine which of these conflicting rules governs the case: this is the very essence of judicial duty.

America's most conspicuous device for obliging government to control itself does not give the Court any superiority. When the Judiciary resolves a conflict between an act of Congress and the Constitution, it acts under the Constitution, not over it. Whereas the President and Congress exert will, the Court exercises only judgment. The President and Congress make law; judges merely interpret it. Both Congress and the President may pervert or violate the instrument; the Court merely elucidates it. The Court simply makes clear what the instrument means and requires. Judicial review insures the dominance of the people's will as embodied in the Constitution against the inroads that may be made upon it by the President and Congress. "Courts," Marshall declared in a subsequent opinion, "are the mere *instruments* of the law and can *will* nothing" (*Osborn* v. *U.S. Bank*, 9 Wheat. 738, 1824). Commenting on Marshall's reasoning in 1931, Judge Cardozo observed: "The thrill is irresistible. We feel the mystery and awe of inspired revelation."

Certain incumbents of the White House, notably Jefferson and Jackson, have been wont to query this theory of the Court's role in American politics. The Court was, they agreed, undoubtedly entitled to read the Constitution for the purpose of deciding cases. But the President and Congress also enjoyed authority and independence in interpreting the Constitution in matters before them. Writing Mrs. John Adams in 1804 as to the hated alien and sedition laws, Jefferson commented:

> The judges, believing the law constitutional, had a right to pass a sentence of fine and imprisonment; because that power was placed in their hands by the Constitution. But the Executive, believing the

law to be unconstitutional, was bound to resist the execution of it; because that power has been confided to him by the Constitution. The instrument meant that its co-ordinate branches should be checks on each other. But the opinion which gives to judges the right to decide what laws are constitutional and what not, not only for themselves in their own sphere of action, but for the Legislative and Executive also in their spheres, would make the Judiciary a despotic branch of government.

JUDICIAL REVIEW ESTABLISHED

John Marshall was not our first Chief Justice—before him there had been Jay, Rutledge and Ellsworth. To date there have been only fourteen Chief Justices of the United States. John Marshall towers above them all as "the great Chief Justice." For all practical purposes, constitutional interpretation begins with him. John Marshall won for the Supreme Court the power to construe the Constitution with finality. He made the Court's interpretation binding on all others, including Congress and the President. Marshall inaugurated, as Holmes said, "a new body of jurisprudence, by which guiding principles are raised above the reach of statute and State, and judges are entrusted with a solemn and hitherto unheard-of authority and duty." The result is that although we study the Constitution, we study it only as Supreme Court Justices read it.

Marbury v. Madison is notable not only because it established judicial review, but also because Marshall, in asserting this power, set forth the notion that the judicial process is essentially an exercise in mechanics. Supreme Court Justices discover law; they do not make it. Constitutional interpretation consists in finding meanings which are clear only to judges. To judges the meaning of the Constitution is obvious. To others, whether legislators or executives, its meaning is hidden and obscure. Outsiders, including the President and members of Congress, have not this transcendental wisdom. The only final and authoritative mouthpiece of the Constitution is the Supreme Court, and its every version gleaned from a sort of "brooding omnipresence in the sky" has the special virtue of never mangling or changing the original instrument.

Of Marshall's decision in Marbury v. Madison, Albert J. Beveridge writes: "By a coup as bold in design and as daring in execution as that by which the Constitution had been framed, John Marshall set up a landmark in American history so high that all the future could take its bearings from it, so enduring that all the shocks the nation was to endure could not overturn it."

Beveridge's praise seems extravagant, for Marshall's argument is not unanswerable. The Chief Justice's biographer projects back into history an appraisal that does not square with the contemporary significance of the case. *Marbury* v. *Madison* aroused comment and criticism in 1803, and for quite some time thereafter, not because the great Chief Justice asserted the power of judicial review, but because he went out of his way to lecture President Jefferson and Secretary of State Madison as to their official duties under the Constitution. Earlier the Court had been severely criticized by Democratic-Republicans themselves, including Jefferson, not because it declared an act of Congress unconstitutional, but because it did not invalidate the Alien-Sedition law and incorporation of the national bank. As late as 1798, Jefferson declared: "The laws of the land, administered by upright judges, would protect you from any exercise of power unauthorized by the Constitution of the United States." "That portion of the opinion," Charles Warren writes, "which was of greatest import at the time when it was rendered becomes subordinate to other considerations. Contemporary writings make it very clear that the Republicans attacked the decision, not so much because it sustained the power of the Court to determine the validity of congressional legislation, as because it announced the doctrine that the Court might issue mandamus to a Cabinet official who was acting by direction of the President in a case properly before it."

But Marshall's assertion of judicial review did not escape trenchant criticism at the hands of his contemporaries. One of the most effective replies was that given in the dissenting opinion of Justice Gibson of the Pennsylvania Supreme Court in the otherwise unimportant case of *Eakin* v. *Raub* (12 Serg. and Rawle, Pa., 1825). Pointing out that judicial review of congressional action had not been provided in the Constitution, where an elaborate set of checks and balances was set forth in clear terms, Gibson argued that the legislature was subject to political restraints, while the Supreme Court, an unrepresentative institution, was not amenable to any corrective action. To his mind, the Court's duty in exercising judicial power was to interpret and apply all of the laws enacted by the legislature.

Described by James Bradley Thayer as "much the ablest discussion," Justice Gibson's opinion denounced judicial review as a "proud pre-eminence," outside the scope of judicial authority. "Every power," Gibson writes, "by which one organ of the government is enabled to control another, or to exert influence over its acts, is a political power." Nor did the fact that the Constitution is *written* strengthen the case for judicial review. For Gibson there was no magic in written constitutions. Recurrence to first principles merely "answers the end of an observation at sea with a view to dead reckoning." That is to say, the Constitution's purpose being general rather than specific or technical, it renders first principles familiar to the mass of people. The people, Gibson insisted, must correct legislative abuses by "instructing their representatives to repeal the obnoxious act. . . . There is no effective guard against legislative usurpation but public opinion, the force of which in this country is inconceivably great." Once it is corrupted the predominant party "will laugh at the puny efforts of a dependent power to arrest it in its course."

In Marshall's time and for some years thereafter, the despotic implications Gibson discerned in judicial review were less onerous than is usually supposed. Believing with Madison that "dependence on the people is the primary control on government," Marshall favored narrow review of congressional action. "The wisdom and discretion of Congress," the Chief Justice wrote in *Gibbons* v. *Ogden* (9 Wheat. 1, 1824), "their identity with the people, and the influence which their constituents possess at elections, are in this as in many other instances, as that for example of declaring war, the sole restraints on which they [the people] have relied, to secure them from abuse. They are the restraints on which the American people must rely solely, in all representative governments."

"To the people," James Bryce observed in his *American Commonwealth* of 1886, "we come sooner or later; it is upon their wisdom and self-restraint that the stability of the most cunningly devised scheme of government will in the last resort depend."

JUDICIAL REVIEW OF STATE ACTION

Far less publicized than judicial review of acts of Congress is the control the federal courts exercise over state acts and state court decisions. Yet the former is, from every point of view, of less importance. The number of congressional acts invalidated has been comparatively few, and many of these were of such minor concern as not to affect vitally the course of history. The second act of Congress did not fall under the judicial axe until the ill-fated *Dred Scott* decision of 1857. Between 1889 and 1937 only 69 acts of Congress suffered judicial censorship, thirteen of these occurring within the crucial two-year period, June 1, 1934-June 1, 1936. Judicial pre-eminence then gave rise to President Roosevelt's famous Court-packing proposal. Under fire, the Court retreated and raised the banner of judicial self-restraint. Since 1937, judicial limitation on the power of Congress, at least quantitatively, has been an unimportant aspect of the Court's work.

Of far greater significance, both before and since 1937, has been judicial review of state acts. In 1787 it was considered of first importance to establish an effective barrier against state action hostile to the Constitution and the Union it created. Even Thomas Jefferson expressed the hope "that some peaceable means would be contrived for the federal head to enforce compliance on the part of the States." The Philadelphia Convention delegates, keenly aware of the necessity of establishing some external control over state action, suggested various limitations. One proposal gave Congress a negative on state laws; another provided for federal appointment of state governors, and gave the general government a negative on state acts. All these proposals were rejected. In its final form "this Constitution," and the laws "made in pursuance thereof, and all treaties made, or which shall be made, under the authority of the United States," are declared to be "the supreme law of the land; and the judges in every state are bound thereby, anything in the Constitution or laws of any State to the contrary notwithstanding."

The first Congress, apparently believing that the purpose of this clause was to make the Judiciary a final resort for all cases arising in relation to the states, enacted Section 25, Judiciary Act of 1789, authorizing the Supreme Court to pass upon the validity of state legislation and to review decisions of state tribunals wherein constitutional questions had been answered in favor of the state, or adverse to national power. Though Section 25 recognized the important role state courts might play in interpreting and applying the Constitution, federal law, and treaties, it had the effect of strengthening national power by making explicit a judicial function left to inference in the Constitution itself.

In a period of Democratic-Republican dominance, during which only the Judiciary remained in Federalist hands, invalidation of state acts or acceptance of jurisdiction of appeals on writ of error to a "sovereign" state court was bound to rouse states-rights resentment. *Fletcher* v. *Peck* (6 Cr. 87, 1810), the first case in which the Supreme Court declared a state act violative of the provisions of the federal Constitution, must have exceeded all expectations. Representatives in Congress condemned the ruling as "sapping the foundations of all our Constitutions," and Marshall's associate Mr. Justice Johnson intimated in dissent that the Chief Justice had, as in *Marbury* v. *Madison,* seized an opportunity to assert judicial review of state acts in a moot case. "I have been very unwilling to proceed to the decision of this cause at all," Justice Johnson commented. "It appears to me to bear strong evidence, upon the face of it, of being a mere feigned case. It is our duty to decide on the rights but not on the speculations of parties." There was less antagonism toward the Court's decision in other states than in Georgia, but no one failed to recognize that power in the Supreme Court to review state acts would vitally affect our constitutional development.

The most important area for the operation of judicial review was yet to be conquered—the power to revise state court decisions in order to make them square with the "supreme law." In *Cohens* v. *Virginia* (6 Wheat. 264, 1821), Marshall established this power in a case involving review of a state court judgment in a criminal prosecution. Citing the supremacy clause of the Constitution (Art. VI, par. 2), Marshall brushed aside Virginia's contention that a writ of error directed to her courts was a suit against a state, and hence, prohibited by the Eleventh Amendment. The state's sovereignty was not to be infringed by Supreme Court review. Cases, such as Cohens', coming before the Court on a writ of error, simply bring the record into Court for re-examination. "It does not in any manner act upon the parties."

The Chief Justice foresaw only chaos, if each state court were to be a final judge of constitutional questions "arising" in its jurisdiction. Counsel for Virginia suggested that the framers of the Constitution had provided no forum for the final construction of itself, that federal and state courts have concurrent jurisdiction in "all cases arising under the Constitution, laws and treaties of the United States." Marshall emphatically denied this, saying that "thirteen independent courts endowed with such power would estabish 'a hydra in government.' " Judicial power of the United States was governed by the nature of the case no less than by the character of the parties. "If it [the argument of counsel for Virginia] be to maintain that a case arising under the Constitution, or of a law, must be one in which a party comes into Court to demand something conferred on him by the Constitution or a law, we think the construction too narrow. . . . A case in law or equity . . . may only be said to arise under the Constitution or law of the United States whenever its correct decision depends on the construction of either." Under the construction contended for by the counsel for Virginia each state would "possess a veto on the will of the whole." "There is nothing in the history of the times," Marshall commented, "which would justify the opinion that the confidence reposed in the states was so implicit as to leave in them and their tribunals the power of resisting or defeating, in the form of law, the legitimate measures of the Union."

Marshall's opinion in *Cohens* v. *Virginia* has been described as "one of the strongest and most enduring strands of that mighty cable woven to hold the American people together as a united and imperishable nation." It was for this very reason that Democratic-Republicans, especially Thomas Jefferson, condemned it so harshly. The Judiciary of the United States, under John Marshall's leadership, was determined, Jefferson believed, "to undermine the foundations of our confederated fabrics." That Marshall's ruling did have consolidating effects, no one can deny. However, one may doubt the correctness of Jefferson's charge that this result had been achieved by spurious judicial interpretation rather than by the Constitution itself. Said the Chief Justice:

The American states, as well as the American people, have believed a close firm union to be essential to their liberty and to their happiness. They have been taught by experience that the union cannot exist without a government for the whole; and they have been taught by the same experience that this government would be a mere shadow, that must disappoint all their hopes, unless invested with large portions of that sovereignty which belongs to independent states.

Madison re-enforced Marshall. In the Federal Convention he declared that too much emphasis had been placed on the states as political societies. Even in 1829, after his nationalist sentiments had waned, he wrote: "A political system that does not provide for a peaceable and effectual decision of all controversies arising among the parties is not a Government, but a mere Treaty between independent nations, without any resort for terminating disputes but negotiations, and that failing, the sword." Failure to lodge this power in the federal judiciary, he added in 1832, "would be as much a mockery as a scabbard put into the hands of a soldier without a sword in it."

The theory of the Court's power, as propounded by John Marshall, remains today virtually unchanged. "Judicial power," the Chief Justice commented in 1824, "as contradistinguished from the power of the laws, has no existence." Two generations later, Justice Brewer maintained that, "There is nothing in this power of the judiciary detracting in the least from the idea of government of and by the people. The courts hold neither purse nor sword. . . . They make no laws, they establish no policy, they never enter into the domain of popular action. They do not govern." Justice Owen J. Roberts reiterated this doctrine in 1936.

It is sometimes said that the Court assumes a power to overrule or control the action of the people's representatives. This is a misconception. . . . When an act of Congress is appropriately challenged in the courts as not conforming to the constitutional mandate, the judicial branch of the Government has only one duty, to lay the article of the Constitution which is invoked beside the statute which is challenged and to decide whether the latter squares with the former. All the court does, or can do, is to announce its considered Judgment upon the question. The only power it has, if such it may be called, is the power of judgment. This court neither approves nor condemns any legislative policy. [*United States* v. *Butler*, 297 U.S. 1.]

In this same case, Justice Roberts' colleagues—Brandeis, Cardozo, and Stone—had performed this "squaring" operation and reached the opposite conclusion.

The Justices themselves have on occasion evidenced sensitiveness to the bearing of judicial review on the democratic process. Justice Frankfurter speaks of judicial review as "a limitation on popular government," and reminds his colleagues that "to the legislature no less than courts is committed the guardianship of deeply cherished constitutional rights. . . . Holding democracy in judicial tutelage is not the most promising way to foster disciplined responsibility in a people," Frankfurter has written.

Justice Stone indicated in a sentence the Court's awesome power: "While unconstitutional exercise of power by the executive and legislative branches of the government is subject to judicial restraint, the only check upon our own exercise of power is our own sense of self-restraint." Justice Sutherland sharply rebuked his colleague: "The suggestion that the only check upon the exercise of the judicial power, when properly invoked, to declare a constitutional right superior to an unconstitutional statute is the judge's own faculty of self-restraint, is both ill considered and mischievous." Justice Stone's observation was considered unfortunate because it undermined the claim that judges exercise no will, no power. From time to time the Justices have, nevertheless, invoked certain cautionary considerations to keep the exercise of judicial power within bounds. Justice Brandeis summed these up in a concurring opinion in 1936 (*Ashwander* v. *T.V.A.*, 297 U.S. 288, 346):

1. The Court will not pass upon the constitutionality of legislation in a friendly, non-adversary, proceeding. . . .
2. The Court will not "anticipate a question of constitutional law in advance of the necessity of deciding it. . . ."
3. The Court will not "formulate a rule of constitutional law broader than is required by the precise facts to which it is applied. . . ."
4. The Court will not pass upon a constitutional question although properly presented by the record, if there is also present some other ground upon which the case may be disposed of. . . .
5. The Court will not pass upon the validity of a statute upon the complaint of one who fails to show that he is injured by its operation.
6. The Court will not pass upon the constitutionality of a statute at the instance of one who has availed himself of its benefits.
7. "When the validity of an act of the Congress is drawn in question,

and even if a serious doubt of constitutionality is raised, it is a cardinal principle that this court will first ascertain whether a construction of the statute is fairly possible by which the question may be avoided."

In addition to these self-denying ordinances, or rules for side-stepping and limiting review of legislative acts, the Court has evolved still others, *viz.*: one who relies on the invalidity of a statute has the burden of proving its invalidity. If this burden is not sustained, the Court will presume the statute is constitutional. The Court may not pass on the expediency or wisdom of legislation. Nor may the motives of the legislature be subjected to judicial scrutiny. If "judges can open it [the Constitution] at all," as Chief Justice Marshall commented in *Marbury* v. *Madison*, "what part of it are they forbidden to read or obey?" The answer was given in *Luther* v. *Borden* (7 How. 1, 1849), where the Justices decided that since the question of whether the government of Rhode Island or any other state is "republican" (as guaranteed by Article IV, Sec. 4) was "political" in nature, it must be determined either by Congress through its acceptance of state representatives, or by Presidential acts in response to requests for assistance in putting down domestic violence. Other questions termed "political," and therefore requiring solution, if at all, through political agencies, are determination of whether a state has ratified a proposed constitutional amendment (*Coleman* v. *Miller*, 307 U.S. 433, 1939); or whether use by a state of the initiative and referendum is a denial of "a republican form of government" (*Pacific States T. & T. Co.* v. *Oregon*, 223 U.S. 118, 1912); or whether officials have "districted" the state in a proper manner (*Colegrove* v. *Green*, 328 U.S. 549, 1946). Decisions of the political departments concerning the international relations of the United States are likewise considered binding on the Court.

There is, however, no touchstone for determining what is, and what is not, a "political question." Justices have dissented from decisions in which this principle has been invoked. On occasion they have attempted in vain to press it upon the Court (see Frankfurter's dissenting opinion in *U.S.* v. *California*, 332 U.S. 19, 43, 1947). According to one view, the Court should invoke this self-imposed limitation more frequently in an effort to avoid judicial solutions of what are essentially policy questions. A contrary view, however, regards excessive use of the "political question" label as a cowardly evasion of the Court's duty to provide peaceful solutions to any and all issues arising in a constitutional system.

In spite of self-imposed limitations, the Court has played an important role in maintaining and developing the "vague and admonitory" Constitution—in preserving the federal system; in upholding the sovereign authority of the national government in the field of foreign relations; in helping shape economic, social, and political policy at both the state and the national level. In all these areas, judicial interpretation has been infinitely variable. Judges do not live in a vacuum. They are, and by inheritance, education, and environment ought to be, influenced by the social and economic forces of their time. On occasion, the Justices have expressly reversed or modified precedents, explaining that altered conditions permitted no other course.

"There is a tendency," Justice Holmes wrote Harold Laski, on January 29, 1926, "to think of judges as if they were independent mouthpieces of the infinite, and not simply directors of a force that comes from the source that gives them their authority. I think our court has fallen into the error at times and it is that that I have aimed at when I have said that the common law is not a brooding omnipresence in the sky and that the U.S. is not subject to some mystic overlaw that it is bound to obey." "The felt necessities of the times," Justice Holmes said on another occasion, "the prevalent moral and political theories, intuitions of public policy, avowed or unconscious, even the prejudices which judges share with their fellowmen, have had a good deal more to do than the syllogism in determining the rules by which men should be governed."

"While an 'over speaking' Judge," Justice McReynolds commented in a Supreme Court opinion of 1921, "is no well-tuned cymbal, neither is an amorphous dummy, unspotted by human emotion, a becoming receptacle for judicial power." "I have never known any judges, no difference how austere of manner," Justice John H. Clark has observed, "who discharged their judicial duties in an atmosphere of pure, unadulterated reason. Alas, we are all 'the common growth of Mother Earth,' even those of us who wear the long robe." Writing in 1958, Judge Learned Hand suggested that judges discharge their function in less occult ways:

Judges are seldom content to annul the particular solution before them; they do not, indeed may not, say that, taking all things into consideration, the legislator's solution is too strong for the judicial stomach. On the contrary they wrap up their veto in a protective veil of adjectives such as 'arbitrary,' 'artificial,' 'normal,' 'reasonable,' 'inherent,' 'fundamental,' or 'essential,' whose office usually, though quite innocently, is to disguise what they are doing and impute to it a derivation far more impressive than their personal preferences, which are all that in fact lie behind the decision. If we do need a third chamber it should appear for what it is, and not as the interpreter of inscrutable principles.

Justice Stone's dictum that the only restraint on the Court's exercise of power "is our own sense of self-restraint" overlooks the possibility that such self-restraint may be stimulated by outside pressure, as in 1937 when President Roosevelt, facing stubborn judicial resistance to his legislative program, tried to "pack" the Court. Justice Roberts, on January 29, 1954, in discussing a proposed constitutional amendment that would prevent Court packing, told Senators that he had been at the time "fully conscious of the tremendous strain and threat to the existing Court" inherent in Roosevelt's plan, which he summed up as "a political device to influence the Court." Whether President Roosevelt's threat did, in fact, influence judicial decisions is the subject of considerable controversy, but following closely on the heels of the proposal reversals and qualification of judicial decisions did occur.

The nature of the Constitution itself has allowed, even required, Justices to reconsider and revise their judgments. We must always remember, Chief Justice Marshall was accustomed to remark, that "it is a *Constitution* that we are expounding." Unlike a code of laws, its provisions are stated in general terms. Our basic law was, as Marshall said, "intended to endure for all ages to come." To avoid the necessity of wholesale revision, or revolution, it had to be adapted, in Marshall's words, to "various crises in human affairs." Chief Justice White once admitted that the Court had "relaxed Constitutional guarantees for fear of revolution."

Since it is a Constitution that is being applied, judges do something more than merely interpret its written provisions. The Justices not only formulate the principles that govern the working of the federal system and the relations of Congress, Court, and

President; they sit in judgment over the policy that controls the social and economic life of the country. There are limits to the power of judicial review, to be sure, but they are largely self-imposed and on occasion have been disregarded. "Government by judiciary" is no idle phrase when applied to the politics of the United States.

From Justice Cardozo, who candidly explored the nature of the judicial process, comes the reminder that the court plays more than a negative role:

> The restraining power of the judiciary does not manifest its chief worth in the few cases in which the legislature has gone beyond the lines that mark the limits of discretion. Rather shall we find its chief worth in making vocal and audible the ideals that might otherwise be silenced, in giving them continuity of life, and of expression, in guiding and directing choice within limits where choice ranges. This function should preserve to the courts the power that now belongs to them, if only the power is exercised with insight into social values, and with suppleness of adaptation to changing social needs. (*The Nature of the Judicial Process*, p. 94.)

THE ROLE OF PRECEDENT
IN CONSTITUTIONAL LAW

The doctrine of *stare decisis*, under which a court is compelled to recognize as binding in the case before it such prior decisions as were rendered in cases involving the same or similar fact situations, is not followed as rigidly in determining constitutional questions as it is in other branches of the law. Prior adjudications are often regarded as tentative conclusions to be abandoned when proved false by the test of experience. Prevailing theories and modes of thought, and the social and economic views impressed in argument on the court, color and determine constitutional decisions. As a result, the reports abound with contradictions in theory and reversals of position, discrepancies that can be harmonized only by a study of the historical background of particular cases and of the legal philosophies of the Justices who decided them. "Doubtless the doctrine of *stare decisis* is a salutary one, and to be adhered to on all proper occasions," the Court said in *Pollock v. Farmers Loan and Trust Co.* (158 U.S. 601, 1895), in holding the federal income taxes invalid and thereby overcoming what it termed "a century of error." "Manifestly," the Court continued, "as this court is clothed with the power and entrusted with the duty to maintain the fundamental law of the Constitution, the discharge of that duty requires it not to extend any decision upon a constitutional question if it is convinced that error in principle might supervene."

"*Stare decisis* is not," Justice Brandeis declared, "a universal, inexorable command. . . . In cases involving the Federal Constitution, where correction through legislative action is practically impossible, this Court has often overruled its earlier decisions. The Court bows to the lessons of experience and the force of better reasoning, recognizing that the process of trial and error, so fruitful in the physical sciences, is appropriate also in the judicial function." Going further, Judge Jerome Frank holds that uncertainty of law, resulting from a refusal to adhere rigidly to precedent, may be of social value. "When men are free of childish compulsions away from or toward the traditional, it will be possible for them to have an open mind on the question of the advisability of radical alterations of law." Taking much the same position, Justice Douglas has observed:

> From age to age the problem of constitutional adjudication is the same. It is to keep the power of the government unrestrained by the social or economic theories that one set of judges may import into the Constitution. It is to keep one age unfettered by the fears or limited vision of another. In that connection, there is a fundamental tenet of faith that has evolved from our long experience as a nation. It is this: If the social and economic problems of state and nation can be kept under political management of the people, there is likely to be long-run stability. It is when a judiciary with life tenure seeks to write its social and economic creed into the charter that instability is created. For then the nation lacks the adaptability to master the sudden storms of an era.

The distinctive feature of our Constitution is not, as Chief Justice Marshall suggested, that it is written. All constitutions are more or less written, more or less unwritten. The British Constitution, though supposedly made up of custom and tradition, is partly written. Magna Charta, Petition of Right, Bill of Rights, Act of Settlement, Parliament Act of 1911—all are fundamental parts of the British Constitution, and these basic documents are written.

The three fundamental laws of the French Constitution of 1875 were written. No constitution, including our own, is either altogether written or altogether unwritten. In our fundamental law of 1789, there is no mention of the President's cabinet, no reference to Senatorial courtesy or to the national nominating conventions for choosing candidates for election. At the same time, usage has discarded, for all practical purposes, the electoral college, expressly provided for in the written Constitution itself.

Thus the Constitution of 1789 is only the original trunk. Important new branches have been added, including not only custom but also amendments, statutory enactments, and judicial decisions.

DEVELOPMENT OF THE CONSTITUTION—FORMAL AMENDMENT

The first ten amendments, the first eight constituting the Bill of Rights, were proposed by Congress in 1789 in order to assure both the people and the states that their rights would be protected against encroachment by the federal government. The Eleventh Amendment was adopted in 1795 to correct "the judicial error" perpetrated by the Supreme Court in *Chisholm* v. *Georgia* (2 Dall. 419, 1793); it reglorified the sovereignty of the states by prohibiting suits against them. The Twelfth Amendment (1804) arose from the tie vote in the electoral college in 1800; it amended the method of choosing the President and Vice-President. The Thirteenth (1865), Fourteenth (1868), and Fifteenth (1870) Amendments were Civil War products; they guaranteed, respectively, personal liberty, the rights of federal citizenship, and due process of law on the part of the states, and immunity from discrimination in the right to vote based on race, color, or previous condition of servitude. These three amendments, ratified a half century after the Twelfth Amendment, dealt, as did the previous ones, with the relation of the government to the people.

The Sixteenth Amendment (1913) made possible the passage of a federal income tax law. The Seventeenth (1913) provided for the direct election of Senators. The Eighteenth (1919) was the prohibition amendment; it was novel in that it grafted the branch of direct social legislation onto the rigid constitutional tree. The Nineteenth Amendment (1920) extended the vote to women. The Twentieth (1933) again affected the Presidency by calculating the terms of the President and Vice-President from noon of the 20th day of January following their election; it also abolished the "lame duck" session of Congress by directing that both houses of Congress convene on January 3, at which time the terms of office of congress-men of the previous session are terminated. The Twenty-First Amendment (1933) repealed the prohibition amendment and in effect placed the old Webb-Kenyon Act into the fundamental law by freeing state prohibition laws from the limitations imposed by Congress' power to regulate interstate commerce. The Twenty-Second Amendment (1951) prevents any person from being elected to the Presidency for more than two terms.

Generally speaking, amendment of the Constitution is a rare event, but there has hardly been a time in our history when proposed new amendments have not been legion. In the first century under the Constitution more than 1,800 amendments were proposed. Though the prospect of success is slim, the effort continues unabated.

STATUTORY DEVELOPMENT

"If we regard as constitutional," the late Charles A. Beard wrote, "all that body of law relative to the fundamental organization of the three branches of the federal government—legislative, executive, and judicial—then by far the greater portion of our constitutional law is to be found in the statutes." Examples include legislation dealing with the organization of the executive and judicial departments, and the various changes, previous to the Seventeenth Amendment, in the method of electing Senators. Legislative construction of the Constitution by early Congresses has been accorded almost conclusive effect in the courts.

JUDICIAL DEVELOPMENT

The Constitution's most important growth comes from its interpretation by the Supreme Court. "A constitution," said Chief Justice Marshall in *McCulloch* v. *Maryland*, "to contain an accurate detail of all the subdivisions of which its great powers will admit, and of all the means by which they may be carried into execution, would partake of the prolixity of a legal code, and could scarcely be embraced by the human mind. It would probably never be understood by the public. Its nature, therefore, requires that only its great outlines should be marked, its important objects designated, and the minor ingredients which compose those objects be deduced from the nature of the objects themselves." The work of the Supreme Court is thus eminently practical: it must reduce the broad statements of the Constitution to a form applicable to particular cases; it must determine the source of powers sought to be exercised by the government and, by construing the relevant provisions, decide how far those powers extend; and it must at all times be prepared to protect individual rights against arbitrary government action.

Perhaps the most distinctive feature of our Constitution is that it is *law*, paramount, *supreme law*, and hence subject to interpretation by the Supreme Court in cases properly before it. Thus, judicial review is an implied power; it is implied from, and is incidental to the power to interpret law and decide cases. Under Chief Justice Marshall's theory, judicial review is less a necessary adjunct to the written Constitution than a supplement to popular government. His argument makes judicial review a means of safeguarding and upholding the Constitution—that "original right" of the people, that "very great exertion," as Marshall describes it, against encroachments by either Congress, the President or the States. Nor does this power in the Supreme Court give to it any practical or real omnipotence. The Court is simply exercising a power granted by the Constitution—judicial power. The effect, at least in theory, is not to elevate Court over legislature, but rather to make "the power of the people superior to both."

In *Federalist*, No. 85, Hamilton described the Constitution as "a compound as well of the errors and prejudices, as of the sense and wisdom" of the delegates, "a compromise of the many dissimilar interests and inclinations," without "claim to absolute perfection." Surely such a document was not intended to be, nor in practice has it proved to be, a strait jacket. At times the Supreme Court has exerted a retarding influence, gratuitously throwing obstacles into the path of effective government. But, by and large, the effect of judicial decisions has been to expand and enlarge, rather than qualify and restrict, the power to govern. The history of the United States is, as James Bryce has said, "in a large measure a history of the arguments which sought to enlarge or restrict" national power. More often than not, the palm of victory has gone to that generous view of national authority to which Chief Justice Marshall contributed so heavily. Had this not been so, a document framed in 1787 in the simplified context of agrarianism, with major provisions still largely unamended, could not serve the expanding needs of a complex industrialized society. It is largely to the credit of the Supreme Court that the Constitution has been in fact what Woodrow Wilson in 1908 presumed it to be—"a vehicle of the Nation's life."

II

THE COURT
AND CONGRESS

*A*s EXPOUNDED BY 17TH AND
18th century political philosophers, *viz.*, Harrington, Locke, and
Montesquieu, the primary purpose of the separation of powers
principle was to take from the monarch some or most of his
ancient lawmaking authority and vest it in a legislature. The
American version of this doctrine went further. Instead of the
simple division of powers into legislative and executive advocated
by European writers, the colonies adopted a threefold separation,
elevating the judiciary to coequal position and placing all three
under the rule of law established by a written constitution.

At the Philadelphia Convention of 1787, separation of powers
was endorsed with virtual unanimity. Madison declared that no
political truth was of "greater intrinsic value." Controversy, apart
from that over the nation-state relationship, concerned mainly
the respective powers and the relations between each of the three
branches of the national government. Because of dominance in the
states of the legislative branch and the demonstrated tendency of
most legislatures to favor rural and small propertied interests rather

than the wealthy and commercial classes, members of the convention deliberately strengthened the presidency and the independent judiciary at the expense of Congress. Madison in *The Federalist*, No. 48, repeatedly warned against the tendency of all power to flow into the legislative vortex, and emphasized the need to check its "ambition."

KEEPING THE DEPARTMENTS SEPARATED

In spite of the recognized importance of the separation of powers principle, no specific declaration concerning it appears in the Constitution. Separation of powers is implied from the opening statements of the first three articles: (1) "ALL LEGISLATIVE POWERS HEREIN GRANTED SHALL BE VESTED IN A CONGRESS OF THE UNITED STATES"; (2) "THE EXECUTIVE POWER SHALL BE VESTED IN A PRESIDENT OF THE UNITED STATES"; (3) "THE JUDICIAL POWER SHALL BE VESTED IN ONE SUPREME COURT AND IN SUCH INFERIOR COURTS AS THE CONGRESS SHALL . . . ORDAIN AND ESTABLISH." From this separation is derived the doctrine that certain functions, because of their essential nature, may properly be exercised by only a particular branch of the government; that such functions cannot be delegated to any other department; and that one branch may not interfere with another by usurping its powers or by supervising their exercise.

So far as the Constitution is concerned, the doctrine of separation of powers applies only to the national government and need not be adhered to by the states. Nor does the doctrine apply to the governments established by Congress in the territories and in the District of Columbia.

The freedom of one department to operate without interference from another has been constantly recognized. Thus the courts will not attempt to compel the legislature to perform its constitutional duties, nor will they compel or prevent the performance of discretionary duties by executive officers. In *Mississippi* v. *Johnson* (4 Wall. 475, 1867), where a state sought to restrain the President from carrying out post-Civil War Reconstruction Acts, the Court held that it was powerless to restrain the President in carrying out his executive duties. "Neither [Congress nor the President] can be restrained in its action by the judicial department; though the acts of both, when performed, are, in proper cases, subject to its cognizance."

Nor will the courts attempt to pass upon political questions, or determine the province of the executive or legislative departments. In *Luther* v. *Borden* (7 How. 1, 1849) the Court refused to decide between the opposing governments in Rhode Island as a result of Dorr's Rebellion, maintaining that the political departments had decided the question. The enforcement of the constitutional guarantee of a republican form of government in each state (Art. IV, Sec. 4) rests solely within the power of Congress, and the court will not substitute its judgment for that of the legislature. In *Pacific States Telephone & Telegraph Co.* v. *Oregon* (223 U.S. 118, 1912) the Court refused to determine whether the constitutional provision is violated by state initiative and referendum statutes. In *Ohio* v. *Akron Metropolitan Park District* (281 U.S. 74, 1930) the Court would not invalidate a provision in the state constitution requiring the concurrence of all judges but one in holding statutes unconstitutional. The judiciary cannot exercise legislative power, nor will it undertake administrative duties. In turn the legislature cannot directly interfere with the judicial process. At one time the freedom of the courts from external control was carried so far as to prevent the levy of even a nondiscriminatory income tax on the salaries of federal judges (*Evans* v. *Gore*, 253 U.S. 245, 1920). The President's power of arbitrary removal cannot be exercised against officers vested with judicial and legislative functions, even though such officers are technically a part of the executive department (*Humphrey Executor* v. *U.S.*, 295 U.S. 602, 1935).

COMMINGLING OF POWERS

The separation of powers rule is by no means absolute. The constitutional system of checks and balances not only permits but requires the commingling of powers. Thus the President may veto legislation (Art. I, Sec. 7, Cl. 2) and may grant pardons (Art. II, Sec. 2, Cl. 1); the legislature may impeach members of the executive and judicial departments (Art. I, Sec. 3, Cl. 6; Art. II, Sec. 4) and participate in the appointment of government officials (Art. II,

Sec. 2, Cl. 2). Although the Constitution does not expressly so provide, the judiciary may declare legislation unconstitutional and may restrain subordinates of the executive from acting illegally.

Because of the criticism directed against the blending of powers in the debates on ratification of the proposed Constitution, Madison in *The Federalist*, No. 47, restated the traditional theory. The mingling of powers was, he explained, a valuable additional restraint on government. Not only did the sharing of powers limit government itself; it also provided weapons by which each department could defend its position in the constitutional system. The President's veto protected him against legislative encroachments, and his power of appointment gave him influence against judicial assault. The Court had the power to pass on legislation, and was protected by life tenure. The Congress could impeach a President and members of the Court. The national lawmakers control the purse upon which both other departments depend, the Senate passes on Presidential appointments, and the Congress may control the appellate jurisdiction as well as the size of the Supreme Court. In short, Madison's design was to separate and blend the powers of government so as to make the ambitions of one department a check on the power drive of other departments.

Nor is this the full extent of the mingling of powers. The legislature may exercise the executive power of pardon in the form of a grant of amnesty or immunity from prosecution. It may punish contempts, and provide in minute detail the rules of procedure to be followed by the courts. Congress's power to control the issuance of injunctions by federal courts and to restrict their power to punish disobedience has also been sustained. Although the courts do not legislate in the proper sense of the word, their decisions may be regarded from a realistic point of view as lawmaking and policy determining. The courts, within limits, may exercise the executive power of appointment; and Congress may confer on them authority to suspend sentence, even though such power is legislative in nature. The President's control over foreign relations is such that advising and consenting to treaties and declaring war, apparently entrusted by the Constitution to the legislature, have come largely under his authority. Executive officers and administrative bodies also exercise functions that belong to other departments. Thus the Commissioner of Patents exercises judicial power in determining whether a patent shall be issued or renewed; the Tax Court of the United States makes judicial decisions; and both the Federal Trade Commission and the Interstate Commerce Commission exercise legislative and judicial functions.

DELEGATION OF LEGISLATIVE
AUTHORITY TO THE EXECUTIVE

The rule prohibiting the delegation of legislative authority, already mentioned in connection with the separation of powers, is relaxed when executive officers or boards are the grantees of the power. Statutes cannot be so detailed as to contain every regulation and form of procedure by which the legislative policies they embody are to be carried out. The courts have consequently recognized that administrative officers must be permitted some discretion in the enforcement of laws. Effective operation of government often requires the exercise of legislative authority by the executive. Thus Congress may permit executive officers to determine when a given statute shall become operative, and fill in the details of legislative enactments by appropriate regulations. An early case, *The Aurora* v. *United States* (7 Cranch 382, 1813) sustained the grant of power to the President to revive the Non-Intercourse Act when he shall have ascertained that certain conditions exist. *Field* v. *Clark* (143 U.S. 649, 1892) upheld a grant of power to the President to suspend the provisions of the tariff act relating to the free introduction of certain articles into this country, when he shall be satisfied that foreign governments impose on such articles duties that "he shall deem to be reciprocally unequal and unreasonable." *Hampton & Co.* v. *United States* (276 U.S. 394, 1928) sustained a flexible tariff act that authorized the President to raise or lower tariff rates by 50 per cent in order to equalize the costs of production in the United States and competing foreign countries.

An administrative officer may be authorized to determine whether the facts of a particular case bring it within the operation of a given law. Such delegation does not violate separation of powers if the legislature has established a reasonable or "primary" standard to guide the action of the executive. Within the limits so established considerable latitude is permitted. The delegation of an unconfined discretion is, however, equivalent to conferring legislative power on the executive and therefore invalid.

Prior to 1935 no statute had ever been held invalid because of an unconstitutional delegation of power to the executive. In each instance the standard set up by the legislature was held to be sufficiently definite, although some rather vague criteria were thus sustained. In *Panama Refining Co.* v. *Ryan* (Hot Oil Case, 293 U.S. 388, 1935), however, the Supreme Court held unconstitutional a provision of the National Industrial Recovery Act that authorized, but did not command, the President to prohibit the interstate shipment of oil produced or withdrawn in violation of state regulations. The court declared that an absolute and uncontrolled discretion had been vested in the executive since the statute stated no policy and provided no standard by which the validity of the President's action could be judged. Though Justice Cardozo, dissenting, found that the declaration of policy in the preamble to the entire act provided a sufficiently definite standard, the majority could see no relationship between the broad generalities of that section and the power conferred on the President. Whereas the majority thought that Congress had "left the matter to the President without standard or rule, to be dealt with as he pleased," Cardozo feared lest the classical separation of powers between executive and Congress become "a doctrinaire concept to be made use of with pedantic rigor." "Discretion is not unconfined and vagrant," he concluded. "It is canalized within banks that keep it from overflowing."

In *Schechter Poultry Corporation* v. *United States* (294 U.S. 495, 1935), shortly after the Hot Oil decision, the Court again found that the discretion of the President under the National Industrial Recovery Act was "virtually unfettered"; in a concurring opinion Cardozo termed it "delegation run riot."

The infirmities of these laws in respect to the attempted delegations were for the most part the result of hasty draftsmanship. By 1941, however, Congress had learned its lesson. In *Opp Cotton Mills* v. *Administrator* (312 U.S. 126, 1941) the Court found that Congress, by adding a rather detailed, though uninstructive, list of factors to guide the administrators' judgment, had provided satisfactory limits within which administrative discretion was to be exercised.

Where international relations are concerned the power delegated need not be encumbered by restrictions. *United States* v. *Curtiss-Wright Export Corp.* (299 U.S. 304, 1936) sustained an embargo on arms to warring South American countries, proclaimed by the President pursuant to a joint resolution of Congress authorizing such action upon a finding that it "may contribute to the re-establishment of peace between those countries." The Justices emphasized the distinction between delegations of power over internal affairs and over foreign relations. In wartime, delegations must of necessity be made on a tremendous scale, with fewer standards than are contained in peacetime delegations. All such delegations have been sustained, both in and following World Wars I and II.

ADMINISTRATIVE AGENCIES AND THE COURTS

Whether in time of war or peace, the Court now seems more kindly disposed toward the efforts of legislative bodies to accomplish policy objectives through delegation. In an era of increasingly detailed regulation of virtually all phases of social and economic life, administration has become a prominent feature of the governmental process. More than one-third of current decisions of the Supreme Court involve judicial review of administrative action, including review of the decisions of administrative agencies engaged in (1) making rules to fill in the gaps in statutes as enacted; (2) enforcing the basic statute, and rules announced by the agency; (3) adjudicating the rights of persons who allegedly violate the terms of the statute or agency rules, or who dispute the asserted authority of the agency. The starting point in any controversy arising from administrative action is the statute enacted by Congress. As has been shown, Congress may not surrender its "legislative" powers; it may not accomplish by delegation to an administrative agency a purpose beyond the range of legislative power under the Constitution. Similarly, administrative agencies have to meet the requirements of fair hearing or proceeding under the due process clause. If Congress fails to provide for a hearing, the Court will require one in order to save the act from the pitfalls of unconstitutionality. (*Yamataya* v. *Fisher*, 189 U.S. 86, 1903; *Wong Yang Sung* v. *McGrath*, 339 U.S. 33, 1950).

The President, a favorite beneficiary of Congressional delegations, may subdelegate power granted him whether or not the statute specifically empowers him to do so unless it is expressly prohibited. (*Wilcox* v. *Jackson* ex dem McConnel, 13 Pet. 498, 1839). However, responsibility for whatever action is taken remains that of the President. (*Williams* v. *U.S.* 1 How. 290, 1843.) A statutory scheme covering this problem was provided by the Presidential Subdelegation Act of 1950 (3 U.S.C. ch. 4).

Even if the basic statute is free of these constitutional infirmities, important questions still remain. Has the agency properly construed its authority and duties? A specific agency action may be valid under the Constitution, and still be inconsistent with statutory provisions. In practice challenge to an agency's interpretation of the law is usually combined with attack on agency procedures or decisions. Has the agency used proper procedures? These may be set forth in the statute establishing the agency, or in the Administrative Procedure Act of 1946 (not all agencies are bound by this act) or in rules previously announced by the agency. In answering this question, courts look to the realities as well as the forms of procedure. Is the agency decision, whether in formulating a rule having the force of law, or in adjudicating a disputed issue between itself and an affected citizen, fair or defensible? An agency is not required to adhere to any particular standard, but under one formula or another it must reach decisions having support in facts and logic. Thus, in reviewing decisions of an agency under the Administrative Procedure Act, a court will reverse where the decision is "arbitrary, capricious or unsupported by substantial evidence" or "unwarranted by the facts" on the whole record, or portion cited by the affected party. [Sec. 10(e)]

It need hardly be added that the role of the federal courts, and especially that of the Supreme Court in reviewing administrative actions is one of considerable delicacy. Separation of powers issues of great difficulty are inevitable. Without the specialized competence of members of administrative boards, the Court must review agency decisions affecting railroads, motor carriers, airlines, television and radio networks, stock exchanges, tax levies, labor relations, minimum wages, and myriad other matters. A backward-looking Court might become a brake on needed measures of social reform. If it scrutinizes administrative action with a suspicious eye, it may encourage extensive litigation and frustrate the achievement of important goals sought by Congress.

If the Court abandons its reviewing function in this area, agencies may become careless or arbitrary allowing vital personal and property rights to lie at the mercy of politically oriented administrators. To an extent not yet fully appreciated, the relationship of the citizen, and the various associations through which he acts, to the modern state is defined in the present era by the action or inaction of administrative agencies exercising wide discretionary powers. The evident unwillingness or incapacity of Congress to maintain an effective surveillance of our administrative system, and the impossibility, except in theory, of Presidential control, means that for better or worse the principal barrier to arbitrary administrative action is the judiciary.

The Supreme Court's varying responses since 1887 to the questions raised above fall into three periods: that terminating in World War I; a second ending in the period 1937-39; a third extending through the present.

1887 TO WORLD WAR I—OVERT HOSTILITY

Initially, the Supreme Court exhibited fierce hostility toward administrative agencies. Despite the legalistic outlook of the first chairman of the Interstate Commerce Commission, former Michigan Supreme Court Justice and Law School Dean, Thomas N. Cooley, the Supreme Court between 1887 and 1905 decided fifteen of the sixteen cases involving railroad rate regulation in favor of the railroads. A body blow was struck in the Maximum Freight Rate case (*ICC* v. *Cinn., N.O. & T.P.R.*, 167 U.S. 479, 1897) which held that the ICC lacked the power to prescribe "fair" railroad rates, and could only veto "unfair" rates. This construction of the Act by Justice Brewer and his fellow judges reflected their view of the administrative process as a dangerous innovation, the proponents of which were "constantly seeking to minimize the power of the courts." In other decisions the Court removed the teeth from certain sections of the Act by reading them in a light most favorable to the railroads and most restrictive of ICC powers. Confronted with judicial frustration of its intentions, and pressed politically by its shipper and farmer constituents, Congress, by a series of acts between 1903 and 1910, removed most of the weaknesses created by adverse court decisions. After 1906 (when the Hepburn Act was adopted) the Supreme Court showed greater respect for decisions of the ICC, an agency whose actions after 1920 have characteristically tended to promote, rather than attack the interests of carriers.

1920 TO 1937—GRUDGING ACCEPTANCE
AND SELECTIVE RESISTANCE

The second significant period of Supreme Court-administrative agency relations came after the close of the first World War. While many of the cases appear to involve technical issues, for the most part they reveal a running debate among the justices concerning the Court's proper role in reviewing agency action, or more specifically, the judicial limits that should be placed on the power of agencies to reach binding and final decisions.

An interesting example of the Supreme Court's divided views are revealed in a series of FTC decisions involving Section 7 of the Clayton Act. The first case concerned the Clayton Act's prohibitions of inter-corporate stockholding, a provision enforceable by the Antitrust Division of the Department of Justice. The real issue was whether under Section 7, earlier illegally acquired stock interests (that had led eventually to the merger of physical assets of established competitors) were subject to Federal Trade Commission action (*FTC* v. *Western Meat Co.* et al, 272 U.S. 554). Five Justices, speaking through McReynolds held the FTC powerless, and in effect sanctioned illegal stock purchases, so long as they went undetected, even though acquisition of physical assets resulted. Brandeis, for Holmes, Stone and Chief Justice Hughes, dissented, pointing out that Section 11 of the Clayton Act provided for Commission action whenever it "shall have reason to believe that any person is violating or has violated any of the provisions" of the Act.

The same section (7) of the Clayton Act was weakened further by a 1930 decision permitting acquisition by the largest shoe manufacturing company of the stock of the fourth or fifth ranking shoe manufacturing company, on the ground that the competition between the companies in the production and sale of mens' dress shoes had not been substantial, hence, not a violation of the act, which prohibited acquisition of the stock of competitors only where the effect was to "substantially lessen competition." Justice Stone dissented. Speaking for Holmes and Brandeis, he thought the record contained an abundance of evidence supporting the District Court and Circuit Court of Appeals findings that competition in certain types of shoes was substantially diminished by the stock acquisition.

In 1934 the meaning of this Clayton Act provision was diluted even further when by vote of 5 to 4 the Court validated a series of transactions in which a corporation purchased stock of competing companies, merged them, and then sold the stock while the FTC hearing was in process (*Arrow-Hart & Hegeman Electric Co.* v. *FTC*, 291 U.S. 587). Justice Roberts, for the majority, took an extremely narrow view of FTC powers, saying in effect, that its power to prevent certain prohibited business transactions did not imply a power to undo a wrongful act once it had been accomplished. Again Justice Stone, speaking for Brandeis, Cardozo and Chief Justice Hughes, dissented. Protesting against the strict construction of the majority, he argued that "no plausible reason has been advanced for interpreting this remedial act (Clayton) as though it were a penal law" (where strict construction is the rule). In reviewing such agency action, Stone remonstrated, "the function of courts is constructive not destructive . . . to make them [agencies], whenever reasonably possible, effective agencies for law enforcement and not to destroy them."

A potent judicial weapon for intervention and hence, limitation of administrative action in the 1930's, was the doctrine of "jurisdictional facts." Given its fullest expression in *Crowell* v. *Benson* (285 U.S. 22, 1932) it meant that whenever a question of the agency's jurisdiction (authority to hear a case) turned on disputed facts, the agency's findings were subject to review *de novo* (a new hearing of the facts) in the appropriate district court. The Crowell case involved the question of whether the Longshoremen's and Harbor Workers' Act applied to an injured worker who was classified an "employee" by Benson, a Compensation Commissioner, but was held not to be an employee by the District Court, and hence not entitled to compensation under the Act. Speaking through Chief Justice Hughes, the majority of the Supreme Court upheld the finding of the District Court, ruling that a *de novo* hearing was required since the jurisdiction of the Deputy Commissioner depended on affirmative answers to two questions: was the injured man an "employee," and did the injury occur upon navigable waters of the United States? This was so, said the majority, not merely because Congress had so provided, but because the Constitutional power of Congress (under the commerce clause) to enact such legislation required affirmative answers to these two questions. Brandeis, with the support of Stone and Roberts, found nothing in the Act or the Constitution that required a trial *de novo*, a procedure which Brandeis feared would "gravely hamper the effective administration of the Act." He advocated review by a district court sitting as a court of equity, limited to a scrutiny of the record made before the Deputy Commissioner. While never expressly overruled, *Crowell* v. *Benson* has been applied by the federal courts strictly to cases involving virtually identical fact issues; it has not been applied to analogous questions arising under other statutes.

Two other cases in the 1930's reveal the temper of the Court in dealing with administrative findings. In *St. Joseph Stockyards* v. *U.S.* (298 U.S. 38, 1935) the question was whether the District Court was required to make an independent determination of facts where the affected party claimed that administratively-set rates were confiscatory. In holding that constitutional issues involving the "due process" and "just compensation" clauses had been raised and that these were limitations on administrative agencies as well as on Congress itself, Chief Justice Hughes declared that the district court must exercise independent judgment on facts as well as law even though when non-constitutional facts were involved an independent finding was not required. A different position would, he said, place those rights (of liberty and property) "at the mercy of administrative officials and seriously impair the security inherent in our judicial safeguards," to him a serious prospect in view of the "multiplication of administrative agencies." On the merits, the majority thought that in the present case confiscation had not been proved. Brandeis, in a concurring opinion, joined by Stone and Cardozo, favored departing from the few precedents holding that due process required an independent determination of facts in rate cases, and advocated a uniform rule for judicial review of administratively determined facts, namely, that administrative findings if supported by substantial evidence are conclusive.

Perhaps the most striking example of the Courts' truculent attitude toward administrative action was that displayed in the Morgan cases, about which much has been written. In the first Morgan case of 1936, the Supreme Court held erroneous a District Court decision refusing to hear evidence as to whether the then Secretary of Agriculture, Henry Wallace, had heard or read evidence, or read the briefs of parties, before fixing stockyard rates (*Morgan* v. *United States*, 298 U.S. 468). The statute required a "full hearing" and that meant, said Chief Justice Hughes, "the officer who makes the determinations must consider and appraise the evidence which justifies them." However, when the case came up again with evidence of the Secretary's participation in the hearing process the Supreme Court found a new defect, "the absence of any intermediate report by the examiner." (*Morgan* v. *U.S.*, 304 U.S. 1, 1938.) To the Solicitor General's motion for a rehearing on the ground that the Court had, in effect, reversed itself, the Court replied that his assertion was "unwarranted," "wholly unfounded," "futile." In this spirit of antagonism and grudging acceptance, the Court worked manfully, over the protests of dissenters, to confine administrative action by strong judicial fetters.

1938—JUDICIAL RETREAT

The Supreme Court "revolution" of 1937 is most readily observed in the series of cases upholding the second Agricultural Adjustment Act, the Fair Labor Standards Act, the National Labor Relations Act and state minimum wage legislation. Equally important, though less strikingly evident, was the changed view of the Court toward administrative action. Essentially, the new attitude of the Supreme Court after 1938 was that administrative agencies were legitimate arms of government whose functions and processes must be viewed in a more generous spirit, if the purposes of Congress were to be achieved. This new philosophy has several facets which can only be touched upon here.

First, the Supreme Court has been prone to accept an agency's interpretation of its own powers. For example, although the Federal Communications Act (1934) contained no specific authorization for the FCC "Chain Broadcasting Regulations," promulgated in 1941, the Court upheld the Commission's action, sought to be justified by "the public interest, convenience, and necessity" provision in the statute, asserting, ". . . the Act gave the Commission not niggardly but expansive powers. . . . It is not for us to say that the public interest will be furthered or retarded by the Chain Broadcasting Regulations." (Frankfurter, in *NBC* v. *United States*, 319 U.S. 190, 1943)

This tendency is evident even when the agency interpretation might be treated as a legal, rather than factual question. Were newsboys "employees" so that they would be entitled to collective bargaining rights under the National Labor Relations Act? *Hearst* v. *NLRB* (322 U.S. 111, 1944) answered this question in the affirmative. For the Court, Justice Rutledge chose to accept the Board's finding, asserting that "it is not the court's function to substitute its own inferences of fact for the Boards', when the latter have support in the record."

Taking a limited view of the scope of its powers of review, the Supreme Court in *Gray* v. *Powell* (314 U.S. 402, 1941) became almost deferential. In administering a code with price-fixing, the Bituminous Coal Commission refused to hold the railroad a "producer-consumer" of coal and hence exempt from the price-fixing provision. The Circuit Court of Appeals disagreed. Justice Reed's opinion for the Supreme Court, upholding the administrative finding, is flavored with comments reflecting the new tone: "Where as here a determination has been left to an administrative body, this delegation will be respected and the administrative conclusion left untouched. . . . Although we have here no dispute as to the evidentiary facts, that does not permit a court to substitute its judgment for that of the Director." And again, "It is not the province of a court to absorb the administrative function to such an extent that the executive or legislative agencies become mere fact finding bodies deprived of the advantages of prompt and definite action." Justice Roberts and Justice Byrnes, joined by Chief Justice Stone who had so often dissented from decisions hostile to the administrative process, thought the Court was being overly generous in its view of the agency action here. "There are limits," said Roberts, "to which administrative officers may go in reconstructing a statute so as to accomplish aims which the legislature might have had but which the statute itself, and its legislative history, do not disclose."

The requirements of a "hearing," set forth in the first and second Morgan cases were apparently abandoned in 1941, eleven years after the proceedings began, when a wearied Court was confronted by the fourth Morgan case (*U.S.* v. *Morgan*, 313 U.S. 409). Now the Court held that the Secretary of Agriculture should never have been subjected to an examination of the process he followed in reaching a decision after "hearing." Justice Frankfurter, for the Court, observed that "just as a judge cannot be subjected to such a scrutiny, so the integrity of the administrative process must be equally respected." His concluding statement is characteristic. "It will bear repeating that although the administrative process has had a different development and pursues somewhat different ways from those of courts, they are to be deemed collaborative instrumentalities of justice and the appropriate independence of each should be respected by the other."

Judicial deference to agency action carried over to its review of rate making and other substantive activities. Abandoning the long asserted power to re-examine rates in a critical spirit, using the standard of "reasonableness" to determine whether rates were "confiscatory," the Court moved sharply in the other direction. In 1942 it asserted through Chief Justice Stone, that "the Constitution does not bind rate-making bodies to the service of any single formula or combination of formulas." Agencies were "free, within the ambit of their statutory authority to make the pragmatic adjustments which may be called for by particular circumstances. . . . If the Commission's order . . . produces no arbitrary result, our inquiry is at an end." (*FPC* v. *Natural Gas Pipeline Co.*, 315 U.S. 575, 1942.) The Court in 1944 adopted an even friendlier attitude toward rate-making agencies, pushing Frankfurter, Reed and Jackson into dissenting positions (*FPC* v. *Hope Natural Gas Co.*, 320 U.S. 591, 1944). Douglas, for the Court, stated boldly "It is the result reached, not the method employed, which is controlling. . . . It is not theory but the impact of the rate order which counts. If the total effect of the rate order cannot be said to be unjust and unreasonable, Judicial inquiry under the Act is at an end." The Court had indeed come full circle.

THE ADMINISTRATIVE PROCEDURE ACT AND AFTER

Although an estimated two-thirds of federal agencies had been established by 1930, the tempo and range of administrative action increased many-fold during the New Deal era. Critics of the new social policies as well as those adversely affected by specific administrative action naturally launched an attack on the new "bureaucracy." More restrained critics, such as the late Arthur T. Vanderbilt, outstanding lawyer and one time President of the American Bar Association, recognized the essential needs fulfilled by administrative agencies but sought reforms in procedure. In 1938 Congress, now restive under strong Presidential leadership and seeking ways of regaining some of its former power, viewed with sympathy proposals to curb the discretion of administrative agencies by regularizing their procedures and broadening judicial review of their actions. A bill to accomplish these purposes was introduced in 1940, but met with a Presidential veto, based on the argument that a fuller study of the problem was necessary. In 1941 the Attorney General's Committee on Administrative Reform issued a divided report, the majority stating that only modest reforms were called for. The minority, however, wished to impose uniform procedures on the agencies and widen the scope of review. World War II halted the debate, but in 1946 a bill embodying in modified form the recommendations of the minority of the 1941 Attorney General's Committee became law.

The essential features of the Administrative Procedure Act of 1946 are: (1) The functions of the prosecuting agency and the hearing officer are separated, and a separate corps of independent hearing officers has been created. (2) Agencies are required to inform the public of their structure, procedures, and rules by publication in the Federal Register. (3) Notice must be given of proposed rules or changes therein. (4) Hearings are to be conducted in accordance with definite rules. (5) Courts are to review agency action not unconstitutional or unauthorized by statute by the test of whether it is supported by substantial evidence on examination of the whole record. It should be noted that the APA did not purport to control all federal agencies, and agencies could be exempt by Congress from various provisions of the Act.

There is general agreement among competent observers that the act does not alter the relationship of courts to agencies in any fundamental way. The APA "transferred no power back to the courts, did not substantially increase judicial review, . . . improved the administrative process instead of weakening or crippling it, and in general gave assurance that further efforts to check the power of the agencies would be unlikely to succeed."

In an interesting case decided in 1950 (*Wong Yang Sung* v. *McGrath*, 339 U.S. 33, modified, 339 U.S. 908), the Supreme Court held that the hearings of the Immigration Service, which determines whether aliens were deportable, had to conform to the hearing provisions of the Administrative Procedure Act. Douglas, for the majority, viewed the hearing of the Immigration Service as one "required by statute," and by the due process clause of the Constitution. Since deportation might result, the hearing had to meet the procedural requirements of the Administrative Procedure Act. Reed, dissenting on the ground that Congress had not intended this result, saw his judgment vindicated when Congress, by a rider to an Appropriation Act in 1950, exempted such hearings from the coverage of the APA, and in the revision of the Immigration Act in 1952, made a similar exemption in unmistakable terms.

A year after the McGrath case, the Court was brought face to face with a question that goes to the heart of Court-agency relations. The issue in *Universal Camera Corp* v. *NLRB* (340 U.S. 474) was whether the APA requirements, and the Taft-Hartley Act (1947) changed the scope of review of NLRB decisions by the Courts of Appeals. The Wagner Act (1935), establishing the NLRB and its functions, provided that "the findings of the Board as to the facts, if supported by evidence, shall be conclusive." This had been interpreted to mean "substantial evidence," as Frankfurter speaking for the Court, pointed out, but it gradually had come to mean that substantial evidence supporting the Board decision "when viewed in isolation" was a sufficient basis for sustaining the Board. Now, Frankfurter argued, Congress in the APA had added a phrase to the substantial evidence rule, "on the record, considered as a whole," as the Taft-Hartley Act required. Conceding this, however, did not solve the problem, "Did the scope of review now differ from that prevailing before 1946?" While asserting that it did, Frankfurter found the change "so elusive that it cannot be precisely defined." He concluded, nevertheless, that "the Administrative Procedure Act and the Taft-Hartley Act direct that courts must now assume more responsibility for the reasonableness and fairness of Labor Board decision than some courts have shown in the past." In a sense, the Court was announcing its awareness that more, rather than less, judicial review was demanded by Congress, and that affected interests had caught the Congressional ear.

Later cases indicate that the Court has no intention of returning to the spirit of the 1930's, when administrative action was subject to rough treatment at the hands of the Court. Perhaps more important than the threat of more intensive court review in achieving fair and reasonable administrative action, is the increasing tendency of agencies to systematize their procedures and to approach their regulatory functions in a more benign and judicial spirit. The Supreme Court remains, however, the ultimate guardian of individual rights against arbitrary administrative action. Joined with this is the power of Congress, through more effective use of its investigative powers, to maintain watch over its offspring.

CONGRESSIONAL INTENT AND JUDICIAL REVIEW

The most convincing evidence that the Court has taken "self-restraint" to heart is the fact that only a handful of relatively unimportant statutes have been set aside since 1937. But this does not mean that the Judiciary has ceased to exercise effective control over public policy. It means rather that its influence has been exerted in other ways, one of the most important being statutory construction. Over half the cases decided by the Supreme Court since World War II involve problems of statutory interpretation. Justice Frankfurter went so far as to say that by 1947 the number of cases before the Court not in this category were "reduced to zero." The judicial task this presents is one of great significance and almost insuperable difficulty. A statute, usually the product of more than one mind and frequently the result of compromise, must necessarily be couched in ambiguous language. Frequently, legislation in its final form is drafted by overworked counsel under heavy pressure to meet urgent deadlines. Also in framing legislation to meet a general and continuing problem, it is impossible to foresee all the complex situations certain to arise. Hence the Congress, acting through a committee (or an executive agency), will by conscious choice use words designed to cast the widest net possible, one that will empower administrators (with the approval of courts, it is hoped) to adapt law to unforeseen circumstances. As John Chipman Gray put it,

> The fact is that the difficulties of so-called interpretation arise when the legislature has no meaning at all. When the question which is raised on the statute never occurred to it; when what the judges have to do is, not to determine what the legislature did mean on a point that was present to its mind, but to guess what it would have intended on a point not present to its mind, if the point had been present. (*Nature and Sources of the Law*, p. 125)

Where two interpretations are possible the Court adopts that which will render the statute constitutional. A good example is found in *United States* v. *Rumely*, 345 U.S. 41 (1953). A House of Representatives' resolution authorized a select committee to investigate "all lobbying activities intended to influence, encourage, promote, or retard legislation." Most observers thought that the committee was created to study the effectiveness of the Federal Regulation of Lobbying Act (1946), with especial attention to possible exposure of the financial supporters of several right-wing organizations that generally opposed the Democratic party, then in control of the House. Rumely, Secretary of the Committee for Constitutional Government, was asked to reveal the names of those who had made bulk purchases of books distributed by his organization. Citing statements of three former Chief Justices (Taft, Hughes, and Stone) to the effect that the Court's duty in interpreting federal statutes was "to reach a conclusion which will avoid serious doubt of their constitutionality," the Court, speaking through Justice Frankfurter, construed the resolution narrowly and held that the "lobbying" to be investigated referred only to "representations made directly to Congress" and not "efforts to saturate the thinking of the community." By ruling that the committee's questions were unauthorized by the resolution, the Court avoided the difficult constitutional question of whether Congress could have authorized the type of investigation actually undertaken here. Justice Douglas dissented, with Black concurring, arguing that the legislative history and actions of the committee showed that a broad investigation of the type actually pursued had been authorized by Congress. As we

shall see, he urged the Court to face the First Amendment issue thus
squarely presented. The majority, however, did not discover so clear
an expression of congressional purpose.

Another principle guiding statutory construction is that laws imposing criminal penalties, particularly those involving imprison-
ment, are to be construed "strictly." This means that doubts are
to be resolved in favor of those affected and against the government.
This is derived from an old common law rule, and is part of the
principle "nulla poena sine lege" (no penalty without a law)
meaning, of course, a law that is understandable.

This issue was raised in *Abrams* v. *United States,* 250 U.S. 616
(1919). Did the circulars published by Abrams opposing American
participation in the allied intervention of Russia after the 1917
Revolution come within the terms of the statute which seemingly
prohibited acts with intent to interfere with the war effort against
Germany? The majority thought that they did, asserting that "men
must be held to have intended, and to be accountable for, effects
which their acts were likely to produce." Holmes dissenting, with
the concurrence of Brandeis, argued that the "intent" shown was
not that specifically prohibited by the statute, and that the words
of the statute should be given their "strict and accurate" meaning.

A more recent example of strict construction of a penal statute
occurs in *Yates* v. *United States* (354 U.S. 298, 1957). Reversing
the conviction of fourteen West Coast Communist Party leaders,
the Court held that the term "organize" in the Smith Act should
be construed narrowly to mean activities directed toward the
original organization of the Communist Party in its revived status
in 1945, and not to include the continuing efforts of Party leaders
to expand the Party by adding new units and expanding existing
ones. As authority, Justice Harlan invoked Marshall's decision in
United States v. *Wiltberger* (5 Wheat. 76, 95-96, 1820) where the
great Chief Justice said: "The rule that penal laws are to be construed strictly is perhaps not much less old than construction itself.
It is founded on the tenderness of law for the rights of individuals,
and on the plain principle that the power of punishment is vested
in the legislative, not in the judicial department. It is the legislature,
not the court which is to define a crime and ordain its punishment."

Occasionally, the language of a statute is found so vague that
it is held to violate due process in failing to afford sufficient notice

and guidance to those affected. In *Lanzetta* v. *New Jersey* (306 U.S. 451, 1939) the Court held invalid on due process grounds a New Jersey law punishing anyone found to be a "gangster," defined as "any person not engaged in any lawful occupation, known to be a member of any gang consisting of two or more persons, who has been convicted at least three times of being a disorderly person, or who has been convicted of any crime in this or any other state."

In *Winters* v. *New York* (333 U.S. 507, 1948) the Court on similar grounds invalidated a New York statute making it an offense to publish or distribute publications "principally made up of criminal news, police reports or accounts of criminal deeds or pictures or stories of deeds of bloodshed, lust or crime." The New York Court had interpreted the law as prohibiting "the massing of pictures and stories so as to become vehicles for inciting violent and depraved crimes against the person." Frankfurter, Jackson, and Burton dissented, arguing that the policy of the act was clear even though its application to each case could not be determined in advance.

Three theories have been advanced to explain what the Court does or should do when it deals with statutory construction problems. The one most frequently cited is the "legislative intent" theory, meaning that the judge should try to discover legislative purpose. A second theory, known as "verbal meaning," views the process as simply one of reading into words their settled meaning. A third, rather iconoclastic theory, is that of "free interpretation," where the judge does whatever seems wise.

On the whole, the Supreme Court has tended more and more to use the "legislative intent" theory. The separation of power principle confirms the appropriateness of this judicial approach, and the availability of substantial amounts of data in the form of debates, committee reports, and hearing transcripts, facilitates it. At times an overabundance of materials complicates the quest for legislative intent, tempting a Justice with available evidence to support whatever preconceived idea he holds.

Where a Justice is convinced that the search for legislative intent is fruitless, or that the correct answer lies in the statute's plain language, he resorts to the verbal meaning theory. The late Justice Jackson was a strong advocate of this approach. One may find this theory being applied by one or more judges in the same case. While the common sense of laymen finds the "plain words" appealing, Judge Learned Hand has warned that "there is no surer way to misread any document than to read it literally." (*Guiseppi* v. *Walling*, CA 2nd, 144 F. 2d 608, 624.)

A good example of unwillingness to read a statute literally is the decision in *United States* v. *United Mine Workers* (330 U.S. 258, 1947). Here the Court held that the United States, being sovereign, was not bound by the provision of the Norris-LaGuardia Act limiting injunctions against strikes unless it explicitly agreed to be covered by the apparently general statute. Frankfurter, who had helped draft the Norris-LaGuardia Act, emphasized that an amendment providing for injunctive relief at the government's insistence was voted down. His reading of legislative history caused him to dissent from that of the majority.

Rejecting the search for legislative intent, Justice Murphy, dissenting, stated that "an objective reading of the National Labor Relations Act removes any doubt as to its meaning. Section 4 (Norris-LaGuardia Act) provides in clear unmistakable language that no court of the United States shall have jurisdiction, etc. in any case involving or growing out of any labor dispute." In other words Murphy advocated the verbal meaning theory.

Of course no judge ever avowedly uses the "free interpretation theory." Rather this is the product of legal commentators' efforts to explain realistically what the judges are doing, their belief being that neither the legislative intent nor the verbal meaning theories furnish satisfactory answers. Under the "free" theory a judge behaves as a super-legislator who, in the guise of interpreting what the legislature had done, in reality supplies a meaning which he— the judge—believes to be desirable. To the commentator, a judge may be doing this even while proclaiming adherence to other theories.

A good illustration of judges reading predilections into law through statutory construction is the decision in the 1911 *Standard Oil Company* v. *United States* case, 221 U.S. 1. The Sherman Act (1890) had stated (Sec. 1) that, "*Every* contract, combination in the form of trust or otherwise, or conspiracy in restraint of trade or commerce . . . is hereby declared to be illegal." Speaking through Chief Justice White, the Court, with only Harlan disagreeing, held that Congress must have intended to adopt the old common law principle against "undue or unreasonable restraints." The Chief Justice spent a great deal of time showing what the English law was before, and contemporaneously with, 1890 and makes only the vaguest reference to debates in Congress. While the anti-trust laws were interpreted so as to favor the business community in this and many other cases in the period 1920-1940, the Supreme Court view of these problems in the period after 1945 had a somewhat different flavor. Two examples will be cited.

By 1945 it was generally assumed that size alone was not a crucial determinant of monopoly, and that only where predatory practices or collusive agreements led to the achievement of great size would the anti-trust laws apply. But in *United States* v. *Aluminum Company of America* (Alcoa) the Supreme Court, unable to muster a quorum, sent the case to the Court of Appeals (Second Circuit) for decision. That court, speaking through Judge Learned Hand, held that Alcoa's consciously achieved size and its control of 90 per cent of the market constituted monopoly and hence, a violation of the anti-trust laws. *United States* v. *Aluminum Company of America* (148 F. 2d 416, 1945). This was a significant modification of the accepted anti-trust rules generally accented since the Standard Oil decision of 1911.

Even more dramatic was the Supreme Court's holding in 1957 that DuPont's acquisition in 1917-1919 of 23 per cent of General Motors Stock violated Section 7 of the Clayton Act. (*United States* v. *DuPont*, 353 U.S. 586). Section 7 provided "that no corporation engaged in commerce shall acquire directly or indirectly, the whole or any part of the stock or of other share capital of another corporation engaged also in commerce, where the effect of such acquisition may be to substantially lessen competition between the corporation whose stock is so acquired and the corporation making the acquisition, or to restrain such commerce in any section or community, or tend to create a monopoly of any line of commerce." Although the Government had not invoked this section against vertical acquisitions such as this (i.e., where the companies are not competitors) for a period of 35 years, the majority refused to accept this interpretation as binding. Rather, the Court found that the pressures on General Motors to purchase auto paint and fabrics from DuPont because of the stock ownership constituted a

"probable restraint or monopoly within the meaning of Section 7."
In support of this decision the Justices found that those sponsoring
the Clayton Act (1914) in the Senate intended the act to cover
vertical acquisitions, and cited letters of John J. Raskob and Pierre
S. DuPont of DuPont, as well as J. A. Haskell, onetime DuPont sales
manager and vice-president, and later vice-president of General
Motors, showing a mutual interest in increasing DuPont sales to
the motor company.

Judicial endorsement of congressional control of an ever-ex-
panding sector of our economic and social life has not meant judicial
abdication. Without resort to the judicial veto, as the DuPont case
shows, the Court may exert effective control over public policy.
In the words of Charles P. Curtis: "The less clearly and the less
certainly Congress speaks out, the more power it gives to the Court.
It is a delegation of legislative power to the Court. An unavoidable
and necessary, often politic and advisable, sometimes careless and
unfortunate, occasionally rather appalling, delegation of legislative
power." (*Lions Under the Throne*, p. 236). So while the Court has
accepted with good grace a lesser policy-making role, often
deliberately sidestepping the constitutional issue, it still exercises
great policy-making power by giving authoritative meaning to an
expanding body of important statutes.

Legislative investigations. As Congressional investigations increase
in number and importance, the search for legislative purpose of the
investigation becomes less significant. The power to conduct investigations, derived from the necessary and proper clause, is sus-
tainable solely on the basis of the inherent power of a legislature to
inform itself for purposes of legislation. *Kilbourn* v. *Thompson*
(103 U.S. 168, 1881) announced the principle that neither house
of Congress possessed "general power of making inquiry into the
private affairs of the citizen," that its power must be related to some
legislative purpose. But in 1927, in *McGrain* v. *Daugherty* (273
U.S. 135), the Court upheld an investigation of corruption in the
Department of Justice, though the resolution authorizing it failed
to mention possible legislation. The Court reasoned that "the subject
was one on which legislation could be had, . . . the only legitimate
object the Senate could have in ordering the investigation was to
aid it in legislating; and . . . the subject matter was such that the
presumption should be indulged that this was the real object."

A 1953 decision indicated, however, that a committee may not extend by its own interpretation the scope of investigation set forth in the resolution creating it (*United States* v. *Rumely*, 345 U.S. 41, 1953). Five Justices held that the investigation was limited, by the terms of the resolution, to activities constituting direct contact with Congress and did not extend to other lobbying activities, such as attempts to influence congressional thinking through publication of books and pamphlets. Justice Douglas, in a concurring opinion, suggested that the First Amendment might bar such investigations:

> A requirement that a publisher disclose the identity of those who buy his books, pamphlets, or papers is indeed the beginning of surveillance of the press. True, no legal sanction is involved here. Congress has imposed no tax, established no board of censors, instituted no licensing system. But the potential restraint is equally severe. The finger of government leveled against the press is ominous. Once the government can demand of a publisher the names of the purchasers of his publications, the free press as we know it disappears. Then the spectre of a government agent will look over the shoulder of everyone who reads. The purchase of a book or pamphlet today may result in a subpoena tomorrow. Fear of criticism goes with every person into the bookstall. The subtle, imponderable pressures of the orthodox lay hold. Some will fear to read what is unpopular, what the powers-that-be dislike. When the light of publicity may reach any student, any teacher, inquiry will be discouraged. The books and pamphlets that are critical of the administration, that preach an unpopular policy in domestic or foreign affairs, that are in disrepute in the orthodox school of thought will be suspect and subject to investigation. The press and its readers will pay a heavy price in harassment. But that will be minor in comparison with the menace of the shadow which government will cast over literature that does not follow the dominant party line. . . . Congress could not do this by law. The power of investigation is also limited. Inquiry into personal and private affairs is precluded. [*United States* v. *Rumely*, 345 U.S. 41, 57-58.]

With the increase of congressional investigations, courts were not disposed to scrutinize committee procedures with care or to impose rules of fairness derived from the due process clause of the Fifth Amendment. The only effective limitation on committee action was the ever more frequent invocation by witnesses of the Fifth Amendment privilege against self-incrimination. The federal district courts took a generous view of the scope of the privilege

(*United States* v. *Yio Abe*, 95 F. Supp. 991, 1950; *United States* v. *Emspak*, 95 F. Supp. 1012, 1951) and recent Supreme Court decisions affirmed the doctrine that the privilege against self-incrimination was as effective in barring investigatory interrogation as interrogation in a court of law (*Quinn* v. *United States*, 349 U.S. 155, 1955; *Emspak* v. *United States*, 349 U.S. 190, 1955; *Bart* v. *United States*, 349 U.S. 219, 1955). Hence, witnesses who would have preferred to challenge a committee's line of questioning by "taking" the First Amendment or by attacking its pertinency or propriety, resorted to the Fifth Amendment, protesting possible self-incrimination. The result is that, in the public mind, the privilege against self-incrimination is synonymous with the Fifth Amendment. To secure testimony, the demand has arisen that immunity from prosecution be given witnesses whose testimony was considered vital. The Immunity Act of 1954 containing this provision was upheld in *Ullman* v. *United States* (350 U.S. 422, 1956). Because of the recognized reluctance of the Supreme Court to become entangled in congressional procedures some observers thought that this situation was likely to prevail for the foreseeable future. Writing in early 1957, Bernard Schwartz stated that decisions in the modern era indicated that *Kilbourn* v. *Thompson* "must now be regarded with caution," that a majority of the Court saw "few, if any, constitutional restrictions of consequence on inquiries." As on many previous occasions in its history, the Supreme Court belied this prediction on June 17, 1957 by its decision in *Watkins* v. *United States* (354 U.S. 178).

John T. Watkins, a former labor union leader, was convicted for contempt of Congress because of his refusal to answer certain questions put to him by the Committee on Un-American Activities. Watkins had given full replies to questions about his relations with Communists during earlier union activities, but refused to respond to questions about persons he knew in the past to be Communist Party members unless he believed that they still were members. Of thirty names read to him, seven were completely unconnected with organized labor. To the Court, this indicated that the subject before the subcommittee was not defined in terms of communism in labor. The government had thought that the remarks of the subcommittee chairman, mentioning specifically a bill that would penalize unions controlled by members of "Communist-action," indicated that his group was inquiring into Communist infiltration. Rejecting this contention, the Court ruled that neither the resolution itself, nor the action of the full committee, made clear the pertinency of such questions. "We remain unenlightened," the Court concluded, "as to the subject to which the questions asked petitioner were pertinent."

The power to investigate is, of course, inherent in the legislative process, but the Chief Justice, noting the broad resolution establishing the committee in 1938 and the equally vague words elevating it to the status of a Standing Committee, declared that "there is no congressional power to expose for the sake of exposure." Legislative investigations are, he pointed out, subject to the restrictions of the First Amendment. The "due process" clause requires that the witness know whether the questions put to him are pertinent to the question under inquiry. In language that recalled the bitter criticism publicists had directed against the procedures of the Committee on Un-American Activities, the Chief Justice declared that investigations conducted solely for the investigators' "personal aggrandizement" or to "punish" those under investigation are "indefensible."

Perhaps anticipating unfavorable congressional reaction, the Court suggested that "a measure of added care" in authorizing the use of compulsory process was "a small price to pay if it serves to uphold the principles of limited, constitutional government without constricting the power of the Congress to inform itself." In effect the Chief Justice threw down the gauntlet to Congress. Threats of judicially imposed restraint run through his opinion. "Curb your committees or else the Court will exert its power to do so." Overlooked in much of the critical discussion of the opinion, however, is Chief Justice Warren's alertness to the "complexities of modern government" and his disinclination to curb its power.

> We are mindful of the complexities of modern government and the ample scope that must be left to the Congress as the sole constitutional depository of legislative power. Equally mindful are we of the indispensable function, in the exercise of that power, of congressional investigations. The conclusions we have reached will not prevent the Congress, through its committees, from obtaining any information it needs for the proper fulfillment of its role in our scheme of government. The legislature is free to determine the kind of data that should be collected. It is only those investigations

that are conducted by use of compulsory process that give rise
to a need to protect the rights of individuals against illegal encroachment. That protection can be readily achieved through procedures which prevent the separation of power from responsibility
and which provide the constitutional requisites of fairness for witnesses. A measure of added care on the part of the House and
Senate in authorizing the use of compulsory process by their committees in exercising that power would suffice.

Montesquieu's great "political truth" was thus given a new
twist—"no separation of power from responsibility." Dissenting
vehemently, Justice Clark criticized the majority for converting
the judiciary into a "grand inquisitor and supervisor of Congressional investigations," making "operation of the committee system
of inquiry both unworkable and unnecessary." The majority opinion
would, Clark suggested, result in a "mischievous curbing of the
informing function of Congress."

A different problem arises when congressional committees seek
to procure the attendance of executive officials, or to obtain
documents in the possession of the President. Though a subpoena
cannot be directed to the President, subordinate officials may be
required by Congress to attend committee meetings. In practice
the refusal of the President to yield documents has been conclusive.

It is unlikely that the Court will go beyond its Watkins' ruling,
and attempt to prescribe in any detail what constitutes a "fair"
investigating procedure. Apart from the difficulties of that task,
the Court is well aware of the dangers to judicial power inherent
in congressional power to prescribe the Court's appellate jurisdiction.
The introduction of bills to limit the Court's jurisdiction, following
Watkins and other decisions unpopular with Congress, suggest that
Congress is not disposed to accept the Court as final arbiter of the
powers of Congress. Whatever the eventual outcome of such measures, the warning to the Court is clear and ominous.

III

THE COURT
AND PRESIDENT

*L*IKE MOST MODERN GOVERN-
ments the United States has manifested a tendency toward concentration of power in the hands of the executive. The President is
the political head of the country in extraconstitutional affairs; he
exercises the power of pardon, the veto power, and extensive war
powers, and has almost absolute control over foreign relations.
Moreover, in certain situations, Congress may give the executive its
own power to be used when swift and coordinated action is required. Finally, the efficient conduct of government, increasingly
in the multiple hands of administrative authority, has given rise to
the expressions "government by commission" and "government by
executive order"—terms indicative of the important position of the
President in present-day government.

The members of the Convention of 1787 who feared that the
executive inevitably would succumb to an all-powerful legislature
have proved to be poor prophets. Although the Supreme Court has
from the time of Marshall asserted and maintained a role of great
significance, it is the presidential office that has expanded most in
power and has shown the greatest increase in both the number and

the variety of its activities. The grand age of the legislature, when the dominance of the concept of limited government both required and permitted long debate preceding any change in governmental policy, when paucity of governmental programs facilitated legislative surveillance of administration, is past. War, economic crises, and the complexity of problems confronting industrialized societies have thrust upon the executive power and responsibility not contemplated in an earlier age. The American Presidency has proved no exception to this worldwide trend.

Three strikingly divergent theories purport to describe the nature and scope of presidential power: the constitutional theory, the stewardship theory, and the prerogative theory. The constitutional theory holds that Article II contains an enumeration of executive powers, and that the President must justify all his actions on the basis of either a power enumerated or a power implied from a specified power. In his book, *Our Chief Magistrate and His Powers* (1916), ex-President Taft endorsed this view. In opposition to Taft, President Theodore Roosevelt believed that the President is a "steward of the people," and is therefore under the duty to do "anything that the needs of the nation demanded unless such action was forbidden by the Constitution and the laws." Taft denounced Roosevelt's theory as calculated to make the President a "universal Providence." As Chief Justice, however, he indicated, as we shall see, greater sympathy for it. Going beyond the first Roosevelt's "stewardship" theory, Franklin D. Roosevelt's concept of his duties conforms essentially to John Locke's concept of "prerogative"— "the power to act according to discretion for the public good, without the prescription of the law and sometimes even against it." During his long incumbency, President Roosevent often glossed over constitutional and legal restrictions if, in his opinion, "emergency" and a commanding public interest justified bold action.

Many dicta in the Curtiss-Wright case (299 U.S. 304, 1936) seem to justify "inherent" power, at least in foreign affairs, where the President speaks and acts for the nation. In the domestic sphere, however, this is, as the steel seizure case suggests, a highly dubious rationale for presidential action (*Youngstown* v. *Sawyer*, 343 U.S. 579, 1952). Decided during a period in which the Justices were still flying the judicial self-restraint banner, this case represents a notable pronouncement.

On April 8, 1952, President Truman, in an attempt to head off a threatened steel strike, issued an executive order directing the Secretary of Commerce to seize and operate the steel mills. "A work stoppage," the President declared, "would immediately jeopardize and imperil our national defense and the defense of those joined with us in resisting aggression, and would add to the continuing danger of our soldiers, sailors, and airmen engaged in combat in the fields." The President's action seizing the steel mills indicates his assumption that he possessed means other than those provided in the Taft-Hartley Act of dealing with such an emergency. When the case was before the District Court, counsel for the United States was asked to specify the source of the President's seizure power in peacetime. "We base the President's power on Sections 1, 2, and 3 of Article II of the Constitution, and whatever inherent, implied or residual powers may flow therefrom," the government's lawyers replied. "So you contend the Executive has unlimited power in time of an emergency?" the Judge inquired. Government counsel said that the President "has the power to take such action as is necessary to meet the emergency," and indicated that the only limitations on Executive power in an emergency are the ballot box and impeachment (Transcript, 371 House Doc. 534, Pt. I, 82nd Sess., 1952). In argument before the Supreme Court, however, government counsel stressed the President's specific powers derived from the duty to execute the laws, and as Commander-in-Chief.

The steel company brought action in a federal court, asking for a declaratory judgment and injunctive relief. The district court issued relief, and the Court of Appeals confirmed it. Before the Supreme Court on certiorari, the Justices upheld the district court's order 6 to 3. Speaking for the Court, Justice Black voiced the dubious proposition that "inasmuch as Congress could have ordered the seizure of the steel mills the President had no power to do so without prior congressional authority." This ruling not only evoked a sharp dissenting opinion from Chief Justice Vinson and Justices Reed and Black, but also elicited five concurring opinions. It should be noted, further, that only Justices Black and Douglas held that seizure of private property must in every instance be based on statute. The other concurring Justices reserved the question whether, in the absence of any legislation providing for seizure, or expression of congressional intent, presidential action based on inherent power would be constitutional.

The steel case decision demonstrates that, although the President himself may not be the subject of judicial orders limiting his actions in executing laws or implementing policy (*Mississippi* v. *Johnson*, 4 Wall. 475, 1867), his subordinate officers may be the objects of injunctive and other forms of relief, when they act, or threaten to act, illegally. Commenting on the steel seizure case, the London *Economist* observed: "The Supreme Court, although it does not possess and never has possessed any means of enforcing its decisions, has once more brought to heel the mighty: the President, the union, the industry, and Congress."

APPOINTMENT AND REMOVAL OF OFFICERS

The Constitution provides that the President "shall nominate and, by and with the advice and consent of the Senate, shall appoint ambassadors . . . judges of the Supreme Court, and all other officers of the United States, whose appointments are not herein otherwise provided for and which shall be established by law; but the Congress may by law vest the appointment of such inferior officers, as they think proper, in the President alone, in the courts of law, or in the heads of departments" (Art. II, Sec. 2, Cl. 2). Persons appointed in a manner not specified by the Constitution are not "officers of the United States"; and while the courts have given us no definition of the term "inferior officers," it would seem to include all except those in whom the power of appointment might be vested.

The Constitution makes no provision for the removal of officers appointed under the clause above quoted. While the power of removal is generally regarded as a power derived from the power to appoint, it rests within the sole discretion of the President only when exercised with respect to a purely executive or ministerial office.

Following the decision in the leading case of *Myers* v. *United States* (272 U.S. 52, 1926), where the Court invalidated an 1876 act requiring the consent of the Senate to the removal of Postmasters, it was generally thought that the power of the President to remove officials appointed by him was plenary, free from any limitations imposed by Congress. Dicta in the Myers opinion written by Chief Justice Taft, one-time advocate of the "weak President" theory, seemed to suggest this doctrine. It is notable that Justices Holmes, McReynolds, and Brandeis dissented, the latter two writing lengthy opinions. All dissenting Justices cast doubt on the majority's argument that the President either possessed or required an unlimited authority to remove inferior officers. Taking issue with the Chief Justice's contention that considerations of efficiency upheld the President's power to remove all officers appointed by him, Justice Brandeis observed:

> The doctrine of separation of powers was adopted by the Convention of 1787, not to promote efficiency but to preclude the exercise of arbitrary power. The purpose was, not to avoid friction, but, by means of the inevitable friction incident to the distribution of the governmental powers among three departments, to save the people from autocracy. In order to prevent arbitrary executive action, the Constitution provided in terms that presidential appointments be made with the consent of the Senate, unless Congress should otherwise provide; and this clause was construed by Alexander Hamilton in *The Federalist*, No. 77, as requiring like consent to removals. Limiting further executive prerogatives customary in monarchies, the Constitution empowered Congress to vest the appointment of inferior officers, "as we think proper, in the President alone, in the Courts of Law, or in the Heads of Departments." Nothing in support of the claim of uncontrollable power can be inferred from the silence of the Convention of 1787 on the subject of removal. For the outstanding fact remains that every specific proposal to confer such uncontrollable power upon the President was rejected. In America, as in England, the conviction prevailed then that the people must look to representative assemblies for the protection of their liberties. And protection of the individual, even if he be an official, from the arbitrary or capricious exercise of power was then believed to be an essential of free government.

Nine years after the Myers decision, the Court whittled down Chief Justice Taft's sweeping dicta. Removal of officials from certain independent agencies, such as the Federal Trade Commission, the Court ruled, could be limited to causes defined by Congress (*Humphrey's Executor* v. *United States*, 295 U.S. 602, 1935). The Court emphasized the distinction between positions in the traditional executive departments for whose administration the President assumed primary responsibility, and those in agencies established by Congress to carry out legislative policy essentially free from any executive influence other than that resulting from appointment.

Failure of Congress to provide for removal for cause in no way
diminishes the essential principle of Humphrey's decision, namely,
that the function of the agency is determinative. In a 1958 ruling
President Eisenhower was held powerless to remove a member of
the War Claims Commission for political reasons similar to those
offered in the Humphrey's affair by President Roosevelt because
the "nature of the function" of the Commission as expressed in the
1948 act under which it was established, revealed a congressional
intention that its members should be free of such presidential control
(*Wiener* v. *United States,* 78 S. Ct. 1275, 1958).

PARDONING POWER

The President is empowered to grant "reprieves" (a suspension
of legally imposed penalties) and "pardons" (a remission of sentence) except in cases of impeachment. A pardon is effective whether
or not the recipient accepts it (*Biddle* v. *Perovich,* 274 U.S. 480,
1927). Further, the effect of a pardon is the restoration of the civil
rights of the recipient, but not his political rights (this stipulation
becomes significant where conviction of a crime is a bar to public
office holding). In *Ex parte Grossman* (267 U.S. 87, 1925) the
pardoning power of the President seemed to collide head on with
the power of the courts to punish for contempt. Nevertheless, the
Supreme Court, taking a generous view of the pardoning power,
held that the President's power in this field was as great as that of
the English kings, who had frequently pardoned those guilty
of contempt of court.

PROTECTION AGAINST DOMESTIC VIOLENCE

The President has the duty under Article IV, Section 4, to furnish
military assistance to repress domestic violence upon call of a state
legislature or governor. From the Whiskey Rebellion to the present,
presidents have been called upon for aid, either because of insurrection against the lawful state government, or because of disorders
arising from social unrest. The action of the President in sending,
or even agreeing to commit, troops to the aid of one of the contending factions in a state dispute, is a recognition that there is a
lawful government in that state (*Luther* v. *Borden,* 7 How. 1, 1849).
If the disorder results in the violation of federal laws, the President
may then act in accordance with his duty to "take care that the

laws be faithfully executed. . . ." In either case, in the actual direction of troops, he acts in his capacity of Commander-in-Chief.

EXECUTING THE LAWS

The constitutional authority of the President has been spelled out by specific legislation: "Whenever the President considers that unlawful obstructions, combinations, or assemblages or rebellion against the authority of the United States make it impracticable to enforce the laws of the United States in any state or territory by the ordinary course of judicial proceedings, he may call into Federal service such of the militia of any state, and use such of the armed forces, as he considers necessary to enforce these laws or to suppress the rebellion." With or without approval of a state governor, the President may use military force, or any other means deemed necessary to fulfill his obligation faithfully to execute the laws of the United States. In defiance of Governor Altgeld of Illinois, President Cleveland invoked such authority during the great Pullman strike (*In re Debs*, 158 U.S. 564, 1895). Earlier the Court had exempted from state prosecution a special officer appointed by direction of the President to guard Supreme Court Justice Field, when the officer shot and killed a man who had threatened and accosted the Justice (*In re Neagle*, 135 U.S. 1, 1890). The justification given in the Neagle case was the President's duty to execute the laws, interpreted broadly to include the protection of officials carrying out their lawful duties. The President was not required to cite a specific statute authorizing his action. His power to protect the "peace" of the United States and execute the laws seemingly has no effective judicial limits.

National authority to enforce a Federal Court order against the opposition of a state governor was brought sharply into focus in September 1957 when President Eisenhower ordered federal troops to enforce the desegregation orders of the United States District Court in Little Rock, Arkansas. The Arkansas Governor's use of state troops to prevent integration in Central High School—for the professed purpose of maintaining the peace—in the face of the Supreme Court's decision of May 17, 1954, raised some interesting questions.

Two cases, *Moyer* v. *Peabody* (212 U.S. 78, 1909) and *Sterling* v. *Constantin* (287 U.S. 378, 1932), were relevant to this situation.

In the first case the Governor of Colorado, declaring a county to be in a state of insurrection called out troops to put down the trouble. The plaintiff in error, leader of the outbreak, had been arrested and ordered detained until he could be discharged with safety. Speaking for a unanimous Court, Justice Holmes upheld the governor's power. "So long as such arrests are made in good faith and in the honest belief that they are needed in order to head the insurrection off, the Governor is the final judge. . . ." "It is not alleged," Holmes added, "that his judgment was not honest, if that be material, or that the plaintiff was detained after fears of the insurrection were at an end."

In the second case, the Governor of Texas, proclaiming "a state of insurrection, tumult, riot and breach of peace," invoked martial law to override a Federal Court decision. The Federal Court, ruling that there was no emergency, enjoined the Governor from further use of troops in defiance of the Court's order. The Governor, contending that the Federal Courts had no power to review the facts on which his action was based, appealed to the Supreme Court. Speaking for a unanimous Court, Chief Justice Hughes held that, although the Governor has wide discretion to use troops in an emergency, it did not follow "that every sort of action the governor may take . . . is conclusively supported by mere executive fiat." If a governor's use of troops to enforce his will could not be reviewed by the Courts, "a state Governor, and not the Constitution of the United States, would be the supreme law of the land." In language that seems particularly applicable to the Little Rock situation, the Court concluded:

> If it be assumed that the Governor was entitled to declare a state of emergency and to bring military force to the aid of civil authority, the proper use of that power in this instance was to maintain the Federal court in the exercise of its jurisdiction and not to attempt to override it, to aid in making its process effective and not to nullify it; to remove and not to create obstructions to the exercise by the complainants of their rights judicially declared.

MILITARY POWERS

The power of the federal government over the armed forces of the nation is divided between the President and Congress. The legislature has been given the important powers of raising armies and providing a navy (Art. I, Sec. 8, Cl. 14); the President, as

Commander-in-Chief of the armed forces (Art. II, Sec. 2, Cl. 1), may issue regulations of his own and may take charge of all military operations in time of peace as well as in war. Article I, Section 9 of the Constitution limits Congress' power to suspend the writ of habeas corpus to "cases of rebellion or invasion." Yet Lincoln, during the Civil War, suspended the privilege of the writ without congressional authorization, and ordered his officers to refuse service of a writ of habeas corpus issued by Chief Justice Taney. Subsequently, Congress authorized the President to suspend the writ in certain cases; the Supreme Court, however, refused to pass on the validity of the President's action (*Ex parte Vallandigham*, 1 Wall, 243, 1864). Lincoln provided another extreme example of executive power when he imposed martial law on portions of the northern states, and substituted trial by military commission for the regular processes of law in dealing with traitors and others charged with violations of wartime statutes.

In the famous case of *Ex parte Milligan* (4 Wall. 2, 1866), decided after the end of hostilities, the Court held that Lincoln had exceeded his authority, since the regular courts of Indiana, where the military commission had convicted Milligan, were open and prepared to handle the charges against him. Five members of the Court went further and stated that martial rule could never exist where the courts were open. Four members thought that Congress could have sanctioned what the Executive could not.

In World War II a similar result followed, where the Governor-General of Hawaii, pursuant to presidential authorization, invoked martial rule, and gave to military commissions jurisdiction over all criminal offenses. In a 6-2 decision, the Court held such action invalid on the basis of the Milligan decision (*Duncan* v. *Kahanamoku*, 327 U.S. 304, 1956).

War does not suspend the guaranties of the Constitution. However, the war powers may furnish a basis of reasonableness for governmental action that in normal times would be invalid (as a denial of due process of law).

Two different approaches to the problem of waging war successfully can be found in American history. Under Lincoln, Congress was ignored or asked to ratify executive actions already accomplished or under way. In World Wars I and II, on the other hand, Congress passed numerous statutes of wide scope delegating to the President, or to persons designated by him, vast discretionary powers. The widest of these delegations were upheld (e.g. *Bowles* v. *Willingham*, 321 U.S. 503, 1944). When statutory authority is thus added to the President's already large powers as Commander-in-Chief, constitutional limitations virtually disappear. The Japanese relocation cases indicate that, even without the support of statute, presidential power in wartime is subject to few limitations. The President can control the movement of the armed forces, and prescribe rules, including judicial procedures, for the government of captured territory. He may convene special military commissions to try saboteurs (*Ex parte Quirin*, 317 U.S. 1, 1942), and direct the seizure of former enemy officers and officials after the conclusion of hostilities, and set up military commissions to try them in proceedings that are not limited by the Constitution (*In re Yamashita*, 372 U.S. 1, 1946).

In *Ex parte Quirin*, the Supreme Court upheld the President's determination that seven captured German saboteurs, who had been landed from submarines off the East coast, should be tried by Military commission rather than by the regular courts. Refusing to issue a writ of habeas corpus, it held that enemy aliens who violate laws of war may be tried by military commissions established by the President, acting under the Articles of War, and by virtue of his own power as Commander-in-Chief. Similarly, the Court ratified extreme applications of the war powers against Japanese-Americans in World War II, citizens and aliens alike. By refusing to examine critically the "reasonableness" of military action imposing a curfew followed by relocation and detention, the Court, in effect, granted to the President, when supported by Congress, virtually unchecked power to do all that may seem necessary to save the nation (*Hirabayashi* v. *U.S.*, 320 U.S. 81, 1943, and *Korematsu* v. *U.S.*, 323 U.S. 214, 1944). However one may deplore the specific course of action taken by the President and his commander in the World War II relocation program, it is easy to comprehend why judicial "self-restraint" was invoked as the only realistic course to follow.

In 1959 questions of presidential power to impose martial law and suspend the privilege of the writ of habeas corpus are "live" issues. During a national mock "alert" in 1955, President Eisenhower, acting on the advice of the Attorney-General, took both of these steps without arousing adverse public reaction. The likelihood of widespread breakdown of normal governmental procedures in a future atomic war reinforces the assumption that the President alone can determine the necessity of drastic departures from the normal operation of the "rule of law."

"The war power of the Federal Government," Chief Justice Hughes declared in 1934, "is a power to wage war successfully, and thus . . . permits the harnessing of the entire energies of the people in a supreme cooperative effort to preserve the nation."

FOREIGN AFFAIRS

In foreign affairs, presidential power is limited by Congress only with great difficulty and on rare occasions. Congressional control of the purse provides a check in theory, but in practice it has been of little effect. The Court has upheld, as we have seen, delegation of power by Congress to the President that would have been invalidated if it had been made in domestic legislation. Sustaining presidential power is the theory of sovereignty set forth in Justice Sutherland's Curtiss-Wright opinion, and the great reservoir of inherent power possessed by the President as representative of the United States in dealing with other nations.

A political society cannot endure without a supreme will somewhere. Sovereignty is never held in suspense. When, therefore, the external sovereignty of Great Britain in respect of the colonies ceased, it immediately passed to the Union.

It results that the investment of the Federal government with the powers of external sovereignty did not depend upon the affirmative grants of the Constitution. The powers to declare and wage war, to conclude peace, to make treaties, to maintain diplomatic relations with other sovereignties, if they had never been mentioned in the Constitution, would have vested in the Federal government as necessary concomitants of nationality. [*U.S.* v. *Curtiss-Wright*, 299 U.S. 304, 1936.]

TREATY-MAKING POWER AND THE STATES

The treaty-making power belongs exclusively to the national government, since the Constitution expressly delegates the power to the President and the Senate (Art. II, Sec. 2, Cl. 2) and prohibits its exercise by the states (Art. I, Sec. 10). Treaties entered into by the national government are "the supreme law of the land" and so stand on a parity, insofar as their operative effect is concerned, with acts of Congress (Art. IV, Sec. 2).

By virtue of the treaty-making power, the national government may exercise greater power over the states than can Congress under its specific grants of power. Treaties must, of course, receive the consent of two-thirds of the Senate. But once it is passed, a treaty may then be the basis of implementing legislation that otherwise would not be within the power of Congress. The ordinary legislative power of Congress, for example, was thought insufficient to permit regulation of migratory birds (*Missouri* v. *Holland*, 252 U.S. 416, 1920); nor might Congress regulate, without a treaty, the rights of aliens to own or inherit property. Yet in each of these cases, treaties in conflict with state laws have been held valid and supreme despite their obvious encroachment on the reserved powers of the states. This does not mean that the constitutional distribution of powers between the states and the national government has been destroyed by an unlimited treaty power. The power is limited by implication in that it can be exercised only in relation to matters that are common subjects of international agreements. That is to say, the power may be used only in connection with foreign relations; it may not be used in violation of an express constitutional prohibition. Whether a treaty may alter the form or character of the federal system of government is not so clear. A treaty has two aspects: as an international engagement, and as law of the land. The former can be changed or modified only by action of the President; the latter can be altered or negatived by an Act of Congress.

The tendency of modern Presidents to use executive agreements rather than the cumbersome treaty procedure has freed them from dependency on the Senate. Such agreements have the same legal effect as treaties (*United States* v. *Belmont*, 301 U.S. 324, 1937; *United States* v. *Pink*, 315 U.S. 203, 1942). In 1952 and again in 1953 resolutions were introduced in the Senate seeking to limit presidential power through a constitutional amendment requiring congressional action before treaties or executive agreements would become effective as domestic law. These efforts, vigorously championed by Senator Bricker of Ohio, have been successfully resisted primarily because of the serious adverse impact such an amendment would inevitably exert on the President's control of foreign relations. Congress has the power, should it choose to exercise it, to exert a substantial influence upon presidential conduct of foreign affairs, through its power to pass joint resolutions and by employing its hitherto largely unexercised power of monetary control. The Senate also remains a partner in the treaty-making process, but with the increasing importance and complexity of foreign policy, the President finds it necessary to play a role unhindered by the ability of one-third-plus-one of the Senate to frustrate his actions.

IV

FEDERALISM

ALTHOUGH JUDICIAL REVIEW has been considered America's unique contribution to political science, it may be that our federalism will continue to be of greater influence on other nations. With growing interest in world organization after World War II, attention again centers on American experience. Unfortunately, for those who look upon federalism as the key to world order under law, American history—unless one takes the long view—is not altogether reassuring.

The United States is governed by a federal system, a duality in which governmental powers are distributed between central (national) and local (state) authorities. The reason for its adoption are both historical and rational. The Colonies of the revolutionary period regarded themselves as independent sovereignties; even under the Articles of Confederation, little of their power over internal affairs was actually surrendered to the Continental Congress. But local patriotism necessarily yielded before the proved inability of the Confederation to cope with the problems confronting it. When the Constitutional Convention met, compromise between the advocates of a strong central government and supporters of states' rights was inevitable. Federalism also fitted into Madison's basic requirement of free government. It reflected his purpose to so con-

69

trive "the interior structure of the government as that its several constituent parts may, by their mutual relations, be the means of keeping each other in their proper place."

Hamilton, in *Federalist*, No. 23, listed four chief purposes of union: common defense, public peace, regulation of commerce, and foreign relations. General agreement that these objectives required unified government drew together representatives of small and large states alike. To Madison and other nationalists, it seemed certain that the people would remain firmly attached to their state governments. It was thought that their ability to resist encroachments by the central government was immeasurably greater than the national government's capacity to withstand adverse state action. To allay criticism, Madison and other supporters of the Constitution agreed, nevertheless, to the Ninth and Tenth Amendments, as reassurance that all powers not delegated to the central government were reserved to the states or to the people.

What Madison said in the debates of the first Congress on the proposed Tenth Amendment bears out Chief Justice Marshall's observation in *McCulloch* v. *Maryland* (4 Wheat. 316, 1819) that this amendment was designed "for the purpose of quieting excessive jealousy which had been excited." The amendment was intended, Madison explained, "to extinguish from the bosom of every member of the community any apprehensions that there are those among his countrymen who wish to deprive them of the liberty for which they valiantly fought and honorably bled. And if there are amendments desired, of such a nature as will not injure the Constitution, and they can be ingrafted so as to give satisfaction to the doubting part of our fellow citizens, the friends of the Federal Government will evince that spirit of deference and concession for which they have hitherto been distinguished." Madison stated his position more tersely on August 15, 1789: "While I approve of these amendments I should oppose the consideration at this time of such as are likely to change the principles of the government." Three days later, when it was proposed that the word "expressly" be added to the proposed Tenth Amendment, making it read, "the powers not *expressly* delegated by this Constitution," Madison objected. "It was impossible to confine a Government to the exercise of express powers; there must necessarily be admitted powers by implication." This motion was defeated. On August 21, still another effort to

get the word "expressly" inserted suffered the same fate. The vote
was 32 to 17.

The distribution of powers agreed upon in the Convention, and
the reassurance given the states by the Ninth and Tenth Amendments, did not preclude conflict. The struggle continued in politics
and in the courts. When prolonged debate and bitter controversy
failed to yield a conclusive verdict, the contestants carried this
baffling issue as to the nature of federalism to the battlefield for
settlement by arbitrament of the sword. Even this holocaust
was not conclusive. The Civil War merely established the supremacy of the Union over individual states. The problem of
determining the extent of national and state power and of resolving
conflicts between the two centers of authority was ultimately left
to the Supreme Court. "A federal polity," Roscoe Pound has noted,
"is necessarily a legal polity. Only a constitution which is the
supreme law can hold the whole and the part to their appointed
spheres."

The problems discussed in this chapter concern the *nature* of the
powers of the national government, the extent to which state
government and national government are free from interference
by each other, the extent of cooperation between them, and the
means whereby federal supremacy is achieved where conflict is
unavoidable. The *extent* of national power is reserved for later
chapters where specific powers are discussed.

NATURE OF NATIONAL AUTHORITY

Theoretically, the powers of the national government are limited
to those delegated to it by the Constitution, expressly or by implication; the powers "not delegated . . . nor prohibited by it to the
states" are "reserved to the states respectively or to the people."

EXPRESS AND IMPLIED POWERS

As a sort of second dimension, the national government may
choose the means of carrying specifically granted power into effect.
Implied powers find verbal basis in Article I, Section 8, Clause 18—
the so-called elastic clause. No new or additional powers are granted
by the "necessary and proper" clause; it merely enables the federal

government to maintain its supremacy in the limited sphere of its activity. Article VI, Paragraph 2, the keystone of the federal system, supplies a third dimension of national power. It indicates that if the legitimate powers of state and nation conflict, that of the national government shall prevail. As Professor Corwin puts it: "When national and state power, correctly defined in all other respects, come into conflict in consequence of attempting to govern simultaneously the same subject-matter, the former has always the right of way."

Thus national power is of three dimensions: (1) the enumeration in which the grant of power is couched; (2) the discretionary choice of means that Congress has for carrying its enumerated powers into execution; (3) the fact of supremacy (Art. VI, Par. 2). Under this three-dimensional theory of national authority, no subject matter whatever is withdrawn from control or regulation by the United States simply because it also lies within the usual domain of state power. Since, as pointed out above, the Tenth Amendment merely asserts a truism—powers not delegated are reserved—powers granted to the national government are not reserved. In short, coexistence of state governments does not limit national power.

Hamilton believed that neither the necessary and proper clause nor the supremacy clause were necessary to national supremacy. In *Federalist*, No. 33, he declared that the constitutional operation of the national government would be precisely the same, if these clauses were "entirely obliterated. . . . They are only declaratory of a truth which would have resulted by necessary and unavoidable implication from the very act of constituting a federal government, and vesting it with specified powers." Though the necessary and proper clause might, he suggested, be "chargeable with tautology or redundancy, [it] is at least perfectly harmless."

Just as those sponsoring the Tenth Amendment feared encroachment by the federal government on the states, so those favoring the necessary and proper clause feared that states rights partisans would "sap the foundations of the Union." Hamilton suggests that the Convention did not want, with respect to "so cardinal a point" as that of the broad scope of national authority, "to leave anything to construction." National supremacy was "a truth which flows immediately and necessarily from the institution of a federal gov-

ernment" (*Federalist*, No. 33). "A law, by the very meaning of
the term, includes supremacy"; laws enacted by the national government "pursuant to the powers entrusted to it by its constitution
must necessarily be supreme" over states "and the individuals of
whom they are composed."

Madison (*Federalist*, No. 44) took precisely the opposite view
of the supremacy clause. He believed that "without the substance
of this power, the whole Constitution would be a dead letter."
Without its inclusion the Constitution would "have been evidently
and radically defective."

RESULTING POWERS

Certain powers of the national government are derived by implication from the mass of delegated powers or from a group of
them. Such powers include the taking of property by eminent
domain for a purpose not specified in the Constitution, the power
to carry into effect treaties entered into by the United States, the
power to maintain the supremacy of the national government within
its sphere of authority, and the power to control relations with
the Indians.

EXCLUSIVE AND CONCURRENT POWERS

The powers of the national government may also be classified
as exclusive or concurrent. Powers delegated to Congress by the
Constitution are exclusive under the following conditions:

(1) Where the right to exercise the power is made exclusive by
    express provision of the Constitution. Article I, Sec. 8, Cl. 17,
    for example, gives Congress exclusive power over the District
    of Columbia and over property purchased from a state with the
    consent of the legislature.
(2) Where one section of the Constitution grants an express power
    to Congress and another section prohibits the states from ex-
    ercising a similar power. E.g., Congress is given the power to
    coin money (Art. I, Sec. 8, Cl. 5), and the states are expressly
    prohibited from exercising such power (Art. I, Sec. 10, Cl. 1).
(3) Where the power granted to Congress, though not in terms
    exclusive, is such that the exercise of a similar power by the
    states would be utterly incompatible therewith. In *Cooley* v.
    Board of Wardens (12 How. 299, 1851) the Court admitted the
    existence of a concurrent power to control interstate commerce,
    but limited state power to matters of local concern. Where the

subject matter is national in scope and requires uniform legislative treatment, such as the federal government alone can provide,
the power of Congress is exclusive. "Exclusive" is here used in
a special sense, since the disability of the states arises not from
the Constitution but from the nature of the subject matter to
which the power is applied. Such power has been termed "latent
concurrent power," since Congress may consent to its exercise
by the state.

The only example of a power expressly declared to belong con-
currently to both federal and state governments was the power
to enforce the Eighteenth Amendment. Although the word "concurrent" is not used elsewhere, other clauses make specific provision
for the exercise of concurrent power, e.g., Article I, Sec. 4, Cl. 1
(elections) and the Twenty-First Amendment (transportation of
liquor). In most instances, however, the grant of a power to
Congress has been held not inconsistent with the exercise of a
similar power by the states. The concurrent power of the states is
potentially subordinate to that of the national government; it
cannot be exercised unless Congress consents. The consent of
Congress may be given expressly, as in the Wilson Act of 1890 (In
re Rahrer, 140 U.S. 545, 1891) where Congress consented to state
legislation affecting interstate commerce in liquor. The consent
may also be implied. Thus the fact that Congress has enacted legislation in a particular field may be construed as assenting to further
state legislation or it may be construed as the negative of such
consent; and the failure of Congress to act at all is also subject
to these alternative constructions. The best illustrations of the
interaction between state and national legislation are to be found
under the commerce power. If congressional consent is given, or
if the Constitution itself makes provision for legislation by both
governments, both state and nation may exercise coordinate jurisdiction over the field.

As was inevitable, the formal distribution of powers between
the national government and the states led to widely diverse interpretations. Those who strove to safeguard state sovereignty feared
a broad construction of national powers; those who viewed the
continuance of state power as the enemy of vested rights and of
national strength, tended for tactical reasons to conceal their satisfaction with the increased scope of national authority.

THE FEDERALISM OF JOHN MARSHALL

As John Adams left the Presidency he installed John Marshall, a strong party man and ardent nationalist, as Chief Justice. Marshall read into our constitutional law a concept of federalism that magnified national at the expense of state powers. Aiding his pronationalist labors were important matters of record and of precedent. Besides the House of Representatives debates out of which the Tenth Amendment emerged, there was the leading case of *Chisholm v. Georgia* (2 Dall. 419, 1793) in which it was claimed unsuccessfully that the judicial power extended only to suits by a "state against a citizen of another state." Georgia's protestations against the Court's taking jurisdiction of the case could not stand, Justice Blair said, in the face of "clear and positive directions . . . of the Constitution." Chief Justice Jay declared that "words are to be understood in their ordinary and common acceptation, and the word, party, being in common usage applicable to both plaintiff and defendant, we cannot limit it to one of them. . . . If that [party plaintiff] only was meant, it would have been easy to have found words to express it." State sovereignty pretensions were denied by a vote of 4 to 1.

Justice Iredell's states-rights preference, like the nationalistic leanings of Justice Wilson's majority opinion, is rooted in a theory of the Constitution and of the Union: "A State does not [Iredell reasoned] owe its origin to the government of the United States. . . . It derives its authority from the same . . . source [as the government of the Union]: the voluntary and deliberate choice of the people. . . . A State, though subject in certain specified particulars to the authority of the government of the United States, is in every other respect totally independent upon it. The people of the State created, the people of the State can only change, its Constitution."

The Court's decision holding that the state of Georgia, as defendant sued by a citizen of another state, was amenable to the jurisdiction of the national judiciary provoked prompt reaction. One newspaper interpreted it as a veiled attempt to reduce the states to mere corporations; another saw it as part of a grand design to bring about eventual monarchy. The *Independent Chronicle* of July 25, 1793 surmised the practical grounds of attack—fear of the "numerous prosecutions that will immediately issue from the various claims of refugees, Tories, etc., that will introduce such a series of litigations as will throw every State in the Union into the greatest confusion." The apparent soundness of the Court's reading of the Constitution stimulated immediate steps toward constitutional amendment. On January 8, 1798, three years before Marshall was appointed Chief Justice, the Eleventh Amendment became a part of the Constitution.

Marshall's tenure (1801-1835), covering a period in which his enemies dominated the political branches of the government, made his fervent nationalism stand out all the more dramatically. As early as 1804, in the obscure case of *United States* v. *Fisher* (2 Cranch 358) the new Chief Justice had taken his stand in favor of a liberal construction of the necessary and proper clause. It was not, however, until the famous case of *McCulloch* v. *Maryland* (4 Wheat. 316, 1819) that he found himself face to face with the dreaded issue of "clashing sovereignties."

The case resulted from a tax levied by the Maryland legislature on banks not chartered by the state, a measure aimed at the unpopular nationally chartered Bank of the United States. Counsel for Maryland asserted unsuccessfully that the power to charter banks was not one of those specifically delegated by the states to the national government in Article I, Section 8. As usual Marshall built his decision on broad theoretical foundations.

The Constitution, he argued, was "ordained and established in the name of the people"; it was not a compact of sovereign states. Nor did it result from the action of the people of the states or of their governments. The Constitution altered the former position of the states as sovereign entities. Unlike the Congress under the Articles of Confederation, the national government operated directly on individuals. Within the sphere of its enumerated powers Congress was supreme. Furthermore, the "necessary and proper clause" gave Congress a discretionary choice of means for implementing the granted powers, and the Tenth Amendment served in no way to limit this freedom of selection. In reply to the argument that the taxing power was reserved to the states by the Tenth Amendment, and hence could operate even against a legitimate national instrumentality, Marshall contended that the supremacy clause permitted no such conclusion. At the same time, he went out of his way to uphold national power to tax state instrumentalities. Thus, Marshall established not only the proposition that national powers must be liberally construed, but the equally decisive principle that the Tenth Amendment does not create in the states an independent limitation on such authority.

In Cohens v. Virginia (6 Wheat. 264, 1821) two years later, where Virginia resisted the right of a defendant in a state criminal proceeding to obtain review by the Supreme Court, Marshall refuted the argument that the highest state court had a power coequal with that of the Supreme Court in interpreting and applying the Constitution. Counsel for Virginia, believing that state courts had not only concurrent but final authority to interpret the Constitution and laws of the United States in cases arising in its courts, argued that the Supreme Court could not take jurisdiction of such a case on appeal from a sovereign state court.

A case in law or equity to which the judicial power of the United States extends, Marshall countered, "consists of the right of the one party, as well as of the other, and may truly be said to arise under the Constitution or a law of the United States whenever the correct decision depends on the construction of either." This was not only the mandate of the "American people"; it was also the conviction of "the American States." All believed that "a close and firm Union" was "essential to their liberty, and to their happiness." Both the supremacy clause and the principle of judicial review required that final decisions on constitutional issues "arising" in state courts be made only by the Supreme Court.

In Gibbons v. Ogden (9 Wheat. 1, 1824) Marshall again seized the opportunity to expound the nature of the Union. "It has been contended," he observed, "that if a law, passed by a state in the exercise of its acknowledged sovereignty, comes in conflict with a law passed by Congress in pursuance of the Constitution they affect the subject, and each other, like equal opposing powers." "The framers of the Constitution foresaw this state of things, and provided for it, by declaring the supremacy not only of itself, but of laws made in pursuance of it." Marshall warned of the danger that the powers granted by the Constitution might by petty or scholastic construction prove inadequate to maintain a system "intended to endure for all ages to come." "Powerful and ingenious minds," he wrote in Gibbons v. Ogden, "taking as postulates, that the powers expressly granted to the government of the Union, are to be contracted, by construction, into the narrowest possible compass, and that the original powers of the states are retained if any possible construction will retain them, may, by a course of well-digested but refined and metaphysical reasoning, founded on these premises, explain away the Constitution of our country, and leave it, a magnificent structure, indeed, to look at, but totally unfit for use."

To sum up, Marshall's doctrine of national supremacy rests on the proposition that the central government and the states confront each other in the relationship of superior and subordinate; that if the exercise of Congress' enumerated powers be legitimate, the fact that their exercise encroaches on the state's traditional domain is of no significance whatsoever. Finally, the Court's duty is not to preserve state sovereignty but to protect national power against state encroachments. For Marshall, as for Madison in 1788, the principal danger to the federal system lay in erosive state action. Effective political limitations existed against national efforts to impinge on state power, but only the Supreme Court could peacefully restrain state action from infringing upon the authority of the national government.

Marshall's doctrine of federalism did not go unchallenged. Madison, who became an increasingly severe critic of national power, as interpreted by the Federalists, wrote that "the very existence of the local sovereignties was a control on the pleas for a constructive amplification of national power" (*Writings*, Vol. 8, pp. 447-453). John Taylor, the Chief Justice's most vociferous critic, thought that Marshall's doctrine destroyed the limiting effect of enumerated powers. In a review of Kent's *Commentaries* in 1828, South Carolinian Hugh Swinton Legaré, later Attorney General and Secretary of State under President Tyler, commented: "The government has been fundamentally altered by the progress of opinion—that instead of being any longer one of enumerated powers and a circumscribed sphere, as it was beyond all doubt intended to be, it knows absolutely no bounds but the will of a majority of Congress . . . and threatens in the course of a few years, to control in the most offensive and despotic manner, all the pursuits, the interests, the opinions and the conduct of men."

Legaré went on to say that under John Marshall's decisions, "Congress is omnipotent in theory and that if in practice it prefers moderate counsels and a just and impartial policy it will be owing not to any check in the Constitution but altogether to the vigilance, the wisdom and the firmness of a free people." "That argument," Legaré concluded, "cannot be sound which necessarily converts a government of enumerated into one of indefinite powers, and a confederacy of republics into a gigantic and consolidated empire." Legaré also took exception to Marshall's view of the Court as an instrument of the national government, empowered to maintain its supremacy. Rather he thought of the Court as an "umpire in questions of constitutional law between the states and the confederacy."

Marshall's death in 1835 was the occasion of considerable satisfaction among states rights partisans. "We can but experience joy," the New York *Post* editorialized, "that the chief place in the supreme tribunal of the Union will no longer be filled by a man whose political doctrines led him always to pronounce such decisions on constitutional questions as was calculated to strengthen the national government at the expense of the states. We lament the death of a good and exemplary man, but we cannot grieve that the cause of aristocracy has lost one of its chief supporters."

As if in answer to states rights fears of nationalist aggrandizement, President Jackson chose, as Marshall's successor, Roger Brooke Taney, who during the next generation (1835-1864) redefined federalism in terms more favorable to state power and so as to enhance the role of the judiciary.

Within two years after Taney's appointment, the Court was reconstituted—or, as Daniel Webster put it, "revolutionized." "Politics has gotten possession of the Bench at last," Webster wrote. "It is in vain to deny or attempt to disguise it. Taney is smooth and plausible, but cunning and jesuitical, and as thoroughgoing a party judge as ever got onto a court of justice." Webster described and denounced Jackson's judicial appointees one by one on the score of their fear or hatred of national power and their "devotion to states rights."

"The Constitution is now in these hands," Webster concluded, "and God only knows what is to save it from destruction."

TANEY AND DUAL FEDERALISM

Under the concept of federalism, common to Marshall's critics, the Constitution was a compact of sovereign states, not an ordinance of the people. This idea—largely the handiwork of Jefferson, Taylor and Madison—had been embodied in the Virginia-Kentucky Resolutions of 1798; it was the premise of John Taylor's view that the national government and the states face each other as equals across a precise constitutional line defining their respective jurisdictions. This concept of national-state equality had been the basis of Virginia's anarchical arguments in *Cohens* v. *Virginia*.

The states rights doctrine, or a variant thereof, was clearly reflected in the Court's decision in *New York* v. *Miln* (11 Peters 102) of 1837 decided after extensive change had occurred in judicial personnel. Involved was the apparent conflict between a New York statute enacted under the police power (but affecting the admission of foreigners as well as citizens from other states) and the power of Congress over interstate commerce. Justice Barbour, speaking for the Court, upheld the state regulation against the contention that the New York act was in direct conflict with the federal commerce power.

> We shall not enter into any examination of the question, whether the power to regulate commerce, be or be not exclusive of the states, because the opinion which we have formed renders it unnecessary: in other words, we are of opinion, that the act is not a regulation of commerce, but of police; and that being thus considered, it was passed in the exercise of a power which rightfully belonged to the states. . . . A state has the same undeniable and unlimited jurisdiction over all persons and things, within its territorial limits, as any foreign nation; where that jurisdiction is not surrendered or restrained by the constitution of the United States. That, by virtue of this, it is not only the right, but the bounden and solemn duty of a state, to advance the safety, happiness and prosperity of its people, and to provide for its general welfare, by any and every act of legislation, which it may deem to be conducive to these ends; where the power over the particular subject, or the manner of its exercise is not surrendered or restrained, in the manner just stated. That all those powers which relate to merely municipal legislation, or what may, perhaps, more properly be called internal police, are not thus surrendered or restrained; and that, consequently, in relation to these, the authority of a state is complete, unqualified and exclusive.

Commenting on Barbour's decision Professor Corwin says,

> The thought here is that the police powers of the state constitute
> a reserve of exclusive powers, with the result that any subject
> matter that falls within their jurisdiction is, for that reason, outside
> the scope of the delegated powers of the United States. In effect
> this sets the Tenth Amendment on its head by requiring that state
> power or at any rate a part of it, be defined prior to the definition
> of the national power and not vice versa.

Marshall is also set on his head. Whereas he had permitted state
regulation under the police powers to affect commerce so long as
they did not interfere with federal regulation, it now appeared
that the federal government would be permitted to regulate under
its commerce powers so long as such regulation did not impinge
upon the exclusive police power of the states.

But the contrast between Marshall and Taney is less sharp than
sometimes supposed. In the words of Professor Ribble: "A state
quarantine law would be to Taney a regulation of interstate or
foreign commerce. Its effect on such commerce was direct and
immediate, although it was not designed to serve an economic or
commercial purpose. To Marshall such laws did not proceed from
a power, shared by Congress to regulate interstate and foreign
commerce. These laws were simply means employed to carry out
their systems of police."

The Taney Court accepted the basic creed of nation-state equality but stripped it of its anarchic implications. Within the powers
reserved by the Tenth Amendment, the states were sovereign, but
final authority to determine the scope of state powers rested with
the national judiciary, which was not, as Marshall had insisted,
merely an instrument of the national government, but an arbitrator
standing aloof from the sovereign pretensions of both nation and
states. "This judicial power [Taney wrote in *Ableman* v. *Booth*,
21 Howard 506, 1859] was justly regarded as indispensable, not
merely to maintain the supremacy of the laws of the United States,
but also to guard the states from any encroachment upon their
reserved rights by the general government. . . . So long . . . as
this Constitution shall endure, this tribunal must exist with it, deciding in the peaceful forms of judicial proceeding the angry and
irritating controversies between sovereignties, which in other countries have been determined by the arbitrament of force."

For John Marshall's concept of national supremacy, the Taney Court substituted a theory of federal equilibrium. Marshall himself, a somewhat less extreme nationalist than his critics supposed, had contributed to the reaction by his recognition that the states retain a great mass of legislative power to protect the health and general welfare of its citizens, and that under the police power the states may govern subject matter also within the reach of the national government under its enumerated powers. This doctrine, later called "dual sovereignty," is well expressed by Justice Daniel in upholding state action affecting commerce in the *License Cases* (5 How. 504, 1847): "Every power delegated to the federal government must be expounded in coincidence with a perfect right in the states to all that they have not delegated; in coincidence, too, with the possession of every power and right necessary for their existence and preservation."

Still other differences between the two great Chief Justices may be noted. In contrast to Marshall's theory of a fundamental law "intended to endure," Taney thought of the Constitution as speaking "not only in the same words, but with the same meaning and intent with which it spoke when it came from the hands of the framers." Taney stated these views in the Dred Scott case (19 How. 393, 1857), holding that a Negro, not being a citizen, could not sue in the federal courts. Nor could Congress prohibit slavery in the territories. The Court, Taney insisted, was powerless to rule otherwise. Yet his decision has been denounced as indicative of "the systematic and conscious aim of the South to make the Supreme Court the citadel of slaveocracy." Representing as it did his arbitrary determination to apply a theory of federalism no longer relevant to rapidly changing American society, the Dred Scott case discredited the Supreme Court as an arbiter of the federal system. In 1928, Charles Evans Hughes described the decision as "a public calamity." "It was many years before the Court, even under new judges, was able to retrieve its reputation."

Taney's passionate concern for states rights and preservation of state control of slavery should not, however, obscure the fact that in the context of his times, state police power was the only available weapon with which government could face the pressing problems of the day. In a period in which the national government was not yet prepared to deal realistically with economic and social problems, national supremacy had the effect of posing the unexercised commerce power of Congress, or the contract clause (Art. I, Sec. 10), as barriers to any governmental action. Taney's dual federalism in the period 1837-1855 enabled the states to deal experimentally with problems that the national government would not face until another half-century had elapsed. Thus Marshall and Taney left as legacies two official conceptions of federalism that succeeding Justices were free to apply as their inclinations or needs of the time dictated.

NATIONAL SUPREMACY AND DUAL FEDERALISM—1864-1937

In *Texas* v. *White* (7 Wall. 700, 1869) the Court was called upon to answer a perplexing question as to the constitutional status of the states that had claimed the right to withdraw from the Union during the Civil War. Although Chief Justice Chase's answer for the Court, upholding actions of the provisional government of Texas after the war, seemed to express the inviolability of the Union, thus officially repudiating the claim of the extreme states rights advocates, he pointed out that "the preservation of the states, and the maintenance of their governments, are as much within the design and care of the Constitution as the preservation of the Union and the maintenance of the National Government. The Constitution, in all its provisions, looks to an indestructible Union, composed of indestructible states." That this was not mere rhetoric was soon evident. In a series of cases arising under the Civil War amendments, and various laws designed to fasten national standards on state political and social systems, the Supreme Court displayed stubborn resistance to extreme theories of national supremacy (*Slaughterhouse cases*, 16 Wall. 36, 1873 and *Civil Rights cases*, 109 U.S. 3, 1883).

In the Slaughterhouse cases, Justice Miller told Louisiana butchers, seeking national protection under the Fourteenth Amendment against a discriminatory state monopoly law, that the Supreme Court refused to become a "perpetual censor" of all state legislation. The Justice bolstered his argument by the suggestion that the federal system itself is immune to the amending process:

> The argument we admit is not always the most conclusive which is drawn from the consequences urged against the adoption of a

particular construction of an instrument. But when, as in the case before us, these consequences are so serious, so far-reaching and pervading, so great a departure from the structure and spirit of our institutions; when the effect is to fetter and degrade the State governments by subjecting them to the control of Congress, in the exercise of powers heretofore universally conceded to them of the most ordinary and fundamental character; when in fact it radically changes the whole theory of the relations of the State and Federal governments to the people; the argument has a force that is irresistible. . . .

As a sort of corollary to its refusal to "degrade the State governments," the Court, until 1890, regarded legislation enacted under the police power with considerable deference.

INDEPENDENCE OF STATE AND NATIONAL
GOVERNMENTS

In addition to the express limitations and prohibitions on national and state power contained in the Constitution, the Justices have developed a considerable number of limitations from federalism itself. Practical considerations involved in the maintenance of a federal form of government in which two sovereignties must operate side by side led to adoption of the doctrine that neither government may interfere with the governmental functions of the other, nor with the agencies and officials through which those functions are executed.

The doctrine of governmental immunity had its inception in *McCulloch* v. *Maryland.* On the premise that "the power to tax involves the power to destroy," Chief Justice Marshall declared: "There is a plain repugnance, in conferring on one government a power to control the constitutional measures of another, which other, with respect to those very measures, is declared to be supreme over that which exerts the control. . . . If the states may tax one instrument employed by the [national] government in the execution of its powers, they may tax any and every other instrument [and] they may tax all the means employed by the government, to an excess which would defeat all the ends of government. . . . The states have no power, by taxation or otherwise, to retard, impede, burden, or in any manner control the operations of the constitutional laws enacted by Congress to carry into execution the powers vested in the general government."

Marshall's immunity doctrine was based upon the theory of the supremacy of the national government in its sphere of activity. Regarded in this light, it is quite consistent with his attitude toward the role of the central government in a federal system. Accordingly, he denied emphatically the proposition that "every argument which would sustain the right of the general government to tax banks chartered by the states will equally sustain the right of the state to tax banks chartered by the general government." "The difference," he explained, "is that which always exists, and always must exist, between the action of the whole on the part, and the action of a part on the whole—between the laws of a government declared to be supreme, and those of a government, which, when in opposition to those laws, is not supreme."

In *Collector* v. *Day* (11 Wall. 113, 1871), however, the Court repudiated Marshall's dictum. Ruling that the salaries of state court judges are immune from a national income tax, the Justices established the doctrine of reciprocal immunity, based on the theory of the equality of national and state authority under our federal system. Said Justice Nelson:

> In respect to the reserved powers, the State is as sovereign and independent as the general government. And if the means and instrumentalities employed by that government to carry into operation the power granted to it are, necessarily and, for the sake of self-preservation, exempt from taxation by the States, why are not those of the States depending upon their reserve power, for like reason, equally exempt from Federal taxation? Their unimpaired existence in the one case is as essential as in the other. . . . In both cases the exemption rests upon necessary implication, and is upheld by the great law of self-preservation; as any government, whose means employed in conducting its operation, if subject to the control of another and distinct government can exist only at the mercy of that government.

Justice Bradley, dissenting, attacked the Court's decision as "founded on a fallacy" that would lead to "mischievous consequences."

> It seems to me that the general government has the same power of taxing the income from officers of the state governments as it has of taxing that of its own officers. It is the common government of all alike. . . . The limitation of the power of taxation in the general government . . . will be found very difficult to control.

Where are we to stop in enumerating the functions of the state governments which will be interfered with by Federal taxation? If a state incorporate a railroad to carry out its purposes of internal improvement, or a bank to aid its financial arrangements, reserving, perhaps, a percentage of stocks or profits, for the supply of its own treasury, will the bonds or stocks of such an institution be free from Federal taxation? . . . I cannot but regard it as founded on a fallacy, and that it will lead to mischievous consequences.

Bradley proved to be right. In time, the doctrine of reciprocal immunity of governmental instrumentalities was carried to such lengths as to deny to both governments fruitful sources of taxation. On the basis of Marshall's doctrine that a national governmental instrumentality is immune even from a nondiscriminatory state tax, it was later held that a state may not reach by a general tax national officials' salaries or incomes from national bonds (*Evans* v. *Gore*, 253 U.S. 245, and *Pollock* v. *Farmers Loan and Trust Co.*, 158 U.S. 601). Private companies doing business with or rendering service to the United States were held immune to state taxation on the privilege of doing such business. Nor could transactions to which the United States was a party be taxed in such a way that the cost to the government would be directly affected by the amount of the tax. *Panhandle Oil Co.* v. *Mississippi* (277 U.S. 218, 1928) even invalidated a state sales tax on gasoline purchased by the United States for use in Coast Guard vessels.

This was an extreme case, and Justice Holmes, sharply adverting to Marshall's famous aphorism, quipped: "The power to tax is not the power to destroy while this court sits. . . . The question of interference with government, I repeat, is one of reasonableness and degree, and it seems to me that the interference in this case is too remote." Three years later, in *Indian Motorcycle Co.* v. *United States* (283 U.S. 570, 1931) the Court struck down a federal tax on sales of motorcycles to a municipality for use in its police service. Justice Stone dissented, invoking the authority of *Educational Films Corp. of America* v. *Ward* (282 U.S. 379, 1931), in which he had set forth the modern doctrine as follows: "This court, in drawing the line which defines the limits of the powers and immunities of state and national governments, is not intent upon a mechanical application of the rule that government instrumentalities are immune from taxation, regardless of the consequences of the operations of government. The necessity for marking those boundaries grows out of our constitutional system, under which both the federal and state governments exercise their authority over one people within the territorial limits of the same state. The purpose is the preservation to each government, within its own sphere, of the freedom to carry on those affairs committed to it by the Constitution, without undue interference by the other."

In recent cases, the Court has gone far toward undermining the doctrine of reciprocal immunity. *O'Malley* v. *Woodrough* (307 U.S. 277, 1939) made the "salaries" of federal judges subject to income taxation, and specifically disapproved of *Evans* v. *Gore.* Under the "necessary and proper" clause, however, Congress may still exempt a national instrumentality from state taxation, as in *Pittman* v. *H.O.L.C.* (308 U.S. 21, 1939).

In *Graves* v. *New York* (306 U.S. 466, 1939), *Collector* v. *Day* and other precedents were overruled so far as they recognized "an implied constitutional immunity from income taxation of salaries of officers or employees of the national or state government or their instrumentalities." The immunity doctrine as to the states had been qualified earlier in *South Carolina* v. *U.S.* (199 U.S. 437, 1905), which upheld a federal tax on South Carolina's liquor-dispensing business. The Court ruled that "the exemption of state agencies and instrumentalities from national taxation is limited to those which are of a strictly governmental character, and does not extend to those which are used by the state in carrying on of an ordinary private business." In *New York* v. *U.S.* (326 U.S. 572, 1946) the Court upheld a federal tax on mineral waters bottled and sold by a New York state public benefit corporation.

In refusing to distinguish South Carolina's traffic in liquor from New York State's traffic in mineral waters, the Justices split three ways. Justice Frankfurter, dispensing with criteria used in past decisions, formulated a new basis for immunity. He would reduce tax immunity by a rule merely forbidding discriminatory taxation of one government by another, except where the tax hit the "state as a state." Stone refused to go along. Holmes was "plainly mistaken," he told Frankfurter, when he intimated that the courts could invalidate federal taxes simply because they were destructive. Stone's own Sonzinsky decision (300 U.S. 506, 1937) had sustained a prohibitive federal license on dealers in "gangster" weapons.

"Are you intending to suggest," Stone asked Frankfurter, "that the rule is different where such a tax is imposed on a state as well as the citizen without discrimination?" Stone had no doubt Congress might lawfully destroy liquor traffic by exorbitant taxation, and taking this tack, he attacked Frankfurter's argument by pointed queries: "Would such a tax be invalid if levied on a liquor business conducted by a state? If it would be valid, why cite Justice Holmes' statement? If it would be invalid, then what becomes of your thesis that a tax laid upon a state in the same way that it is laid on ordinary taxpayers is not invalid?"

"Nothing was further from my thought," Frankfurter responded, "than to suggest that 'a federal tax in other respects constitutionally laid,' could be set aside because it is too large. I entirely agree with you that Congress could lay a tax on intoxicating liquors involving a state 'calculated to destroy the traffic.' The point of my reference to the two Holmes' opinions [Panhandle case and *Long* v. *Rockwood*, 277 U.S. 142, 1928, p. 148] was the support of my statement that in Marshall's time absolutes were more frequently employed in opinion than the complexities of our times have rendered permissible. . . ."

"All I claim for my opinion," Frankfurter continued, "is that it tidies up one corner of the law by removing the messy criteria on which previous cases sustaining taxes falling directly on states have been based. It does so by giving a generalizing limitation upon such taxing power, i.e., that it must be nondiscriminatory, so that every producer of mineral water is taxed and not merely the state as a producer of mineral water, and by making it clear that whatever other freedom from taxation the state may enjoy because of our federal system, is to be left for future adjudication unembarrassed by anything we now say."

Frankfurter's purpose was less drastic than Stone supposed. He merely wished to "clear the ground" of faulty generalization about "proprietary vs. governmental" and "find an empirical binder for all these cases." "I think I am breaking no fresh eggs," Frankfurter concluded, "and merely throwing away some putrid ones."

Reiterating the stand he had taken earlier, Stone upheld a less simplified view of the judicial function. The problem was not one to be solved by a formula, but the structure of the Constitution may be looked to as the guide to decision.

In a broad sense, the taxing power of either government, even when exercised in a manner admittedly necessary and proper, unavoidably has some effect upon the other. The burden of federal taxation necessarily sets an economic limit to the practical operation of the taxing power of the states, and vice versa. . . . But neither government may destroy the other nor curtail in any substantial manner the exercise of its powers. Hence the limitation upon the taxing power of each, so far as it affects the other, must receive a practical construction which permits both to function with the minimum of interference each with the other; and that limitation cannot be so varied or extended as seriously to impair either the taxing power of the government imposing the tax . . . or the appropriate exercise of the functions of the government affected by it.

Justice Douglas, dissenting, contended that the South Carolina precedent should be overruled. The distinction there made between governmental and nongovernmental functions, he argued, is a distinction without a difference, and one extremely harmful to state power. Since the national excises imposed on the sale of both liquor and mineral waters did not seriously affect state finances, it is reasonable to suppose that Justice Douglas had other considerations in mind—the possibility of hostile national tax policy designed to frustrate state experiments in social democracy. In the years ahead the states might be inclined, through necessity, to enter all sorts of businesses now considered private. If the Court upheld national taxes on these new activities on any such flimsy basis as that established in the South Carolina case, the states might be greatly embarrassed financially.

COOPERATIVE FEDERALISM

Older than national supremacy or dual federalism, is the concept of cooperative federalism. Cooperation has been a continuing feature of federal-state relations since 1789. A sort of federalism characterized the unhappy relations between the colonies and the mother country. Without considerable collaboration between the states and the Continental Congress, conditions, after 1776, would have been well-nigh disastrous. The Constitution itself was the result of state and national cooperation. The Philadelphia Convention delegates were appointed by the states, but the product of their deliberations was reported to the Continental Congress. The Congress, in turn, adopted the suggestion of the framers that the proposed Constitution be referred to state constitutional conventions elected by the people.

The expectation that the state and federal governments would cooperate is manifest in the provisions of the Constitution itself. Under Article IV, Section 4, the United States is under obligation to guarantee to every state a republican form of government. Amendments may be proposed and ratified by the state legislatures; state court judges are bound to observe and apply federal law. Lincoln relied heavily on state governments to raise his Union army in the first years of the Civil War. Before the introduction of the draft, he requisitioned men from a given state, the governor mustered them into service, named a ranking politician a general and sent them off to war. After the Civil War, as now, the process was sometimes reversed—the ranking general became a politician! Under the Seventeenth Amendment, the election of United States Senators demanded state-federal action. In 1880 the Supreme Court held that Congress might adopt measures for the effective enforcement of state election laws. The Court would not listen to the plea that a state's election laws were its own business when these concerned the election of federal officers.

"The greatest difficulty in coming to a just conclusion arises," Justice Bradley said, "from mistaken notions with regard to the relations which subsist between the State and National governments. It seems to be often overlooked that a National Constitution has been adopted in this country, establishing a real government therein, operating upon persons and territory and things. . . . If we allow ourselves to regard it as a hostile organization, opposed to the proper sovereignty and dignity of the state governments, we shall continue to be vexed with difficulties as to its jurisdiction and authority. . . . The true interest of the people of this country requires that both the national and state governments should be allowed, without jealous interference on either side, to exercise all the powers which respectively belong to them according to a fair and practical construction of the Constitution. State rights and the rights of the United States should be equally respected." (*Ex parte Siebold*, 100 U.S. 371, 1800.) "The true doctrine," the Court concluded, "is that whilst the states are really sovereign as to all matters which have not been granted to the jurisdiction and control of the United States, the Constitution and constitutional laws of the latter are . . . the supreme law of the land; and, when they conflict with the laws of the States, they are of paramount authority and obligation" (*Ex parte Siebold*, p. 398).

Comity governs the relations between state and federal courts. Where both courts may take jurisdiction of the same subject matter, that court which first obtains jurisdiction may not be interfered with by the other, although it may voluntarily waive its rights. In 1922, Chief Justice Taft held that the national government may honor a writ of habeas corpus issued by a state court and directed to the warden of a federal penitentiary ordering him to produce a federal prisoner in the state court so he might be tried for a state offense, the prisoner to be returned to the federal prison after such trial. "We live," Taft said, "in the jurisdiction of two sovereignties each having its own system of courts to declare and enforce its laws in common territory. . . . One accused of crime has the right to a full and fair trial according to the law of the government whose sovereignty he is alleged to have offended, but he has no more than that. He should not be permitted to use the machinery of one sovereignty to obstruct his trial in the courts of the other. . . . He may not complain if one sovereignty waives its strict right to exclusive custody of him for vindication of its laws in order that the other may also subject him to conviction of crime against it. . . . The situation requires, therefore, not only definite rules in cases of jurisdiction over the same persons and things in actual litigation, but also a spirit of reciprocal comity and mutual assistance to promote due and orderly procedure. . . ." (*Ponzi* v. *Fessenden*, 258 U.S. 254, 1922.)

Here, clearly, was cooperative federalism in action. A decade earlier, Justice McKenna, upholding the Mann White Slave Act, suggested that cooperation, rather than competition, was appropriate in the achievement of social objectives:

> Our dual form of government has its perplexities, State and Nation having different spheres of jurisdiction . . . but it must be kept in mind that we are one people; and the powers reserved to the States and those conferred on the Nation are adopted to be exercised, whether independently or concurrently, to promote the general welfare, material and moral. [*Hoke* v. *U.S.*, 227 U.S. 308, 1913, p. 322.]

But the constructive social purposes federalism may serve have been sometimes frustrated. Especially when controversial social and economic policies are involved federal-state relations have been less amicable. Conflict has arisen from two sources: when the states, in pursuit of normal objectives, under their police power, encroached on Congress' power to regulate interstate commerce; when the federal government pursued a national policy normally thought of as lying within the province of the state. A good example of the first source of trouble is found in state liquor control laws.

Beginning in the late nineteenth century various states tried to stem the flow of good liquor into the dry areas established within their own borders. In a series of cases, the Supreme Court held that such interference flew in the face of the constitutional grant to Congress of the power to regulate commerce. No matter how desirable prohibition might be as a social goal, the states must not "obstruct" commerce in a genuine article among the states. (*Leisy* v. *Hardin*, 135 U.S. 100, 1890.)

Opposition has arisen from the other side when Congress, under its commerce power, sought to achieve a purpose or reach subject matter normally confined to state regulation. Examples of this type of government action are the grant-in-aid program to land-grant colleges, the national regulation of child labor, and federal prohibition of interstate traffic in prostitution and stolen automobiles.

The Justices themselves sensed the dilemma. In 1890, while striking down a state law licensing inter- and intra-state liquor merchants, Chief Justice Fuller held that regulation of interstate commerce was not "within the jurisdiction of the police power of the state, *unless placed there by Congressional action.*" Here was a clear invitation to the legislators to lead the judiciary out of the wilderness—an invitation repeated in the opinion no less than five times. Following Chief Justice Fuller's suggestion, Congress, in 1890, passed the Wilson Act depriving liquor shipments of their interstate character "on arrival" within the state. The next year, the Justices honored their own invitation by stamping on the Act its judicial approval (*In re Rahrer*, 140 U.S. 545, 1891). National and state cooperation was thus launched upon the tides of constitutional history.

The idea was attractive, practical—and it caught on. In the next four decades Congress prohibited the introduction of alcoholic beverages into a state in contravention of state law (Webb-Kenyon

Act of 1905, *Clark Distilling Co.* v. *West Md. Ry.*, 242 U.S. 311, 1917); permitted the states to set up plant quarantine inspection systems in the absence of action by federal Secretary of Agriculture; subjected dead game birds and animals to state regulation even though the game had been taken in another state (Lacey Act of 1900, *Silz* v. *Hesterberg*, 211 U.S. 31, 1908); proscribed shipment of Black Bass taken in violation of state law; closed channels of interstate commerce to convict-made goods where the state of shipment forbade sale of such articles (Hawes-Cooper Act of 1929, *Kentucky Whip & Collar Co.* v. *Illinois Central*, 299 U.S. 334, 1936). In each of these cases the federal government stepped in, plugged the gap and assisted local law enforcers in their task. Each of the state laws varied in detail and in major outline, added to rather than subtracted from the states' power to affect interstate commerce, yet the Court approved federal action. It did this, despite the ruling in *Leisy* v. *Hardin* that the subject matter involved was national in character, and therefore any regulation would have to be uniform. Senator Hoar answered this objection at the time the Wilson Act was under consideration by saying that the act was uniform with respect to the article rather than as to the states—the statute simply had the effect of uniformly withdrawing the protection of the commerce clause from traffic in the particular article.

While the Court was permitting Congress to relax the death-hold of the commerce clause on regulation of "local" subject matter and conditions, it also (with certain important exceptions) permitted Congress to utilize its power over commerce to stifle objectionable traffic, despite the fact that state law permitted, and in some cases positively encouraged, such commerce. Proceeding on this basis, the Congress banned transportation of lottery tickets from one state to another; blocked the movement in interstate commerce of impure and falsely branded goods, of "filled" milk, of liquor, of stolen automobiles, and of stolen goods in general. Under the so-called Lindbergh law of 1932, kidnapping, if the victim was carried across state lines, was made an offense against the United States. The Justices sustained all these measures specifically or by implication.

The fly in the ointment was that—as formulated by the Supreme Court—cooperative federalism was practically limited to enforcement of the Ten Commandments. "Congress," Chief Justice Taft declared in 1925, "can certainly regulate interstate commerce to the extent of forbidding and punishing the use of commerce as an agency to promote immorality, dishonesty, or the spread of any evil or harm to the people of other States from the State of origin. In doing this it is merely exercising the police power, for the benefit of the public, within the field of interstate commerce" (*Brooks* v. *United States*, 267 U.S. 432, 436, 1925). The full power of the national government and of the states could be used cooperatively to enforce the commandments "thou shall not steal, thou shall not commit adultery," but the Justices could see no taint of immorality—no evil within the reach of Congress to correct—in child labor, in sweatshops. Underlying these refinements was economic dogma, reinforced by a theory of the Union, not the Constitution of 1789.

After 1890 the doctrine of "dual federalism" was invoked in several important cases to thwart national legislation regulating property rights and the "freedom of business enterprise." In the Sugar Trust case (*United States* v. *E. C. Knight*, 156 U.S. 1, 1895) the concept of "reserved power" (Tenth Amendment) was used, as we shall see, to invalidate the application of the Sherman Anti-Trust Act to a sugar refining monopoly on the grounds that manufacturing was local. "Dual federalism" frustrated national attempts to regulate child labor under both the commerce power (*Hammer* v. *Dagenhart*, 247 U.S. 251, 1918) and the federal taxing power (*Bailey* v. *Drexel Furniture Co.*, 259 U.S. 20, 1922). In each case the Court viewed manufacturing and labor relations as wholly local, beyond the reach of national power. Dual federalism reached its climax in a series of New Deal cases invalidating acts passed under both the taxing and commerce power. Congressional effort to create orderly conditions in the bituminous coal industry was defeated by the Court's decision in *Carter* v. *Carter Coal Co.* (298 U.S. 238, 1936). A complex plan to impose quotas on farm production, financed by a tax on processors, was invalidated because agriculture was a subject matter reserved to the states (*United States* v. *Butler*, 297 U.S. 1, 1936). An attempt to aid bankrupt municipalities under the national bankruptcy power was rejected as an interference with state sovereignty (*Ashton* v. *Cameron County*, 298 U.S. 513, 1936).

But the Court was not always unanimous in enforcing economic dogma on the altar of a highly conceptualized theory of the federal system. In *Hammer* v. *Dagenhart* Holmes, in a dissenting statement, declared that he could see no reason why a rule that permitted the prohibition of traffic in strong drink could not be extended so as to stop traffic in articles made by the warped fingers of child labor. Three of his colleagues agreed with him. Furthermore, in spite of allegations that congressional acts constituted intrusions on state power, the Court on occasion, during the period 1890-1937, sustained national authority. In the Shreveport cases (234 U.S. 342, 1914), the Justices endorsed congressional regulation of intrastate railroad rates and national regulation of the stockyards was upheld in *Stafford* v. *Wallace* (258 U.S. 495, 1922). In both cases, activities that in one sense were local, were viewed as necessarily within the reach of national commerce power because of their effect upon interstate commerce.

Thus when New Deal legislation came under the microscope of the judiciary, two lines of precedents, both in good standing, had been established. Until 1937, the restrictive precedents won majority approval. The theory behind judicial obscurantism has roots going deep into our history and even deeper into the minds of businessmen, lawyers, and judges who had succeeded in the fifty years following 1870 in making the Constitution a bulwark of laissez-faire. Liberty for them, as for their philosopher-king, Herbert Spencer, was measured solely by the paucity of restraints which *government* imposes on the individual. In striking down government regulations the Court was "not to strike down the common good; it was to exalt it." At last the Court's unwarranted insistence that the Tenth Amendment inhibited the exercise of national powers precipitated such an impasse between Court and Congress that President Roosevelt proposed his plan to "pack" the Court. The outcome was the triumph of Marshall's doctrine of national supremacy as, one by one, precedents restricting national power were reversed. "Our conclusion is unaffected by the Tenth Amendment," Justice Stone announced in upholding the Fair Labor Standards Act (*United States* v. *Darby*, 312 U.S. 100, 1941). "The Amendment states but a truism, that all is retained which has not been surrendered."

A significant change had occurred in 1932. In rallying behind the banner of President Roosevelt's New Deal, the people over-whelmingly registered their conviction that liberty also needed protection by government from the unrestrained economic power in the no-man's-land carved out by the Supreme Court between federal and state authority. Then, even businessmen, overwhelmed by the ravages of their own short-sightedness, turned to government.

From the first days of his administration, the New Deal President gave evidence of his determination to extend national power into that sacrosanct area lying between nation and state, into the pre-serve made immune to regulation by economic dogma, and zealously guarded by the high priests of the law. During the remarkable first one hundred days of FDR's administration, federal authority illuminated more dark corners, penetrated more swiftly and com-pletely into national life than ever before. At the same time, the states were, on occasion, encouraged to renew their efforts to remedy evils consequent upon an economic disaster.

In the spring of 1937 a key piece of FDR's reform program—Social Security—came before the Supreme Court. Two suits were brought—one challenged the authority of the United States to institute a broad program of social insurance, charging that such use of the taxing and spending power invaded areas reserved to the states by the Tenth Amendment. The other suit made a similar charge with respect to a joint federal-state program to provide unemployment compensation. The states had been "coerced" into cooperating in these schemes by generous handouts from the federal government. In sustaining this far-flung cooperative effort, the Justices had much to say about federalism.

In *Steward Machine Co.* v. *Davis* (301 U.S. 548, 1937) Justice Cardozo, recognizing vastly changed conditions in American life, held that to "serve the interests of all" the national government must do things the Court had long held reserved to the states by the Tenth Amendment:

> The problem [of old age pensions] is plainly national in area and dimensions. Moreover, laws of the separate states cannot deal with it effectively. . . . States and local governments are often lacking in the resources that are necessary to finance an adequate program of security for the aged. . . . Apart from the failure of resources, states and local governments are at times reluctant to

increase so heavily the burden of taxation to be borne by their residents for fear of placing themselves in a position of economic disadvantage as compared with neighbors or competitors. . . . A system of old age pensions has special dangers of its own, if put in force in one state and rejected in another. The existence of such a system is a bait to the needy and dependents elsewhere, encouraging them to migrate and seek a haven of repose. Only a power that is national can serve the interests of all.

In the second case, sustaining the validity of national unemployment compensation, Justice Stone refuted the contention that generous grant-in-aid funds had "coerced" the states into surrendering their own powers to the federal government. Denying that the federal unemployment legislation involved state coercion, he said:

The United States and the State of Alabama are not alien governments. They coexist within the same territory. Unemployment within it is their common concern. Together the two statutes now before us embody a cooperative legislative effort by state and national governments, for carrying out a public purpose common to both, which neither could fully achieve without the cooperation of the other. The Constitution does not prohibit such cooperation. [*Carmichael* v. *Southern Coal & Coke Co.*, 301 U.S. 495, 525.]

In the next four years, the Chinese wall which the Court had built around manufacturing, agricultural production, and employer-employee relations was breached again and again. Congress was permitted to set minimum wages and regulate hours of work in the smallest factories, encourage union organization, compel employers in the same shops to adopt a hands-off policy, regulate agricultural production from the seed-bed to the grain elevator. What is more, the same Justices simultaneously allowed state laws to determine the width and length and weight of giant interstate trucks used on their highways. The Court even allowed some state taxes on interstate instruments to stand—all against the objection that such regulation burdened interstate commerce.

Finally, in 1941, Mr. Justice Stone confirmed the death of dual federalism. Invoking the jurisprudence of John Marshall, he held that the Tenth Amendment constitutes no limitation on the powers actually delegated to the national government.

Stone's opinion was greeted with cries of despair. The Court had forsaken the states; the line between matters local in character and those of national concern had been erased; all power now lay in the grasp of a power-hungry central government. That these sweeping decisions opened vast preserves of national power, there can be no doubt. Could the Court thereafter insist that any matter lay beyond the reach of national authority? Had Hugh Legaré's prophecy at last come true? Was there "no end to the consequences that may be deduced" once the commerce clause is loosed from the fetters of the Tenth Amendment? "The new concept," Charles P. Curtis observed, "was one of degree which had no logical stopping place. It was a ramp, with no convenient landings for a logical mind, slightly out of breath perhaps, to rest on."

Two insistent questions pressed for attention: Could the Justices prevent Congress from using its power completely to obliterate the state's control over its own affairs? Was the Supreme Court now without obligation with respect to the federal system? Early in 1943, critics of the Court thought they had a negative answer to such queries in its unanimous decisions in *Wickard* v. *Filburn* (317 U.S. 111) and *Parker* v. *Brown* (317 U.S. 341).

Filburn ran a small farm in Ohio, his primary business being the raising of chickens. Each year he planted some acres of wheat for his poultry. Having accepted an Agricultural Marketing Agreement allotment of 11 acres, he planted 23 and raised 269 bushels in excess of his assigned quota. The penalty provisions of the act were invoked by the Secretary of Agriculture and suit was brought to collect the penalties. Filburn's defense was seemingly unanswerable: national regulation was unconstitutional because he had grown the wheat, not for a national market, but for his own chickens and livestock. How could his 269 bushels of wheat have any effect whatever on interstate commerce?

Farmer Filburn's question was a hard one, even for Supreme Court Justices. When the case was first argued in the spring of 1942—all but three of them requested reargument. Much troubled, Justice Jackson told Chief Justice Stone that, unless justification could be found in the effect of such economic activity on commerce itself, he could not see how Congress got the power to regulate "activities that are neither interstate nor commerce." Pleading for reargument, he confessed that "if a completely baffled mind can be called an open one, mine is."

For all his doubts, Jackson had put his finger on the core of

the matter—the Court's power to inquire into the factual justification for congressional control over acts not interstate and not in
themselves commerce—but which affected commerce. After a
second hearing, the Chief Justice assigned Justice Jackson the task
of writing the opinion. The federal government, the Court held,
could penetrate a chicken yard; the farmer could be penalized for
his non-quota wheat even though he never intended it to reach
the market or leave his farm. "Such wheat," Justice Jackson explained, "overhangs the market, and if induced by rising prices
tends to flow into the market and check price increases." Even
"if we assume it is never marketed," the Justice went on, "it supplies
a need of the man who grew it which would otherwise be reflected
by purchases in the open market. Homegrown wheat in this sense
competes with wheat in commerce."

The worst fears of the calamity howlers seemed to have been
borne out—federal bureaucrats stood between the farmer and his
chickens; national agents took over where few state authorities had
dared to enter.

The second case carries further judicial deference to the power
to govern. The state of California had enacted detailed regulation
of agriculture, and two months after the Court sustained regulations
affecting a farmer's barnyard, the Court sustained the state's far-
reaching agricultural regulations (*Parker* v. *Brown*, 317 U.S. 341,
1943).

California farmers grow nearly all of the raisins consumed in
the United States. Ultimately about 90 per cent of their annual
product is shipped interstate. A state sponsored monopoly was given
control of all marketing for California raisins, and all growers were
required to comply with its rules. By these regulations all raisins
were handed over to a central committee for marketing; the grower
was permitted to sell only 30 per cent of his crop in the open
market, the remainder being divided into surplus or stabilization
pools from which the committee controlled the flow of raisins into
the interstate market so as to raise and maintain prices.

Could the same judges who had approved federal control of
the farmer and his wheat also approve California's control of its
raisins? Yes, the Justices approved state power unanimously. The
Sherman Act enjoining combinations in restraint of trade had no
application because it made no mention of the states. "In a dual

system of government in which the states are sovereign, save only as Congress may constitutionally subtract from their authority, an unexpressed purpose to nullify a state's control over its officers is not lightly to be attributed to Congress." Nor could the Court find the alleged conflict between California's plan and the federal agricultural program. By adoption of the Agricultural Marketing Agreement Act, Congress had not completely occupied the legislative field, so as to preclude the effective operation of a state program. The fact that the Secretary of Agriculture believed there was no clash between the scheme he administered and California's was persuasive that Congress had not intended to exclude the states altogether. But what about the judgment of the lower court that this California arrangement interfered with interstate marketing? The Court agreed that the regulation of raisins before they were ready for shipment out of state might properly be described as a local activity, but courts are not confined to so mechanical a rule. Summing up the cooperative conception of state-federal relations, Chief Justice Stone concluded:

> When Congress has not exerted its power under the commerce clause, and state regulation of matters of local concern is so related to interstate commerce that it also operates as a regulation of that commerce, the reconciliation of the power thus granted with that reserved to the state is to be attained by the accommodation of the competing demands of the state and national interests involved.

Until the Congress gave further directions, the judiciary was to adjust any conflicts. California's protection scheme was valid "because upon a consideration of all the relevant facts and circumstances it appears that the matter is one which may appropriately be regulated in the interest of the safety, health, and well-being of local communities, and which because of its local character and because of the practical difficulties involved, may never be adequately dealt with by Congress."

By decisions such as these, the Roosevelt Court turned the pre-1937 Court's no-man's-land—an area immune from governmental regulation, state or national—into a neutral zone within which either nation or state could control economic activity largely free from judicial interference. Today, the Court has approved solutions that seem more adequate to the necessities of modern times. As cooperation replaces conflict and competition between state and nation the states rights slogan remains vital primarily for political purposes.

Back of the shift of judicial decision was a significant change of political and constitutional theory. Originally, the existence of national powers was used to inhibit the exercise of state power, and vice versa, by those who found all government regulation distasteful. Before 1932, the laissez-faire dogma accorded each individual nearly complete freedom over wages, prices, and profits. Liberty then meant the union of social power and private right. After 1932 the orientation of American political thought became basically collectivistic. Thereafter it was recognized that no individual, no group can profit or suffer without affecting the interests of all. Economic rights had therefore to be added to the roster of our freedoms; government, rather than industrial management of ownership, became the dominant power. Promotion of the general welfare became recognized as inherent in government.

President Roosevelt stated the transformation in these words:

> The big choice before the American people in 1932 had been to determine whether they should continue the old type of administration or install a new one—definitely committed to the proposition that the federal government had not only the power, but the duty, to step in to meet with bold action the economic forces at play. The people had made their choice in 1932, and had emphasized it in 1934.

The shift in judicial decision that occurred in 1937 reflected these political pressures. As Professor Corwin puts it: "The doctrines, formulas, and devices of constitutional law . . . which had been hitherto chief sources of the Court's broadly supervisory powers over congressional legislation simply dried up. In choosing pro-New Deal doctrines, they eliminated the competing formulas." Once it was conceded that the national government was entitled to employ all its powers to promote the objectives of free government, the role of the Court was considerably reduced.

After more than 150 years of constitutional debate, the issue of federalism is now more or less settled. Cooperative federalism provides the necessary flexibility in the federal system. Without heeding the full claims of either states' rights partisans, or the extreme followers of John Marshall and Alexander Hamilton, it gives full scope, as the recent decision in the Steve Nelson case

(350 U.S. 497, 1955) shows, to the power intrusted to the national government. It recognizes that Congress, legislating for the whole people, may formulate its own policies, establish its own laws, and so arrange its action as to enable the states to effectuate their own particular programs. In the words of Justice Cardozo, cooperative federalism is based on the view that the Constitution was "framed on the theory that the people of the several states must sink or swim together, and that in the long run, prosperity and salvation are in union and not in division." The Supreme Court's role in achieving this balance has been and is considerable.

V

COMMERCE POWER
AND THE STATES

REMOVAL OF RESTRICTIONS ON commercial relations imposed by the "sovereign" states was a moving cause of the Philadelphia Convention. For protection against these burdens, Madison, as a member of the Continental Congress, had advocated general authority over commerce. Later on he was conspicuous among those who set in motion the sequence of events leading to the successful meeting at Philadelphia. There seems to be no doubt that the commerce clause was inserted in the Constitution primarily to prevent the states from interfering with the freedom of commercial intercourse. Yet all the plans offered by the Convention apparently envisioned positive power in the national government to regulate commerce, and subsequent developments have converted this clause into a most important source of national authority. But the records of the Convention of 1787 afford no conclusive answer as to whether this was the intention of those who framed the Constitution. There was, however, general disinclination to impose restrictions.

It is proper, General Pinckney commented, that "no fetter should be imposed on the power of making commercial regulations . . .

as we are laying the foundations for a great empire." In the same vein, Rutledge declared that "we ought to take a permanent view of the subject and not look at the present moment only."

On September 15, 1787, Madison, commenting on the question whether a tonnage tax could be levied by the states under Article I, Section 10, for purposes of clearing and dredging harbors, said: "It depends on the extent of the commerce power. These terms— to regulate commerce—are vague but seem to exclude this power of the states. He [Madison] was more and more convinced that the regulation of commerce was in its nature indivisible and ought to be wholly under one authority." Immediately following this statement, Sherman of Connecticut observed: "The Power of the United States to regulate trade, being Supreme, can control interferences of the State regulations where such interferences happen; so that there is no danger to be apprehended from a concurrent jurisdiction."

"Had the issue been clearly posed and unequivocally settled," Albert S. Abel has commented, "it must perhaps have eliminated decades of judicial groping and guessing; on the other hand it might have broken up the convention."

Certain inferences about the nature and scope of the commerce power may be drawn from changes made by the Convention in the wording of the commerce clause itself. In the Pinckney Plan the word "exclusive" was used before "power." Draft VIII of the Committee of Detail used "exclusive," but in Draft IX it was deleted and reported out in its present form. No evidence has been presented concerning the significance of this deletion. "Exclusive" is used as a description of congressional power only in Clause 17 (laws for the District of Columbia). Even the power of Congress to declare war is not stated to be "exclusive," but Article I, Section 10 explicitly limits state action.

Comparison of the commerce clause with other provisions suggests that where specific restraints are placed on the states, as in Article I, Section 10, the only restriction of a commercial nature forbids duty on imports (or exports), except for the amount necessary to meet inspection cost. This seems to mean freedom of the states to pass other laws regulating commerce.

Because of the partisan motives of the speakers, contemporary opinion is no sure guide. Those opposed to the new Constitution stressed its centralizing tendencies in lurid colors; supporters, on the other hand, minimized the significance of commerce power. McHenry of the Maryland delegation said: "We almost shuddered at the fate of commerce of Maryland should we be unable to make any change in this extraordinary power." In the Virginia ratifying convention, Randolph agreed that the broad power over commerce was a *sine qua non* of the union, and yet he favored a two-thirds vote by Congress for national commerce acts. Richard Henry Lee, also of Virginia, reported a widespread fear that the clause would be used to discriminate against Southern states by the establishment of northern monopolies.

The writers of that skillful campaign document *The Federalist* employed their usual tactics. They made clear the dangers of not giving a broad power over commerce to the General Government, but blurred the precise limits of national power. In No. 7 Hamilton writes: "The competitions of commerce would be another fruitful source of contention. . . . Each state or separate confederacy, would pursue a system of commercial policy peculiar to itself. . . . The infractions of these [state] regulations on one side, the efforts to prevent and repel them on the other, would naturally lead to outrages, and these to reprisals and war." In essay No. 42 Madison glosses over the commerce power, discussing it chiefly as a supplement to the power over foreign commerce, and stressing the unfairness of permitting coastal states to levy a toll on states in the interior. In *Federalist*, No. 45 Madison again hints that the commerce power will be exercised chiefly on foreign commerce.

Many years later, in 1829, after the "Father of the Constitution" had become a proponent of state sovereignty, he insisted that the power to regulate commerce was designed to prevent abuses by the states rather than for positive purposes of the national government. "I always foresaw," Madison wrote J. C. Cabell,

> that difficulties might be started in relation to this power which could not be fully explained without recurring to views of it, which, however just, might give birth to specious though unsound objections. Being in the same terms with the power over foreign commerce, the same extent, if taken literally, would belong to it. Yet it is very certain that it grew out of the abuse of the power of the importing state in taxing the nonimporting, and was intended as a negative and preventive provision against injustice among the States themselves, rather than as a power to be used for the positive pur-

poses of the General Government, in which alone, however, the remedial power could be lodged.

For those opposed to the use of the commerce power as a basis for positive national regulation, Madison's words have done yeoman service.

THE MARSHALL DOCTRINE

The intriguing question of just what the commerce clause meant was first presented to the Court in 1824. *Gibbons* v. *Ogden* (9 Wheat. 1, 1824) involved the unpopular New York "steamboat monopoly." Chancellor Kent of New York, in upholding the state granted monopoly against the claim of Gibbons, operating under authority of a 1793 federal licensing act, maintained that Congress did not have any direct jurisdiction over internal commerce or waters. Webster, arguing for Gibbons on appeal to the Supreme Court, asserted that the power of Congress to regulate commerce was exclusive. Counsel for the monopoly claimed that a concurrent power existed wherever such a power was not clearly denied by the Constitution. Webster's prophetic definition of commerce as comprehending "almost all the business and intercourse of life" was countered by the definition of commerce as "the transportation and sale of commodities." Both sides agreed that if an actual collision of state and national power occurred, the latter must prevail, but the spokesman for the monopoly held that state power gave way only to the extent needed to give effect to the federal law. Accordingly navigation on state waters remained under state control.

Marshall could have solved the case simply by finding that both state and nation had acted within their powers, but since the state law conflicted with the federal licensing act it must give way. He chose instead to examine the nature of national commerce power before finding the existence of a conflict. Commerce is more than traffic; "it is intercourse. It comprehends navigation." Commerce "among" the states cannot stop at state lines but "may be introduced into the interior." "Among" meant "that commerce which concerns more states than one." Though the states retain authority to enact inspection, pilotage, and health laws, even here Congress could enter the field if it chose.

"What is this power?" Marshall asks. And he answers,

It is the power to regulate; that is, to prescribe the rule by which commerce is to be governed. This power, like all others vested in Congress is complete in itself, may be exercised to its utmost extent, and acknowledges no limitations, other than are prescribed in the Constitution . . . the power over commerce with foreign nations, and among the several states, is vested in Congress as absolutely as it would be in a single government, having in its constitution the same restrictions on the exercise of the power as are found in the Constitution of the United States.

Justice Johnson, concurring, went beyond Marshall. Even in the absence of the federal licensing act, the state monopoly must give way. Johnson's forthright remarks on the scope of the commerce power stand in bold contrast to those of Marshall. The national commerce power, Johnson contended, embraces all the power enjoyed by the states before the Constitution. It is a grant of the whole power carrying the whole subject exclusively into the hands of the national government. "The power must be exclusive; it can reside but in one potentate; and hence, the grant of this power carries with it the whole subject, leaving nothing for the state to act upon."

"The immediate cause that led to the forming of the convention," Johnson recalled, was the "iniquitous laws and unpolitic measures . . . destructive of the harmony of the states, and fatal to their commercial interests abroad." The commerce power was that power to regulate commerce which "previously existed in the states." Speaking out on the question Marshall sidestepped, Johnson ruled that the "inferences to be drawn" from Article I as a whole "seem to me altogether in favor of the exclusive grant to Congress of power over commerce."

Johnson's definition of the subject-matter of commerce is equally sweeping. Commerce

means an exchange of goods; but in the advancement of society, labor, transportation, intelligence, care and various mediums of exchange, become commodities, and enter commerce; the subject, the vehicle, the agent, and their various operations, become the objects of commercial regulations. Shipbuilding, the carrying trade, and propagation of seamen, are such vital agents of commercial prosperity, that the nation which could not legislate over these subjects, would not possess the power to regulate commerce.

Commenting on Marshall's more circumspect reading of the commerce clause, Professor Crosskey explains: "The effect . . . was undeniably to narrow ostensibly and quite unwarrantly, the power of Congress over commerce. And since it is impossible to suppose that John Marshall, a man of the 18th century, did not understand aright the subject of commercial regulation, and equally impossible to assume that he restricted willingly, without warrant, the authority of Congress over commerce, the rational surmise would seem to be that he was again making compelling concessions for the sake of unanimity in the court." The Chief Justice may have been moved, Crosskey suggests, by the desire "to prevent dissents by some of his 'States' Rights' brethren, and also in all probability to keep the writing of the Court's opinion in his own hands." Marshall's biographer, Albert J. Beveridge, suggests even subtler motives, pointing out that the Chief Justice may have availed himself of the political status of the South Carolinian as well as of his remarkable talents, to have Johnson state the real views of the master of the Supreme Court.

With the exception of spokesmen for monopolists and Southern slave-owners who feared the consequences of a broad definition of national power over commerce, public opinion welcomed the Court's rebuke to holders of special privilege. Following the decision, the number of steamboats plying in and out of New York harbor increased in one year from 6 to 43.

Three years later, in *Brown* v. *Maryland* (12 Wheat. 419, 1827) the Court held that national power over foreign commerce excluded state regulation in the form of licensing and taxing importers. Marshall pointed out that state actions of this nature violated both the prohibition of state taxes on imports (Art. I, Sec. 10) and the limitations on state power implicit in the commerce clause. In his effort to draw a line between commerce that could be regulated by the states and commerce that could not, the Chief Justice formulated the "original package" doctrine—the protection of national power over imported goods continues until they are incorporated into the mass of property within a state. To this proposition Marshall added the dictum that "we suppose the principles laid down in this case to apply equally to importations from a sister state." Two generations later, in *Brown* v. *Houston* (114 U.S. 622, 1885) the Court, refusing to follow Marshall, established another rule for drawing the line between national control over commerce "among the states" and the state taxing power. Whenever an article shipped from another state reaches its final destination or is interrupted for business purposes, it loses its national immunity from general state taxation—at least "in the absence of Congressional action."

Though Marshall described the subject matter of commerce and national power to regulate it in sweeping terms, he did not overlook the tremendous power reserved to the states. As to the "inspection laws," he said in *Gibbons* v. *Ogden:* "They form a portion of that immense mass of legislation which embraces everything within the territory of the State not surrendered to the general government; all which can be most advantageously exercised by the States themselves. Inspection laws, quarantine laws, health laws of every description, as well as laws for regulating the internal commerce of the State, and those which respect turnpike-roads, ferries, etc., are component parts of this mass." Commerce wholly within a state, which did not affect more than one state, was not within national authority, unless and until Congress acted positively. Said Marshall: "No direct general power over these objects is granted to Congress, and, consequently, they remain subject to State legislation. If the legislative power of the Union can reach them, it must be for national purposes." Marshall neatly sidestepped the question of whether the power was still in the states in the absence of congressional action, saying: "We may dismiss that inquiry because it [national power] has been exercised, and the regulations which Congress deemed it proper to make are now in full operation."

Reverting to the same problem in *Brown* v. *Maryland,* Marshall commented: "It has been observed that the powers remaining with the States may be so exercised as to come in conflict with those vested in Congress. When this happens, that which is not supreme must yield to that which is supreme. . . . The taxing power of the States . . . cannot interfere with any regulation of commerce." Marshall was but reiterating the point established in the Gibbons case, that wherever a conflict exists between national and state authority, the state must yield. But did the Constitution, in conferring upon Congress the power to regulate commerce "among the several States," deny to the states all concurrent authority?

Marshall's views on this question come out most clearly in *Willson* v. *Blackbird Creek Marsh Co.* (2 Peters 245, 1829). The Delaware legislature had authorized the Blackbird Creek Company to build a dam across the creek for the purpose of redeeming marshland. Willson, who owned a sloop licensed under national authority, broke through the dam and continued to navigate the creek. The company sued for trespass. Upholding the Delaware act, Marshall ruled:

> The act of assembly by which the plaintiffs were authorized to construct their dam, shows plainly that this is *one of those many creeks*, passing through a deep, level marsh, adjoining the Delaware, up which the tide flows for some distance. The value of the property on its banks must be enhanced by excluding the water from the marsh, and the *health of the inhabitants probably improved*. Measures calculated to produce these objects, provided they do not come into collision with the powers of the general government, are undoubtedly within those which are reserved to the states. . . .
>
> The counsel for the plaintiffs in error insist that it comes in conflict with the power of the United States "to regulate commerce . . . among the several states." If Congress had passed any act which bore upon the case; any act in execution of the power to regulate commerce; the object of which was to control state legislation over *those small navigable creeks* into which the tide flows, and *which abound throughout the lower country of the middle and southern states*, we should feel not much difficulty in saying that a state law coming in conflict with such act would be void. But Congress has passed no such act. . . .
>
> We do not think, that the act empowering the Blackbird Creek Marsh Company to place a dam across the creek, can, *under all the circumstances of the case*, be considered as repugnant to the power to regulate commerce in its dormant state, or as being in conflict with any law passed on the subject. [Italics are the authors'.]

Marshall is at considerable pains to show the bearing of the dam on land values and the health of the community. As a health measure, enacted under the police power of the state, the act was valid until it collided with national authority. The Chief Justice passes over the fact that the sloop was licensed under an act of Congress—the vital point in the Gibbons case. "Marshall could have made this little incident the occasion for another great opinion," said Charles Fairman, but "for some reason had let it pass."

Marshall's position may be summarized as follows:

(1) The power of Congress over commerce is "plenary," "absolute," "complete," subject to no limitations except those expressly stated in the Constitution. The following observation set the tone of Marshall's nationalism:

> Reference has been made to the political situation of the States, anterior to its [the Constitution's] formation. It has been said, that they were sovereign, were completely independent, and were connected with each other only by a league. This is true. But when these allied sovereigns converted their congress of ambassadors, deputed to deliberate on their common concerns, and to recommend measures of general utility, into a legislature, empowered to enact laws on the most interesting subjects, the whole character in which the States appear, underwent change.

What was formerly a league became a government. To the same effect, Marshall observed in *Cohens* v. *Virginia* (6 Wheat. 264, 1821):

> In war, we are one people. In peace we are one people. In all commercial regulations we are one and the same people. In many other respects the American people are one; and the government which is alone capable of controlling and managing their interests in all these respects, is the government of the Union. It is their government, and in that character they have no other. America has chosen to be, in many respects and to many purposes, a nation; and for all these purposes, her government is complete; to all these objects, it is competent.

(2) The commerce power is capable of acting on any aspect of commercial life, even that wholly within one state—if such commerce "affects more than one State."

(3) The power to regulate is the power to "prescribe the rules" by which commerce is to be governed, and this includes measures designed to prohibit, direct, and control as well as measures to foster and promote.

(4) The commerce clause operates of its own force to invalidate state regulations that obstruct or hinder the flow of commerce or discriminate against it. Such "mischief" is precisely what the commerce clause was designed to prevent. In the absence of such purpose or effect, state regulation can stand—unless and until a conflict exists with national regulation.

THE DOCTRINE OF THE TANEY COURT

During Taney's tenure as Chief Justice (1835-1864) the Court squarely faced the question that Marshall had pointedly circumvented in *Gibbons* v. *Ogden:* May the states regulate commerce in the absence of federal regulation? The importance of the answer cannot be overstressed. Congress was not likely to react positively to commercial problems during this period. Invalidation of state laws regulating commerce meant that commerce would probably be free from all regulation.

In *New York* v. *Miln* (11 Pet. 102, 1837) the Taney Court, in a confused set of opinions, upheld as a police-power regulation a state act requiring the ship's master on incoming vessels to furnish information concerning his passengers. Justice Thompson, who was originally assigned the task of writing the opinion, treated the state act as a police measure and as permissible commerce regulation—in the absence of national action. Because four Justices balked at Thompson's analysis, Justice Barbour wrote an opinion holding the state law valid under the police power. Barbour added some expressions about the commerce power with which other Justices did not agree, but since it was delivered on the last day of the term, they could do nothing to show their displeasure. Barbour's gratuitous remarks on commerce, with which Taney later indicated agreement, stated in effect that persons were not "subjects of commerce," a pronouncement highly pleasing to the slave states.

In 1847, the even more confused opinions in the *License Cases* (5 How. 504) revealed how difficult it was for the Court to settle on any one view of commerce power. Taney favored state regulation of the liquor trade. In one case, upholding the state act, he adopted the "original package" doctrine, since the amount involved was only two quarts. In another he said that a state could regulate articles in the original package in absence of national regulation, thus countering Marshall's dictum in *Brown* v. *Maryland* (12 Wheat. 419, 1827), a case in which Taney had been counsel for the state. Some members of the Court talked in terms of "police power"; others argued that only intrastate commerce was involved.

In the *Passenger Cases* (7 How. 283, 1849) state taxes on passengers on incoming vessels were challenged. These cases were argued on three different occasions over a four-year period. Webster, who as counsel opposed the state acts, was convinced of the accuracy of his position, but feared the absence of a "strong and leading mind" on the Court. Van Buren, for the states, stressed the popular support for the state acts and state sovereignty. Webster won a 5-4 decision. But each of the five Justices stated his views in such a way that the reporter could enter as a headnote only that the act was invalid. Three of the four dissenters wrote separate opinions. Taney held that since states could expel undesirable immigrants, they could reject them in the first place, and cited *New York* v. *Miln* to the effect that persons were not "subjects of commerce." The majority split—two Justices ruling congressional power over foreign commerce to be exclusive, three holding that this was unnecessary for the decision—since the state act conflicted with existing national legislation. The one happy note in this confusion was that the judges did not follow sectional or party lines. Nevertheless disappointment and frustration greeted the decision. Charles Warren, referring to the diversity of judicial views, points out that the confusion was "so great that the Reporter himself, in perplexity, very frankly declared that there was no opinion of the Court as a Court."

The law was in this muddle when President Fillmore, in 1851, appointed Benjamin R. Curtis to the Court. Curtis, a brilliant young Massachusetts lawyer, was destined to be the mediator between two tenuous coalitions, the effective medium through whom a compromise was reached. In the famous case of *Cooley* v. *Board of Port Wardens* (12 How. 299, 1851) a Pennsylvania law imposing a one-half pilotage fee on vessels leaving Philadelphia without a pilot was declared valid against the charge that it conflicted with the national power over commerce. Complicating the situation was a congressional act of 1789 stating that pilots should be regulated in conformity "with such laws as the states may hereafter enact . . . until further legislative provision shall be made by Congress." Curtis, combining elements of the "exclusive" and "concurrent" doctrines, fashioned a new formula that still commends itself to a majority of the Supreme Court. His middle ground was this: subjects national in scope admit only of uniform regulation; these require congressional legislation, and in the absence of such legislation the states cannot act. As to subjects of a local character, not requiring uniform legislation, the states may legislate until Congress, by acting on the same subject, displaces the state law. Where national and state laws are in conflict the national supremacy rule prevails. Though Taney did not agree with Curtis' analysis, he silently joined in the opinion. With the Cooley doctrine, Warren comments, "the law received considerable clarification and fixity."

Despite the "balanced" formula Justice Curtis created in the Cooley case, difficult questions remained unanswered. What was a subject matter requiring a national (or uniform) regulation? When was a state law affecting commerce in conflict with national legislation? The awkward question of the extent of state power to tax one or more aspects of interstate commerce was left to the future. The answers the Court might give had more than logical or semantic importance because with the national government incapable or unwilling to govern, a theory of broad national power (a narrow definition of what required local regulation) meant that commerce would be free of all regulation.

COMMERCE POWER AND STATE ACTION: 1865-1890

Under the Cooley doctrine, and in the absence of congressional legislation, the Court's first duty was to determine the nature of the subject matter of the regulation. If it required national regulation, then state action was foreclosed. If the subject matter permitted state or local regulation, two questions remained: Did the state law discriminate against interstate commerce, and in favor of local commerce? Did the state act, although nondiscriminatory, place an unreasonable burden on interstate commerce? A host of socio-economic fact and theory, flavored by judicial bias, entered inevitably into the attempt to answer these questions. Theories of federalism marched, as we have seen, hand in hand with social and economic theory.

A variety of aims motivate state governments in passing laws affecting interstate commerce. One purpose is to protect the safety and promote the well-being of state citizens. In other words, invocation of the "police power," to protect the public health, safety, morals, and general welfare, frequently has the effect of prescribing

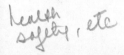
health, safety, etc

a rule affecting one or more aspects of commerce. Legislation requiring trains to have certain lights, to sound horns, and to proceed at limited speeds has this effect, as does legislation forbidding the sale of harmful food or drink.

Another state purpose is to create, protect, and foster intrastate commerce, to construct and improve roads, canals, and streams. In the consideration of all such measures, the line between intra- and interstate activities is hard to draw. A third objective is to tax commercial activities within the state in order to raise revenue, and in many instances to compensate the state for services rendered those using its commercial facilities. A tax on gasoline, for example, provides revenue for road repairs.

In the post-Civil-War period, especially, state legislatures were under pressure to solve the problems arising from a burgeoning industrialism. It seemed not unlikely, at least prior to 1880, that regulation, if it were to come at all, had to be state imposed. Such legislation had first to run the gauntlet of challenge on the ground of invalidity under state constitutions. Then it was possible for its opponents to interpose the Constitution of the United States, especially the commerce clause, and later the due process clause of the Fourteenth Amendment, as weapons against state action. Since due process in the federal courts before 1890 had only procedural significance, the commerce clause was the chief weapon available to those who wished to frustrate state effort to regulate the rapidly expanding world of business and commerce.

In the 1869 case of *Paul* v. *Virginia* (8 Wall. 168) the Court upheld a state act requiring all insurance companies to obtain a license before issuing policies within the state. State power was sustained against the contention that insurance is essentially an interstate business, and in the absence of national legislation could not be regulated by the states. Justice Field, speaking for a unanimous court, met this argument by declaring that insurance transactions are local because, technically considered, the delivery of the contract took place in Virginia. That the Justices did not view national power narrowly when Congress chose to act was shown by a Court decision two years later holding a federal licensing act applicable to a steamboat engaged in carrying goods and passengers on a navigable river between two points wholly within a state (*The Daniel Ball*, 10 Wall. 557, 1871). The river was a "highway of commerce," Justice Field said, and the federal licensing act was an appropriate means of insuring the safety of navigation. Though the steamer did not itself travel in interstate commerce, it was an "instrument" by which such commerce was carried on, since some of the persons and goods continued across state lines. A Missouri statute that licensed and taxed pedlars of goods not grown or produced in Missouri was invalidated in the 1876 case of *Welton* v. *Missouri* (91 U.S. 275). Here Justice Field emphasized the element of discrimination against interstate commerce.

After 1870, state legislation regulating the railroads focused judicial attention on the limits of state power in the absence of congressional action. In *Munn* v. *Illinois* (94 U.S. 113, 1877) and the other "Granger" cases (94 U.S. 77, 155, 179, 180, 187) the Court upheld an Illinois regulation of grain elevator and railroad rates, saying that although "instruments" of interstate commerce were the subject of the legislation and that these instruments "may become connected with interstate commerce," they were not necessarily so, and until Congress acted the states could control the rates, even though this regulation had an indirect effect on interstate commerce. Shortly after this decision the Court held that (in the absence of Congressional legislation) the states were free to tax goods held within a state even if the goods were subjects of interstate commerce (*Brown* v. *Houston*, 114 U.S. 642, 1885). By 1886, however, the Court was ready to shift ground. The facts in the historic Wabash case (118 U.S. 557) showed that the railroad charged 15 cents per pound from Peoria, Illinois, and 25 cents per pound from Gilman, Illinois, on shipments of similar chattels to New York City. The state court had allowed the application of the state law forbidding price discrimination by measuring the discrimination on the intrastate portion of the journey, but the Supreme Court held that since these were single trips such measurement was invalid. "This is commerce of a national character," Justice Miller said, "and national regulation is required." Bradley, Waite, and Gray objected, stating that in the absence of congressional action the states should be allowed to act so long as the effect on interstate commerce was indirect. It is noteworthy that between 1877 and 1886 the Court set aside fourteen state commercial regulations, and in only two instances was national legislation involved.

While state railroad rate regulation became virtually meaningless with the passage of the Interstate Commerce Act in 1887, state police-power legislation affecting transportation continued unabated. In 1888 in *Smith* v. *Alabama* (124 U.S. 465) a state law requiring a license for locomotive drivers was accepted as a police regulation, despite its effect on interstate commerce. In 1890 a state law requiring railroads carrying passengers in the state to provide equal but separate facilities for Negroes was upheld in *Louisville Railway* v. *Mississippi* (133 U.S. 587).

STATE LEGISLATION AND THE COMMERCE POWER AFTER 1890

After 1890, two dominant themes began to pervade the application of the commerce clause: use of the commerce power by Congress to accomplish broad social and economic purposes; continuation and further development of the commerce clause as a restriction on state action affecting interstate commerce.

At the outset, cases on the latter subject reveal no clear pattern. In *Leisy* v. *Hardin* (135 U.S. 100, 1890), the Taney Court's ruling in the License Cases, upholding state prohibition laws, was rejected on the ground that beer was a genuine article of commerce, the sale of which could be prohibited only by congressional action. Yet four years later in *Plumley* v. *Massachusetts* (155 U.S. 461), the Court held that a Massachusetts law forbidding the sale of colored oleo only "incidentally affected" trade between states and was, therefore, a legitimate police measure to prevent the defrauding of purchasers. Increasingly, the Court, after ascertaining that the subject matter was not one requiring national regulation, examined the state law to see whether it discriminated against or burdened interstate commerce. Whether the statute challenged was labeled a police regulation, a tax law, or an attempt to control intrastate commerce is largely irrelevant, although the language of the decisions on this point is frequently confused.

The Court has been rather generous in upholding state acts regulating motor transportation, such as the licensing of vehicles using state roads (*Buck* v. *Kuykendall*, 267 U.S. 307, 1925). In the important 1938 case of *South Carolina* v. *Barnwell* (303 U.S. 77),

a statute prohibiting trucks with loads over 20,000 pounds and
widths exceeding 90 inches from using state roads was upheld.
Justice Stone thought it a reasonable measure to protect roads built
and maintained by the state in the absence of congressional legislation, especially since no discrimination or attempt to burden
interstate commerce had been shown. Similarly a large number of
state taxes, ostensibly designed to force interstate traffic to bear
its share of the cost of maintaining and policing highways, were
upheld (in 11 of 16 cases, 1915-1950) on the theory that they
neither discriminated against interstate vehicles nor imposed unreasonable burdens on interstate commerce. However, where the
tax is viewed as one on the privilege of doing business within the
state (*Spector Motor Service* v. *O'Connor*, 340 U.S. 602, 1951),
or where the tax formula bears no resemblance to highway use
(*McCarroll* v. *Dixie Greyhound Lines*, 309 U.S. 176, 1940), state
legislation has been invalidated.

Problems arising from state attempts to tax one or more incidents
of interstate commerce have posed vexing issues. The early case of
State Freight Tax (15 Wall. 232, 1873) held that a state could not
tax interstate freight carried by railroads operating within its
borders. In *Robbins* v. *Shelby County* (120 U.S. 489, 1887) a
license tax on all salesmen, interstate and local, was declared invalid
as a regulation of interstate commerce, which Congress by its
silence intended to be free from all regulation. The sale of goods,
by means of sample, which are to be brought in from another
state is interstate commerce and therefore free from state taxation.

In the depression of the 1930's the Court seemingly relaxed this
view and approved a state "use" tax, a suspiciously close relative
of the sales tax (*Henneford* v. *Silas Mason*, 300 U.S. 577, 1937).
Here a Washington statute levied a sales tax of 2 per cent on sales
made within the state, and a use tax of 2 per cent on sales made
outside Washington for use within the state unless a tax of 2 per
cent or more had already been paid at the time of the sale. Upholding the "use" tax, Justice Cardozo wrote:

> Equality is the theme that runs though all sections of the statute.
> . . . When the account is made up, the stranger from afar is sub-
> ject to no greater burdens as a consequence of ownership than the
> dweller within the gates.

In *Gwin, White and Prince* v. *Henneford* (305 U.S. 434, 1939), however, the Court invalidated a state business activities tax measured by gross income, because the majority thought it posed the danger of multiple burdens; other states could seize upon other events in interstate transactions for tax purposes. In *Best* v. *Maxwell* (311 U.S. 459, 1940) a license tax obviously aimed at out-of-state merchants was deemed discriminatory. Yet in *McGoldrick* v. *Berwind-White* (309 U.S. 33, 1940) the Court approved a New York general sales tax as applied to coal originating in Pennsylvania and sold from a New York City office. Chief Justice Hughes's dissenting opinion pointed out that the risk of multiple burdens existed in the McGoldrick case quite as much as it had in earlier cases where the state tax had been rejected. Later cases seem less charitable to such taxes. In *McLeod* v. *Dilworth Co.* (322 U.S. 327, 1944) a tax on sales completed by acceptance of orders in, and shipment of goods from another state, in which title passed upon delivery to the carrier, was set aside by a divided Court. For the majority Justice Frankfurter explained:

> A sales tax and a use tax in many instances may bring about the same result. But they are different in conception, are assessments upon different transactions. . . . A sales tax is a tax on the freedom of purchase. . . . A use tax is a tax on the enjoyment of that which was purchased. In view of the differences in the basis of these two taxes and the differences in the relation of the taxing state to them, a tax on an interstate sale like the one before us and unlike the tax on the enjoyment of the goods sold, involves an assumption of power by a state which the commerce clause was meant to end.

In *Nippert* v. *Richmond* (327 U.S. 416, 1946) a municipal ordinance imposing upon solicitors of orders for goods a license tax of fifty dollars, and one-half of one per cent of the gross earnings, commissions, etc. for the preceding year in excess of $1,000, was also invalidated. For the Court, Justice Rutledge noted that the drummer "is a figure of a bygone day," but that his "modern prototype persists under more euphonious appellations. So endure the basic reasons which brought about his protection from the kind of local favoritism the facts of this case typify." Broadly speaking, the doctrine of the classic case of *Robbins* v. *Shelby Taxing District* still holds. A nondiscriminatory tax on goods brought from another state is valid, but a tax on the negotiation of sales by means of samples of goods to be brought in from another state is invalid as a burden on interstate commerce.

State taxation in relation to the Commerce Clause is still a troublesome issue. On February 24, 1959 (*North-Western States Portland Cement Co.* v. *Minnesota*, 358 U.S. 450) the Court sustained the constitutionality of state income tax laws levying taxes on that portion of a foreign corporation's net income earned from and fairly apportioned to business activities within the taxing state, even though those activities are exclusively in furtherance of interstate commerce. Three Justices (Whittaker, Frankfurter and Stewart) dissented, holding that the Commerce Clause precluded the state from laying taxes directly on exclusively interstate commerce. Taking sharp issue with the dissenters, Justice Harlan's reading of the precedents clearly sustained the taxing act. "As I read the cases," Harlan observed, "the existence of some income from *intrastate* business on the part of the taxed corporation, while sometimes adverted to, has never been considered essential to the valid taxation of such 'interstate' income."

Problems of a different nature have been presented by state police regulations, such as that challenged successfully in *Di Santo* v. *Pennsylvania* (273 U.S. 34, 1927) where the state tried to license sellers of steamship tickets. Invoking the direct and indirect effects formula that had proved so effective in restricting the scope of the Sherman Anti-Trust Act, Justice Butler ruled that the Pennsylvania statute "directly interferes with or burdens foreign commerce" and was therefore invalid. Justice Stone, dissenting, objected that the "traditional test of the limit of state action by inquiring whether the interference with commerce is direct or indirect seems to me too mechanical, too uncertain in its application, and too remote from actualities, to be of value." Rejecting the "direct" and "indirect" interference test, Stone argued that state interferences with congressional control over commerce should be sustained, "not because the effect on commerce is nominally indirect, but because a consideration of all the facts and circumstances, such as the nature of the regulation, its function, the character of the business involved and the actual effect on the flow of commerce, lead to the conclusion that the regulation concerns interests peculiarly local and does not infringe the national interest in maintaining the freedom of commerce across state lines."

It was not, however, until well over a decade later that Stone's realistic approach prevailed. In *California* v. *Thompson* (313 U.S. 109, 1941), a law requiring licenses of those selling interstate bus tickets was sustained. "The decision in the Di Santo case," Justice Stone commented, was a "departure . . . which has been recognized since *Cooley* v. *Port Wardens*. . . . It cannot be reconciled with later decisions of this court . . . and it can no longer be regarded as controlling authority." Applying the realism Stone advocated in 1927, the Court ruled that "in the absence of pertinent congressional legislation there is constitutional power in the states to regulate interstate commerce by motor vehicles whenever it affects the safety of the public or the safety and convenient use of the highways, provided only that the regulation does not in any other respect unnecessarily obstruct interstate commerce."

The most extreme case of permissible state regulation—*Parker* v. *Brown* mentioned in the previous chapter—was yet to come. The act permitted a state-sponsored monopoly to control all marketing of California raisins, and required that all growers comply with its rules. Three objections were leveled against the act: (1) A federal District Court judge had enjoined the act as an unconstitutional burden on interstate commerce; (2) the act appeared to be a violation of the Sherman Anti-Trust Act (there seemed no doubt that if the farmers themselves had banded together to do what they actually did through the agency of the state the program would have been outlawed under the Sherman Act); (3) the state act may have been in conflict with a comprehensive scheme of federal regulation. Against all these objections, the Court upheld the act unanimously, stressing the importance of the industry to the state, and the apparent acceptance by the national government of the state program.

Among the cases decided in the last two decades few have stimulated greater controversy than *United States* v. *South-Eastern Underwriters* (322 U.S. 533, 1946). Speaking through Justice Black, the Court ruled, in the face of a 75-year-old precedent, that insurance is interstate commerce, at least insofar as the Sherman Anti-Trust Act was applicable. In dissent both Justices Stone and Jackson apparently proceeded on the assumption that the commerce clause operates automatically to wipe out state regulation, even in the absence of congressional legislation concerning the subject matter.

For Black, on the other hand, the commerce clause does not of itself appropriate anything exclusively to the national government —except possibly the duty to see to it that state laws do not discriminate against interstate commerce. In Black's view the consequences were less disastrous than Stone and Jackson supposed, since state legislation regulating the insurance business was still valid.

Certain legislators, notably Senator Radcliffe of Maryland, interpreted the Court's decision as placing insurance under the supervision of the national government. President Roosevelt denied this: "The Attorney General advises me," he wrote the Maryland Senator on January 25, 1945, "that he does not believe that this alternative is inevitable or even probable. He tells me that there is nothing in the decision which prevents regulation by the states of insurance rates as long as that regulation does not interfere with the provisions of the Sherman Act."

Following the Court's decision, considerable uncertainty arose as to the validity of state tax laws and other regulatory provisions governing the insurance companies. To stabilize the situation, Congress passed the McCarran Act of 1945, confirming the long-exercised state power over insurance that some thought they had lost as a result of judicial decision. "The Congress," the Act reads, "hereby declares that the continued regulation and taxation by the several states of the business of insurance is in the public interest, and that the silence on the part of the Congress shall not be construed to impose any barrier to the regulation or taxation of such business by the several states."

The Act, in effect, ratified the Court's decision by leaving intact state regulation of insurance business, except as such regulation, after January 1, 1948, permitted practices in conflict with the antitrust laws. If at the end of the three-year moratorium provided under the Act the states had not brought themselves into compliance, if they had not regulated the business of insurance, then they would be obliged to take the consequences because, after that period, the Sherman Act and other acts were to come immediately into force as regards the business of insurance. The Supreme Court ratified this legislative decision and suggested that coordinated state and national action could "achieve legislative consequences, particularly in the great fields of regulating commerce and taxation, which, to some extent, at least, neither could accomplish in isolated action" (*Prudential Ins. Co.* v. *Benjamin*, 328 U.S. 408, 1946).

It may not be too much to say that Black's opinion in the South-Eastern Underwriters case is the first since Marshall's day to give the commerce clause an all-embracing yet state-power-saving construction. The confusion throughout seems to have arisen from the Court's persistent tendency to consider state regulation "affecting" interstate commerce as though it involved power in the states to regulate such commerce. In Marshall's view, as in Black's, such regulating power as the states possess derives from their police power. Furthermore, state legislation enacted thereunder will prevail unless and until supplanted by national legislation. In a word, the states possess, as Marshall said, that "immense mass" of power designated "police"; Congress has the power to regulate commerce. When the two conflict, that which is "supreme" must prevail over that which is not supreme. The question turns, therefore, on whether or not there is a conflict, or whether state action "burdens" interstate commerce. As to this there is, as recent decisions indicate, plenty of opportunity for debate. *where should court rule?*

Not least, indeed, among the subjects on which the Justices are divided is the question of what role the Court should play in this important area. Three basic positions have emerged. All Justices agree that even in the absence of congressional action, no state can discriminate against interstate commerce in order to gain for itself a commercial advantage. Black, leading one group of Justices, would stop there—that is, he would restrict judicial inquiry to the question of whether or not state law discriminates against interstate commerce. In all other cases he would remand the solution of difficulties to Congress. Black believes that this idea was rejected in the Arizona Train Limit case (325 U.S. 761, 1945), where the Court, led by Chief Justice Stone, invoked the "balancing of interests" rule to determine whether the state's regulation limiting interstate or intrastate freight trains to 70 cars could stand. A majority, considering this a subject requiring uniform regulation, set the state act aside. In a vigorous dissent, Justice Black wrote:

> What the Court decides today is that it is unwise policy to regulate the length of trains. . . . The determination of whether it is in the interest of society for the length of trains to be governmentally regulated is a matter of public policy. Someone must fix that policy

—either the Congress, or the State, or the courts. A century and a half of constitutional history and government admonishes this Court to leave that choice to the elected legislative representatives of the people themselves where it properly belongs both on democratic principles and the requirements of efficient government. . . . Representatives elected by the people to make their laws, rather than Judges appointed to interpret those laws, can best determine the policies which govern the people. That at least is the basic principle on which our democratic society rests.

Convinced later that he could not persuade the majority to accept his limited view of the scope of judicial review in commerce cases, Justice Black, in *Morgan* v. *Virginia* (328 U.S. 373, 1946) joined the majority. In this case, Justice Reed, speaking for the Court, and employing Stone's "balancing of interests" formula, ruled that a state "Jim Crow" law could not be enforced against passengers on interstate buses.

A group within the majority, led by Justice Jackson, found Black's and Stone's positions about equally objectionable. Neither gave due weight to the danger the commerce clause was designed to avert—"Balkanization" of the United States, by permitting individual states to raise barriers against interstate commerce. Even in the absence of congressional legislation, Justice Jackson held, the commerce clause of its own force prohibits the state from doing anything to burden, obstruct, hinder, or restrain interstate commerce, and it is the duty of the Supreme Court to guard national commerce from such local encroachments.

As this group gained strength, Justice Black turned from his limited-review theory to defend the "balance of interests" role he had formerly opposed. *Hood* v. *DuMond* (336 U.S. 525, 1949) brought the conflict between the two approaches to a head.

Hood, a Massachusetts dairyman, bought his milk in New York state through three receiving stations licensed by that state. His application for a fourth station was denied on the ground that expansion of his facilities would reduce the milk supply for New York state markets and lead to destructive competition in a market already adequately served. New York, it was said, had the right to prevent its milk from being bought for use out of the state until local needs were first satisfied. Denying that New York state could refuse a license for expanding facilities to receive out-of-state milk, Justice Jackson ruled that the Constitution does not say clearly where the line is to be drawn between federal and state power. Nor does it indicate what the states can do in the absence of congressional action. These, he says, are among "the great silences of the Constitution." Giving meaning to these silences had been quite as significant a part of the Court's work as interpretation of the written word. It is the Court's job under the commerce clause to "advance the prosperity and solidarity of the nation." Lack of power in the states to "retard, burden or constrict the flow of commerce for their economic advantage, is one deeply rooted in both our history and our law."

"Our system," Jackson went on, "fostered by the Commerce Clause, is that every farmer and every craftsman shall be encouraged to produce by the certainty that he will have free access to every market in the Nation, that no home embargoes will withhold his exports, and no foreign state will by customs duties or regulations exclude them. Likewise, every consumer may look to the free competition from every producing area in the Nation to protect him from exploitation by any." "Such," he said, "was the vision of the Founders; such has been the doctrine of this Court which has given it reality."

Justice Jackson was able to secure the assents of but four colleagues—Justices Black and Frankfurter in separate dissents spoke for the remaining four judges. Black distrusted Jackson's reasoning as leading to the reconstitution of an area immune from governmental regulation—not because Congress lacks power to intervene in this sphere (Mr. Justice Jackson's opinion was quite clear on that), but because it concerned a local detail that could never be adequately controlled from Washington. "It is inconceivable," Black argued, "that Congress could pass uniform national legislation capable of adjustment and application to all the local phases of interstate activities that take place in the 48 states. It is equally inconceivable that Congress would attempt to control such diverse local activities through a 'swarm of statutes only locally applicable and utterly inconsistent.'"

Furthermore, Black doubted whether authority could be found in the Constitution for judicial protection of interstate commerce as against the weight of the state's interest—"even in its great silences." He detected reaction in the majority's new approach, a rebirth of the due-process philosophy which utilized the Court "as an emancipator of business from regulation." In his own words: "The due process clause and commerce clause have been used like Siamese twins in a never-ending stream of challenges to governmental regulation. Both clauses easily lend themselves to inordinate expansion of this Court's power at the expense of the legislative power."

"The basic question here," he concluded, "is not the greatness of the commerce clause concept, but whether all local phases of interstate business are to be judicially immunized from state laws."

From this survey, certain conclusions can be drawn. First, the rule in the Cooley case has not been used to frustrate state legislation simply because one might argue that a national rule would be more efficient or desirable. Second, judicial generosity toward state action has in fact permitted the erection of certain trade barriers (motor carrier limitations, taxes, inspection laws, safety laws). Third, Congress for many reasons has not chosen to regulate all subjects that lie within the reach of its commerce power. Fourth, the permissible limits of the state taxing power are not clearly defined, although, in general, nondiscriminatory and apportioned taxes have a good chance of being upheld. The commonly held view that growth of the national commerce power would in time completely displace state power has not been borne out. The Supreme Court has undertaken, however, the role of guardian of the national market against obviously discriminatory and parochial efforts to re-erect the type of trade barriers that marked the preconstitutional era. At the same time, it has recognized the danger of leaving large areas of commercial activity free from all regulation, which would be the inescapable result if Congress cannot or will not act and the states are forbidden to act.

barriers to interstate commerce

complete freedom from regulation

VI

NATIONAL TAXING
AND SPENDING

*under
articles
depended on contrib.*

GOVERNMENT, LIKE INDIVIDUAL
citizens, must have regular income to pay bills and maintain credit.
Government must also have coercive power to collect taxes. No
government can carry on if it has to depend, as the Congress did
under the Articles of Confederation, on requisitions and voluntary
contribution.

Indeed, the principal weakness of Congress under the Articles
of Confederation was its lack of power to levy taxes. National
expenditures were defrayed out of a common treasury, supplied
by the states in proportion to the occupied land in each state, and
upon requisition from Congress. The states reserved the right to
levy taxes for this purpose and were, in fact, very delinquent in
making payments.

Therefore, it is not surprising that although members of the
Federal Convention were sharply divided on many issues, they
were almost unanimous in believing that Congress should have
broad power to tax. Heading the list of enumerated powers in
Article I, Section 8 stands the provision that Congress shall have

power "to lay and collect taxes, duties, imposts and excises, to pay the debts and provide for the common defense and general welfare of the United States."

It would be difficult to fashion more sweeping language. In the exercise of its taxing power the national government reaches individual citizens and their property, acts as directly as though there were no states. Nor are there any limits (apart from those imposed on the law makers at the ballot box) on the amount Congress may attempt to collect through taxation. The only specific limitations on taxing power are those mentioned in Article I, Section 9. This Article expressly prohibits the national government from granting a preference to one state's ports over another's, and forbids a tax on exports—a concession made in 1787 to Southern exporters.

LIMITATIONS THROUGH INTERPRETATION

In addition to these express limitations the Supreme Court has developed two others through interpretation. The first is the doctrine of reciprocal immunity of the state and national governments and their instrumentalities from taxation by the other. Chief Justice Marshall argued, as we have seen, that this immunity was enjoyed only by the national government. With the ascendancy of the concept of dual federalism the Court, under Chief Justice Taney's influence, extended the immunity to state governments and their instrumentalities. *Collector* v. *Day* (11 Wall. 113, 1871) recognized an implied immunity of state and municipal officers from income taxation, establishing a limitation not overruled until *Graves* v. *New York* (306 U.S. 466, 1939). However, the immunity of the states was qualified in 1905. In *South Carolina* v. *United States* (199 U.S. 437, 1905), involving a federal tax on the state of South Carolina's liquor-dispensing business, the state claimed immunity under the doctrine of *Collector* v. *Day*, but without success. The Court made this distinction: whenever the state embarks on business or proprietary enterprises, in contrast to what the Court called the exercise of governmental functions, the state loses its Court-created immunity. This is still good law. But with state governments entering more and more fields previously under private management (e.g., water and power utilities, transit systems), what is and what is not a governmental function is not easily decided.

A second judge-made limitation on the national taxing power was not fully established until 1936. In the famous AAA case (*United States* v. *Butler*, 297 U.S. 1, 1936) Justice Roberts, speaking for the Court, at the height of the controversy stimulated by the New Deal's legislative program, declared that the reserved powers of the states prevented Congress from using the taxing and spending power as an indirect method of regulating certain activities traditionally belonging to them, of which agricultural production was one example. In short, the general welfare clause was a grant of power to use public money for any purpose that concerns the general welfare, but this did not include power to enact supporting legislation, unless that power is conferred by some other clause of the Constitution. The Court's elaboration of this theory is reserved for later consideration in this chapter.

The Constitution declares that taxes are of two kinds, and sets forth briefly the rules by which Congress may use each. Direct taxes shall be levied according to the rule of apportionment among the several states on the basis of census enumeration or population. Indirect taxes shall be levied according to the rule of uniformity, which means geographical uniformity (as *Knowlton* v. *Moore*, 178 U.S. 41, made clear). That is to say, a tax must be laid at the same rate and on the same basis throughout all parts of the United States. The meaning of indirect taxes, which include all excises and duties, has never troubled the Court deeply, but the meaning of direct taxes has provided substantial difficulties.

Madison's notes throw no light on the mystery of what is a direct tax. The single entry on this question runs as follows: "Mr. Davies of North Carolina rose to ask the meaning of the direct taxes. Mr. King said he did not know." Like so many other terms in the Constitution, the meaning of direct taxes had to be spelled out by judicial construction. The Court first spoke on the subject in 1796 in the leading case of *Hylton* v. *United States* (3 Dall. 171). In this most unusual moot or test case, the attorneys on both sides were paid by the government. Even the facts were fictitious, the government alleging that Hylton possessed 125 "chariots exclusively for the defendant's own use and not to let out for hire." Hylton had, in fact, only one chariot. He contested the case merely to "ascertain a constitutional point and not by any means to delay the payment of a public duty." The Court's holding, that the federal tax on carriages was indirect and therefore not subject to apportionment, was based, first, on the nature of the carriage tax, which it considered one on the privilege of *using* carriages; and second, on the impossibility of fairly apportioning a tax of this kind, since the ratio of carriages to population was obviously not the same in each state. The Justices agreed that the only direct taxes (which the Southern delegation at the Constitutional Convention had feared would be directed at their slaves or land) were capitation and land taxes. These categories remained frozen for a century.

In accordance with its belief that the Court would adhere to this definition, Congress levied an income tax during the Civil War. It was challenged unsuccessfully before the Supreme Court in *Springer* v. *United States* (102 U.S. 586, 1881), and stood until the 1890's when Congress enacted another income tax law, levied, as the Civil War tax had been, as if it were indirect. This time, in *Pollock* v. *Farmer's Loan and Trust Co.* (158 U.S. 601, 1895), the Court, changing its mind, boldly corrected "a century of error."

With a fortune at stake, an extraordinary galaxy of legal talent had been joined in opposition to the tax—Benjamin H. Bristow, a United States Attorney who came into the national limelight when he cracked down on the Ku Klux Klan in Kentucky; George F. Edmunds, veteran Vermont Senator and formerly chairman of the Judiciary committee, among several others. Towering above them all was Joseph H. Choate. Only the lawyers appearing in the Dartmouth College case could match the eminence of these legal luminaries. Attorney General Richard Olney, implying that the Justices felt themselves overshadowed, cautioned them against being unduly influenced by this "great array of counsel, this elaborate argumentation, and these many and voluminous treatises mislabeled by the name of briefs."

"An income tax," Olney argued, "is preeminently a tax upon the rich, and all the circumstances just averted to prove the immense pecuniary stake which is now played for. It is so large that counsel fees and costs and printers' bills are mere bagatelles. It is so large and so stimulates the efforts of counsel that no legal or constitutional principle that stands in the way . . . is suffered to pass unchallenged. . . ."

The opposition was not inclined to dispute the government's class-struggle approach. Underscoring the explosive social aspects of the case, Choate observed:

I believe there are private rights of property here to be protected. . . . The act of Congress which we are impugning before you is communistic in its purposes and tendencies, and is defended here upon principles as communistic, socialistic—what shall I call them— populistic as ever have been addressed to any political assembly in the world.

Admitting that he was spokesman for a privileged minority and insisting that the Court was its guardian, Choate defied popular reaction:

If it be true . . . that the passions of the people are aroused on this subject, if it be true that a mighty army of sixty million citizens is likely to be incensed by this decision, it is the more vital to the future welfare of this country that this Court . . . declare . . . that it has the power to set aside an act of Congress . . . no matter what the threatened consequences of popular or populistic wrath may be.

On April 18, 1895, after listening to arguments five days, the Court delivered its opinion. Because Justice Jackson was absent the Court was evenly divided. On a rehearing the Justices listened to three more days of argument. Counsel for the appellants insisted that income taxes are direct. This was the framers' intentions; John Marshall himself had endorsed it. A tax on real estate, Choate argued, is undoubtedly direct, and "the rent of real estate issuing from it is indistinguishable from a tax on the real property itself." Similarly if municipal bonds are exempt from federal taxation, it is clear that this is recognition that the source of a person's income can be taken into account in computing income taxes. Five Justices accepted this line of argument and set the income tax aside as wanting in the constitutional requirement of apportionment. Chief Justice Fuller, speaking for them, accepted Choate's argument almost verbatim:

Taxes on real estate being indisputably direct taxes, taxes on the rents or income of real estate are equally direct taxes. We are of the opinion that taxes on personal property, or on the income of personal property, are likewise direct taxes.

Justice Field, practically adopting Choate's sulphurous language along with the lawyer's class-struggle view of the issue, warned in a concurrence that "The present assault upon capital is but the beginning . . . the stepping stone to others . . . till our political contests will become a war of the poor against the rich." The Justice made clear his view that this kind of spoilation had to be stopped.

Justices Brown, Harlan, Jackson and White dissented, each writing a separate opinion. After reviewing a long list of relevant precedents, including the Hylton and Springer cases, Harlan regretted that the majority had "not given to the maxim of *stare decisis* the full effect to which it is entitled." The decision, he said, "may, not improperly, be regarded as a judicial revolution that may sow the seeds of hate and distrust among different sections of our common country." Taking the same line, Justice White observed:

> This Court said that direct taxes within the meaning of the Constitution were only taxes on land and capitation taxes. And now, after a hundred years, after long-established action by other departments of the government, and after repeated adjudications of this Court, this interpretation is overthrown, and the Congress is declared not to have a power of taxation. . . .

Justice Jackson called the decision "the most disastrous blow ever struck at the constitutional power of Congress," while Justice Brown suggested the decision might "prove the first step toward the submergence of the liberties of the people in a sordid despotism of wealth." Spelling out the implications, Harlan concluded:

> This Court, for the first time in all its history, declares that our government has been so framed that, in matters of taxation for its support and maintenance, those who have incomes derived from the renting of real estate . . . or who own invested personal property . . . have privileges that cannot be accorded to those having incomes derived from the labor of their hands, or the exercise of their skill, or the use of their brains.

Criticism of the Court was bitter and widespread. Some critics advocated a drastic curb on the Judiciary, while others suggested that Congress simply pass an act reversing the Court's reactionary decision. Senator Hernando DeSoto McLaurin (Miss.) did not see "that the Congress of the United States should be called upon to zig-zag around inconsistent rulings of the Supreme Court." Senator Anselm J. Money's (Miss.) irreverence went even further:

> I am not one of those who regard the judgment of the Supreme Court as an African regards his particular deity. I respect such a decision just exactly to the extent that it is founded in common sense and argued out on reasonable logic, but when it violates the law of common sense, then I cease to so regard it, except as a citizen I am bound by it.

"As a legislator," the Senator continued, "I have no more regard for it than I have for the decision of a magistrate in one of the counties of the state of Mississippi, especially when I know it runs counter to the decisions of a hundred years and was decided by a vote of five to four and that one judge who voted in the affirmative changed his mind somewhat in the shadows between two different hearings." (*Congressional Record*, July 3, 1909, Vol. 42, pp. 4067, 4115.)

Discussion of possible ways of overcoming the disabling effects of the income tax decision reached its height during the Presidency of William Howard Taft. The 1909 session of Congress discussed the matter at length. A measure introduced by Senator Bailey of Texas, as an amendment to the tariff bill, was essentially the same as that the Supreme Court invalidated in 1895, except omission of the tax on income from state and municipal bonds. Said Senator Bailey: "Instead of trying to conform the amendment to the decision of the Court, the amendment distinctly challenges that decision. I do not believe that that opinion is a correct interpretation of the Constitution and I feel confident that an overwhelming majority of the best legal minds in the Republic believe it was erroneous."

President Taft himself agreed that the decision was wrong. He favored the income tax, and believed that an ordinary act of Congress was sufficient to reverse the Court's decision. In his acceptance speech of July 28, 1908, he had declared that, in his judgment, "an amendment to the Constitution, for an income tax, is not necessary." Taft, nevertheless, advised against congressional action alone and urged recourse to the time-consuming amending procedure. The President reasoned this way:

> Although I have not considered a constitutional amendment as necessary to the exercise of certain phases of this power, a mature

134

consideration has satisfied me that an amendment is the only proper
course for the establishment to its full extent. . . . This course is
much to be preferred to the one proposed of re-enacting a law
once judicially declared to be unconstitutional. For the Congress
to assume that the Court will reverse itself, and to enact legislation
on such an assumption, will not strengthen popular confidence in
the stability of judicial construction of the Constitution. It is much
wiser policy to accept the decision and remedy the defect by
amendment in due and regular course.

Senator Root of New York, eminent constitutional authority,
spelled out Taft's views:

> . . . what is it that we propose to do with the Supreme Court?
> . . . It is that the Congress of the United States shall deliberately
> pass, and the President of the United States shall sign, and that the
> legislative and executive departments thus conjointly shall place
> upon the statute books as a law a measure which the Supreme Court
> has declared to be unconstitutional and void. And then . . . what
> are we to encounter? A campaign of oratory upon the stump, of
> editorials in the press, of denunciation and imputation designed to
> compel that great tribunal to yield to the force of the opinion of
> the executive and the legislative branches. If they yield, what then?
> Where then would be the confidence of our people in the justice
> of their judgment? If they refuse to yield, what then? A breach
> between the two parts of our Government, with popular acclaim
> behind the popular branch, all setting against the independence,
> the dignity, the respect, the sacredness of that great tribunal whose
> function in our system of government has made us unlike any
> republic that ever existed in the world, whose part in our Govern-
> ment is the greatest contribution that America has made to political
> science. [*Congressional Record*, July 1, 1909, Vol. 42, p. 4003.]

President Taft and Senator Root placed high value on maintaining the fiction of an unchanging Constitution, even in the face
of judicial action that did incalculable violence to it. The popular
image of identity between the judicial version of the Constitution
and the Constitution itself had to be maintained at all cost. Neither
was under the illusion that law either is or can be stationary, but
both were wary of sanctioning the notion that Congress could
reverse an avowedly erroneous decision by an ordinary act.

But the damage President Taft and Senator Root were at such
pains to avert had already been inflicted by the Court itself. Writing
in the *American Law Review* of 1895, shortly after the Income

Tax decision came down, Oregon's former Governor Sylvester
Pennoyer wrote:

> The Supreme Court has not contented itself with its undisputed
> judicial prerogative, of interpreting the laws of Congress, which
> may be ambiguous for the sole purpose of ascertaining its intent
> and enforcing it, but it has usurped the legislative prerogative of
> declaring what the laws shall not be. Our constitutional government
> has been supplanted by a judicial oligarchy. The time has now
> arrived when the government should be restored to its constitu-
> tional basis. The duty is plain and the road is clear. If Congress, at
> its next session, would impeach the nullifying judges for the usurpa-
> tion of legislative power, remove them from office, and instruct
> the President to enforce the collection of the income tax, the
> Supreme Court of the United States would never hereafter presume
> to trench upon the exclusive power of Congress; and thus the
> government, as created by our fathers, would be restored with all
> its faultless outlines and harmonious proportions.

Later on the *American Law Review* editor charged that a narrow
majority in cases such as *Pollock* enforced not the Constitution but
their own economic predilections:

> Nay, we have reached the stage of constitutional development
> when acts of the legislature are set aside on economic and casuistic
> theories, and on the ground of being opposed to implied limitations
> upon the legislative power in every free government,—that is, upon
> limitations not found in any constitution, but found in the imagina-
> tions of the judges. It is said that, in the original argument in this
> income tax case, the court allowed itself to be harangued upon the
> economic features of the law,—questions with which the court had
> nothing to do. Nay, it appears, at least from one of the opinions
> which was rendered, that the Justice who rendered it proceeded
> with an imagination inflamed by the socialistic tendencies of the
> law, as involving an attack upon private property: considerations
> which lay totally outside the scope of his office as a judge inter-
> preting the constitution. It is speaking truthfully, and therefore not
> disrespectfully, to say that some of the judges of that court seem
> to have no adequate idea of the dividing line between judicial and
> legislative power, and seem to be incapable of restraining themselves
> to the mere office of a judge.

The immediate effect of this decision was to add income taxes
to the category of direct taxes, and since it was not feasible to
apportion income taxes Congress was deprived of this fruitful source

of revenue for nearly twenty years. To correct this judge-made amendment of the Constitution, resort was had finally to the cumbersome formal amending process, which in 1913 resulted in the Sixteenth Amendment: "The Congress shall have power to lay and collect taxes on incomes, from whatever source derived, without apportionment among the several states, and without regard to any census or enumeration."

The proposed Amendment passed the Senate 77 to 0 and the House 318 to 14. Little or no light on the meaning of the words "from whatever source derived" can be gleaned from the congressional debates. But the evidence from other sources—debates in the ratifying states, contemporary newspapers and journals—indicate that these words meant just what they said. In a letter to the New York legislature opposing ratification, Governor Charles Evans Hughes wrote: "The comprehensive words 'from whatever source derived,' if taken literally, in their natural sense, would include not only incomes from real and personal property, but also incomes derived from state and municipal securities." Professor Corwin has assembled an impressive body of evidence, including the statements of six governors, in support of Hughes's opinion as to the Amendment's scope.

This seemingly comprehensive language, however, was not allowed to mean all that it seemed to say. By judicial construction, the Amendment was held to mean only that income taxes need not be apportioned, and was not interpreted as authorizing taxes on all incomes. "It does not extend the taxing-power," the Court ruled, "to new or excepted subjects, but merely removes all occasion otherwise existing for an apportionment among the states of taxes laid on incomes whether derived from one source or another." (*Peck* v. *Lowe*, 247 U.S. 165, 1918.) Stock dividends were not taxable as income because they were held to involve neither payment nor receipt. (*Eisner* v. *Macomber*, 252 U.S. 189, 1920.) The salaries of federal judges were still exempt from the income tax, prompting Justice Holmes to declare in dissent that he saw nothing in that clause of the Constitution, protecting the compensation of judges, "to indicate that judges were to be a privileged class, free from bearing their share of the cost of the institutions upon which their well-being if not their life depends." (*Evans* v. *Gore*, 253 U.S. 245, 1920.)

The Justices not only preferred their own judge-made exemptions to the clear language of a constitutional amendment but they went out of their way to achieve this feat. "The Supreme Court is chargeable," Professor Corwin observes, with having "settled" by the mere process of "heaping obiter dictum upon obiter dictum a most important question of constitutional power."

What the Court could settle, it could unsettle. In 1939, without any revision of the Sixteenth Amendment, it overruled *Evans* v. *Gore* (*O'Malley* v. *Woodrough*, 309 U.S. 297). Echoing Holmes, Justice Frankfurter remarked: "To suggest that it [a nondiscriminatory income tax] makes inroads upon the independence of judges . . . by making them bear their aliquot share of the cost of maintaining the government is to trivialize the great historic experience on which the framers based the safeguards of Article 3, Section 1."

REGULATION THROUGH TAXATION

The most obvious and normal purpose of taxation is the raising of revenue, but this is not taxation's only legitimate purpose and effect. Whether a tax is primarily for revenue or for regulation is frequently a highly difficult question, a matter of degree, for strictly speaking no tax is or can be solely a revenue measure. The taxes open to challenge by the taxpayer are those which are laid in such circumstances or are of such a nature that their primary purpose is clearly regulation rather than revenue.

One aspect of this question has been definitely settled: Congress may use its taxing power primarily for purposes of regulation, or even destruction, when the tax is used to aid Congress in exercising one of its other delegated powers, such as regulating interstate commerce, controlling the currency, or maintaining a postal service. An illustrative case is *Veazie Bank* v. *Fenno* (8 Wall. 533, 1869), involving an act of Congress placing a 10 per cent tax on state bank note issues in order to protect the notes of the new national banks from the state banks' competition. The tax was, of course, destructive, as it was intended to be; yet the Court upheld it on the ground that Congress could have achieved the same end by absolute prohibition of state bank notes under the currency power.

A more controversial question remains. May Congress use a tax primarily as a regulatory device, that is, to enforce some social and economic policy, when no enumerated power of Congress can be invoked in justification? For a long period the Court's answers to this question wavered between a clear "yes" and an equally clear "no."

The leading affirmative case is *McCray v. United States* (195 U.S. 27, 1904), which involved the validity of a destructive tax on oleomargarine colored to resemble butter. That the primary purpose of the tax was regulation and not revenue was clear from the much higher tax on colored oleomargarine (10 cents per pound) as compared with uncolored oleomargarine (¼ cent per pound). Yet, the Court held that since Congress had virtually unlimited discretion in the selection of the objects of taxation, it was no part of the judicial function to explore congressional motives. "The right of Congress to tax within its delegated powers being unrestrained, except as limited by the Constitution, it was within the authority conferred on Congress to select the subjects upon which an excise should be laid." Under this judicial hands-off policy Congress proceeded to regulate by taxation the manufacture of phosphorus matches, narcotics, and the retail sale of certain firearms. It should be observed that the doctrine of the McCray case, acceptable as it was to those who felt that Congress should use all regulatory weapons available to it, came close to making the question of the validity of destructive and regulatory taxation a "political question."

In due course, the Court evolved a more effective technique for imposing limitations upon the destructive use of the federal taxing power for purposes of social control and regulation. The change came in 1922 in the second child labor case (*Bailey v. Drexel Furniture Co.*, 259 U.S. 20), which involved the constitutionality of a 10 per cent federal tax on the net income of any employer of child labor, regardless of the number of children employed. In addition the act set up an elaborate code for regulating each employer's conduct, a matter over which Congress admittedly had no direct control under existing precedents. Speaking through Chief Justice Taft the Court condemned the Act primarily because it was a "penalty" and not a true tax, and secondarily because by regulating production the Act invaded the reserved powers of the states. Said the Chief Justice:

Grant the validity of this law, and all that Congress would need to do, hereafter, in seeking to take over to its control any one of the great number of subjects of public interest, jurisdiction of which the States have never parted with, and which are reserved to them by the Tenth Amendment, would be to enact a detailed measure of complete regulation of the subject and enforce it by a so-called tax upon departures from it. To give such magic to the word "tax" would be to break down all constitutional limitation of the powers of Congress and completely wipe out the sovereignty of the States.

For reasons to be indicated later, even Holmes and Brandeis joined in this judicial limitation on national power. Only Justice Clark dissented, unfortunately, without opinion.

Thus in 1935-36, when the New Deal program was subjected to the test of constitutionality, the Court could choose between two lines of precedents. If it chose to sustain a measure under the taxing power, it could employ the general principle of the McCray case. If, on the other hand, the Justices decided to set aside the legislation, it could look upon the tax—as Chief Justice Taft did in the Bailey case—as a "penalty," a form of "regulation," federal usurpation of state power.

One of the planks in the platform on which F.D.R. was elected—a commitment equal in emphasis to the Democratic candidate's campaign promise to balance the budget—was his solemn vow to restore agricultural prosperity. Under the famous Agricultural Adjustment Act (AAA), a processing tax was levied on basic commodities such as wheat, corn, and cotton. From the funds thus accumulated money was paid out to farmers as "inducement" to reduce their acreage. Here, at long last, was a self-financing scheme to subsidize farmers as the protective tariff had long subsidized industry.

High expectations arose from the first years of its administration, until one December day in 1935 the entire scheme became shrouded in constitutional doubt. The Court room was filled to capacity. Attacking the Act's constitutionality was Philadelphia's eminent lawyer, George Wharton Pepper. He was perfectly cast for the role. "I have tried very hard to argue this case calmly and dispassionately," Mr. Pepper told the Justices, "because it seems to me that this is the best way in which an advocate can discharge his duty to this Court. But I do not want Your Honors to think my feelings are not involved and that my emotions are not deeply stirred. Indeed, may it please Your Honors, I believe I am standing here today to plead the cause of the America I have loved; and I pray Almighty God that not in my time may 'the land of the regimented' be accepted as a worthy substitute for 'the land of the free.' "

The former Senator's prayers were soon answered. Within a month, on January 6, the Court announced its decision in *United States* v. *Butler* (297 U.S. 1, 1936). Justice Roberts spoke for the majority, which included Chief Justice Hughes. The vote was 6 to 3, Brandeis, Cardozo, and Stone dissenting.

The keystone of AAA, the processing tax, could not be upheld as a tax. "The word has never been thought to connote the expropriation of money from one group for the benefit of another," the Court ruled. If valid, the exaction could be supported only as an exercise of the disputed power to tax and spend for the general welfare. The Court was thus face to face with an unresolved issue dating from Washington's first administration.

Through many administrations, regardless of party, appropriation of money had been made to accomplish purposes not identified with those Congress is authorized to promote under its other powers. The records of the Constitutional Convention seemed to support this practice. On six different occasions the delegates approved a broad general welfare cause. A weak clause, written by Roger Sherman of Connecticut, was rejected and a stronger version sent by the Committee on Detail to the Committee on Unfinished Portions. It read: "And to provide, as may become necessary from time to time, for the well-managing and securing the common property and general interests and welfare of the United States. . . ." This clause was accepted in somewhat revised form and moved from the bottom to the top of the list of powers. Both clauses, the narrow version and the broad, were written by Sherman. The weight of the evidence appears to be that in the end he supported a general welfare clause of broad scope. It was, Sherman explained, intended to be a power which "involves many others."

In *Federalist* essays Nos. 30-36, Hamilton upheld the broad view. "Every power ought to be in proportion to its object"; "a government ought to contain in itself every power requisite to the full accomplishment of the objects committed to its care." The objects committed to the federal government are such that "no possible limits can be assigned" to them. Therefore the revenue power, the primary means a government has of achieving its ends, is unlimited. "Constitutions of civil government," he wrote in *Federalist* No. 34,

> are not to be framed upon a calculation of existing exigencies, but upon a combination of these with the probable exigencies of ages, according to the natural and tried course of human affairs. Nothing, therefore, can be more fallacious than to infer the extent of any power, proper to be lodged in the national government, from an estimate of its immediate necessities. There ought to be a *capacity* to provide for future contingencies as they may happen; and as these are illimitable in their nature, it is impossible safely to limit that capacity.

Continuing, Hamilton argues:

> It is true, perhaps, that a computation might be made with sufficient accuracy to answer the purpose of the quantity of revenue requisite to discharge the subsisting engagements of the Union, and to maintain those establishments which, for some time to come, would suffice in time of peace. But would it be wise, or would it not rather be the extreme of folly, to stop at this point, and to leave the government intrusted with the care of the national defense in a state of absolute incapacity to provide for the protection of the community against future invasions of the public peace, by foreign war or domestic convulsions? If, on the contrary, we ought to exceed this point, where can we stop, short of an indefinite power of providing for emergencies as they may arise?

Hamilton elaborated these views in 1791, as a member of Washington's cabinet. After arguing the propriety—indeed the necessity —of using government funds for the encouragement of various forms of manufacturing, he noted that, "A question has been made concerning the constitutional right of the Government of the United States to apply this species of encouragement. . . ." "But," he added, "there is certainly no good foundation for such a question."

> The National Legislature has express authority "to lay and collect taxes, duties, imposts, and excises, to pay the debts, and provide for the common defence and general welfare," with no other qualifications than that "all duties, imposts, and excises shall be uniform throughout the United States; and that no capitation or other direct tax shall be laid, unless in proportion to numbers ascertained by a census or enumeration, taken on the principles prescribed in the

Constitution," and that "no tax or duty shall be laid on articles exported from any State."

These three qualifications excepted, the power to raise money is plenary and indefinite. . . .

Moreover, the objects to which this plenary and indefinite power could be applied were "no less comprehensive," embracing, as they did, "the payment of the public debts, and the providing for the common defense and general welfare." The latter phrase is "as comprehensive as any that could have been used, because it was not fit that the constitutional authority of the Union to appropriate its revenues should have been restricted within narrower limits than the 'general welfare,' and because this necessarily embraces a vast variety of particulars, which are susceptible neither of specification nor of definition."

The contrasting view is that of James Madison, namely, that the power to tax and spend for the general welfare is not derived from the tax clause, but is implied from Congress' other enumerated powers and is limited to such general welfare objects as are covered by its other powers. In short, the general welfare clause grants no power at all. On the contrary, it is a limitation on power, the intention being to prevent spending for local, as opposed to general welfare purposes.

Hamilton's interpretation was followed by the Supreme Court in upholding the Morrill Act of 1862, establishing federal and state colleges of agriculture and mechanical arts. On the other hand, several Presidents, following the Madisonian interpretation, had vetoed appropriations they believed unconstitutional. But the dominant opinion favored the Hamiltonian construction. It was not until 1936, in a Supreme Court opinion of unprecedented ambiguity, that Madison's restrictive view momentarily gained the ascendency. Justice Roberts emphatically embraced the Hamiltonian doctrine. No sooner had he adopted it, however, than he proceeded to enforce, for all practical purposes, the narrow Madisonian theory he had just repudiated. Congress, the Justice agreed, might appropriate money for any objective designated the general welfare, but it could attach no terms or conditions on the use of funds so appropriated unless the condition was itself authorized by another specific congressional grant. Federal money might be spent for the broad purposes outlined by Hamilton, but Congress could control the expenditure only if the objectives were within the narrow scope Madison gave the general welfare clause.

"From the accepted doctrine that the United States is a government of delegated powers," Roberts reasoned, "it follows that those not expressly granted, or reasonably to be implied from such as are conferred, are reserved to the states or to the people. To forestall any suggestion to the contrary, the Tenth Amendment was adopted. The same proposition, otherwise stated, is that powers not granted are prohibited. None to regulate agricultural production is given, and therefore legislation by Congress for that purpose is forbidden."

Roberts thus placed the taxing and spending provisions in a special category, doing for Congress' power to tax and spend what Justice Day had done in 1918 for Congress' power to regulate interstate commerce. In both instances the Judiciary wrote "expressly" into the Tenth Amendment. "It is an established principle," Justice Roberts concluded, "that the attainment of a prohibited end may not be accomplished under the pretext of the exertion of powers which are granted."

Such drastic restriction on the scope of the national taxing power evoked sharp reaction within the Court and the country. The intramural judicial war, developing since 1930, now reached its climax. Six Justices, including Hughes and Roberts, were solidly united against the power to govern. Thus Stone's dissent does more than attack the majority's view of the taxing and spending power. He blasts judicial usurpation as such.

The power to use money for the general welfare, the dissenter began, is a substantive power, granted "in specific and unambiguous terms," and therefore equal in force to any other enumerated power. It, like Congress' authority to coin money or declare war, comes within the general proposition that the powers of Congress carry with them a choice of means for their execution. It comes also within the proposition that such power and such means enjoy supremacy over any conflicting state power whatsoever. The majority opinion, Stone asserted, reverses "the time-honored principle of constitutional interpretation that the granted power includes all those which are incident to it. . . ." Justice Roberts' opinion, he charged, subjects a grant of power "to limitations which do not find their origin in any express provision of the Constitution and to which other expressly delegated powers are not subject."

By an elaborate display of "coercive effect which rests on nothing more substantial than groundless speculation," the majority ignored the traditional presumption of constitutionality. It is, Stone wrote, a "contradiction in terms to say that there is a power to spend for the national welfare, while rejecting any power to impose conditions reasonably adapted to the end which alone would justify the expenditure." Any such gratuitous, inconsistent limitation would lead to the most absurd consequences: "The government may give seeds to farmers, but may not condition the gift upon their being planted in places where they are most needed or even planted at all. The government may give money to the unemployed, but may not ask that those who get it shall give labor in return, or even use it to support their families. It may give money to sufferers from earthquake, fire, tornado, pestilence or flood, but may not impose conditions—health precautions designed to prevent spread of disease. . . . All that, because it is purchased regulation infringing state powers, must be left for the states, who are unable or unwilling to supply the necessary relief."

Stone conceded that there were "widely held and strongly expressed differences of opinion on the wisdom of the Agricultural Adjustment Act." But, however a judge may feel about legislation in terms of policy, such views should not be permitted to influence his consideration of the Act's validity. Therefore, in the "interest of clear thinking and sound result," he listed "guiding principles of decision which ought never to be absent from judicial consciousness": that courts are properly concerned not with matters of policy but of power; that even in this narrow province, courts should be deferential to legislative findings of fact out of which controverted statutes emerge, and ever mindful of the awesome nature of judicial power.

Justice Roberts had raised the spectre of "legislative power, without restriction or limitation, . . . vested in a parliament . . . subject to no restrictions except the discretion of its members." But, Stone countered, consider the status of our own power. While the Executive and Congress are restrained by "the ballot box and the processes of democratic government," and "subject to judicial restraint, the only check upon our own exercise of power is our own sense of self-restraint." Precisely because it is unfettered, Stone suggested, judicial responsibility should be discharged with finer conscience and humility than that of any other agency of government.

Of course "governmental power of the purse" was, as Stone conceded, fraught with frightening possibilities of abuse. But the majority's inference that such power, unless judicially limited, might be put to undesirable and constitutionally prohibited ends, Stone said, "hardly rises to the dignity of argument. . . . So may judicial power be abused," he commented curtly, and continued:

> A tortured construction of the Constitution is not to be justified by recourse to extreme examples of reckless congressional spending which might occur if courts could not prevent [it]. . . . Such suppositions are addressed to the mind accustomed to believe that it is the business of courts to sit in judgment on the wisdom of legislative action. Courts are not the only agency of government that must be assumed to have capacity to govern. Congress and the courts both unhappily may falter or be mistaken in the performance of their constitutional duty. But interpretation of our great charter of government which proceeds on any assumption that the responsibility for the preservation of our institutions is the exclusive concern of any one of the three branches of government, or that it alone can save them from destruction is far more likely, in the long run, "to obliterate the constituent members" of "an indestructible union of indestructible states" than the frank recognition that language, even of a constitution, may mean what it says. . . .

The redundancy embodied in the Tenth Amendment—"powers not delegated are reserved"—had long been conspicuous in the armory of judicial devices for defeating national power. Justice Stone had been troubled by the inferential sanction Chief Justice Hughes gave this notion in his Schechter opinion; he went out of his way to discredit it in the AAA dissent. Several weeks later he was still pondering the subject: "Have you ever found in your researches in our constitutional history," the Justice asked Charles A. Beard, "any indication that the framers of the [Tenth] Amendment intended the reserve powers of the states to constitute a limitation on the power of Congress?"

"I do not find in the records of the Convention," Beard replied, "any discussion of future interpretation of the clauses of the Constitution by the judiciary. But there is plenty of evidence that the majority of the framers intended to put all 'general interests' under the federal government and to restrict the states to matters of local interest. . . . When the Tenth Amendment was pending in the House of Representatives, an attempt was made to add the word 'expressly.' That would have limited the Federal Government to 'powers not expressly delegated.' Madison said that no government could endure on express powers, and the proposal was defeated, leaving the Constitution really unamended, for no person in his right mind contended that the Federal Government had any powers not given to it."

Beard's research served only to confirm Stone's conviction. "I have always held," the Justice wrote the historian, April 21, 1936, "that the framers of the Constitution intended to create a strong government, adequate to deal with every situation. I think they would have been surprised, even after the Tenth Amendment, to learn that the Constitution reserved a legislative field to the states. It granted power to the National Government and, in the vernacular of the farmer, 'the tail goes with the hide.' " The Tenth Amendment framed, as John Marshall said, "for the purpose of quieting excessive jealousy which had been excited," was quite innocuous, unusable even as a means of limiting the implied powers "without smuggling into the text what was not there—the word 'expressly.' " In 1936, six Supreme Court Justices had performed precisely this feat, doing then what the first Congress, after due consideration, had specifically refused to do.

Another significant item had been added to the list of functions that neither the Federal Government nor the States could effectively exercise. "What we face now," Dean Lloyd K. Garrison said, "is not how governmental functions shall be shared but whether, in substance, we shall govern at all." Democratic legislators denounced the Justices for usurping powers of Congress, for substituting their individual views on basically political issues for that of the people's elected representatives. But the sharpest indictment had come from one of the Court's own members. "Never before," Professor Howard L. McBain declared in a *New York Times* article, "has a dissenting minority gone quite so far toward calling into question the motives of the majority and clearly implying that they have abused their judicial prerogative."

An immediate response was forthcoming from the Justice himself. "I thought your article in yesterday's *New York Times* very interesting and able," Stone wrote McBain, "but perhaps I should enter one disclaimer. I do not question the motives of my brethren, and did not intend to do so in the vigorous language which I used in my dissenting opinion. I do question a method of thinking which is perhaps the greatest stumbling block to the right administration of judicial review of legislation." Elaborating the point, Stone continued:

> We see it frequently enough in the common untrained mind, which is accustomed to think that legislation which it regards as bad or unwise must necessarily be unconstitutional. Where there is a choice of interpretations of a constitutional provision such a habit of thought is very likely to make a choice of the interpretation which would lessen the possibility of enacting a bad law. The difficulty with this method is that lessening the power to enact bad laws likewise lessens the power to enact good ones, and the judgment of what is good or bad, which is essentially a legislative function, is likely to be affected by the passions and prejudices of the moment. Such an approach to constitutional construction tends to increase the dead areas in the Constitution, the lacunae in which no power exists, either state or national, to deal with the problems of government.

Justice Stone's inference that his colleagues' approach to the consideration of constitutional issues was essentially the same as that of the "common untrained mind," recalls the story James Landis tells of Justice Brandeis' disillusionment. The Justice and Landis, his law clerk, had just finished preparation of an opinion the logic of which seemed incontestable. Yet there were members of the Court who disagreed. The law clerk was sorely puzzled. "Mr. Justice," Landis commented, "this is one of those cases which is a matter of following certain premises to their logical conclusions, not one where disagreement stems from differing social viewpoints. If you think you are right and I think so, why doesn't the rest of the Court go along?" "Sonny," Brandeis commented, "when I first came to this Court I thought I would be associated with men who really cared whether they were right or wrong. But sometimes, sonny, it just ain't so."

In *United States* v. *Butler*, the Court had chosen to follow Taft's narrow construction of the taxing power, only to revert, after President Roosevelt's proposal to "pack" the Court, to the more generous construction laid down in the McCray case. In the term of Court following the AAA decision, Justice Cardozo set forth a strongly nationalist theory, upholding a tax on employers and employees to provide unemployment benefits under federally approved state plans. In 1938, the Court sustained the National Firearms Act, imposing a $200 annual license tax on dealers in firearms. Writing for a unanimous Court, Justice Stone said: "Every tax is in some measure regulatory. . . . But a tax is not any the less a tax because it has a regulatory effect. . . . In going into the hidden motives which may move Congress to exercise a power constitutionally conferred upon it, is beyond the competency of Courts."

Among the factors contributing to these enlarged views of the taxing and spending power was a book written by a newspaper man, Irving Brant. After a most devastating analysis of Justice Roberts' circuitous reasoning in *United States* v. *Butler*, Brant concluded:

> . . . the framers of the Constitution agreed, without dispute, that the taxing power could be used for purposes totally unrelated to revenue, that one of its principal functions was the regulation of commerce, that it could be used to destroy commerce, that it could be used to regulate morals, and that, in the absence of a special restriction, it could be employed for a social purpose involving destruction of a huge vested property over which the federal government had been granted no direct control whatever —it could be used to turn slaves into free men.

In an enthusiastic review of Brant's findings, Professor Corwin observed: "It was high time that somebody should turn to and show up the preposterous law-office constitutional history . . . for what it is worth."

That Congress now has full power to tax and spend for the general welfare is indicated by the Court's approval of a federal statute of 1952, forcing gamblers to procure a license and pay a substantial tax, or incur the risk of federal as well as state criminal prosecution. This Act had been declared invalid by a federal district judge. Upholding the tax, Justice Reed observed: "It is axiomatic that the power of Congress to tax is extensive and falls with crushing effect on businesses deemed unessential or inimical to the public welfare. . . . As is well known, the constitutional restraints on taxing are few. . . . The remedy for excessive taxation is in the hands of Congress, not the Court's" (*United States* v. *Kahriger*, 345 U.S. 22, 1953).

Taft's forebodings in the Bailey case that the taxing power might be used as a weapon (if the Court did not intervene) by which the national government could take over, one by one, subjects traditionally within the orbit of the state police power seems to have been borne out. Making precisely this point and quoting Chief Justice Taft's own words, Justice Frankfurter wrote a vigorous dissent. Like Taft he saw the Act as "an attempt to control conduct which the Constitution left to the responsibility of the states, merely because Congress wrapped the legislation in the verbal cellophane of a revenue measure. . . . To allow," Frank-furter went on, "what otherwise is excluded from congressional authority to be brought within it by casting legislation in the form of a revenue measure could, as so significantly expounded in the Child Labor Tax case, offer an easy way for the legislative imagination to control 'any one of the great number of subjects of public interest, jurisdiction of which the states have never parted with.' "

Taft's reasoning was "significant," Frankfurter explained, because Holmes and Brandeis who had dissented in *Hammer* v. *Dagenhart*, joined Taft in the Child Labor Tax opinion. But Frankfurter's inference that Brandeis would have invalidated the tax on its merits seems mistaken. In an early draft of an unpublished opinion, in *Atherton Mills* v. *Johnston*, Brandeis wrote: "I should have no difficulty in holding the Act [Child Labor Tax] valid on the authority of *Veazie Bank* v. *Fenno*, . . . and *McCray* v. *United States* . . . , and for reasons expressed in the dissent by Justice Holmes in *Hammer* v. *Dagenhart* . . . in which I joined." Brandeis, believing that the Atherton case should be dismissed for want of jurisdiction, found it unnecessary to discuss the case on its merits. He apparently joined in invalidating the Child Labor Tax Act for reasons of judicial strategy, not because he doubted the Act's validity. (For the full story see A. M. Bickel, *The Unpublished Opinions of Mr. Justice Brandeis*, 1957, pp. 14-17.)

Enthroned, at last, were Hamilton's bold nationalistic views. For him co-existence of the states and the federal government did not mean that the states restrict or qualify federal power. This notion would, Hamilton wrote in the *Federalist*, "leave the general government in a kind of tutelage to the state governments, inconsistent with every idea of vigor or efficiency. . . . How [could] . . . it undertake or execute any liberal or enlarged plans of public good?" In light of recent Supreme Court opinions Hamilton's query appears altogether rhetorical.

VII

GOVERNING UNDER
THE COMMERCE POWER

*U*NTIL 1890 THE SUPREME
Court was concerned with the commerce clause primarily as it
limited state action affecting interstate commerce. By and large,
the Court was generous as to the range of state action. In a leading
case of 1876, the Justices held that the states—in the absence of
legislation by Congress—could regulate railroad and other rates
for interstate as well as for intrastate shipments. The resulting confusion was so great that ten years later the Court (*Wabash Railway
Co.* v. *Illinois*, 118 U.S. 557, 1886) repudiated its former view as
ill-considered.

THE NEED FOR NATIONAL ACTION

The Illinois act under consideration in the Wabash case had
been applied as a corrective of long- and short-haul rate dis-
criminations on shipments originating in Illinois and terminating in
New York City. "As restricted to a transportation which begins
and ends within the limits of the state," the Court said, "it may be

very just and equitable. . . . But when it is attempted to apply to transportation through an entire series of states a principle of this kind, and each one of the states shall attempt to establish its own rates of transportation . . . the deleterious influence upon the freedom of commerce among the states . . . cannot be overestimated." The Court concluded by suggesting that since the subject was of "national character" any regulation "should be done by the Congress of the United States under the commerce clause of the Constitution." The upshot was enactment, in 1887, of the Interstate Commerce Act—the first major effort by Congress to use the commerce power to achieve regulatory purpose. Three years later the Sherman Anti-Trust Act manifested Congress' determination to use its power over interstate commerce to accomplish purposes far beyond anything hitherto attempted. The business community strenuously resisted this bold national effort to regulate and control American industrial and commercial life. We consider in this chapter only major cases involving acts of a controversial nature by which the national government sought to accomplish various far-reaching economic or social objectives. Conventional measures regulating commerce (e.g., acts and administrative orders prescribing rules for railroads, motor carriers, aircraft, telephone, and other industries), have of necessity been ignored.

Difficult questions arose at the very outset concerning the applicability of the Sherman Anti-Trust Act (1890) to industrial and commercial enterprise. The rationale of the Act was that contracts, combinations, and conspiracies, "in the form of trust or otherwise," which restrain, or attempt to monopolize interstate trade should be prohibited. In the Sugar Trust case (*United States* v. *E. C. Knight*, 156 U.S. 1, 1895), however, a virtual monopoly of the production of refined sugar was held exempt from the Act. To Chief Justice Fuller, commerce meant primarily transportation—the physical movement of goods across state lines. The effect of contracts and combinations to control manufacture, "however inevitable and whatever its extent," would be "indirect," the Chief Justice commented, and therefore beyond congressional reach. Yet he recognized that goods are manufactured *only* because they can be sold, that manufacture and commerce are part of a seamless web. Much disturbed by the implications of an integrated national economy for federal power, the Chief Justice said: "Slight reflection will show that if the national power extends to all contracts and combinations in manufacture, agriculture, mining, and other productive industries, whose ultimate result may affect external commerce, comparatively little of business operations and affairs would be left for state control."

To achieve this limitation of the scope of national power, the Court redefined "commerce" so as practically to restrict it to what Marshall considered its narrowest signification—"transportation." Fuller recognized that "traffic," buying and selling, "affected" interstate commerce, as the goods were sold and distributed among the states, but this "was no more than to say that trade and commerce served manufacture to fulfill its function." In support of transportation as the aspect of commerce within the reach of federal power, Fuller reasoned:

"There must be a point of time when articles cease to be governed exclusively by domestic law and begin to be governed and protected by the national law of commercial regulation, and that moment . . . [occurs when] they commence their final movement from the state of their origin to that of their final destination."

In support of this curtailment of Marshall's broad concept of "commerce," Chief Justice Fuller invented one of the most enduring formulas in the Court's arsenal of power crippling devices—that of direct and indirect effects. Manufacturing is local, and therefore beyond the reach of Congress' power. Said Fuller:

"Doubtless the power to control the manufacture of a given thing involves in a certain sense the control of its disposition, but this is a secondary and not the primary sense; and although the exercise of that power may result in bringing the operation of commerce into play, it does not control it, and affects it only incidentally and indirectly."

The commercial life of the nation had, it is true, become inextricably intertwined, interdependent, but the control over such industrial complexity must be divided between the national government and the states, lest the former bring all commercial enterprise within its orbit. Fuller's attempt to draw the line between federal and state power so as to keep the national government from absorbing the entire field has been summarized under four headings: (1) Production is always local and under the exclusive domain of the states. (2) Commerce among the states does not begin until goods "commence their final movement from their state of origin to that of their destination." (3) The sale of a product is merely an incident of its production and while capable of "bringing the operation of commerce into play" affects it only incidentally. (4) The restraints on commerce as a result of combinations to control production would be "indirect" and beyond the purview of the Act.

Justice Harlan's dissenting opinion, almost twice as long as Fuller's, represents one of the most pointed pronouncements in the annals of the Supreme Court. To him the majority ruling meant that "the Constitution has failed to accomplish one primary object of the Union," to place commerce *among the states* under the control of the common government of all the people and thereby "relieve or protect it against burdens or restrictions imposed, by whatever authority, for the benefit of *particular localities* or *special interests*." Bearing down on the point, the dissenter suggested that it would be a cause for regret that "the patriotic statesmen who framed the Constitution did not foresee the necessity of investing the national government with the power to deal with gigantic monopolies holding in their grasp, and injuriously controlling in their own interests, the entire trade among the states." After detailed review of the cases from *Gibbons* v. *Ogden* on, Harlan concludes:

> Any combination therefore that disturbs or unreasonably obstructs freedom in buying and selling articles manufactured to be sold to persons in other states or to be carried to other states—a freedom that cannot exist if the right to buy and sell is fettered by unlawful restraints that crush out competition—affects, not incidentally but directly the people of all the states; and the remedy for such an evil is found only in the exercise of powers confided to a government which this Court has said was the government of all, exercising powers delegated by all, representing all, acting for all.

Harlan made dire predictions as to the consequence that would follow the Court's restriction of federal power to regulate the national economy.

> If this be not a sound interpretation of the Constitution, it is easy to perceive that interstate traffic, so far as it involves the price to be paid—may pass under absolute control of overshadowing combinations having financial resources without limit and an audacity in the accomplishment of their objects that recognizes none

of the restraints of moral obligation controlling the action of individuals; combinations, governed entirely by the law of greed and selfishness—so powerful that no single state is able to overthrow them and give the required protection to the whole country, and so all pervading that they threaten the integrity of our institutions.

In this landmark case the Court was not enforcing the Constitution, nor Chief Marshall's version of it. Rather it applied a theory of the Union, and thus enthroned an economic dogma—laissez-faire. Under Chief Justice Fuller's ruling, industrial monopolies were free to exercise the very power the Court had denied Congress. Moreover, the states were equally powerless to control modern business enterprise. For under Fuller's reasoning such an effort would more than likely be construed as an encroachment on Congress' power to regulate commerce.

The impact of Chief Justice Fuller's Sugar Trust decision was far-reaching. It made, as Justice Rutledge pointed out in 1948, the Sherman Act "a dead letter for more than a decade and, had its full force remained unmodified, the Act today would be a weak instrument, as would also the power of Congress, to reach evils in all the vast operations of our gigantic national industrial system antecedent to interstate sale and transportation of manufactured products. Indeed it, and succeeding decisions embracing the same artificially drawn lines, produced a series of consequences for the exercise of national power over industry conducted on a national scale which the evolving nature of our industrialism foredoomed to reversal." (*Mandeville Island Farms* v. *American Cane Sugar Co.*, 334 U.S. 219.)

Though *United States* v. *E. C. Knight* was cited in a majority opinion of 1936 (*Carter* v. *Carter Coal Co.*) as embodying the law of the land, subsequent decisions had already undercut its restrictive implications. In 1904 (*Northern Securities Co.* v. *United States*, 193 U.S. 197) a scheme by which a holding company had been established to hold the stock of competing railroads was held contrary to the Sherman Act. In *Swift* v. *United States* (196 U.S. 375, 1905), a combination of meat packers was held unlawful under the Act, on the ground that their activities, though geographically "local," were important incidents in a current of interstate commerce. "Although the combination alleged," Justice Holmes observed, "embraces restraint and monopoly of trade within a single state, its effect upon commerce among the states is not accidental, secondary, remote or merely probable. . . . Here the subject matter is sales and the very point of the combination is to restrain and monopolize commerce among the states in respect to such sales."

For Chief Justice Fuller's compartmentalized view of commerce as manufacture, traffic and transportation, Holmes substituted the realistic view of commerce as a "current." The buying and selling of cattle was actually part "of a single plan," Holmes wrote, in which "cattle are sent for sale from place in one state, with the expectation that they will end their transit, after purchase, in another." This, he said, is "a typical, constantly recurring course, the current thus existing is a current of commerce among the states, and the purchase of cattle is a part and incident of such commerce."

Of *Swift* v. *United States*, Chief Justice Taft said in 1922 (*Board of Trade of Chicago* v. *Olsen*, 262 U.S. 1): "That case was a milestone in the interpretation of the commerce clause of the Constitution. It recognized the great changes and development in the business of this vast country and drew again the dividing line between interstate and intrastate commerce where the Constitution intended it to be. It refused to permit local incidents of great interstate movement, which, taken alone, were intrastate, to characterize the movement as such. The Swift case merely fitted the commerce clause to the real and practical essence of modern business growth."

JUDICIAL CHOICES IN CONSTITUTIONAL INTERPRETATION

But only three years after the Swift case, the Court refused to find sufficient connection between membership in a labor organization and the free flow of commerce (*Adair* v. *United States*, 208 U.S. 161, 1908). The federal act in dispute had made it unlawful for railroad employers to discharge employees because of their union membership, in this period a frequent source of strikes. Apart from his view that the government should not interfere with an alleged "equality" of bargaining between employer and employees, Justice Harlan expressed ideas on the scope of the commerce clause often repeated in later cases. The rules prescribed by Congress under the commerce power must, he said, have a "real" or "substantial" relation to the commerce regulated. In other words, Harlan narrowed Marshall's broad definition of interstate commerce by determining in each case, according to standards created by the Supreme Court, whether the congressional conception of commerce squared with its own. Justice McKenna, dissenting, thought that removing a cause of frequent strikes was more important to the health of commerce than most safety regulations, and Holmes, also dissenting, chided the majority for confusing questions of economic policy with those of constitutional power. In answer to the Court's assertion that an employee's membership in a labor union "cannot have, in itself and in the eye of the law any bearing upon commerce with which the employee is connected by his services," Holmes retorted that it was not unreasonable for Congress to believe that the law in question would have a direct effect on interstate commerce. Upholding the wisdom and propriety of judicial self-restraint in an area so fraught with conflicting emotions, the dissenter wrote:

> Where there is, or generally is believed to be, an important ground of public policy for restraint the Constitution does not forbid it, whether this Court agrees or disagrees with the policy pursued. . . . I quite agree that the question what and how much good labor unions do, is one on which intelligent people may differ, —I think that laboring men attribute to combinations of capital disadvantages, that really are due to economic conditions of a far wider and deeper kind—but I cannot pronounce it unwarranted if Congress should decide that to foster a strong union was for the best interest, not only of the men, but of the railroads and the country at large.

A series of cases between 1903 and World War I clearly established the principle that the commerce power could be used to accomplish purely social objectives. In the leading case of *Champion* v. *Ames* (188 U.S. 321, 1903) a federal act prohibiting the interstate shipment of lottery tickets was upheld. Noting that the facilities of interstate commerce were used to promote and spread the evil, the Court reasoned that if a state under its police power could suppress lotteries within its limits, the Congress, invested with the power to regulate commerce among the states, could provide that such commerce "shall not be polluted by the carrying of lottery tickets from one state to another." Since Congress was the only authority capable of destroying this "widespread pestilence," "we should hesitate long before adjudging that an evil of such appalling character, carried on through interstate commerce, cannot be met and crushed by the only power competent to that end."

On similar grounds, the Pure Food and Drug Act withstood attack in 1911 (*Hipolite Egg Co.* v. *United States,* 220 U.S. 45). In *Hoke* v. *United States* (227 U.S. 308, 1913), the Court approved the Mann Act, making it a felony to transport a woman from one state to another for immoral purposes. In the *Shreveport Case* (234 U.S. 342, 1914), the Court upheld an Interstate Commerce Commission order fixing intrastate railroad rates because of their effect on interstate commerce.

"Wherever the interstate and intrastate transactions of carriers are so related," Justice Hughes ruled, "that the government of the one involves the control of the other, it is Congress, and not the state, that is entitled to prescribe the final and dominant rule, for otherwise Congress would be denied the exercise of its constitutional authority, and the state, and not the nation, would be supreme within the national field." These words suggest approval of Chief Justice Marshall's dictum that the national power extends to that commerce which "affects more than one state."

After 1918 the pattern became confused. In the frequently cited case of *Hammer* v. *Dagenhart* (247 U.S. 251, 1918), the Court, following the seriously qualified Sugar Trust precedent, again drew a distinction between commerce and manufacturing. Congress had prohibited transportation in interstate commerce of products produced by child labor (age 16 in mines, age 14 in factories, or more than 48 hours a week for the age group 14-16 years). Justice Day, for the Court, characterized the precedents involving lotteries, food, and white slavery as attempts to regulate where transportation was used to accomplish harmful results; production and its incidents were (in Day's opinion) local matters beyond the reach of Congress. Returning to Chief Justice Fuller's narrow view of commerce, Justice Day reasoned: "Over interstate transportation, or its incidents, the regulatory power of Congress is ample, but the production of articles, intended for interstate commerce, is a matter of local regulation." As in the case of Fuller's Sugar Trust opinion, Day bolstered his reasoning by recourse to a theory of federalism.

"A grant of authority over a purely federal matter," he wrote, "was not intended to destroy the local power always existing and carefully reserved to the states in the Tenth Amendment to the Constitution. . . . It must never be forgotten that the nation is made up of states to which are entrusted the powers of local government, and to them the powers not expressly [sic] delegated to the national government are reserved."

In a dissenting opinion, however, Justice Holmes pointed out that powers granted are not reserved. "The Act does not meddle with anything belonging to states. The states . . . may regulate their internal affairs and their domestic commerce as they like. But when they seek to send their products across the state line they are no longer within their rights." To Holmes there was no greater justification for examining the motives of Congress in this case than in those involving lottery tickets, food, or women. The dissenter, speaking for himself and three others, made clear his view that the different result followed from the Justices' ideas concerning acceptable social policy.

Two subsequent cases seemed to indicate once again that the Court might be prepared to endorse broad construction of the commerce power. In *Stafford* v. *Wallace* (258 U.S. 495, 1922) Chief Justice Taft delivered an opinion upholding the Packers and Stockyards Act of 1921, designed to regulate trade practices in the Chicago meat-packing industry. Taft stated that although in a geographic sense the packers were conducting a local business at Chicago, in an economic sense their activities were but an incident in a continuing interstate market. Justice Holmes's "clear and comprehensive exposition" in the Swift case, Taft said, "leaves to us in this case little but the obvious application of the principles there declared." The application of the commerce clause in the Swift case was "the result of the natural development of interstate commerce under modern conditions. It was the inevitable recognition of the great central fact that such streams of commerce from one part of the country to another, which are ever flowing, are, in their very essence, the commerce among the states and with foreign nations which historically it was one of the chief purposes of the Constitution to bring under national protection and control." Continuing, the Chief Justice observed:

The stockyards are not a place of rest or final destination. Thousands of head of live stock arrive daily by carload and trainload lots, and must be promptly sold and disposed of and moved out to give place to the constantly flowing traffic that presses behind. The stockyards are but a throat through which the current flows, and the transactions which occur therein are only incidents to this current from the West to the East, and from one state to another. Such transactions cannot be separated from the movement to which they contribute and necessarily take on its character. The commission men are essential in making sales without which the flow of the current would be obstructed, and this, whether they are made to producers or dealers. The dealers are essential to the sales, to the stock farmers and feeders. The sales are not in this aspect merely local transactions. They create a local change of title, it is true, but they do not stop the flow; they merely change the private interests in the subject of the current, not interfering with, but, on the contrary, being indispensable to its continuity. . . . This is the definite and well-understood course of the business. The stockyards and sales are necessary factors in the middle of the current of commerce.

Chief Justice Taft's opinion restores to the broad concept commerce (a word, as Marshall said, of many significations) two important aspects which Fuller had destroyed—manufacture and traffic. At the same time Chief Justice Taft threw down a caveat against judicial aggrandizement at the expense of Congress:

Whatever amounts to more or less constant practice, and threatens to obstruct or unduly to burden the freedom of interstate commerce is within the regulatory power of Congress under the Commerce Clause, and it is primarily for Congress to consider and decide the fact of danger and meet it. This Court will certainly not substitute its judgment for that of Congress in such a matter unless the relation of the subject to interstate commerce and its effect upon it are clearly non-existent.

Following the same line of reasoning, the Court in 1925 upheld the National Motor Theft Act, making it a crime to transport in interstate commerce a stolen automobile (*Brooks* v. *United States*, 267 U.S. 432). These cases cast grave doubt on the Sugar Trust case and *Hammer* v. *Dagenhart* as precedents. They seemed to portend a return to the broad doctrines of Chief Justice Marshall. They had not, however, been specifically overruled. So, in 1935, when the Court was faced with the necessity of passing on the New Deal legislation enacted under the commerce clause, it had before it two viable lines of precedents: (1) The doctrines established by John Marshall, which had inspired the Court's decisions in *Swift* v. *United States* and *Stafford* v. *Wallace;* (2) The restrictive interpretations of the Sugar Trust case and *Hammer* v. *Dagenhart.* Commenting on the latitude of judicial choices open to the Court, Professor Corwin has observed: "Prior to the New Deal its conceptualistic equipment in the field of constitutional law was often such that the Court was able to translate into judicial idiom almost any result which it might decide to be for the best interest of the country; . . . This was definitely the situation when the issue of constitutionality arose under the commerce clause. . . . At the same time, any student of the subject must feel that the Court's interpretation of the Constitution frequently exhibits considerable continuity and self-consistency over considerable periods —falls, in other words, into a describable pattern for such periods. To some extent this fact has been due to the principle of *stare decisis;* but to a vastly greater extent it has been due to other circumstances: to the influence of certain dominant personalities on the Court or at the Bar; to the concern felt by its members for the security of certain great interests or institutions and to certain doctrines which were congenial to those interests. . . ."

The influences of which Professor Corwin speaks—dominant personalities, interests and doctrines—were especially conspicuous during the first seven years of Charles Evans Hughes's Chief Justiceship.

When Chief Justice Taft retired in 1930 the Court was sharply divided into two camps: Taft, Butler, McReynolds, Van Devanter, Sutherland and Sanford construed the powers of government narrowly, thus disabling in advance any effort to deal with social and economic complexities. Holmes, Brandeis, and Stone deplored judicial review of such dimensions as discouraging experiment and change. Their persistent plea stressed judicial self-restraint. Writing in 1924, Judge Cardozo referred to this cleavage as representing "a problem in the choice of methods."

> On the one hand the right of property, as it was known to the fathers of the republic, was posited as permanent and absolute. Impairment was not to be suffered except within narrow limits of history and precedent. No experiment was to be made along new lines of social betterment. The image was a perfect sphere. The

least dent or abrasion was a subtraction from its essence. Given such premises, the conclusion is inevitable. The statute becomes an illegitimate assault upon rights assured to the individual against the encroachments of society. The method of logic or philosophy is at work in all its plentitude.

The opposing view, if it is to be accepted, must be reached through other avenues of approach. The right which the assailants of the statute posit as absolute or permanent is conceived of by the supporters of the statute as conditioned by varying circumstances of time and space and environment and degree. The limitations appropriate to one stage of development may be inadequate for another. Not logic alone, but logic supplemented by the social sciences becomes the instrument of advance.

By 1930 the divergence Cardozo had described was clearly marked. Yet the margin of safety for conservatism remained perilously narrow. Chief Justice Taft had horrid premonitions of what might happen when he died. Though failing in health, he was determined to stick it out.

"The most that can be hoped for," he wrote Justice Butler September 14, 1929, "is continued life of enough of the present membership to prevent disastrous reversals of our present attitude. With Van and Mac and Sutherland and you and Sanford there will be five to steady the boat. We must not give up at once."

Recruitment of Supreme Court Justices was, as Taft realized, a matter of major political importance. He knew, as did North Carolina Chief Justice Walter Clark in 1906, that "if five lawyers can negative the will of 100,000,000 men, then the art of government is reduced to the selection of those five lawyers." Taft distrusted President Hoover as a "progressive," and in the Senate, recent Supreme Court decisions had reinflamed the "radical spirit." A decision bearing the name "O'Fallon" had become a rallying point.

This embattled litigation had arisen under the Transportation Act of 1920. In Section 15A thereof, Congress had directed that the Interstate Commerce Commission give "due consideration to all the elements of value recognized by the law of the land for rate-making purposes." A minority of the Commission objected to the valuation of the railroad's property in the case because preponderant weight had not been given the "reproduction-cost" theory. Chief Justice Taft disliked the whole problem and candidly confessed his incompetence but, he commented, "We have some experts on our Court. One is Pierce Butler, the other is Brandeis." The "experts," however, were in complete disagreement. Butler, a former railroad attorney, upheld "reproduction cost" and, with the aid of like-minded colleagues, the Court elevated this theory to the status of a constitutional directive. Billions were thus construed into the total railroad valuation. Increased rates and profits became inevitable.

In the backwash of public resentment against the O'Fallon and similar cases, and within a year after Taft had penned his frantic words as to the Court's future, death claimed the Chief Justice and his colleague, Sanford—both veterans of the Court's conservative wing. To fill the center chair President Hoover nominated New York's most eminent lawyer, Charles Evans Hughes who along with John W. Davis had been of counsel for the O'Fallon railroad, upholding the controversial theory of reproduction-cost.

Superficially the President's choice seemed admirable. As a man of unquestioned integrity, Hughes had been appointed to the Court in 1910 by President Taft. As an Associate Justice until 1916, he had demonstrated qualities of judicial statesmanship. But in 1930 the nominee was strangely apprehensive when President Hoover broached his appointment: "I don't want a fight over the nomination. . . . If you are convinced that the nomination will be confirmed by the Senate without a scrap, I will accept it. But I don't want any trouble about it." The President was confident there would be no trouble, and it looked at first as though he might be right. Senator George Norris, insurgent Nebraska Republican, and chairman of the Senate Judiciary Committee, told reporters "that favorable action would be taken at the regular meeting of the Committee."

"The chorus of approval is as emphatic as it is unanimous," the *Literary Digest* announced. The *Troy Times* suggested that "if there had been a nation-wide straw vote to determine popular choice for the vacancy, at least a plurality and probably a large majority would have voted for the man President Hoover has nominated." The *New York Times* blazoned the headline: *Speedy Confirmation is Forecast for New Head of Supreme Court, Old Opposition Passes.* A few days later, however, the Judiciary Committee recommended confirmation by a split vote of 10 to 2, with Norris himself in opposition. What had been seen as a foregone conclusion was destined to become the subject of bitter partisan controversy. The Washington *Daily News* referred to it as "one of the most significant developments in the political life of this nation."

The opposition leader, Senator Norris, questioned the propriety of Hughes's resignation from the Court in 1916 to enter the race for the Presidency. Norris believed that "we have reached a time in our history when the power and influence of monopoly and organized wealth are reaching into every governmental activity." "Perhaps," the Senator explained, "it is not far amiss to say that no man in public life so exemplifies the influence of powerful combinations in the political and financial world as does Mr. Hughes."

Other Senators voiced the same objection. "If the system of judicial law that is being written in defiance of state legislation and of congressional legislation, is continued," Senator Dill of Washington observed prophetically, "there is no human power in America that can keep the Supreme Court from becoming a political issue, nation-wide, in the not far distant future." The very struggle which the Senator foresaw in 1930 became conspicuous, as we shall see, in 1937.

Hughes's confirmation, 52 to 26, seemed almost an anticlimax. But the crusade against the Court was resumed a few weeks later when, to fill the Sanford vacancy, President Hoover nominated John J. Parker, a Federal Circuit Court Judge, 4th Circuit. A North Carolina Republican, Parker's nomination had been successfully urged on Hoover as a "master political stroke." But Parker was not confirmed. Hoover at once nominated Owen J. Roberts, well known as prosecutor in the Teapot Dome scandal, and confirmation quickly followed.

The campaign against Hughes and Parker had been both exploratory and educational. Accepting Hughes's confirmation as a foregone conclusion, the insurgents merely wished, as Senator Dill said, "to place in the record . . . a warning." The Senators wanted "to call attention to the fact that if the American people . . . would free themselves and have justice at the hands of their Government they must reach the Supreme Court of the United States by putting men on that bench who hold economic theories which are fair and just to all, and not in the interest of the privileged few."

"We all realized from the very beginning," Senator Norris

commented, "that we had no hope of victory." The insurgents had been motivated by the "conscientious belief that . . . profit will come perhaps even to the Supreme Court if they read the debates of the Senate, and if the majority members of that Court will even read the dissenting opinions of their brethren Brandeis, Holmes, and Stone." Implicit in the Senate debates was stern admonition that the Justices take to heart their own oft-professed principle of judicial self-restraint. A well-known commentator, Frank Kent, suggested that Hughes might be "a better Chief Justice for the experience." "To have permitted without protest," Kent observed, "such a man, graciously accepting as merely his due the almost unanimous chorus of journalistic eulogy to become Chief Justice would have been a pity." Kent believed that the votes against the new Chief Justice "will have their effect upon the sitting members of the Court . . . and upon Mr. Hughes."

The next day after confirmation the Senate insurgents joined in the broadside attack on the Court itself, denouncing "judge-made law," "government by injunction," "federal interference in the internal concerns of the states," etc. There were suggestions of constitutional amendment, stripping the Court of its power to declare acts of Congress unconstitutional, and a call for popular election of the Justices. The magic that had shielded the high court and its decisions came in for special attack. "There has not been a criticism of the Supreme Court anywhere, even on the floor of the Senate, . . . for a good many years," Senator Norris observed, "because we have set it up on a pedestal, beyond human criticism, a tribunal composed of human beings who are subject to the same passions and the same feelings that apply to me. We have made idols of them. . . . They have black gowns over their persons. Then they become something more than human beings." As the Washington *Daily News* pointed out, the debates had broken through "the hush-hush and ah-ah atmosphere surrounding the Court, daring to examine the political and very human institution for what it is worth."

The Senate's daring assult raised a warning flag at a crucial hour. Never before was the power to govern so urgent. Yet the effectiveness of that power—even its existence—turned absolutely on the votes of nine men appointed for life and politically responsible to no one. "The Supreme Court fight is not over," the

New York Times noted ten days after Hughes was confirmed. "It will continue as long as the property issue divides the country politically and economically."

THE NEW DEAL IN COURT

The first New Deal reform measure reached the Supreme Bench December 10, 1934, under circumstances that did not augur well for the validity of executive orders issued under N.I.R.A. The Panama Refining Company had challenged the Act's prohibition against shipment of "hot oil" (that exceeding state allowances) across state lines. Early in the argument government counsel disclosed that criminal penalties attaching to the violation of the relevant code provisions had been inadvertently omitted from the executive order. Judicial curiosity was immediately aroused; concern deepened when opposing counsel bitterly complained that his client had been arrested, indicted, and held several days in jail for violating this nonexistent "law." With these points against it the government was at a disadvantage in pressing the argument that Congress could constitutionally empower the President in his discretion to ban "hot oil" from interstate commerce. Hughes and seven other Justices held Section 9(c) of the N.I.R.A. invalid as an unconstitutional delegation of legislative power to the Chief Executive (*Panama Refining Co.* v. *Ryan*, 293 U.S. 388). Congress, they said, established no "primary standard," thus leaving "the matter to the President without standard or rule, to be dealt with as he pleased."

For the first time the maxim *delegata potestas non potest delegari*, a principle not found in the Constitution, formed the basis of a judicial decision overturning an act of Congress. Justice Cardozo, dissenting, wrote: "If we look at the whole structure of the statute the test is plainly this, that the President is to forbid the transportation of oil when he believes, in the light of the conditions of the industry as disclosed from time to time, that the prohibition will tend to effectuate the declared policies of the act—not merely his own conception, of its policies, . . . but the policies announced in section 1 in the forefront of the statute." Cardozo was convinced that the policy of Congress, express or implied, as declared in this section was "a sufficient definition of a standard to make the statute valid." "Discretion," he wrote, "is not unconfined and vagrant. It is canalized within banks that keep it from overflowing."

Before the dust thrown up by the Justices in the "hot oil" decision had fairly settled, the Court made headlines again in a 5 to 4 ruling that scuttled the recently enacted railroad retirement scheme, which required the carriers to subscribe to a pension plan for old employees (*Railroad Retirement Board* v. *Alton R. R. Co.*, 295 U.S. 330, 1935). Mr. Justice Roberts' objections riddled and ridiculed the enactment. Brushing the legislation contemptuously aside as based on "the contentment and satisfaction theory" of social progress, he inquired: "Is it not apparent that they [pensions] are really and essentially related solely to the social welfare of the worker, and therefore remote from any regulation of commerce as such?" Congress might, he agreed, require outright dismissal of all aged workers, but it could not give them pensions. If superannuation is a danger, Roberts argued in effect, the commerce clause authorizes compulsory retirement—without a pension! Congressional effort to compel railroads to pension off older workers must fail for want of any relation between the pensioning system and the efficiency or safety of the national rail network.

The discouraging aspect of Justice Roberts' opinion is implicit in Hughes's dissent. ". . . the majority finally raise a barrier against all legislative action of this nature by declaring that the subject matter itself lies beyond the reach of the congressional authority to regulate interstate commerce. In that view, no matter how suitably limited . . . or how appropriate the measure of retirement allowances, or how sound actuarily the plan, or how well adjusted the burden, still under this decision Congress would not be at liberty to enact such a measure. . . . I think that the conclusion thus reached is a departure from sound principles and places an unwarranted limitation upon the commerce clause of the Constitution."

Taken together, the Panama Refining and the Railroad Retirement cases clearly forecast the New Deal's doom. The blow fell May 27, 1935, "Black Monday," when NIRA, sloppily drafted and symbolized by the Blue Eagle, was eliminated from the recovery program (*Schechter Poultry Co.* v. *United States*, 295 U.S. 495).

The Schechter brothers, wholesale poultry dealers in Brooklyn, were charged with violating NIRA's Live Poultry Code by ignoring minimum wage and maximum hour requirements, and by giving special treatment to preferred customers. The Court, speaking through the Chief Justice, found the act wanting as an unconstitutional delegation of legislative power. Government counsel conceded that congressional authority to regulate the Schechter business had to be based on the commerce clause, but the Court held the defendants' business was neither interstate commerce in itself, nor closely enough connected with it to "affect" such commerce.

"In determining how far the Federal Government may go in controlling intrastate transactions, upon the ground that they 'affect' interstate commerce," the Chief Justice declared, "there is a necessary and well-established distinction between direct and indirect effects. The precise line can be drawn only as individual cases arise, but the distinction is clear in principle. . . ."

For authority in support of the proposition that he enunciated, the Chief Justice went back to 1890 and the Sugar Trust decision. He did not cite that old case. Instead he mentioned *Brown* v. *Houston*, but in so doing failed to point out that in the latter case the Court had ruled that barges of coal shipped down the river to New Orleans, even though the coal remained in its "original package," were subject to local taxation—*"in the absence of congressional action."* Justice Bradley expressed the qualification five times. The Chief Justice ignored it, though the very question in the case before him concerned the validity of "congressional action."

Echoing Chief Justice Fuller in the Sugar Trust case, Hughes said that if the direct-indirect distinction were ignored "the federal authority would embrace practically all activities of the people and the authority of the state over its domestic concerns would exist only by sufferance of the federal government." The processes of production had to be immune to national control because "in the application of our formula [direct and indirect] we find a direct effect in so many intrinsically local matters that the sphere of state autonomy would be pretty much ended. The effect here is indirect because the perpetuation of the federal system requires us to say so." On the altar of a theory of the union, rather than on the basis of the Constitution, "a few sick chickens," as Fred Rodell put it, "had murdered the mighty Blue Eagle."

Stone and Cardozo, in a separate opinion written by the latter, agreed with the Court's disposition of the case. "This," they said, "is delegation running riot." Nor could they find support in the commerce clause "for the regulation of wages and hours of labor in the intrastate transactions that make up the defendants' business." Without characterizing all production as "local," Stone and Cardozo rejected "a view of causation that would obliterate the distinction between what is national and what is local in the activities of commerce." Somewhat more cautious than their brethren, however, they subtly indicated a desire to treat such problems as they arose without anticipating and deciding in sweeping language all the constitutional issues of the decade.

President Roosevelt reacted vehemently, intemperately. In a famous press interview, he spoke of the decision as a "social setback of fifty years," taking us back to the "horse and buggy" days. The Justices seemed to the President and to others the prisoners of rigid conceptualism. Even Stone and Cardozo, though they stood slightly to the side in the Schechter case, did not disavow the lengths to which the Court had gone to make certain that nothing like NIRA would be tried again. Justice Stone's correspondents expressed their disappointment. His replies were somewhat less than convincing.

Still other setbacks were in store. On May 18, 1936, the Justices ruled, 5 to 4, that Congress had failed in its effort to salvage NRA remedies for the notoriously distressed bituminous coal industry in the form of wage and price agreements, marketing quotas and a special sales' tax, refundable to code participant (*Carter* v. *Carter Coal Co.*, 298 U.S. 238). The situation in the bituminous coal industry was so urgent and the benefits of the legislation so evident that President Roosevelt had taken the unusual step of asking the congressional subcommittee, while the Guffey coal act was pending, not to "permit doubts as to constitutionality, however reasonable, to block the suggested legislation." Five Justices, apparently undisturbed by the consequences of inaction, were moved by considerations (to them) of even greater concern. ". . . it is of vital moment," Justice Sutherland said for a 5 to 4 majority, "that, in order to preserve the fixed balance intended by the Constitution, the powers of the general government be not so extended as to embrace any not within the express terms of the several grants or the implications necessarily to be drawn therefrom."

Sutherland's opinion is clear-cut and unequivocal on one point that Chief Justice Hughes had left somewhat obscure—the nature of the distinction between direct and indirect effects. "The local character of mining, of manufacturing, and of crop growing is a fact, and remains a fact, whatever may be done with the products," Sutherland said. Going straight back to Chief Justice Fuller's opinion in the Sugar Trust case and paraphrasing his words, Sutherland declared: "Such effect as they [working conditions] may have upon commerce, however extensive it may be, is secondary and indirect." Sutherland reinforced his opinion by invoking Chief Justice Hughes's opinion in the Schechter case, especially the Chief Justice's insistence on the fundamental character of the distinction between "direct" and "indirect" effects. But, unlike Hughes, he spelled it all out in detail:

> Whether the effect of a given activity or condition is direct or indirect is not always easy to determine. The word "direct" implies that the activity or condition invoked or blamed shall operate proximately—not mediately, remotely, or collaterally—to produce the effect. It connotes the absence of an efficient intervening agency or condition. And the extent of the effect bears no logical relation to its character. The distinction between direct and indirect effect turns, not upon the magnitude of either the cause or the effect, but entirely upon the manner in which the effect has been brought about. . . . If the production by one man of a single ton of coal intended for interstate sale and shipment, and actually so sold and shipped, affects interstate commerce indirectly, the effect does not become direct by multiplying the tonnage, or increasing the number of men employed, or adding to the expense or complexities of the business, or by all combined. . . . The relation of employer and employee is a local relation. . . . The wages are paid for the doing of local work. Working conditions are obviously local conditions. . . . Such effect as they may have upon commerce, however extensive it may be, is secondary and indirect. An increase in the greatness of the effect adds to its importance. It does not alter its character.

In the teeth of the congressional declaration that the Act's price-fixing and labor provisions were separable, Sutherland held that they were united inextricably, and therefore must stand or fall together. They must fall, he ruled, because the labor provisions here, like those involved in the Schechter case, bore no "direct" relation to interstate commerce. Chief Justice Hughes, in a concurrence, declared that Sutherland had been in error only in denying the separability of the price-fixing provision and the hours of labor regulation. But Hughes and Sutherland were in agreement as to the nature of the distinction between direct and indirect effects.

"I agree," the Chief Justice continued, "that . . . the power to regulate commerce among the several states is not a power to regulate industry within the state. The power to regulate interstate commerce embraces the power to protect that commerce from injury. . . . But Congress may not use this protective authority as a pretext for the exertion of power to regulate activities and relations within the states which affect interstate commerce only indirectly. Otherwise, in view of the multitude of indirect effects, Congress in its discretion could assume control of virtually all the activities of the people."

The distinction between direct and indirect being one of kind rather than degree, national regulation of the conditions of production must await the cumbersome process of constitutional amendment. "If the people desire to give Congress the power to regulate industries within the State, and the relations of employers and employees in those industries," Hughes wrote, "they are at liberty to declare their will in the appropriate manner, but it is not for the court to amend the Constitution by judicial decision."

To maintain his concept of the federal system, Hughes, like Sutherland, returned to Chief Justice Fuller's formula of 1895: "the distinction between direct and indirect effects of intrastate transactions upon interstate commerce must be recognized as a fundamental one, essential to the maintenance of our constitutional system. Otherwise, as we have said, there would be virtually no limit to the federal power and for all practical purposes we should have a completely centralized government."

Yet even as the Court exalted the so-called "constitutional system" to outlaw major New Deal enactments, it handed down two decisions—*Whitfield* v. *Ohio* (297 U.S. 431, 1936) and *Kentucky Whip and Collar Co.* v. *Illinois Central Railroad Co.* (299 U.S. 334, 1937)—that seemed to revitalize national authority over interstate commerce. The first involved the constitutionality of a congressional act which, following the pattern of the Wilson Act of 1890, deprived convict-made goods of their interstate character, and submitted them to state regulation upon arrival, "in the same manner as though such goods . . . had been manufactured, pro-

172

duced or mined in such state." The Whip and Collar Company case involved the validity of another congressional enactment, modeled after the Webb-Kenyon Act of 1913, prohibiting transportation in interstate or foreign commerce of convict-made goods "into any state where the goods are intended to be received, possessed, sold, or used in violation of its laws." Upholding this Act Chief Justice Hughes declared that "in certain circumstances an absolute prohibition of interstate transportation is constitutional regulation. . . . The contention is inadmissible that the Act of Congress is invalid merely because the horse collars and harness which petitioner manufactures and sells are useful and harmless articles. . . . The pertinent point is that where the subject of commerce is one as to which the power of the state may constitutionally be exerted by restriction or prohibition in order to prevent harmful consequences, the Congress may, if it sees fit, put forth its power to regulate interstate commerce so as to prevent that commerce from being used to impede the carrying out of the state policy."

Although the Court tried to distinguish *Hammer* v. *Dagenhart*, little of its substance seemed to remain after these decisions. Nor was this all. Only 12 months before the Schechter decision, the broad scope of the national commerce power was again recognized in *Baldwin* v. *Seelig* (294 U.S. 511, 1935). Here the Court invalidated a New York law prohibiting the sale in New York of milk purchased outside the state at prices lower than those fixed by local law for similar purchases within the state. Upholding "our national solidarity" and deploring "nice distinctions . . . made at times between direct and indirect burdens," the Court declared the New York act void, whether applied to milk out of the original package or enforced against milk while so packaged. The Court's decision here stood on the proposition that the national commerce power operated to destroy the states' power to establish "an economic barrier against competition with the products of another state or the labor of its residents."

It is hard to make out any differences between the Schechter and Seelig businesses. The rulings in the two cases are all the more puzzling when one takes into account the fact that in *Baldwin* v. *Seelig* the national commerce power was "dormant," whereas in Schechter it had been exercised, only to encounter "nice distinction

. . . between direct and indirect burdens" and the sanctity of a preconceived theory of "our constitutional system."

So far as the commerce power was concerned, the Court by 1936 seemed to have adopted the view that certain subjects are local in nature and beyond the power of Congress even though they required national or uniform regulations if they were to be regulated at all. On the other hand, effective state-by-state regulation was clearly impossible; if it were attempted it might be found to have a substantial effect on interstate commerce, and hence run afoul (as in *Baldwin* v. *Seelig*) of the "silence of Congress" doctrine. The Court thus had narrowed the commerce doctrines of Marshall by withdrawing from congressional power certain subject-matters, such as production, agriculture, and the employer-employee relationship. In effect, the Court had created a category additional to those classes enumerated in the Cooley case, viz.: those objects which could not in practice be regulated by either government— a "twilight zone," a "no man's land."

"Through constitutional interpretation the United States shifted," Irving Brant wrote in 1936, "from a Constitution of implied powers under the express powers [of Congress] to a Constitution of implied limitations upon express powers. It was virtually the same as writing a new, and infinitely narrower, Constitution." To the same effect, Professor Corwin suggested that "the chief result of Judicial review" had been the "Court's emancipation from the constitutional document."

"The way out must be found shortly," the *St. Louis Star-Times* predicted, June 4, 1936, "because it must be found." The forebodings Senate insurgents voiced in 1930 had been vindicated. The Supreme Court was the issue of the hour.

VIII

CONSTITUTION OF POWERS
OR OF RIGHTS?

*I*NVALIDATION OF A DOZEN NEW
Deal measures, some of them central to the administration's recovery effort, had put the New Deal firmly on the rack of unconstitutionality. Loud acclaim resounded among adherents to the
status quo. Raoul E. Desvernine, vice-president of the American
Liberty League, declared that "the Judiciary has again proved itself
to be the bulwark of defense against the subtle and skillful manipulation of democratic processes to achieve unsanctioned theories."
Herbert Hoover expressed his heartfelt thanks "to Almighty God
for the Constitution and the Supreme Court." "I am happy to
report," Chief Justice Hughes remarked in his American Law
Institute address, May 1936, "that the Supreme Court is still functioning." Members and guests of the Institute vigorously applauded
the announcement, obliging the speaker "to pause for more than
two minutes."

All this rejoicing was in response to the stark fact that in certain
crucial cases the Justices of the Supreme Court, usually only five
or six, had rendered government impotent. "The general purpose
of the court conservatives is plain," one pro-Roosevelt newspaper

said. "It is to create the largest possible vacuum in government authority between the powers of the states and the powers of the nation."

Though the people had replaced the executive and legislative branches of the government with a party which advocated positive and constructive action, they had been unable to do anything about the Supreme Court, which "seemed," as President Roosevelt said, "almost invariably to lean" toward the preservation of the special privileges of private economic power. In the decade before 1937, the President commented, the Court's tendency had been toward "an unwarranted, restrictive interpretation of the legislative and executive powers of government, federal, state, and local; an unwillingness to tolerate legislative protection of ordinary men, women, and children—laborers and others—from the control and domination of private economic forces; and a refusal to permit reasonable governmental curbs upon vast, monopolistic, aggregations of concentrated industrial and financial power." The entire legislative program overwhelmingly approved by the American people in 1932, 1934, and 1936 was, as Assistant Attorney-General Jackson said, in danger of being lost in "a maze of constitutional metaphors." The President went even further, declaring that by June 1936 his program had been "fairly completely undermined."

The President denied that the Constitution was to blame. "The only trouble was with some of the human beings then on the Court" —with judges who "were torturing its meaning, twisting its purposes, to make it conform to the mould of their own outmoded economic beliefs." The President was absolutely certain in his diagnosis of the trouble. He knew that a remedy would inevitably involve the Judiciary.

"As I returned to Washington after election day, I knew that the great interests and the great newspapers which had opposed my reelection in 1936 by violently attacking the policies and objectives of the last four years, were all ready and set again to transfer the scene of battle from the legislative halls to the Court room. Defeat at the poles would never deter them from seeking ultimate victory from the courts."

The impasse between Congress and the Court had not been brought about overnight, nor had it come about without persistent protest within the Court itself. Justice Brandeis had railed against the Court's exercise of "the powers of a super-legislature." Justice Holmes had deplored the lack of any limit to the Court's willingness to invalidate legislation that struck a "majority of this Court as for any reason undesirable." Justice Stone had accused his colleagues of torturing the Constitution, reminding them that "Courts are not the only agency of government that must be assumed to have the capacity to govern." The Constitution as a straitjacket or "vehicle of the Nation's life"—that was the basic issue. "With a competent, detached, and courageous judiciary," Justice Stone said, "most of the problems of adequate administration would disappear." The Justice had repeatedly alerted his colleagues to the perils of "self-inflicted" wounds. Time and again writers and speakers alluded to or quoted from Stone's dissents to prove from the mouth of this "most highly respected Justice" how the majority had perverted the judicial function.

By January 1936, the constitutional crisis reached the explosive stage; popular pressure then rose to the point of exasperation. "The time has come," the *New York Post* proclaimed in March 1936, "for a showdown with Judicial autocracy."

A legislative ground swell mounted perilously after the Agricultural Adjustment Act case holding regulation of agriculture to be solely within state power (*United States* v. *Butler*, 297 U.S. 1, 1936). "This detached group," Oregon's Representative Walter M. Pierce said of the Court majority, "did not hold the Triple A Act was in contravention of the rights of man or the laws of God, but it did say that by its passage the Congress had interfered with the rights of the states. What an arbitrary, unjust, and reactionary opinion it seems to those of us who hold that the minority opinion is more logical, more legally sound, more just, and helpfully constructive in a changing social order."

Legislators mentioned several remedies for the constitutional blockade. One innovator, reproached for suggesting a remedy that meant "putting the Court on the spot," heatedly replied: "Exactly . . . the Court ought to be put on the spot when it subscribes to such labored and far-fetched opinions as that of the Chief Justice in the poultry case." As the insurgent senators of 1930 confidently had predicted, the Court had now become the storm center of politics.

The militant lawmakers were not without press support. A small but remarkably vocal group of newspapers took up the cry: "Curb this Court before it destroys the nation." The people should bring the Justices down from "the pedestal of fetish and deal with them as men and not supermen," the *Philadelphia Record* clamored. From the obscure Danville, Pennsylvania, *Morning News* came the editorial caveat: "Everybody knows there will be nothing the Court can do about it when elected officials finally say to it: 'Your ruling is stupid and doesn't make sense, according to our opinion and according to the bristling protests of four of your number. Therefore we shall ignore you.' " "By their own admission," the *Philadelphia Record* observed, drawing on Stone's outraged dissents, "they read their personal bias, their individual economic predilections into our fundamental law. Instead of utilizing their unequaled independence to serve the Constitution, they twist the Constitution to serve their notions. And today the document dedicated to the general welfare is employed to destroy the general welfare. . . . The Supreme Court's usurpation of power is the issue of the hour."

Various correctives were open. The President and Congress might limit the jurisdiction of the Supreme Court, increase the number of judges to override the present arrogant majority, or sponsor constitutional amendments limiting the Court's power. Though many Congressmen urged that something be done, they were uncertain what to do, not quite sure whether the trouble was the fault of the Constitution or of judges "callously insensible to the needs and demands of our people." The President and his party were uncertain, too, at least on what was the most feasible remedy politically. The Democratic Party Platform of 1936 was ambiguous: "If these problems [social and economic] cannot be effectively solved by legislation within the Constitution, we shall seek such clarifying amendments as [we] . . . shall find necessary, in order adequately to regulate commerce, protect public health and safety, and safeguard economic liberty. Thus we propose to maintain the letter and spirit of the Constitution." Throughout the campaign Democratic orators muted the discord between the Court and New Deal, giving no hint that President Roosevelt would, if re-elected, wage an all-out war on the judiciary.

THE COURT-PACKING THREAT

But Roosevelt could not be sure, even in the face of his over-whelming electoral triumph, that the Court would give ground. The traditional theory that the Justices are, and must be, immune to election returns, not Finley Peter Dunne's witticism about the Court's ready response to them, pervaded the political atmosphere. In no mood to take chances, the President, on February 5, 1937, fresh from his second triumphant inauguration and at the very peak of personal prestige, sent to Congress his message proposing a drastic shakeup in the judiciary. In a word, the President's solution was to give a Supreme Court Justice past 70 six months in which to retire. A Justice who failed to quit within the appointed time could continue in office, but the Chief Executive would appoint an additional Justice—presumably younger and better able to carry the heavy load. Since there were six Justices in this category, Roosevelt would have six appointments to make at once. The maximum membership of the Court was to be fifteen.

In presenting his proposal the President gave no hint of wishing to stem the tide of anti-New-Deal decisions. He tendered the hemlock cup to the elderly jurists on the elevated ground that they slowed the efficient dispatch of judicial business. Alluding to the volume of denials of petitions for certiorari, F.D.R. observed: "Can it be said that full justice is achieved when a court is forced by the sheer necessity of keeping up with its business to decline, without even an explanation, to hear 87 per cent of the cases presented to it by private litigants?"

Roosevelt had awaited the propitious moment. Early February of 1937 seemed well-nigh perfect. The election had, as one news-paper said, yielded "a roar in which cheers for the Supreme Court were drowned out." Congressional opinion appeared overtly hostile. "The boys on Capitol Hill have their knives out, and how they do ache to use them," one news commentator had reported in January 1936.

Yet from the very start, "Court-packing" ran into terrific public opposition. Overnight Supreme Court Justices were again pictured as demigods far above the sweaty crowd, weighing public policy on the delicate scales of the law. "Constitutionality" was talked about as if it were a tangible fact, undeviating and precise, not merely the current judicial theory of what ought and what ought not to be done. The same Congressmen who, prior to the President's message, had demanded the scalps of reactionary Justices, were "shocked beyond measure" and turned upon Roosevelt in an attitude of anguished surprise. Closing ranks with Bar Associations, the newspapers lined up almost solidly against Court-packing. The idea implicit in Roosevelt's scheme, that the Court may change its interpretation in such a way as to sustain legislative power to meet national needs, was called as "false in theory, as it would be ruinous in practice."

In a rash of articles and comments published in the *American Bar Association Journal*, lawyers upheld the myth that judges discover law; they do not make it. Typical among them is the stubborn comment of the Association's president, Frederick H. Stinchfield:

> He [F.D.R.] derisively uses the word veto as applied to the Supreme Court. Now, each of us is aware that the Supreme Court, in no sense, exercises a veto. What the Court does is to examine the legislation in the light of the Constitution, to ascertain whether or not any of the liberties retained by the people or by the individual states are invaded by the legislation. If they find that to be true, the Court declares the legislation invalid because of the invasion of retained rights. With the legislation, as such, or with its present significance, the Court has no dealing. [*American Bar Association Journal*, April 1937, Vol. 23, p. 235.]

In the same issue of the *Journal*, Warren Olney, Jr., of the San Francisco Bar, declared with supreme confidence that, in passing on the validity of legislation, "the judicial duty is to decide whether it is in accord with the Constitution and refuse to give effect to the law in conflict with it. . . . *And this, and only this, is all that the Supreme Court has ever done.*" (Italics in the original.) And yet some of the most distinguished Supreme Court Justices, including Holmes, Brandeis, Stone, and Cardozo, are on record in opposition to this over-simplification of the judicial process.

Throughout the ensuing months clergymen, lawyers, and educators trekked to Washington and testified for and against the plan. "No issue so great or so deep has been raised in America since secession," Walter Lippmann commented. Edward S. Corwin, historian and political scientist, viewing the struggle more realistically than the *American Bar Association Journal* writer, commented: "It [the Supreme Court] is a hybrid body. It exercises political functions as well as judicial functions." "The chief result of judicial review has to date been the Court's emancipation from the Constitutional document."

Everyone who could read knew that the Justices were not the vestal virgins of the Constitution. Yet, through the years, and despite increasing evidence that judicial interpretation and not Fundamental Law shackled the power to govern, the American people had come to regard the Court as the symbol of their freedom. Tarnished though the symbol was, it made, like the English monarchy, for national stability and poise in crisis; moreover, like its English counterpart, the Supreme Court commanded the loyalty of the citizenry, providing in the minds of many an impregnable barrier against dictatorship and personal government. "The President wants to control the Supreme Court" was the phrase hammered home incessantly. If the plan were accepted, the anti-New-Deal press averred, nothing would stand between Roosevelt and the absolute dictatorship of the United States.

Roosevelt, quick to sense that his initial approach had been a major blunder, moved closer to the real issue on March 4, when he likened the judiciary to an unruly horse on the government gang plough, unwilling to pull with its teammates, the executive and Congress. As he saw it now, the crucial question was not whether the Court had kept up with its calendar, but whether it had kept up with the country.

In a nation-wide Fireside Chat on March 9, the President threw off the cloak of sophistry and frankly explained: "The court has been acting not as a judicial body, but as a policy-making body. . . . That is not only my accusation, it is the accusation of most distinguished Justices of the present Supreme Court. . . . In holding the AAA unconstitutional, Justice Stone said of the majority opinion that it was 'a tortured construction of the Constitution' and two other Justices agreed with him. In the case holding the New York Minimum Wage Law unconstitutional, Justice Stone said that the majority were actually reading into the Constitution their own 'personal economic predilections' . . . and two other Justices agreed with him." This belated strategy of frankness failed. The President's false assertion that the Judges lagged in their work blurred the

issue, diverting public attention so completely that this later effort
to face the difficulty squarely never quite succeeded.

A vigorous campaign against the President's bill was being waged
in the Senate under the leadership of Senator Burton K. Wheeler.
Tom Corcoran, then a White House adviser, tried vainly to dissuade
the Montana Senator from making a fight; the President himself
told Wheeler of the futility of opposing a measure certain to pass
in any event. "A liberal cause," Wheeler retorted bluntly, "was
never won by stacking a deck of cards, by stuffing a ballot box, or
packing a Court."

Meanwhile, those most knowledgeable as to the condition of the
Court's docket—the Justices themselves—maintained discreet silence.
Finally, Senator Wheeler nervously sought an interview with
Justice Brandeis, known to be a stickler for proprieties. Much to
his surprise he found Brandeis most cooperative. "Why don't you
call on the Chief Justice?" Brandeis suggested. "But I don't know
the Chief Justice," the Montana Senator demurred. "Well," said
Brandeis, somewhat impatiently, "the Chief Justice knows you and
knows what you are doing."

This was late Friday afternoon. The next day Senator Wheeler
went to see Chief Justice Hughes. The Senator wanted to know
from the Justices themselves whether the President's oft-repeated
allegations about the swollen Court docket, lack of efficiency, and
so on had any basis in fact. As Brandeis had indicated, the Chief
Justice was friendly and helpful. Though Wheeler did not reach
him until Saturday, March 20, he was able somehow to prepare a
long and closely reasoned document for the Senator's use the following Monday, March 22. "The baby is born," Hughes said with
a broad smile, as he put the letter into Wheeler's hand late Sunday
afternoon.

The Chief Justice's letter not only scotched the President's charge
that the "old men" were not abreast of their docket, but also revealed its composer as a canny dialectician. Though carefully
refraining from open opposition to the plan, the letter suggested
that the President's idea of an enlarged Court and the hearing of
cases in divisions might run counter to the Constitutional provision
for "one Supreme Court." Whether Hughes's words constituted an
advisory opinion remains a moot question. But observers were quick
to note that in his book (*The Supreme Court of the United States,*

pp. 30-31) Hughes had written of the Court's customary rejection of "the overtures of the Congress for opinions on constitutional questions in the absence of a real case or controversy to be decided."

Hughes also managed to convey the erroneous impression that the entire Court endorsed his statement. Ignoring the customary disavowal of authority to speak for members of a body not consulted, he was "confident that it [the statement] is in accord with the views of the Justices," though he admitted "on account of the shortness of time, I have not been able to consult with members of the Court generally." We know that Cardozo and Stone, at least, objected strongly to Hughes's "extra-official-expression on a constitutional question." "I did not see the Chief Justice's letter, or know of it until I read it in the papers," Stone explained later on. "I certainly would not have joined in that part of it which undertakes to suggest what is and what is not constitutional. . . . Although the Court was then in recess," Stone went on, "all its members were in the city. They could have been brought together for a conference on an hour's telephone notice, or less. Throughout the recess, Justices Sutherland, Cardozo, and myself were in our homes, which are within five minutes' walk of the residence of the Chief Justice." If Hughes had taken the trouble to consult his colleagues, there might have been no letter, or, as Hughes may have realized, a very different one.

The Chief Justice's letter put a serious crimp in the President's project. Further, to lessen the chances of its success, the Justices began, as the fight raged about them, shameless destruction of their most recent handiwork.

A SWITCH IN TIME

Toward the end of the 1935-36 term, the really big issue facing Court and country was posed by the Wagner Labor Relations Act, a bold attempt to salvage from the defunct NRA provisions requiring collective bargaining between employers and employees, and protecting the right of labor to organize. The constitutional basis of the Act was that labor disputes disrupted interstate commerce. Several cases were argued on February 10 and 11, 1937. Industrial peace—or war—seemed to hang in the balance when, on

April 12, 1937, in the heat of the Court fight, Chief Justice Hughes put forward a broad and encompassing definition of interstate commerce and conceded to Congress the power to protect the lifelines of the national economy from private industrial warfare (*National Labor Relations Board* v. *Jones & Laughlin Steel Corp.*, 301 U.S. 1, 1937).

Arguments that had proved effective in the Schechter and Guffey Coal cases now availed nothing. "Those cases," the Chief Justice commented summarily, "are not controlling here." They were not controlling because he now chose to consider that "fundamental" distinction between "direct and indirect effects" as one of degree rather than kind. They were not binding now because he minimized the point much stressed in the Schechter case, namely, that the "fundamental" nature of the distinction between direct and indirect effects of intrastate transactions upon interstate commerce arises from the fact that it is "essential" to the maintenance of "our constitutional system." Since interstate commerce was now seen as a "practical conception," interference with that commerce "must be appraised by a judgment that does not ignore actual experience."

Treating the earlier approach somewhat disdainfully, the Chief Justice declared that, in light of the industry's "farflung activities," it was "idle to say" that interference by strikes or other labor disturbances "would be indirect or remote. It is obvious that it would be immediate and might be catastrophic. . . . We are asked to shut our eyes to the plainest facts of our national life," the Chief Justice continued, "and to deal with the question of direct and indirect effects in an intellectual vacuum." This he now refused to do.

"When industries organize themselves on a national scale, making their relation to interstate commerce the dominant factor in their activities, how can it be maintained that their industrial labor relations constitute a forbidden field into which Congress may not enter when it is necessary to protect interstate commerce from the paralyzing consequences of industrial war?" The Chief Justice's sweeping doctrine did not apply solely to large-scale industries, such as steel. He proceeded immediately to apply the same doctrine to two small concerns, a trailer company and a men's clothing manufacturer.

The Chief Justice's colleagues naturally supposed that the man who took a position apparently so completely at odds with his earlier pronouncements must have seen a new light. "Every consideration brought forward to uphold the act before us was applicable to support the acts held unconstitutional in cases decided within two years," Justice McReynolds countered in dissent. The four dissenters bemoaned this flagrant departure from *Schechter* and *Carter*. No "direct" and "material" interference with commerce was threatened here, they argued, and nothing could be more remote and indirect than the relation between the regulation of hours and wages of labor and the flow of interstate commerce. Justice Stone, apparently sharing the dissenter's view as to the Court's drastic shift, thought Jones & Laughlin might properly be regarded as "very revolutionary."

Two things stand out: first, there is nothing in the majority opinion that does not find its counterpart in *Gibbons* v. *Ogden*. Second, this reversion to John Marshall was not the work of a "packed" Court. The same Court had defeated the NRA and the Guffey Coal Act. Justice Roberts himself, the Court's spokesman in *United States* v. *Butler*, delivered the opinion upholding the second Agricultural Adjustment Act (*Mulford* v. *Smith*, 307 U.S. 38, 1939) providing that production quotas be set and enforced against producers of certain agricultural products after a referendum. "Any rule, such as that embodied in the Act, which is intended to foster, protect and conserve that commerce, or to prevent the flow of commerce from working harm to the people of the nation, is within the competence of Congress," he announced. Congress was thus invited to use the commerce clause as the basis of a national police power.

Chief Justice Hughes's insistence that these reversals and new interpretations, while the Court was under attack, were unrelated to the President's bold determination to reorganize the Judiciary provoked much reaction, both cynical and sober. "We are told," a skeptical paragrapher noted, "that the Supreme Court's about-face was not due to outside clamor. It seems that the new building has a sound-proof room, to which the Justices may retire to change their minds." President Roosevelt was convinced that "the change would never have come, unless this frontal attack had been made upon the philosophy of the majority of the Court." That is why he regarded the message of February 5, 1937, as one of "the most important and significant events" in his administration on the domestic scene. "I regard it as a turning point in our modern history. For, . . . unless some quick means had been found to give our democracy the power to work out its needs, there is grave doubt whether it could have survived the crisis which was bearing down upon it from within." The President believed that democratic government itself was at stake.

> This was the year which was to determine whether the kind of government which the people of the United States had voted for in 1932, 1934, and 1936, was to be permitted . . . to function. If it had not been permitted to function as a democracy, it is my reasoned opinion that there would have been great danger that ultimately it might have been compelled to give way to some alien type of government—in the vain hope that the new form of government might be able to give the average men and women the protection and cooperative assistance which they had the right to expect.

"Across the seas," the President continued, "democracies had even then yielded place to dictatorships, because they had proven too weak or too slow to fulfill the wants of their citizens. . . . It would have been dangerous to block too long the just and irresistible pressure of human needs."

The President was convinced that America had been saved from this risk because "the Court yielded. The Court changed. The Court began to interpret the Constitution instead of torturing it."

Of this remarkable transformation—"limited revolution," Professor Corwin calls it—Robert H. Jackson has observed: "So the Court reorganization debate came to an inconclusive end. But even as Senators and lawyers shouted ringing defenses of the old and changeless order, the Court made certain that the old order should yield rapidly and decisively. In politics the black-robed reactionary Justices had won over the master liberal politician of our day. In law the President defeated the recalcitrant Justices in their own Court."

The final blow in the legislative forum occurred June 14 when a majority of the Senate Judiciary Committee recommended that the President's bill be rejected. It must "not pass," the committee reported, because the measure was based on the belief that the Court had overstepped its proper limit. Even if the Justices had gone "too far," this remedy, designed to force the Court to alter its decisions, would destroy judicial independence. "If the Court of last resort is to be made to respond to a prevalent sentiment of a current hour, politically imposed, that Court must ultimately become subservient to the pressure of public opinion of the hour, which might at the moment embrace much passion abhorrent to a more calm, lasting consideration." Echoing the Founding Fathers' distrust of pure democracy, the report lashed out furiously, pointing out that "the milestones of liberal progress are made to be noted and counted with caution rather than merely to be encountered and passed. Progress is not a mad mob march; rather, it is a steady invincible stride." Or, as A. Lawrence Lowell put it nearly a half century earlier, "the Constitution is an obstacle to the whim, but not the will of the people."

Signed by ten of its eighteen members, the committee's report concluded:

> We recommend the rejection of this bill as a needless, futile, and utterly dangerous abandonment of constitutional principles. . . .
> It is a measure which should be so emphatically rejected that its parallel will never again be presented to the free representatives of the free people of America.

F.D.R.'s attempt to "pack" the Court has been considered so outrageous that certain Senators are determined that there shall be no repetition of it. In 1953, Senator Butler of Maryland, apparently determined to remove the Court permanently from the political arena, proposed a constitutional amendment that would fix the composition and jurisdiction of the Supreme Court. The Butler amendment seems to rest on three assumptions: (a) Supreme Court Justices can do no wrong; they, unlike other agencies of government, never abuse their power. (b) The Court has not been in politics, except as drawn in by the political organs of government. (c) The proposed amendment, by increasing their political independence, would take the Justices out of politics. There is little or nothing in our history to bolster these assumptions. On the contrary, experience shows that the President's appointing power, along with congressional authority to determine the size of the Court and control its jurisdiction, are useful guns behind the door. The proposed amendment got exactly what it deserved—a quick legislative brush-off.

Vacancies on the Supreme Bench are not always the work of

fate. Not every tired or disabled constitutional warrior is disposed to "bow to the inevitable," retire promptly and unhesitatingly without regard to how his successor will vote on the crucial issues ahead. Judges have, in fact, displayed conspicuous determination and capacity to stay on pending political relief—incumbency of a new president of the right political stripe. On more than one occasion, Presidents or Justices themselves have felt impelled to resort to the embarrassing task of advising a senescent judge to quit.

Though he felt his powers failing, John Marshall held on to the center chair until death in 1835, determined to frustrate Jackson who had triumphed in the 1832 election. In 1875 Justice Miller complained bitterly of his inability to induce colleagues "who are too old, to resign." Taft, mistaking Hoover for a "progressive," faced retirement with trepidation, and urged like-minded colleagues to hang on. Holmes, the most sophisticated of judges, acutely aware of his aging colleagues' tendency to stay on and on, had himself to be asked to step down. For five years after Franklin D. Roosevelt's election in 1932, the Supreme Bench, comprised of judges averaging age 72 plus, remained unchanged, one reason being their hope that the people would return to their senses and elect a Republican president. In seems probable that Chief Justice Stone continued on the bench longer than he might have done except for political considerations. From the side of the Executive our history affords conspicuous illustrations of what Madison aptly called, the "matching of ambition against ambition." The Jeffersonians impeached a Supreme Court Justice; the Jacksonians packed the Court; Teddy Roosevelt put the "fear of God in judges"; F.D.R. made a frontal attack on them. Allowance must be made for play in the constitutional joints—even at the price of injecting politics into judicial appointments. Such flexibility is far more likely to achieve justice and moderation than the futile attempt, as in the Butler Amendment, to create a Supreme Court independent of politics.

The most striking examples of the Court's about-face occurred long after the dust of the 1937 battle had settled. In 1941 the Justices ruled unanimously in favor of the constitutionality of the Fair Labor Standards Act of 1938, a far-reaching enactment fixing, among other things, minimum wages and maximum hours for producers of goods shipped in interstate commerce.

In a case of such moment, one might have guessed that Chief

Justice Hughes himself would speak for the Court. Hitherto he had instinctively recognized those "occasions when an opinion should carry the extra weight which pronouncement by the Chief Justice gives." Surely this was such an occasion. One suspects that Hughes ignored his usual procedure and assigned the writing of this crucial opinion to Stone because of the doubts he entertained as to the Act's constitutionality. For one thing, the undefined phrase, "production *for* commerce," which Congress had used to delimit the scope of the Act, Hughes considered too vague to be valid in a criminal statute. "In attempting to give some appropriate content to this loose phrase," the Chief Justice wrote, "I think that the test should be as objective as possible and should not be centered on the mere *intent* or *expectation* of the employer apart from the usual and normal course of business or actual transactions." "Even with the best possible test," he told Stone, "the statute is a highly unsatisfactory one and as it is a borderline case, I should prefer not to write."

Nor could the Chief Justice accept the unqualified definition of the commerce power required to sustain the Wages and Hours statute. For him, "regulate" meant "facilitate," "promote," "advance," "foster"; only incidentally did it comprehend "restrain," "control," or "prohibit." He agreed that the power "to protect interstate commerce" was plenary. But his understanding of the nature and scope of "commerce" and of the power to regulate it, in spite of his opinion upholding the Wagner Labor Relations Act, was a far cry from John Marshall's grand conception laid down in *Gibbons* v. *Ogden*. There Marshall had boldly sketched this binding tie of Union as the authority to govern commercial intercourse among the states, characterizing the constitutional grant as "sovereign," "complete," "plenary," "absolute," and of the same scope as if it were vested "in a single government," and therefore utterly unaffected by the coexistence of the states. Regulation signified the authority "to prescribe the rules by which commerce is to be governed," and extended to all "that commerce which concerns more states than one." Apart from certain specific constitutional prohibitions, such as that barring discriminatory preference for the ports of one state, the "sole restraints" on congressional exercise of this fundamental power were political—those "on which the people must often solely rely, in all representative governments."

All but ignoring Hughes's refinements in the great commerce cases decided since 1935, Stone, the Court's spokesman, went all the way back to *Gibbons* v. *Ogden*. The definitions he fashioned for the key words "power" and "regulate" carry the majestic sweep of Marshall's classic decision of 1824. The Darby opinion (312 U.S. 100, 1941), Stone explained to Professor Noel T. Dowling, was designed "to make two things clear, namely (1) that the commerce power of Congress is not restricted to intrinsically harmful commodities, and (2) that the motive of Congress in passing commerce clause laws is none of the Court's business." Thus for the first time since Marshall, the Court said flatly that Congress "is free to exclude from commerce articles whose use in the states for which they are destined it may conceive to be injurious to the public health, morals, or welfare." Manufacture of goods, Stone agreed, is not commerce, but their shipment is, and the power to regulate is the power "to prescribe the rule by which commerce is governed. It extends not only to those regulations which aid, foster, and protect the commerce, but embraces those which prohibit." Quoting Chief Justice Marshall, he held that the power "is complete in itself, may be exercised to its utmost extent, and acknowledges no limitations other than are prescribed in the Constitution."

Nor is congressional action a "forbidden invasion of state power merely because either its motive or its consequence is to restrict the use of articles of commerce within the states of destination." "The motive and purpose of a regulation of interstate commerce," Stone said, "are matters for the legislative judgment upon the exercise of which the Constitution places no restriction and over which the courts are given no control. . . . Whatever their motive and purpose, regulations of commerce which do not infringe some constitutional prohibitions are within the plenary power conferred on Congress by the commerce clause."

As Stone afterward explained, his opinion had been "deliberately fashioned on the model of Justice Holmes' dissent in *Hammer* v. *Dagenhart*." Stone, like Holmes, could not understand how the commerce clause, which admittedly empowered Congress to prohibit interstate traffic in diseased livestock, lottery tickets, adulterated and misbranded articles, women for immoral purposes, intoxicating liquors, stolen motor vehicles, kidnaped persons, and convict-made goods, could be construed so as to nullify a law prohibiting trade among the states in commodities manufactured under substandard conditions of labor or by children. The contrary ruling in *Hammer* v. *Dagenhart*, decided twenty-two years before over what Stone called "the powerful and now classic dissent of Mr. Justice Holmes," could no longer stand. The reasoning and conclusion of the Court in the Dagenhart case, Stone said, "cannot be reconciled with the conclusion which we have reached, that the power of Congress under the commerce clause is plenary to exclude any article from interstate commerce subject only to the specific prohibitions of the Constitution."

"*Hammer* v. *Dagenhart*," he wrote, "has not been followed." It was an "aberration" resting on the unacceptable judicial refinement that "congressional power to prohibit interstate commerce is limited to articles which in themselves have some harmful or deleterious property—a distinction which was novel when made and unsupported by any provision of the Constitution. . . . The conclusion is inescapable," he announced, "that *Hammer* v. *Dagenhart* was a departure from the principles which have prevailed in the interpretation of the commerce clause both before and since the decision and that such vitality, as a precedent, as it then had has long since been exhausted. It should be and now is overruled."

The Darby opinion did more than vindicate Holmes. Stone had waited nearly five years for an opportunity to read out of constitutional jurisprudence that mainstay of laissez faire—"dual federalism"—the notion that the Tenth Amendment sets an independent limitation on the powers of Congress. In a now famous passage, Stone wrote:

> Our conclusion is unaffected by the Tenth Amendment. . . . The Amendment states but a truism that all is retained which has not been surrendered. There is nothing in the history of its adoption to suggest that it was more than declaratory of the relationship between the national and state governments as it had been established by the Constitution before the Amendment or that its purpose was other than to allay fears that the new national government might seek to exercise powers not granted, and that the states might not be able to exercise fully their reserved powers. . . . From the beginning and for many years the Amendment has been construed as not depriving the national government of authority to resort to all means for the exercise of a granted power which are appropriate and plainly adapted to the permitted ends.

The press generally interpreted the decision as "clearing away the last legal doubt about major New Deal reforms." Many papers noted how the long struggle for a child labor amendment had been brought to a successful close by the Court itself. The *St. Louis Star-Times* welcomed the decision as further evidence of the Court's determination "to permit the democratic processes to operate free from the autocracy of judicial tyranny." Even the staid *New York Times* approved this "historic decision."

So far as the commerce power is concerned, the so-called constitutional revolution appears in retrospect not so much a revolution as a counter-revolution. In the period from 1890 to 1936 when the Court began to develop a series of implied limitations on the exercise of the commerce power, it was not doing so in response to any rule of law announced by the Marshall or Taney Courts. Marshall, while not denying the power of the states to regulate certain local matters defined the commerce power broadly. Taney's Court, although more generous to local regulation, in the absence of federal legislation, made it clear that Congress' power was broad and to the extent exercised would be upheld, and that the Court would undertake to determine the validity of state acts by measuring the need for uniform regulation in each case. The Court, in other words, was to have the difficult role of ascertaining the limits of state power of commerce until Congress should act.

During the period 1890-1936, the Court inverted the role of the Taney Court. At one time it would use the commerce power to frustrate state acts where they interfered with national commerce; at other times it would imply limits on the national power to regulate certain aspects of commerce by evolving rules denying to mining, agriculture, and manufacturing any relationship with interstate commerce. From 1890 onward "powerful interests" were encouraged, as Robert H. Jackson put it, "by the trend of decision to carry to the Supreme Court all causes lost in Congress, and the power of judicial review came more and more to resemble a political veto." By 1936 a majority of the Justices, like the beneficiaries of the interests their decisions safeguarded, had made it apparent to Jackson that "the great objectives of this administration and this Congress offend their deep convictions and that the methods of this day violate their conceptions of good government."

If one is inclined to protest that the founders never dreamed of AAA, FLSA, and NIRA, and other measures premised on a broad interpretation of national commerce or taxing power, the answer is that of course they did not. This argument could be used to reject the great bulk of modern regulatory legislation. But, as Marshall said in *McCulloch* v. *Maryland:*

> This provision [necessary and proper clause] is made in a constitution, intended to endure for ages to come, and, consequently, to be adapted to the various crises of human affairs. To have prescribed the means by which government should, in all future time, execute its powers, would have been to change, entirely, the character of the instrument, and give it the properties of a legal code. It would have been an unwise attempt to provide, by immutable rules, for exigencies which, if foreseen at all, must have been seen dimly, and which can be best provided for as they occur.

In the light of this philosophy the growth of national power through the commerce clause can be described as the necessary response by government to economic and social change. Those adversely affected by regulation may cry "back to the Constitution" but it may well be asked: Back to which Constitution—that of 1787, as interpreted by John Marshall and Roger Brooke Taney, or that of 1890-1936? Events have dictated the answer.

IX

THE CONTRACT CLAUSE
AND STATE POLICE POWER

*J*UDICIAL REVIEW OF THE POWER
of Congress to regulate commerce and to tax and spend, and the
relation of federal authority to state power in these areas highlights
one of the first great antinomies of American constitutional law—
national supremacy versus dual federalism. By 1937 the Court had
largely resolved that conflict in favor of national power. This
chapter features another major antinomy—the doctrine of vested
rights (the general import of which is that "the effect of legislation
on existing property rights was a primary test of its validity")
versus state police power (the power to promote the health, safety,
morals, and general welfare). Throughout much of our history, the
state police power has been limited by the commerce clause. We
are now to explore the limitations on state power that flow from
the doctrine of vested rights.

The struggle between vested rights and police power is a more
modern form of the earlier conflict between theories of natural
rights, on the one hand, and the principle of legislative supremacy
on the other. On this side of the Atlantic, these two doctrines appeared in the prerevolutionary contest between the natural rights

of the colonists and the legislative supremacy of the mother country. The same phenomenon is manifest after 1776 in the effort of state legislative majorities to regulate the property and contract rights of individual citizens.

VESTED RIGHTS

The doctrine of vested rights is rooted in the notion that property is a basic social institution. Antedating civil society itself, property fixes the limits within which even the supreme legislative authority may properly operate. Indeed, the main function of government, its *raison d'être*, is to protect property. "The right of acquiring and possessing property and having it protected," Justice Paterson wrote in an early Supreme Court opinion, "is one of the natural inherent and unalienable rights of man. Men have a sense of property: property is necessary to their subsistence, and correspondent to their natural wants and desires; its security was one of the objects that induced them to unite in society. No man would become a member of a community in which he could not enjoy the fruits of his honest labor and industry. The preservation of property, then, is a primary object of the social compact." (*Van Horne's Lessee* v. *Dorrance*, 2 Dall. 304, 310, 1795.) Elaborating this same doctrine James Madison gave "property" a more expansive meaning in his essay of 1792:

This term means 'that dominion which one man claims and exercises over the external things of the world, in exclusion of every other individual.' But in its larger and juster meaning, it embraces everything to which a man may attach a value and have a right; and which leaves to every one else the like advantage. In the former sense, a man's land, or merchandise, or money is called his property. In the latter sense, a man has property in his opinions and a free communication of them. He has a property of peculiar value in his religious opinions, and in the profession and practice dictated by them. He has property dear to him in the safety and liberty of his person. He has equal property in the free use of his faculties and free choice of the objects on which to employ them. In a word, as a man is said to have a right to his property, he may be equally said to have a property in his rights. . . . If there be a government then which prides itself on maintaining the inviolability of property, which provides that none shall be taken directly even for public use without indemnification to the owner, and yet directly violates the property which individuals have in their opinions, their religion, their person and their faculties, nay more which directly violates their property in their actual possessions, in the labor that acquires their daily subsistence, and in the hallowed remnant of time which ought to relieve their fatigues and soothe their cares, the inference will have been anticipated that such a government is not a pattern for the United States. If the United States mean to obtain or deserve the full praise due to wise and just governments they will equally respect the rights of property and the property in rights.

Among the major causes of the Federal Convention of 1787 was the "injustice" experienced under state laws during the so-called critical period, 1783-1787. In opening the Convention, Edmund Randolph referred to "the havoc of paper money," and Mercer urged protection of the people "against those speculating Legislatures which are now plundering them throughout the United States." Madison, deprecating the same activity, said that "the fundamental principle of republican government, that the majority who rule in such governments are the safest guardians both of public good and private rights," had become suspect. The urgency of the problem posed by state injustices is well illustrated in the colloquy that occurred in the early days of the Convention between Roger Sherman and James Madison. Sherman had enumerated as objectives of a Constitution, provision for defense against foreign danger and internal disputes, and creation of a central authority to make treaties with foreign nations and to regulate foreign commerce. Madison agreed that these goals were important, but insisted on combining with them "the necessity of providing more effectually for *the security of private rights* and the steady dispensation of justice within the states." "Interferences with these," Madison added, "were evils which had, more perhaps than anything else, produced this convention."

What Madison had in mind was the activity of state legislatures on behalf of the financially embarrassed but politically dominant small farmer class, led by rabble rousers such as Daniel Shays in Massachusetts—men seeking special legislation to alter under the standing law the rights of designated parties; intervention by state legislatures in private controversies pending in, or already decided by, the ordinary courts; legislation setting aside judgments, granting new hearings, voiding valid wills, or validating void wills, and laws promoting the interests of a favored religious sect. Those who wished to see the menace of special legislation and state legislative supremacy abated, those who felt the need for outside protection of the rights of property and of contract, naturally supported the movement afoot for a Constitutional Convention.

Various measures were proposed to secure such protection. Unsuccessful motions were introduced looking to the imposition of property qualification for suffrage or office-holding. The suggestion that the Senate be organized as a barrier for property was also defeated. The difficult and delicate matter of suffrage was ultimately left to the states. As the Constitution came from the hands of the framers, it contained only one brief clause that might afford vested rights protection against state legislative majorities—Article 1, Section 10: "No State shall . . . pass any . . . ex post facto law or laws impairing the obligation of contracts. . . ." And even this clause, when it came up for interpretation in *Calder* v. *Bull* (3 Dall. 386, 1798), was given a very narrow interpretation. The legislature of Connecticut had granted a new hearing to Bull after the expiration of the time for appeal in a dispute over a will. Confining the application of the ex post facto provision to retroactive penal legislation, the Supreme Court held that this clause was not "inserted to secure the citizen in his private rights of either property or contracts." This decision, by creating a wide breach in the constitutional protection afforded civil rights, aroused widespread criticism. Even Justice Chase, who delivered the opinion, suggested that legislation adversely affecting vested rights might be set aside as violation of natural law. "There are certain vital principles," Chase observed, "in our free republican governments which will determine and overrule an apparent and flagrant abuse of legislative power. An act of the legislature (for I cannot call it a law) contrary to the great principles of social compact cannot be considered a rightful exercise of the legislative authority."

But Chase's associate, Justice Iredell, questioned the validity of natural law limitations on legislative power. He characterized such talk as the plaything of "some speculative jurists," and said that if the Constitution itself imposed no limitations on legislative power, "whatever the legislature chose to enact would be lawfully enacted, and the judicial power could never interpose to pronounce it void." "The ideas of natural justice are regulated by no fixed standard,"

Iredell commented. "The ablest and purest of men have differed upon the subject, and all that the Court could properly say in such an event would be that the legislature . . . had passed an act which, in the opinion of the judges, was inconsistent with abstract principles of justice."

In appearance Iredell's views on the scope of judicial power have prevailed, but (as we shall see) by the end of the century Chase's views were for all practical purposes triumphant. By 1890 the Court achieved, under the due process clause of the 14th Amendment, the very power to supervise and control legislative action in relation to abstract principles of justice against which Iredell had so strongly inveighed.

EXPANSION OF THE CONTRACT CLAUSE

Calder v. *Bull*, narrowing the scope of ex post facto so that it outlawed only retroactive penal legislation, was a binding precedent in the year 1810, when the leading case of *Fletcher* v. *Peck* (6 Cr. 87) came before Chief Justice Marshall. Marshall, wrote Professor Corwin, found in *Fletcher* v. *Peck* "a task of restoration awaiting him in that great field of Constitutional Law which defines state power in relation to private rights." In the task of providing an efficient national government, Hamilton had laid solid foundations for Marshall; no such preliminary work had been done in the task now confronting the Chief Justice. Indeed *Calder* v. *Bull* presented a nearly insuperable barrier.

Fletcher v. *Peck* illustrates the speculative spirit rife in America at the close of the 1700's. Land companies found Georgia an especially inviting field. Between 1789 and 1795 speculators badgered the Georgia legislators without success. Finally, however, on January 7, 1795, the Governor of Georgia signed a bill granting the greater part of what is now Alabama and Mississippi to four groups of purchasers, known as the Yazoo Land Companies, at 1½ cents per acre. The "purchasers" included men of national reputations as well as local politicians (all but one member of the Georgia legislature who voted for the act held shares in one or more of the companies). Indignation ran high and in 1796 a new legislature repealed the land-grab act. By the time of repeal some of the lands had passed into the hands of purchasers, mostly Boston capitalists, who in turn sold exclusively to investors in New England and the Middle Atlantic States.

Contending that the repeal act of 1796 could not constitutionally divest them of their titles, these innocent purchasers decided to test their rights in the federal courts. The case, an "arranged" suit, first came before the Supreme Court in the 1809 term; it was re-argued the next year, and a decision was rendered on March 16, 1810. Marshall was profoundly interested in the stability of the contractual relationships involved. His own title to the Fairfield estate had been put in jeopardy by acts of the Virginia legislature, later the subject of controversy in *Martin* v. *Hunter's Lessee* (1 Wheat. 304, 1814). "No man in America," Beveridge writes, "could have followed with deeper anxiety the Yazoo controversy than John Marshall." Sustaining the contention of the Yazoo claimants, the Chief Justice held that the 1796 repeal act was unconstitutional as an impairment of the obligation of a contract. At the outset, Marshall suggested that the rescinding act of the Georgia legislature was void as a violation of vested rights, and hence contrary to the underlying principles of society and government. But, apparently realizing that a decision based on such flimsy ground would be less secure than one grounded in the words of the Constitution, he resorted to the contract clause. In doing this, he was confronted with two difficulties; first, the sort of contract the framers had in mind must have been executory—a contract in which the obligation of performance is still to be performed. Marshall got around this by saying that every grant is attended by an implied contract on the part of the grantor not to reassert his right to the thing granted. Therefore, the clause covered executed contracts, in which performance has been fulfilled, as well as executory contracts.

The greater difficulty was that the contract before the Court was *public*, not private. In the case of private contracts it is easy enough to distinguish the contract as an agreement between the parties from the obligation which comes from the law and holds the parties to their agreement. Who, in this case, was to hold Georgia to its engagement? Certainly not Georgia, which had passed the rescinding act, or the Georgia state court. Marshall finally escaped the dilemma by ruling that Georgia's obligation was moral, and that this moral injunction had been elevated to legal status by Article 1, Section 10 of the Constitution.

But Marshall was uncertain at the very end. In the last paragraph of his opinion he says that the state of Georgia was restrained from passing the rescinding act "either by general principles that are common to our free institutions, or by particular provisions of the Constitution."

Fletcher v. *Peck* went a long way toward bridging the gap opened by *Calder* v. *Bull* in the constitutional protection of private rights. But, since Marshall's ruling was somewhat ambiguous, there remained the question of whether the obligation-of-contract clause safeguarded corporate charters as well as public grants against legislative interference. In 1819, by his opinion in the Dartmouth College case (4 Wheat. 518), Marshall completed the task of filling in the breach Justice Chase had created in the constitutional protection of vested rights.

The college's original charter was granted by the King of England. Parliament could have destroyed it at any time before 1776, and before 1788 the state of New Hampshire could have wiped it out. After that year, Marshall held that it must continue in perpetuity. His opinion adds up to these propositions: the college was not public, but a "private eleemosynary institution"; its charter was the outgrowth of a contract between the original donors and the Crown; the trustee represented the interest of the donors; the terms of the Constitution were broad enough to cover and protect this representative interest.

Marshall was troubled at only one point. The requirement of the obligation-of-contract clause was admittedly designed to protect those having a vested beneficial interest. No one then living, not even the trustees, had any such interest in Dartmouth College. But Marshall held that the case came within the spirit, if not the words, of the Constitution. The gifts, the Chief Justice reasoned, had been

> made in the pleasing, perhaps delusive hope that the charity will flow forever in the channel which the givers have marked out for it. If every man finds in his own bosom strong evidence of the universality of this sentiment, there can be little reason to imagine, that the framers of our Constitution were strangers to it, and that, feeling the necessity and policy of giving permanence and security to contracts, of withdrawing them from the influence of legislative

bodies, whose fluctuating policy, and repeated interferences, produced the most perplexing and injurious embarrassments, they still deemed it necessary to leave these contracts subject to those interferences.

The nub of Marshall's decision is the proposition that any ambiguity in a charter must be construed in favor of the adventurers and against the state. With perpetuity thus implied, the college charter was placed beyond the reach of the legislature. By that same token, the charters of profit-seeking corporations were likewise beyond the control of legislative majorities. In short, the doctrine of vested rights, heretofore having no safeguard except the principles of natural law, now enjoyed the solid protection of a specific provision of the Constitution—the impairment-of-contract clause.

In a separate opinion in the Dartmouth College case, Marshall's scholarly colleague Joseph Story suggested the means by which states might in the future avoid the restrictive effect of Marshall's holding. Speaking of the state's power over corporations, Story observed that there was "no other control, than what is expressly or implicitly reserved by the charter itself."

As early as 1805 Virginia had used a reservation clause (reserving to the state the power to alter, amend, or repeal a charter) in special incorporation acts. In 1827, following the Dartmouth decision, New York enacted a general law making all charters "hereafter granted . . . subject to alteration, suspension and repeal, in the discretion of the legislature." Eventually all states were to have such a provision in either constitutions or general acts, or in both.

Could any society, particularly an industrialized society claiming to rest on the foundation of popular sovereignty, hold rigidly to the doctrine of vested rights? Even John Marshall seemed unwilling to go quite so far. In *Fletcher* v. *Peck*, the doctrine of the public interest gave way to the doctrine of vested rights. But eleven years later, in the Dartmouth College case, Marshall suggested an opposing idea, later designated the "police power." "The framers of the Constitution," he then observed, "did not intend to restrain the states in the regulation of the civil institutions adopted for internal government." In *Gibbons* v. *Ogden* (9 Wheat. 1, 1824), the police-power concept became quite explicit: "The acknowledged power of the state to regulate its police, its domestic trade and to govern its own citizens may enable it to legislate on this subject [commerce] to a considerable extent." Referring to "inspection laws," Marshall conceded that they "form a portion of that immense mass of legislation, which embraces everything within the territory of a state, not surrendered to the general government." The term "police power" itself makes its first appearance in Marshall's opinion in *Brown* v. *Maryland* (12 Wheat. 419, 1827). Marshall here speaks of the police power as residual, comprising what is left over of the state's power beyond those other great prerogatives, eminent domain and taxation.

By 1830, the doctrine of vested rights, as limiting legislative power, was nevertheless accepted in the majority of the states and by leading lawyers and judges—especially by the eminent jurist Chancellor Kent of New York. Kent conceded that the state had the power to "prescribe the mode and manner of using it [property] so far as may be necessary to prevent the abuse of the right to the injury or annoyance of others or to the public." But he denied state power to destroy property values in the hands of owners without paying for them. Implicit in Kent's doctrine was his theory of social progress: "A state of equality as to property is impossible to be maintained, for it is against the laws of our nature; and if it could be reduced to practice, it would place the human race in a restless enjoyment and stupid inactivity which would degrade the mind and destroy the happiness of social life."

The fierceness of the battle between public power and vested rights at the state level was highlighted in the leading case of *Wilkinson* v. *Leland* (2 Peters 627, 1829), involving an act of the Rhode Island legislature, confirming an otherwise "void" title to land. Daniel Webster, attorney for the defendant in error, insisted that: "If at this period, there is not a general restraint on legislatures in favor of private rights, there is an end to private property. Though there may be no prohibition in the constitution, the legislature is restrained from acts subverting the great principles of republican liberty and of the social compact." To this contention Webster's opponent, William Wirt, responded: "Who is the sovereign? Is it not the legislature of the state and are not its acts effectual unless they come in contact with the great principles of the social compact?" Justice Story, speaking for the Court, upheld the retrospective legislation in question, yet he too came out strongly for vested rights: "That government can scarcely be deemed to be free where the rights of property are left solely dependent upon the will of a legislative body without any restraint. The fundamental maxims of a free government seem to require that the rights of personal liberty and private property should be sacred."

These pronouncements suggest that property rights fix the contours within which the legislature might exercise its powers; courts are obliged to enforce these limitations even in the absence of specific provisions of the Constitution.

It seems not unlikely that these developments caught the discerning eye of the French aristocrat, Alexis de Tocqueville. Visiting this country in the middle thirties, at the peak of Jacksonian democracy, Tocqueville saw a counter-force in the Judiciary:

> If I were asked where I place the American aristocracy, I should reply without hesistation that it is not among the rich, who are united by no common tie, but that it occupies the judicial bench and the bar.
> . . . The lawyers, as a body, form the most powerful, if not the only, counterpoise to the democratic element. In that country we easily perceive how the legal profession is qualified by its attributes, and even by its faults, to neutralize the vices inherent in popular government. When the American people are intoxicated by passion or carried away by the impetuosity of their ideas, they are checked and stopped by the almost invisible influence of their legal counselors. These secretly opposed their aristocratic propensities to the nation's democratic instincts, their superstitious attachment to what is old to its love of novelty, their narrow views to its immense designs, and their habitual procrastination to its ardent impatience.

The Court would, Tocqueville suggested, curb democratic excesses. "In ages of equality every man naturally stands alone. . . . He is easily got rid of, and he is trampled on with impunity. . . . The strength of the courts of law has always been the greatest security that can be offered to personal independence; but this is more especially the case in democratic ages. Private rights and interests are in constant danger if the judicial power does not grow more extensive and stronger to keep pace with the growing equality of conditions." In the long run De Tocqueville was a good prophet.

The police power concept dates, for all practical purposes, from the Taney Court, but the idea had been recognized, as we have seen, by Marshall himself. Instances in which he sanctioned state power, though not unknown, are the exception rather than the rule. The total effect of Marshall's leadership was to stifle regulation of property rights.

Growing opposition to Marshall's position became increasingly evident as America shifted toward a more democratic base. As Attorney General, Roger Brooke Taney told President Andrew Jackson that an act of incorporation, particularly those performing public services, such as roads and bridges, could "never be considered as having been granted for the exclusive benefit of the Corporators."

"It would be against the spirit of our free institutions," Taney declared, "to grant peculiar franchises and privileges to a body of individuals merely for the purpose of enabling them more conveniently and effectually to advance their own private interests. . . ." In a critical review of the Dartmouth College case, David Henshaw, a loyal Jacksonian, observed:

> Business corporations, excluding banks and all large corporations for trading in money, when judiciously granted and suitably regulated, seem to me generally beneficial and the natural offspring of our social condition. But if they are to be placed beyond legislative control and are thus to become monopolies and perpetuities, they assume an aspect the reverse of this and become alarming excrescences upon the body politic. . . . With such latitudinous and far fetched constructions, the Federal Constitution is whatever the Federal judiciary may please to make it; and the states are in fact in possession of little more power than the bailiffs who officiate in the Federal courts.

Meanwhile political forces of great significance for the development of constitutional law were rapidly taking shape. The year 1828 had witnesed the election of Jackson. In a single decade Massachusetts, New York, and Virginia met in convention to remove certain constitutional safeguards for economic privilege and to liberalize the suffrage. Out of all this emerged the doctrine of popular sovereignty, the notion that the will of the people is to be discovered at the ballot box, not merely, as Hamilton and Marshall insisted, in a document framed in 1787. The juristic expression of popular sovereignty is the doctrine of the police power, which was given classic expression by Jackson's appointee and Marshall's successor, Roger Brooke Taney, in the famous Charles River Bridge case (11 Peters 420).

At issue was the question whether the Massachusetts legislature, by authorizing construction of a free bridge over the Charles at a point where it interfered with the profits of a privately owned toll bridge, violated the obligation-of-contract clause. The case had been argued before John Marshall's Court in 1831. It was reargued in 1837, with Daniel Webster as counsel for the bridge company.

The Charles River Bridge Co. claimed that its unexpired right to operate a toll bridge between Boston and Charleston had been destroyed by a legislative act of 1828 chartering the Warren Bridge, because the latter was so close to the original bridge that it would deprive it of revenue. Although the original bridge company could not point to a clause in its charter promising freedom from competition, it argued, on the basis of the Dartmouth College decision, that such an implication should be read in. Taney, for the Court, denied this, insisting that the rights of a corporate charter holder should not be enlarged by implication, and that the public interest required a construction of corporate charters in favor of the state.

"The object and end of all government," Taney observed, "is to promote the happiness and prosperity of the community by which it is established; and it can never be assumed that the government intended to diminish its power of accomplishing the end for which it was created. . . . The continued existence of government would be of no great value, if by implications and presumptions, it was disarmed of the powers necessary to accomplish the ends of its creation; and the function it was designed to perform, transferred to the hands of privileged corporations." Rights of private property must, of course, be "sacredly guarded" but, Taney explained, "we must not forget that the community also have rights, and that the happiness and well being of every citizen depends on their faithful preservation."

Justice Story, a hold-over from the Marshall Court, dissented in a long and tedious opinion, studded with citation of precedents. The issue had been so long settled that any reexamination of it might have disruptive effects. "The very agitation of a question of this sort is sufficient to alarm every stockholder in every public enterprise of this sort, throughout the whole country."

Taney's opinion in the Charles River Bridge case suggested a concept of incalculable potentialities—the police power. In upholding a state law regulating the sale of liquor a decade later (*License Cases*, 5 How. 547), he evolved a succinct definition: "The power [of the state] to govern men and things within the limits of its dominion." This power is "inherent in every sovereignty to the extent of its dominion." Justice McLean went further, holding that "over these objects the federal government has no power. They appertain to state sovereignty as exclusively as powers exclusively delegated appertain to the general government." On the other hand, Justice Catron argued that the police power must be subordinate to congressional authority. With the Justices so hopelessly divided, small wonder the Court reporter was puzzled as to just what had been decided.

Although the clause enjoining impairment of the obligation of contracts was used in the 1840's to invalidate state laws giving retrospective relief to mortgage creditors, after the Charles River Bridge decision it never regained its earlier stature as a barrier against legislative encroachment on property rights. Coming in 1837 at the peak of Jackson's power and prestige, Taney's doctrine of the police power stimulated considerable legislative activity. In time it came to mean not only legislative authority to remove government-created privilege, as in the Charles River Bridge case, but also sanction of state legislation having broad social purpose. In *Stone* v. *Mississippi* (101 U.S. 814, 1880) the Court refused to limit state police power by applying the protection of the contract clause to a lottery company charter that had been abrogated by a provision in the new state constitution. The reason for the police-power rule, Chief Justice Waite wrote, lies in the fact that "the power of governing is a trust, committed by the people to the government, no part of which can be granted away. . . . [The agencies of government established by the people] can govern according to their discretion, if within the scope of their general authority, while in power; but they cannot give away or sell the discretion of those that are to come after them, in respect to matters the government of which, from the very nature of things, must 'vary with varying circumstances.' . . . The contracts which the Constitution protects are those that relate to property rights, not governmental." The Court's task was eased by the character of the property right involved, but in terming police power "governmental," in speaking of an "implied understanding" that a grant might be altered, the Court obscured the real clash of interests between property rights and legislative power.

Many years later, amid unprecedented economic depression, the obligation of contracts clause received a well-nigh fatal blow. Now, even in rural areas, law and order ran neck and neck with riot and anarchy. Formerly prosperous Midwestern states such as Minnesota had seen annual cash income of farmers fall in 1932 to an average of $141. That same year more than one-half of the state's farms were mortgaged or foreclosed. "The situation produced a general outcry for relief," one observer reported. "In isolated instances mobs of farmers took the law into their own hands and prevented foreclosure sales by force." These sporadic outbreaks indicated the trend and force of feeling among the debtors, and Minnesota's wheat growers made every effort to impress their plight on the state's lawmakers. "When the legislature assembled, a caravan of two or three thousand farmers descended upon St. Paul from southern Minnesota, in an astonishing array of antediluvian automobiles, and swarmed over the capitol, making demands and threats and uttering dire predictions." Three weeks later the Governor addressed an uproarious gathering on the steps of the capitol: "I want to say to the people of Minnesota that if the legislature—the Senate in particular—does not make ample provision for the sufferers in this state . . . I shall invoke the powers that I hold. I shall declare martial law. A lot of people who are now fighting the measures because they happen to possess considerable wealth will be brought in by provost guards. They will be obliged to give up more than they are giving up now."

The Governor ordered sheriffs "to refrain from proceeding with all foreclosure sales until after the legislative sessions." In due course, a bill modeled on New York's postwar Emergency Housing Act, giving courts power to postpone mortgage foreclosures, was passed without a dissenting vote. Debtors now hastened to bring their holdings under its protection, while creditors challenged in the courts this statutory readjustment of the terms of their contracts.

The first test case under the Act concerned one Blaisdell and his wife, who were struggling to pay off a mortgage on their fourteen-room house by letting rooms and keeping boarders. The state's highest court did not question the legislature's action in bowing to desperation. "The members of the legislature," it observed, "come from every community of the state and from all the walks of life. They are familiar with conditions generally in every calling, occupation, profession, and business in the state. Not only they, but the courts, must be guided by what is common knowledge. It is common knowledge that in the last few years land values have shrunk enormously. Loans made a few years ago upon the basis of then going values cannot possibly be replaced on the basis of present values. We all know that when this law was enacted the large financial companies, which had made it their business to invest in mortgages, had ceased to do so. No bank would directly or indirectly loan on real-estate mortgages . . ."

On November 8 and 9, 1933, in faraway Washington, the case was argued in the Supreme Court, and on January 8, 1934, the Justices sustained the Act, 5 to 4 (*Home Building Loan Association* v. *Blaisdell*, 290 U.S. 398, 1934). Chief Justice Hughes, taking advantage of his prerogative, assigned this strategic majority opinion to himself.

The Minnesota statute seemed to fly in the face of the Constitution's categorical imperative—that no state shall pass any law "impairing the obligation of contracts" (Art. I, Sec. 10). Nevertheless the Chief Justice upheld the act by distinguishing between the *obligation* of contract and the *remedy* given by the legislature to enforce that obligation. In short, he tried to demonstrate that the moratorium did not really impair the *obligation* of Minnesota mortgages; the statute only modified the remedy. Article I, Section 10, is qualified, Hughes argued, "by the measure of control which the state retains over remedial processes," and the mortgage contracts themselves are subject to the "reservation of the reasonable exercise of the protective power of the state," which is "read into all contracts as a postulate of the legal order."

The Chief Justice went out of his way to consider the relation of emergency to power. "Emergency does not create power," he said. "Emergency does not increase granted power or remove or diminish the restrictions imposed upon power granted or reserved." Specific constitutional requirements, such as the representation of each state by two senators, are plainly distinguishable, he noted, from the constitutional provisions against impairing the obligation of contracts. The former provision is not affected by emergency;

the latter is. "While emergency does not create power, emergency may furnish the occasion for the exercise of power."

It was this line of reasoning that opened the way for reactionary attack. The priestly dogma of Sutherland's jurisprudence knew no such loopholes, and he took this occasion to say so. "I can only interpret what is said," the dissenter remarked scornfully, "as meaning that while an emergency does not diminish a restriction upon power it furnishes an occasion for diminishing it; and this, as it seems to me, is merely to say the same thing by the use of another set of words, with the effect of affirming that which has just been denied." Sutherland was especially vehement in opposing Hughes's "adaptive" theory of the fundamental law. Invoking historical evidence, he concluded: "The foregoing leaves no reasonable ground upon which to base a denial that the clause of the Constitution now under consideration was meant to foreclose state action impairing the obligation of contracts *primarily and especially* in respect of such action aimed at giving relief to *debtors in time of emergency*." War constituted an emergency, justifying legislative modification of rent leases, to be sure, but ruinous economic depression was not a comparable holocaust. This was no occasion for slackening the stubborn "strength of the fabric" woven by the Fathers. The aging Justice had seen "economic emergencies" before: "The present exigency is nothing new. From the beginning of our existence as a nation, periods of depression, of industrial failure, of financial distress, of unpaid and unpayable indebtedness, have alternated with years of plenty."

Two hundred billion dollars of private credit had been destroyed, a total national income had been reduced from over eighty billions to under forty billions. But to this Supreme Court Justice all such cataclysmic economic chaos was nothing new. Now, as always, recovery must be achieved by "self-denial and painful effort." As the snapper to his forthright dissent, the former Utah Senator challenged: "If the provisions of the Constitution be not upheld when they pinch as well as when they comfort, they may as well be abandoned."

Cardozo and Stone read the Chief Justice's first draft with misgivings so serious that each considered writing a concurring opinion. The former actually prepared a draft, and Stone submitted a long memorandum. In conflict were two fundamentally different conceptions of the Constitution. For Sutherland, a Constitution, in essence, limited rather than granted power. For him, a Constitution that "grows or changes with every passing popular pain, ceases to exist." The views of Stone and Cardozo, on the contrary, resemble Jefferson's. Jefferson believed that "to lose our country by a scrupulous adherence to written law, would be to lose the law itself, with life, liberty, property and all those who are enjoying them with us; thus absurdly sacrificing the ends to the means."

Their approach was also in the tradition of Marshall and Holmes. The opening paragraph of Cardozo's undelivered concurrence quoted Marshall's famous dictum: "We must never forget that it is *a constitution* we are expounding," a constitution "intended to endure for ages to come, and, consequently, to be adapted to the various *crises* of human affairs." Cardozo also included the bold note Holmes struck in 1920: "The case before us must be considered in the light of our whole experience and not merely in that of what was said a hundred years ago." The Minnesota statute, Cardozo admitted, "may be inconsistent with things" which the men of 1787 believed or took for granted, but "their beliefs to be significant must be adjusted to the world they knew. It is not . . . inconsistent with what they would say today. . . ." For them as for us, Cardozo suggested, "the search was for a broader base, for a division that would separate the lawful and forbidden lines more closely in correspondence with the necessities of government."

Cardozo did not undertake to square the Minnesota statute with the literal requirements of Article I, Section 10. He did not rest his case in favor of the moratorium on "the distinction between right and remedy with all its bewildering refinements." The more general provisions of the Fourteenth Amendment were seen as pointing the way "toward a rational compromise between private rights and public welfare. . . . A promise exchanged between individuals," he concluded, "was not to paralyze the state in its endeavor at times of direful crises to keep its life-blood flowing."

Cardozo's attack on Justice Sutherland's deep-freeze dogmas was equally forthright. "A gospel of laissez faire—of individual initiative—of thrift and industry and sacrifice—may be inadequate in the great society that we live in to point the way to salvation, at least for economic life. The state when it acts today by statutes like the one before us is not furthering the selfish good of individuals or classes as ends of ultimate validity. It is furthering its own good by maintaining the economic structure on which the good of all depends." The Chief Justice took over Cardozo's idea almost verbatim.

Stone also threatened to speak out independently if certain of his points were rejected. "I have taken more than the usual time to study your opinion," he wrote, December 13, 1933, "because of the great importance to the public and to the court of the questions involved." Like Cardozo, he wished to elevate the tone of the opinion and focus the argument on the merits of the case:

> I am not inclined to join in so much of the [opinion] . . . as states that the relief afforded could only be of a temporary character. . . . I think we should be meticulous in not making pronouncements with respect to cases other than that before us. Moreover, the statement itself, without definition, has not very much meaning. We may yet have to deal with cases where the moratorium is for longer periods and where the law itself is made applicable for longer periods than those involved in this case; whether they could be regarded as temporary or not is, of course, a relative matter, and other and controlling considerations might come in. Therefore, it seems to me that we should leave ourselves absolutely unhampered by pronouncements which might be taken to affect situations not presented to us in this case.

Continuing, Stone wrote: "I think the part of the opinion which discusses what the Court has sometimes treated as a distinction between obligation and remedy is somewhat confusing and, to some extent, obscures the point with which we have to deal in the present case. The distinction . . . comes to nothing more than a question of degree, and the net result of the cases seems to be unreasonable. Our present case has no complications of this character, since the statute does cut down both obligation and remedy to a material extent, and the sole question is whether private parties, by their contract, may tie the hands of the state so that it is powerless to deal with a problem vital to the Government itself. I think the opinion would gain in power and directness if the discussion of the right-remedy phase were very much condensed or relegated to a footnote."

Why not, Stone suggested, erect the opinion on more realistic foundations? "We are . . . confronted with a problem permeating the entire economic structure, of which Chief Justice Marshall probably never had any conception. A generation or more ago the state was concerned principally with problems affecting the moral and physical well-being of society. When its concern for public morality had led a state to a judgment different from that which had formerly prevailed, this Court could not say that it exceeded constitutional limitations in curtailing a grant to indulge in public lotteries, even though lotteries had long been accepted as legitimate activity. Today, when the whole economic structure of society is threatened with widespread foreclosures, the state has afforded a measure of relief which tends to prevent the impending ruin of mortgagees, as well as mortgagors, and to preserve the stake of the former as well as of the latter in land mortgages, viewed as a form of investment security. . . . It is, I think, desirable to emphasize the special character of the mortgage situation as affects both mortgagors and mortgagees, to show that, looked at collectively, the legislation protects the interest of both and harms neither. Once conceded, as it must be, that the contract clause is not an absolute and unyielding restriction upon the state, such legislation is demonstrated to be so reasonable in character as to be plainly within state competency."

The Chief Justice's opinion, as finally announced, included long passages from the Cardozo draft opinion and from Stone's memoranda. But he kept intact the legalistic distinction between emergency power, thus exposing himself to Sutherland's broadside. From Cardozo came the verbal formulation of the Court's recognition of "the necessity of finding ground for a rational compromise between individual rights and the public welfare"—the passage that commentators praised as embodying juristic statesmanship. But Hughes retained the stultifying arguments to which Stone and Cardozo objected. So equivocal a result dissatisfied Stone. "Probably if I had been doing the writing, I should have presented the matter in somewhat different form," he remarked to a friend. "Just between ourselves I feel it was too long and discursive." Believing that the Court had really done nothing more than it had in the Rent cases, (*Block* v. *Hirsh*, 256 U.S. 135, 1921) Stone felt that the Chief Justice's views could have been expressed more forthrightly.

THE ORIGINS OF DUE PROCESS

Meanwhile a new judicial formula had been found for defeating government action under the police power, now the mainspring of a growing body of legislation. The 1830's had seen the establishment of the public school system; the 1840's witnessed the first steps toward regulation of the liquor traffic, primitive factory legislation, and emancipation of women. The character and volume of social legislation created the need for a new constitutional weapon. Special credit for the invention of that weapon must go to New York—and to the leading case of *Wynehamer* v. *New York* (13 N.Y. 378, 1856).

The defendant, Wynehamer, was indicted and convicted by a common-law jury in the Court of Sessions of Erie County for selling liquor in small quantities contrary to the act, passed April 9, 1855, "for the prevention of intemperance, pauperism and crime." It was admitted that the defendant owned the liquors in question before and at the time the law took effect. But his counsel insisted that he was entitled to an acquittal on the ground, among others, that the statute was unconstitutional and void. The Court invalidated the act as applied to existing stocks of liquor, but the complexity of the issue and the diversity of judicial opinion concerning it is indicated by the fact that the judges split three ways. The volume reporting the case covers over two hundred pages.

Judge Comstock, who spoke for the Court, noted at the very outset that, though "the legislative power" is vested in the legislature, it is subject to special constitutional limitations, "which are of very great interest and importance" in that they prohibit the deprivation of life, liberty, and property without due process of law.

The Justice had thus introduced a constitutional injunction of tremendous but undefined possibilities—"due process." To the lay mind this phrase suggests procedural limitations—that is, if it limits legislative power at all, it does so in terms not of what can be done, but of *how* something must be done. Comstock and the concurring Justices made clear at once that they had something more sweeping in mind. Since the legislature has only limited powers, it cannot encroach, Comstock contended, on the rights of any species of property, even where the action would be of "absolute benefit" to the people of the state. To allow the legislature such a power, even in the public interest, would "subvert the fundamental idea of property." "In a government like ours," Comstock observes, "theories of public good or public necessity may be so plausible, or even so truthful, as to command popular majorities. But whether truthful or plausible merely, and by whatever numbers they are assented to, there are some absolute private rights beyond their reach, and among these the constitution places the right of property."

Two concurring opinions rejected Comstock's notion of "higher law," i.e., of extra-constitutional limitations, and held that the only limits on legislative power are those clearly stated in the Constitution. The legislature, they said, could regulate property, even to the extent of rendering it virtually worthless; but they, too, held that the present act involved destruction rather than regulation, and was therefore void. The form of the declaration—"No person shall be deprived of life, liberty or property without due process of law"— Justice A. S. Johnson commented, "necessarily imports that the legislature cannot make the mere existence of the rights secured the occasion of depriving a person of any of them, *even by the forms which belong to 'due process of law.'* For if it does not necessarily import this, then the legislative power is absolute."

In his dissenting opinion, Justice T. A. Johnson emphasized legislative supremacy except where specifically limited by the Constitution. Judicial review based upon judges' views of what is reasonable would constitute usurpation, a "veto or dispensing power" that does not "pertain to the judicial functions." Said the dissenter:

> The remedy for unjust legislation, provided it does not conflict with organic law, is the ballot box; and I know of no provision of the Constitution nor fundamental principle of government which authorizes the minority, when defeated at the polls, upon the issue involving the propriety of a law, to appeal to the judiciary and invoke its aid to reverse the decision of the majority and nullifying the legislative power.

Johnson suggested that the courts should approach even doubtful legislation with the greatest of restraint, remembering that their primary function is vigilantly and fearlessly to uphold legislative enactments. "The people have a far more certain and reliable security and protection against mere impolitic, overstringent or uncalled-for legislation than courts can ever afford, in their reserved power of changing . . . the representatives of their legislative sovereignty; and to that final and ultimate tribunal should all such errors and mistakes in legislation be referred for correction." As to the rights of property, they had long been subject to popular control; and if they could ever have been enjoyed as a natural right, that right had long since ceased to exist. Without such governmental control of the misuses of property, those putative rights would be superior to liberty itself.

Due process of law also received a different emphasis in Johnson's hands: it must be considered as protecting physical property itself rather than any rights thereof. To proscribe governmental controls that decrease the value of property would, after all, "place the right of traffic above every other right, and render it independent of the power of government." "A government," the dissenting Justice concluded, "which does not have power to make all needful rules with respect to internal trade and commerce, to impose such restrictions upon it as may be deemed necessary for the good of all, and even to prohibit and suppress entirely any particular traffic which is found to be injurious and demoralizing in its tendencies and consequences, is no government."

Impressive support for the Wynehamer decision is found in an anonymous *American Law Magazine* article of July 1843. Written under the title "The Security of Private Property," this paper argued that property needs "every parchment barrier which has been or can be thrown around it." "In a republic, where the legislature . . . is annually elected, and where . . . legislation partakes . . . of the passions and impulses of the moment, it is important to inquire into the extent of the power possessed by the majority to encroach upon the fruits of honest industry, or interfere with the proprietor in his free and undisturbed possession and enjoyment."

"What," the writer asks, "are the general powers of government in a civilized society? Is there no *lex legum*, independent of express Constitutional restrictions?" The answer is cautious, but decisive.

It may be a wide and dangerous door to open to judicial discretion, to say that they shall apply to the question of validity or invalidity of legislative acts, the general principles of just government as laid down by the most eminent jurists and text writers. Yet suppose the legislature to pass a law arbitrarily depriving a citizen of life or liberty, without fault or crime, must we look to the Constitution for an express disaffirmance of such power? There exists a disaffirmance of it, clear, positive, and unequivocal in the words magna carta transferred into the bill of rights, and standing out in bold relief in the . . . Constitution of Pennsylvania. . . . The same provision which secures our lives and liberties against an arbitrary exercise of power . . . extends to our property.

The constitutional protection this writer found so fully supported in authoritative texts was enforceable, he said, "through an independent judiciary." The article concludes with the happy thought that "the reader . . . will lay it aside with the reflection that the liberty of the republican states of America will owe their perpetuity to their courts, executing the supreme will of the people against acts of tyranny and oppression, whether proceeding from the executive or the legislator."

In 1856, the year that the Wynehamer decision was handed down, the Supreme Court of the United States had occasion in *Murray* v. *Hoboken* (18 How. 272) to state the meaning of due process in the Fifth Amendment. Here the Court said that only a process in conflict with a provision of the Constitution, or in conflict with "settled usages and modes of proceeding existing in the common and statute law of England, before the emigration of our ancestors and which are . . . not . . . unsuited to their civil and political conditions" lacked due process. "That all men of that day [1856]," commented the late Judge Charles M. Hough, "had no conception of due process other than a summary description of a fairly tried action at law, is not asserted; but I do submit that reports before the Civil War yield small evidence that there was any professional conviction that it was more than that."

It is also important to note that contemporaneously with the Wynehamer decision, "several other state courts were deciding similar issues in precisely the opposite way, and invoking the police power in justification." Thus, by mid-19th century two great forces were meeting head on: the doctrine of vested rights and the doctrine of the police power. Professor Corwin suggests that as the Civil War was about to break, courts and country were faced with a reincarnation of that old conundrum: what happens when an irresistible force—the doctrine of the police power—meets an immovable object—the doctrine of vested rights? What, moreover, was to be the role of the courts in this situation?

Confronted with legislation enacted under the police power, Corwin suggests that the courts might have done one of two things: surrender the view that rights of property and of contract set absolute barriers against the exercise of public power; or cast about for a new constitutional formula to protect vested rights against regulatory legislative power. Would "due process" serve this purpose? Could a term suggesting procedural limitations only be fashioned into a limitation on the substantive law-making power of legislature? The great significance of the Wynehamer case is that it evoked as early as 1856, twelve years before the adoption of the Fourteenth Amendment, due process of law as a constitutional measure not only of *how*, but of *what* legislative power should be exercised.

X

THE DEVELOPMENT
OF DUE PROCESS

1868

*E*IGHTEEN HUNDRED AND SIXTY-
eight was a critical year in the development of constitutional law
because of two major events. Laissez-faire capitalism was then given
an authoritative legal ideology by the publication of Thomas M.
Cooley's classic work, *Constitutional Limitations*. The Fourteenth
Amendment, adopted that year, provided exponents of laissez-faire
a constitutional text of great potentialities.

For our purposes Cooley's work contains two chapters of special
interest: Chapter 11, entitled "Protection of Property by the Law
of the Land"; and Chapter 16, entitled "The Police Power and the
States." These two chapters constitute a compendium of state constitutional decisions prior to 1868 in which the courts had upheld
the power and the right indicated in the chapter title. "Thus was
the national Supreme Court," Professor Corwin has written, ". . .
supplied with a double set of answers, each duly authenticated by
supporting precedents . . . touching the vital problem of the
relation of legislative power to the property right." So, just at the
time when the practice of inserting a "reservation clause" in state

217

charters lessened the usefulness of the impairment-of-contract clause, the Fourteenth Amendment added another weapon of untold usefulness to the judicial arsenal. Henceforth the battles to protect property rights against state regulation were destined to revolve around "due process."

JUDICIAL RESTRAINT AND THE FOURTEENTH AMENDMENT

Despite the unlimited potentiality latent in the Fourteenth Amendment for the enhancement of the Court's supervisory power, the Justices seemed reluctant at the outset to exploit this new source of authority. In the *Slaughterhouse Cases* (16 Wall. 36, 1873) where a Louisiana law establishing a New Orleans butchering monopoly was challenged, the Court, speaking through Justice Miller, refused to construe the privileges-and-immunities clause of the Fourteenth Amendment as breaking down the distinction between state and national citizenship. The framers' intention was not to confer on the national government the duty of protecting both kinds of citizenship. National citizenship, said Miller, included the right of coming to the seat of the government, the right to enjoy government offices, and the right to government protection on the high seas, whereas state citizenship included, among other rights, the fundamental right to acquire and possess property. Since the rights allegedly infringed in the *Slaughterhouse Cases* were derived from state citizenship, the butchers of New Orleans could not, in Miller's opinion, look beyond the state for protection.

Miller was equally cool to the application of the equal protection and due process clauses. As for equal protection, he doubted its relevance except in cases involving the rights of Negroes. Due process had not yet been the subject of much construction, but under no interpretation he had yet seen could the statute under complaint be held lacking in due process. Miller's narrow view of judicial power grew out of his conception of the Union—"the structure and spirit of our institutions." The Fourteenth Amendment did not (perhaps could not) change "the whole theory of the relations of the State and Federal governments to each other and of both these governments to the people. . . . Such a ruling," Miller said, "would constitute this Court a perpetual censor upon all legislation of the states, on the civil rights of their own citizens, with authority to nullify such as it did not approve."

Four Justices, including Chief Justice Chase and headed by Justice Field, dissented vehemently and at great length. Field said that the issues were "of the gravest importance, not merely to the parties . . . but to the whole country. It is nothing less than the question whether the recent amendments . . . protect the *citizens of the United States against the deprivation of their common rights by state legislation*." [Authors' italics.] Field thought that the amendment was intended "to place the common rights of American citizens under the protection of the national government." The Louisiana act was invalid quite apart from the Fourteenth Amendment. "Grants of exclusive privilege," Field contended, ". . . are opposed to the whole theory of free government, and it requires no aid from any bill of rights to render them void. That only is a free government, in the American sense of the term, under which the inalienable right of every citizen to pursue his happiness is unrestrained, except by just, equal and impartial laws." The Court's narrow construction of the amendment made it, in Field's opinion, a "vain and idle enactment."

Despite Field's protest, the judicial hands-off position was maintained four years later in *Munn* v. *Illinois* (94 U.S. 114, 1877), where a statute fixing rates for grain elevators was challenged. Though privately owned these were declared in the state Constitution to be "public warehouses." Harking back to principles of common law, Chief Justice Waite reasoned that when a man devotes his property to a use in which the public has an interest, the property ceases to be private; it becomes "affected with a public interest," and hence subject to a greater degree of regulation. The legislature, not the Court, was to determine how much regulation was permissible, whether it was arbitrary, and whether the business was so affected. "We know," the Chief Justice observed, "that this is a power which may be abused; but that is no argument against its existence. For protection against abuses by legislatures the people must resort to the polls, not to the Courts." Against this refusal to censor state legislation, dissenting Justice Field protested strongly. He said that this decision was "subversive of the rights of private property." The principles of "free government" fixed absolute limits on legislative power, and these limits could not be altered even by organic law. "There is no magic in the language," Field commented, "though used by a constitutional convention, which can change a private business into a public one." The dissenter recognized the state's power to tax property, to seize it by right of eminent domain and establish restrictions on its use, but he drew the line sharply on price control. Field absolutely denied "the power of any legislature under our government to fix the price which one shall receive for his property of any kind. . . . A tailor's or a shoemaker's shop would still retain its private character, even though the assembled wisdom of the state should declare, by organic act or legislative ordinance, that such a place was a public workshop, and that the workmen were public tailors or public shoemakers. One might as well attempt to change the nature of colors, by giving them a new designation."

Observers were keenly aware of the magnitude of these issues. The *New York Tribune* (March 11, 1877) called the Court's decision in the Granger cases "the broadest possible affirmation of the right of the state to regulate its own commerce, and their importance can hardly be overestimated." The *Tribune* portrayed the legislation and the Court's decision upholding it as "the advance guard of a sort of enlightened socialism." "What seemed 'thieving' and 'brigandage,' " the *Springfield Republic* of March 13, 1877 said, "proves to have been the vindication of the power of the States over all the public interests in its borders, not merely by the decision of the Supreme Court, but by the revolution in the attitude of Legislatures to corporate power—from a servile deference to a sharply critical and almost inquisitorial sovereignty." J. N. Pomeroy, writing in the *American Law Review* of 1883, called the Munn decision

a menace to business and material interests of all kinds. No other decision has ever been made in the course of our judicial history . . . which threatens such disastrous consequences to the future welfare and prosperity of the country. . . . By the demagogues who are conducting the agitation now going on throughout the country, it is confidently appealed to and relied upon to sustain the yet more communistic and destructive legislation which they demand.

For almost a century the existence of the "due process" clause in the Fifth Amendment had not created any serious limitation on the

substance of national legislation. But the clause was no sooner inserted in the Fourteenth Amendment than it became a rallying point
for those who resisted the effort of government to regulate and
control the expanding industrial economy. The issue was sharpened
in *Davidson* v. *New Orleans* (96 U.S. 97, 1878) where the Court sustained, against "due process" objections, an assessment of New Orleans real estate for draining the city's swamps. While concurring
in the Court's ruling, Justice Bradley felt that the decision "narrows
the scope of inquiry as to what is due process more than it should
do." The due process clause, he argued,

> is a restraint on the legislative, as well as on the executive and
> judicial. . . . I think, therefore, we are entitled, under the four-
> teenth amendment, not only to see that there is some process of
> law, but "due process of law," provided by the State law when a
> citizen is deprived of his property; and that, in judging what is
> "due process of law," respect must be had to the cause and object
> of the taking, whether under the taxing power, the power of
> eminent domain, or the power of assessment for local improvements,
> or none of these: and if found to be suitable or admissible in the
> special case, it will be adjudged to be "due process of law"; but if
> found to be arbitrary, oppressive, and unjust, it may be declared to
> be not "due process of law."

This "strange" turn of events, this sudden resort to the constitutional shield of "due process," puzzled Supreme Court Justices
no less than commentators. Speaking for the Court in the Davidson
case, Justice Miller observed:

> It is not a little remarkable that while this provision has been in
> the Constitution of the United States, as a restraint on the au-
> thority of the Federal Government for nearly a century, and while,
> during all that time, the manner in which the powers of that Gov-
> ernment have been exercised has been watched with jealousy, and
> subjected to the most rigid criticism in all its branches, this special
> limitation upon its powers has rarely been invoked in the judicial
> forum or the more enlarged theatre of public discussion. But while
> it has been a part of the Constitution, as a restraint upon the power
> of the State, only a few years, the docket of this Court is crowded
> with cases in which we are asked to hold that state courts and state
> legislatures have deprived their own citizens of life, liberty, or prop-
> erty without due process of law. There is here abundant evidence
> that there exists some strange misconception of the scope of this
> provision as found in the Fourteenth Amendment. In fact, it would
> seem, from the character of many of the cases before us, and the
> arguments made in them, that the clause under consideration is

looked upon as a means of bringing to the test of the decision of this Court the abstract opinions of every unsuccessful litigant in a State Court of the justice of the decision against him; and of the merits of the legislation on which such a decision may be founded.

But what was "remarkable" about the notion that the property right is basic? What was unusual about the view that vested rights set limits on what the government may do, even though those boundaries are not specifically drawn in the Constitution itself? The notion that due process fixes substance as well as procedural limitations on the lawmaking authority was not lacking in respectable support. Writing in 1953, Howard Jay Graham observed: "Americans may be proud and thankful to discover, certainly in these times, that broadened and discretionary due process, far from being an excrescence or tool of ambition, is in reality so deeply enrooted in our national consciousness that its judicial achievement was quite as much a result as a cause of widespread popular usage." Judicial consideration of the substance of legislation was necessary to protect society from popular majorities, "the fear of which," as Professor Corwin reminds us, "lies at the very basis of the whole system of judicial review, and indeed of our entire constitutional system." ("The Supreme Court and the Fourteenth Amendment," 7 *Michigan Law Rev.*, 1908-1909, p. 670.)

Though the Court persisted for a time in its refusal to use the due process clause as a means of censoring state legislation, another decade was to see the views of Field and the other dissenters prevail. Thus the breach left by the Munn and Davidson cases and others in the wall of protection around vested rights was destined to be closed, just as the same breach had been closed by Chief Justice Marshall when he expanded the scope of the contract clause to overcome the decision in *Calder* v. *Bull*. Various forces and factors were joined in this movement.

FACTORS LEADING TO JUDICIAL CENSORSHIP

In 1878, one year after the Munn and Davidson decisions, the American Bar Association was organized. In the first annual address. President E. J. Phelps urged lawyers of the country "to meet on a common ground" and set "their feet on and their hands against all effort to transgress the true limits of the Constitution." By 1881 the Association was embarked on a deliberate and persistent campaign of education designed to reverse the Court's broad conception of legislative power. The chief burden of the Association's campaign was to convince the nation that judges "discover" law rather than "make" it. In the annual addresses of the president and the titles of various papers read, it is evident that the Association stood with Adam Smith for individualism, agreed with Darwin's view of the inevitability of the human struggle, and accepted Herbert Spencer's evolutionary theories of politics. Extracts from addresses reveal such thoughts as "The great curse of the world is too much government"; "Forces which make for growth should be left absolutely free to all"; "Ownership and responsibility are not individual"; "If trusts are a defensive weapon of property interests against the communistic trend, they are desirable"; "Monopoly is often a necessity and an advantage." In 1892, John Randolph Tucker voiced a conviction, fairly widespread among lawyers, that "government regulation was no cure for the ills of the country; it is instead the worst disease which can come." The "young Hercules" would recover "if left free from the paternal doctors to work out his cure by his own self-reliant efforts on his invincible energy."

In the *Princeton Review* for March 1878, Judge Cooley, taking account of the legislative upsurge, had pointed out that, "By far the larger part of all doubtful legislation which the history of the country presents has taken place since the year 1846 when radical ideas began to be characteristic of state constitutions, and the theory that officers of every department should be made responsible to the people after short terms of service, was accepted as a political maxim." Cooley suggested two safeguards against the rising threat of popular power. One was "*The Constitution, if properly construed. . . .* If principles are not fixed and permanent," he wrote, "they are not constitutional." The second was "higher law," "natural law." Cooley treated the "laws" of supply and demand as if they were part of the Constitution itself. Free government could not support any fixing of prices for service, even if monopoly existed. "Does . . . the *mere* fact," he inquired, "that one owns the whole supply of anything, whether it be of a certain kind of goods or of a certain kind of service, confer upon the state the authority to interfere and limit the price he may set upon his wares or his services?" Cooley's defiant answer was that anyone giving an affirmative response should be expected to show how the power may be harmonized with the general "principles of free government." Private monopolists could thus effect regulations of individual rights in ways not open to politically responsible government.

It is difficult to square Cooley's ideas on the requirements of free government with the facts of our history. The volume *Laws and Liberties of Massachusetts*, published in 1648, shows that price-fixing and wage-fixing were quite common in colonial days. Prior to 1787 at least eight of the thirteen states passed laws fixing the prices of almost everything from butter and beans to shoes and steel. This, the late Justice Robert H. Jackson observed, was the atmosphere "in which the fathers of the Constitution were brought up; this is the way they acted when left to their own devices. Is it likely, then, that when they adopted the Fifth Amendment they meant to select for outlawry that form of legislation which fixed wages or prices? And if they had no such intention, did the states which ratified the due process clause of the Fourteenth Amendment understand that they were renouncing the power?"

Whatever the correct answer, it was clear that if the narrow scope of judicial review adopted in the Munn case were to be overcome, lawyers and judges would have to recapture what the Jacksonian revolution had repudiated—their exclusive responsibility for interpreting and enforcing the Constitution. At the first annual Bar Association meeting, President Phelps had deplored the increasing number of instances in which unhallowed hands had been placed upon the ark of the covenant. The Constitution had, Phelps noted, become "more and more a subject to be hawked about the country, debated in the newspapers, discussed from the stump, elucidated by pothouse politicians, and dung-hill editors, scholars in the science of government who have never found leisure for the graces of English grammar, or the embellishment of correct spelling." Exclusive interpretation of the Constitution had to be regained for that "inner sanctum," that "priestly tribe"—the American Bar. "It is . . . upon entrusting to the judicial department of the whole subject of constitutional law, for all purposes," President Phelps pleaded in 1789, "that our government rests."

A shift in the Court's view, as embodied in *Munn* v. *Illinois*, came swiftly. In 1882, Roscoe Conkling made his famous argument in *San Mateo Co. v. South Pacific R.R.* (116 U.S. 138). Conkling, who had been a member of the Joint Congressional Committee that drafted the Fourteenth Amendment in 1866, revealed for the first time a manuscript Journal of the Committee. From this authoritative source he selected extensive quotations to show that he and his colleagues in drafting the equal protection and due process clauses purposefully used the word "person" as including corporations. "At the time the Fourteenth Amendment was ratified," Conkling told the Justices, "individuals and joint stock companies were appealing for Congressional and Administrative protection against invidious and discriminating state and local taxes. . . . Those who devised the Fourteenth Amendment . . . planted in the Constitution a monumental truth to stand foursquare to whatever wind might blow. That truth is but the Golden Rule, so entrenched as to curb the many who would do to the few as they would have the few do to them."

The inference deducible from Conkling's argument is that the Amendment's framers deliberately concealed their purpose to protect corporations by use of the word "persons." On the basis of this inference Charles and Mary Beard and others developed the "conspiracy theory" of the Fourteenth Amendment. With reference to Conkling's argument the Beards wrote:

> In this spirit, Republican lawmakers restored to the Constitution the protection for property which Jacksonian judges had whittled away and made it more sweeping in its scope by forbidding states, in blanket terms, to deprive any person of life, liberty, or property without due process of law. By a few words *skillfully chosen* every act of every state and local government which touched adversely the rights of persons and property was made subject to review and liable to annulment by the Supreme Court at Washington. [Italics added.]

Conkling and his testimony were impressive. In addition to his vital role in drafting the amendment for submission to both houses of Congress, he had twice refused appointment—once the Chief Justiceship—to the Supreme Court itself. For whatever reason, within a few years after his revelations in the San Mateo case, the Court began veering away from the narrow Negro-race protection theory expounded by Miller in the Slaughterhouse cases, away from the narrow conception of judicial review under due process propounded by Waite in *Munn* v. *Illinois*. Yet scholarly research has revealed that Conkling sold the Court a bill of constitutional goods. Writing in 1938, Howard Jay Graham showed that Conkling's interpretation of the Fourteenth Amendment was a fraud, or at least a trick unworthy of a great lawyer. At certain points in his peroration in the San Mateo case, Conkling indicated that surmise, not factual knowledge, was the basis of his theory ("Those who devised the Fourteenth Amendment may have builded better than they knew. . . . To some of them the sunset of life may have given mystical lore"). Graham's conclusion is that Conkling "suppressed" pertinent facts and misrepresented others; that he "deliberately misquoted the Journal [of the Joint Committee] and even arranged his excerpts so as to give his listeners a false impression of the record and his own relation thereto."

Nevertheless, Conkling's argument received strong support. The impending shift for which the dissenters in the Munn and Slaughterhouse cases had argued was evidenced in majority opinions, beginning with *Hurtado* v. *California* (110 U.S. 516, 1884).

In the Hurtado case, Justice Matthews, speaking for the Court, sustained an act of California substituting a prosecutor's information for grand jury indictment against the charge that it violated due process. But he warned:

> The limitations imposed by our constitutional law upon the action of the government, both state and national, are essential to the preservation of public and private rights. . . . The enforcement of these limitations by judicial process is the device of self-governing communities to protect the rights of individuals and minorities . . . against the power of numbers. . . . It would be incongruous to measure and restrict them [general maxims of liberty and justice embodied in due process] by the ancient customary English law; they must be held to guarantee not particular forms of procedure, but the very substance of individual rights to life, liberty and property.

Two years later, in the Railroad Commission cases (116 U.S. 307, 1886), Chief Justice Waite himself warned legislatures that they must not press their rate-making powers too far. "This power to regulate is not a power to destroy," he admonished, "and limitation is not the equivalent of confiscation." Similarly, Justice Harlan, speaking for the Court in *Mugler* v. *Kansas* (123 U.S. 623, 1887), commented: "It does not at all follow that every statute enacted ostensibly for the promotion of these ends [morals and welfare] is to be accepted as a legitimate exertion of the police powers of the state." Legitimacy was to be determined by the Court. "The courts are not bound by mere forms, nor are they to be misled by mere pretenses. They are at liberty—indeed, are under a solemn duty—to look at the substance of things."

THE FOURTEENTH AMENDMENT
JUDICIALLY AMENDED

Three major factors had been at work to effect a change within the Court as to the scope of its power—the Bar Association's propaganda campaign, Conkling's so-called "conspiracy" theory of the Fourteenth Amendment, and the powerful dissenting opinions. In 1887 a fourth element was added—a change in judicial personnel. Between 1877 and 1890 seven Justices who had participated in the Slaughterhouse and Munn cases resigned or died. Field lived on, and in 1888 he was joined by his nephew David J. Brewer and Melville W. Fuller, the latter as Chief Justice. The judicial about-face that soon occurred is the more remarkable in not being clearly foreseen. At the very time the judicial turnover was completed, Charles C. Marshall supplied impressive historical and analytical justification for the Court's resistance to the use of the Fourteenth Amendment as a barrier against social legislation. A lawyer of conservative sympathies, Marshall said that the police power—the power to govern men and things—hitherto exercised by various ruling classes, belonged to the legislature. Property, previously regarded as an absolute right, was also (in Marshall's opinion) legitimately subject to control by the legislature.

"It is clear," Marshall writes,

> that if, according to law, all property affected by a public use or interest, is in its very nature subject to legislative control, then for the legislature to control its use is in no sense to deprive a citizen of such property contrary to the law of the land. What the citizen owns is not absolute property but a *qualified and contingent interest in property*. Control by the legislature is its necessary incident, and such control, when exercised through a statute, is in its very self "due process of law." It is equally clear, for the

same reasons, that such legislative control is not the appropriation of private property to public use. When the legislature exercises such control it does not appropriate property, for up to the extent of such control there is no property.

Two great questions, Marshall commented, had vexed the American people: personal liberty and property. The Dred Scott decision opened the first, the Munn decision the second. Each decision left "a wide section of human rights unprotected by constitutional guaranties." These decisions were both products of divided courts, and both stimulated great controversy and dispute. "In a commercial emergency," Marshall continues, "the oracles of law have been approached. Dumb for almost a century on the questions involved because no inquirer had sought the shrine, they now give forth a response which startles lawyers and laymen and startles them the more they read and examine. For the first time it is appreciated that there has lain dormant for a century a vigorous principle of the Common Law [the police power], an element of Anglo-Saxon government, which in the hands of an aristocracy has often been an instrument of wrong and oppression and which may in the hands of 'the people' effect a despoliation of property-owners surpassing the encroachments of the crown at the worst periods of English history."

Marshall agreed that the implications of the Munn decision were terrifying: "Our boasted security in property rights falls away for the lack of a constitutional guaranty against this sovereign power thus discovered in our legislatures. It is apparent that against the whim of a temporary majority, inflamed with class-prejudice, envy or revenge, the property of no man is safe. And the danger is even greater in an age teeming with shifting theories of social reform and economic science, which seem to have but one common principle —the subjection of private property to governmental control for the good—or alleged good—of the public."

But far from questioning the soundness of the Court's decision in the Munn case, Marshall argued that the doctrine of legislative supremacy is well established, both historically and constitutionally. He recognized, as did J. K. Edsall in 1884, that "there are some things possessed by every state, for the sale of which a valid contract cannot be made. Among these are the police powers of the state."

But Marshall was concerned about the "wide section of human rights" left unprotected. Noting the misguided "storm of criticism emanating from the advocates of 'higher law,'" and featured in dissenting opinions, Marshall thought of the Munn decision as revealing "a defect where all was supposed to be perfection." That defect, he said, could be "properly remedied only by constitutional amendment." "The possibility of retracing steps," he wrote emphatically, "of reversing or distinguishing, or otherwise nullifying [the Munn doctrine] through the courts is put quite beyond possibility."

Six months before Marshall's article saw the light of day what he said must be done by the formal amending process was already accomplished by the Court's decision in *Chicago, Milwaukee and St. Paul R.R. Co.* v. *Minnesota* (134 U.S. 418, 1890). By vote of 6 to 3 the Justices decided that the question of the reasonableness of railroad rates could not be left by the legislature to a state commission, but must be subject to judicial review. The Minnesota Rate decision, rejecting the principle of *Munn* v. *Illinois* decided only thirteen years earlier, thus completed a judicial revolution. The Court had now become what Justice Miller had feared—a "perpetual censor" of state legislation under the due process clause of the Fourteenth Amendment.

Justice Bradley in a vigorous dissent, joined by Justices Gray and Lamar, protested that this decision "practically overrules *Munn* v. *Illinois*." Said Bradley:

> It is urged that what is a reasonable charge is a judicial question. On the contrary it is preeminently a legislative one, involving considerations of policy as well as of remuneration; and is usually determined by the legislature. . . . When the legislature declares that the charges shall be reasonable, or, which is the same thing, allows the common law rule to that effect to prevail, and leaves the matter there, then resort may be had to the courts to inquire judicially whether the charges are reasonable. Then, and not till then, is it a judicial question. But the legislature has the right, and it is its prerogative, if it chooses to exercise it, to declare what is reasonable.

The decision represented, in Bradley's opinion, an assumption of authority on the part of the judiciary, "which, it seems to me with all due deference to the judgment of my brethren, it has no right to make." In a memorable passage, that foreshadowed Justice Stone's classic dissent in *United States* v. *Butler* nearly half a century later, Bradley concluded:

> It is complained that the decisions of the board are final and without appeal. So are the decisions of the Courts in matters within their jurisdiction. There must be a final tribunal somewhere for deciding every question in the world. Injustice may take place in all tribunals. All human institutions are imperfect—Courts as well as commissions and legislatures. . . . It may be that our legislatures are invested with too much power, open, as they are, to influences so dangerous to the interests of individuals, corporations and society. But such is the Constitution of our republican form of government; and we are bound to abide by it until it can be corrected in a legitimate way.

A majority of the Court disagreed, and in so doing overruled an unbroken line of decisions from *Munn* v. *Illinois* on. "It is from that decision," Judge Charles M. Hough has written, "that I date the flood." Or, to vary the figure, this decision started the Justices down "the slippery slope of due process."

The result could hardly have been cause for surprise. In 1875 Justice Miller, who had written a separate opinion in the Minnesota Rate case, had complained:

> It is vain to contend with Judges who have been at the bar the advocates for forty years of railroad companies, and all forms of associated capital, when they are called upon to decide cases where such interests are in contest. All their training, all their feelings are from the start in favor of those who need no such influence.

"I am losing interest in these matters," Miller concluded wearily. "I will do my duty, but will fight no more."

It was a great triumph for lawyers, especially for John W. Cary, counsel for the Chicago, Milwaukee Railroad. But he was still apprehensive. Speaking before the American Bar Association in 1892, Cary declared:

> It is said that socialism is making rapid progress, and we occasionally hear the fearful mutterings of anarchy; but of all the signs of the times which confront us, the most fearful is this disposition of our courts to sanction the lawless violations, by the Legislature, of rights of property secured and guaranteed by the Constitution. . . . The whole matter of fixing prices by the Legislature is unauthorized, and

an attempt at paternal government, which cannot exist under our free constitution. . . .

Now, virtually a superlegislature, the Court proceeded to discharge the heavy political responsibility of judging "right" and "wrong" in matters of public policy. Since "due process" provided no precise or fixed standard, the Court in raising it against legislative action virtually said that, in the opinion of the judges, the act violated abstract principles of justice. The scorn Justice Iredell leveled against natural law as the limitation on legislative power applied equally to "due process." Under its aegis judicial authority was elevated and economic-industrial oligarchy enthroned. The stage was thus set for one of the longest and most bitterly fought contests in American history—political democracy versus economic oligarchy.

Looking back in 1949 on the momentous developments traced in this chapter, Justice Frankfurter remarked:

Adam Smith was treated as though his generalizations had been imparted to him on Sinai and not as a thinker who addressed himself to the eliminations of restrictions which had become fetters upon initiative and enterprise in his day. Basic human rights expressed by the constitutional concept of "liberty" were equated with theories of laissez-faire. The result was that economic views of confined validity were treated by lawyers and judges as though the framers had enshrined them in the Constitution. [Concurring in *A.F. of L.* v. *American Sash and Door Co.*, 335 U.S. 538, p. 543.]

XI

DUE PROCESS
AFTER 1890

$\mathcal{J}$UST AS POLITICAL DEMOCRACY was coming into its own, the Supreme Court, equating the laissez-faire dogma with the Constitution, safeguarded industrial might against "mere numbers, whether organized in trade unions or in legislative assemblies." In the Supreme Court, powerful vested interests had found "a bulwark of defense against the subtle and skillful manipulation of democratic processes to achieve unsanctioned theories." As if to demonstrate that he had learned the lesson speakers before the American Bar Association had tried to teach, Justice Henry Billings Brown interrupted his judicial labors, in 1893, to discuss "The Distribution of Property":

> While enthusiasts may picture to us an ideal state of society where neither riches nor poverty shall exist, wherein all shall be comfortably housed and clad, and what are called the useless luxuries of life are unknown, such a utopia is utterly inconsistent with human character as at present constituted; and it is at least doubtful whether upon the whole it would conduce as much to the general happiness and contentment of the community which excites

the emulation and stimulates the energies, even if it also awakens the envy, of the less prosperous. Rich men are essential even to the well-being of the poor. . . . One has but to consider for a moment the immediate consequence of the abolition of large private fortunes to appreciate the danger which lurks in any radical disturbance of the present social system.

Private property, Justice Brown said, is a mark of civilization, and the pecuniary motive has always been the goad of social progress:

It is the desire to earn money which lies at the bottom of the greatest efforts of genius. The man who writes books, paints pictures, moulds statues, builds houses, pleads causes, preaches sermons, or heals the sick, does it for the money there is in it. . . . The motive which prompted Angelo [sic] to plan the Dome of St. Peter or paint the frescoes of the Sistine Chapel was essentially the same as that which induces a common laborer to lay brick or dig sewers.

Legislation was powerless to effect "any radical change in the social status or in the relations of employees and employers, and even if such change were possible, it would be attended by evils which would inevitably throw the whole system in confusion." Brown must not, however, be regarded as an unregenerate mossback. Though the legislature was helpless to disrupt the foundations of capitalism, it could ameliorate the conditions of labor, and safeguard society against the tyranny of both organized capital and organized labor. "I am by no means satisfied," he wrote, "that the old maxim that the country which is governed least is governed best, may not, in these days of monopolies and combinations, be subject to revision."

That same year Supreme Justice David J. Brewer, somewhat less flexible in his social views than his colleague Brown, addressed the New York State Bar Association on movements of coercion. "I wish to notice," Brewer told the assembled lawyers, "that movement which may be denominated the movement of 'coercion,' and which by the . . . force of numbers seeks to diminish protection to private property, . . . a movement, which seeing that which a man has, attempts to wrest it from him and transfer it to those who have not." This movement expressed itself in two ways: in the improper use of labor organizations to destroy the freedom of the laborer, and legislation controlling the uses of capital. Brewer called this coercion, force. "It is the effort of the many, by the mere weight of numbers, to compel the one to do their bidding. It is a proceeding outside of the law, in defiance of the law; and in spirit and effect an attempt to strip from one that has, that which of right belongs to him— the full and undisturbed use and enjoyment of his own. . . . It is not in the interest of liberty—it is not in the interest of individual or personal rights. It is the attempt to give to the many a control over the few—a step toward despotism."

What should be done; how was justice to be restored? Brewer's answer was simple: "Strengthen the Judiciary."

> The great body of judges are as well versed in the affairs of life as any, and they, who unravel all the mysteries of accounting between partners, settle the business of the largest corporations and extract all the truth from the mass of sciolistic verbiage that falls from the lips of expert witnesses in patent cases, will find no difficulty in determining what is right and wrong between employer and employees, and whether proposed rates of freight and fare are reasonable as between the public and the owners; while, as for speed, is there anything quicker than a writ of injunction?

The major reason for the widespread use of commissions rather than courts to decide conflicts between the majority and the minority was simply that the commissions could be influenced. Commissions "will the more readily and freely yield to the pressures of numbers, that so-called demand of the majority. . . ." But the judge, who knows nothing can disturb his position, "does not hesitate promptly and clearly to 'lay judgment to the line and righteousness to the plummet.'" Judges dispense the eternal verities of justice— they exercise judgment, not will. To those who argued that Brewer's recipe would substitute government by the Judiciary for government by the people, the Justice replies:

> This involves a total misunderstanding of the relations of judges to government. There is nothing in this power of the judiciary detracting in the least from the idea of government of any by the people. The courts hold neither purse nor sword; they cannot corrupt nor arbitrarily control. They make no laws, they establish no policy, they never enter into the domain of popular action. They do not govern. Their functions in relation to the state are limited to seeing that popular action does not trespass upon right and justice as it exists in written constitutions and natural law. . . . I am firmly persuaded that the salvation of the nation, the permanence

of government of and by the people, rests upon the independence and vigor of the judiciary. To stay the waves of popular feeling, to restrain the greedy hand of the many from filching from the few that which they honestly acquired, and to protect in every man's possession and enjoyment, be he rich or poor, that which he hath, demands a tribunal as strong as is consistent with the freedom of human action and as free from all influences and suggestions other than compassed in the thought of justice. . . .

The Court had already begun to discharge the responsibility Brewer claimed for it. But "due process" was a most uncertain measure of "what is right and what is wrong" in matters of public policy. Attempts to offer a standard or at least a rationalization were made, but few were deceived as to the realities of the judicial process. Having plunged into the thicket of judicial rate-making by its decision in the Minnesota Rate case where it expressed a determination to second-guess administrative bodies and the legislative judgment, the Court felt duty bound to provide some guide to its thinking on this complex issue. The real problem at the heart of each case concerned the proper method of ascertaining the rate base upon which earnings were based. In *Smyth* v. *Ames* (169 U.S. 466, 1898) where the Court invalidated Nebraska rate-fixing action, Justice Harlan confessed that "rates could be more easily determined by a commission composed of persons whose special skill, observation and experience qualified them to so handle great problems of transportation as to do justice" between public and railroad investors. Still the Court could not shrink from its constitutional duty. In determining the fair value of the railroad property, Harlan suggested this formula: "Original cost of construction, the amount expended in permanent improvements, the amount and market value of its bonds and stocks, the present as compared with the original cost of construction, the probable earning capacity of the property under particular rates prescribed by statute, and the sum required to meet operating expenses." All these were to be given such weight as may be "just and right in each case," with the possibility that still other factors might be considered. Thus began almost a half-century of judicial law-making based on what Justice Frankfurter has called the "hodge-podge of the rule in *Smyth* v. *Ames* (dissenting in *FPC* v. *Hope Natural Gas Co.*, 320 U.S. 591, 1954).

Once the Court abandoned its previous attitude of judicial toleration, how could the Justices avoid reading their own predilections into the Constitution? The problem was squarely presented in the famous New York Bake Shop case (*Lochner* v. *New York*, 198 U.S. 45, 1905), which involved a state law limiting the hours of employment in bakeries and confectionary establishments to 10 hours a day and 60 hours a week. Only seven years earlier the Court had upheld a Utah law, imposing an 8 hour day on miners or smelters (*Holden* v. *Hardy*, 169 U.S. 366, 1898). Police power legislation of this type could hardly be deemed novel or radical. But bakery workers and mine workers formed different classes, according to the majority in the Lochner case. In this case Justice Peckham's test of "due process" contrasts sharply with that of Holmes in dissent. Peckham invoked that most unscientific criterion, "common understanding." "To common understanding the trade of a baker has never been regarded as an unhealthy one." A few excerpts from the majority opinion suggest deeper motives: "It might be safely affirmed that almost all occupations more or less affect the health. But are we all, on that account, at the mercy of legislative majorities?" "This interference on the part of legislatures of the several states with the ordinary trades and occupations of the people seems to be on the increase." Peckham said he did "not believe in the soundness of the views" in support of such legislation. Nor was he alone in his opposition. Applauding this bold assertion of judicial pre-eminence, the *New York Times* (April 19, 1905) editorialized: "It is most gratifying to observe that the Supreme Court does not allow of the sanctity of any contracts which may have been made between the demagogues in the Legislature and the ignoramuses among the labor leaders in bringing to naught their combined machinations."

Iredell's assertion of 1798 that personal preferences inevitably dominate the judges who invoke natural law concepts seemed to have been fully realized. This case, Justice Holmes said in dissent, was decided "upon an economic theory which a large part of the country does not entertain." Holmes denounced any such use of due process; the Constitution had not enacted Herbert Spencer's Social Statics or any other social or economic theory. Against Peckham's test of "common understanding," Holmes commented, "I think the word 'liberty,' in the Fourteenth Amendment, is perverted when it is held to prevent the natural outcome of a dominant opinion." The legislature was limited by prohibitory words in the Constitution, and by the test of whether "a rational and fair man necessarily would admit that the statute proposed would in-fringe fundamental principles as they have been understood by the traditions of our people and our law." For Holmes, reasonableness of legislative majorities was to be the rule; unreasonableness, the exception. As a judge he was inclined to accept the resultant forces in a democratic society as the "proximate test." "Considerable lati-tude must be allowed for differences of view," the Justice had ob-served in an earlier opinion. "Otherwise a constitution, instead of embodying only relatively fundamental rules of right . . . would become the partisan of a particular set of ethical or economical opinions, which by no means are held *semper ubique et ab omnibus*" (*Otis* v. *Parker*, 187 U.S. 606, 1903, p. 608).

In rejecting the gospel of Herbert Spencer and all other nostrums, in upholding laissez-faire as the guide to judicial action, Justice Holmes started a legend which, in time, was to mark him, quite mistakenly, as a great liberal. Personally Holmes, hardly less than Peckham, was impressed with Spencer's verities. The important fact is that Holmes's deferential approach placed on those who chal-lenged legislative action the almost insuperable task of taking the case completely out of the realm of rational justification.

Justice Harlan, also, dissenting, came to grips more precisely than Holmes with the proper scope of judicial power. Granting, as Peckham did, that "liberty of contract" is subject to such regula-tions as the state may reasonably prescribe for the common good and well-being of society, what are the conditions under which the judiciary may declare regulations in excess of legislative authority and void? "If," Harlan answered, "the end which the legislature seeks to accomplish be one to which its power extends, and if the means employed to that end, although not the wisest or best, are yet not plainly and palpably unauthorized by law, then the Court cannot interfere."

The dissenter was not content, however, to let the matter rest there. Peckham indicated that if a real and substantial relation be-tween the health of bakers and the hours they worked could be shown, the New York act might be sustained. Acting on this sugges-tion and thus meeting the majority on its own grounds, Justice Harlan proceeded to demonstrate by recourse to nonlegal sources (ignored by both Peckham and Holmes) that " 'the labor of the bakers is among the hardest and most laborious imaginable.' " Not only had hours of labor long been "a subject of consideration among civilized people," said Harlan, but "we also judicially know that the number of hours that should constitute a day's labor in particular occupations . . . has been the subject of enactments by Congress and by nearly all the states." Therefore, the New York statute could "not be held to be in conflict with the Fourteenth Amendment, without enlarging the scope of the amendment far beyond its original purpose, and without bringing under the supervision of this court matters which have been supposed to belong exclusively to the legislative departments of the several states when exerting their conceded power to guard the health and safety of their citizens by such regulations as they in their wisdom deem best."

"Let the state alone in the management of its purely domestic affairs," Harlan implored, "so long as it does not appear beyond all question that it has violated the Federal Constitution."

THE BRANDEIS BRIEF

From the Lochner decision Justice Harlan anticipated "consequences of a far-reaching and mischievous character." Reformers shared these forebodings; they realized that if social legislation were to be saved from judicial obscurantism a different approach would have to be made. In 1907 the National Consumers League, learning that the Oregon ten-hour law for women was soon to be contested in the Supreme Court, began a search for outstanding counsel to present the case in support of the Oregon law. Joseph H. Choate, one of the most distinguished and successful lawyers of his time, the man who had successfully blocked the "march of Communism" in the Income Tax Case of 1895, refused a retainer, saying that he saw no reason why "a big husky Irish woman should not work more than ten hours in a laundry if she and her employers so desired." The day after Choate's refusal, Louis D. Brandeis of Boston accepted a retainer and began work on his now famous factual brief.

At the turn of the century judges generally disliked hours of labor regulation, even for women. In 1895 the Illinois Supreme Court invalidated an eight-hour law for women, and in 1907 the New York Court of Appeals set aside a similar law, saying, "When it is sought under the guise of a labor law, arbitrarily as here to prevent an adult female citizen from working any time of day that suits her. . . . It is time to call a halt." The Lochner decision followed this trend. "In our judgment," Peckham had said, "it is not possible *in fact* to discover the connection between the number of hours a baker must work in a bakery and the healthful quality of the bread made by the workman." Brandeis, accepting this challenge, took a bold and unprecedented step: he furnished the Court with the requisite social and economic statistics to *demonstrate* this factual relationship between working hours and public health and safety. Heretofore no lawyer had had confidence in his ability to make the judges see a "reasonable" relation grounded in facts whether they wanted to see it or not. Brandeis had confidence in both himself and the judges.

So, in place of the usual array of legal precedents, Brandeis produced facts and statistics on women's health needs in order to show that the legislation was within the legal principles already enumerated by the Court. Playing down the revolutionary aspects of his brief (*Muller* v. *Oregon*, 208 U.S. 412, 1908), he agreed with Peckham's opinion in the Lochner case that "no law limiting the liberty of contract ought to go beyond necessity." He diverged from Peckham in following the line suggested by Justice Harlan, asserting that "no logic is properly applicable to these laws, except the logic of facts."

Brandeis' brief was revolutionary in bringing to a court disposed to make unsubstantiated economic and social judgments—a power which, one may well argue, it never possessed—a method for performing its task more intelligently and more fairly. His Muller brief contains two pages of conventional legal arguments and over one hundred pages of factual data drawn from the reports and studies of governmental bureaus, legislative committees, commissions on hygiene, and factory inspections—all proving that long hours are, *as a matter of fact*, dangerous to women's health, safety, and morals, and that short hours result in general social and economic benefits.

The ten-hour law was upheld, and Justice Brewer took the unusual step of commenting on Brandeis' novel technique: "It may not be amiss in the present case, before examining the constitutional question, to notice the course of legislation, as well as expressions of opinion from other than judicial sources. In the brief filed by

Mr. Louis D. Brandeis . . . is a very copious collection of all these matters." The remainder of Justice Brewer's comment clearly indicates that he did not consider Brandeis' "facts" conclusive, perhaps not wholly relevant:

> The legislation and opinions referred to in the margin may not be, technically speaking, authorities, and in them is little or no discussion of the constitutional question presented to us for determination, yet they are significant of a widespread belief that woman's physical structure, and the functions she performs in consequence thereof, justify special legislation restricting or qualifying the conditions under which she should be permitted to toil. Constitutional questions, it is true, are not settled by even a consensus of present public opinion. . . . At the same time, when a question of fact is debated and debatable, and the extent to which a special constitutional limitation goes is affected by the truth in respect to that fact, a widespread and long continued belief concerning it is worthy of consideration.

Brewer's opinion in the Muller case, like that of Peckham in the Lochner case, was based essentially on "common knowledge" rather than on the knowledge gained from Brandeis' brief:

> That woman's physical structure and the performance of maternal functions place her at a disadvantage in the struggle for subsistence is obvious. . . . History discloses the fact that woman has always been dependent on man. . . . Some legislation to protect her seems necessary to secure a real equality of right. . . . It is impossible to close one's eyes to the fact that she still looks to her brother and depends upon him. . . . A widespread and long-continued belief concerning [a fact] is worthy of consideration. We take judicial cognizance of all matters of general knowledge. [208 U.S. 412, 421-2, 1908.]

Following the Muller decision, Brandeis was in heavy demand to appear on behalf of hours-of-labor laws in other states. In 1913 Oregon set up an Industrial Welfare Commission to regulate wages, hours, and the safety, health, and welfare of Oregon employees. A minimum wage requirement for women employed in factories and stores was soon announced. When the validity of the act and the orders issued under it were contested, Brandeis filed a brief; later, after the act was sustained in the Oregon Supreme Court, he appeared for the state before the Supreme Court. Brandeis faced the economic argument squarely: low wages were not cheap wages, he said, and wages insufficient to sustain the worker properly were uneconomical. In other words, he tried to show that this type of legislation, far from interfering with the employer's freedom of contract to his financial detriment, really was to his advantage. Those present during Brandeis' oral presentation noted how the original hostility of the Court was visibly reduced as the lawyer proceeded. The 4 to 4 decision (in *Stettler* v. *O'Hara*, 243 U.S. 629, 1917), sustaining the state court, was a substantial victory.

As a result of these decisions a more tolerant judicial attitude was forecast. A new trend, it was thought, had been started as the result of the "brilliant and distinguished service" of one man— Louis D. Brandeis. In *McLean* v. *Arkansas* (211 U.S. 539, 1909) the Court upheld state legislation regulating the payment of wages to miners. For Louis M. Greeley this case was highly significant.

"Note the method of this opinion," Greeley wrote, "its avoidance of mere closet ratiocination, its sticking to the concrete fact. Note above all how carefully the court observes the constitutional limits of its own powers, and how fully it accords to the legislature the powers conferred upon it by the constitution. For the court says, in effect, that the legislatures, not courts, are to decide what the public good requires. . . ." In 1917 the Court even upheld (in *Bunting* v. *Oregon*, 243 U.S. 426) a ten-hour-day law with an overtime provision for men. "There is a contention made," the Court observed, "that the law, even regarded as regulating hours of service, is not either necessary or useful for the preservation of the health of employees in mills, factories and manufacturing establishments. The record contains no facts to support the contention and against it is the judgment of the legislature and the Supreme Court [of Oregon]." From now on the burden of proof was thrown on those who contested regulatory action designed to advance the public weal.

Such "liberalism" was short-lived. Brandeis himself was appointed to the Bench in 1916, but his appointment did little more than balance Wilson's earlier elevation of his Attorney General, James R. McReynolds, to Associate Justice. Within a few years Warren G. Harding succeeded Wilson and named William Howard Taft Chief Justice and George Sutherland Associate Justice. Under such auspices, the prospect for positive government was dim.

STUBBORN THEORY CONQUERS PLIABLE FACTS

Skepticism continued to mark the conservative Justices' attitudes toward facts. In 1921 Justice Holmes cited the "publicly notorious and almost worldwide fact" of housing shortages following World War I to help justify a rent control act for the District of Columbia in *Block* v. *Hirsh* (256 U.S. 135). But four of his colleagues could not see how an emergency could alter the unchanging limitations of the Constitution. In 1923, when Justice Sutherland was confronted with a mass of sociological data in support of the validity of a District of Columbia act regulating women's wages, he brushed all such extra-legal matter aside scornfully as "interesting, but only mildly persuasive" (*Adkins* v. *Children's Hospital*, 261 U.S. 525). Said Sutherland:

> We are asked upon the one hand, to consider the fact that several states have adopted similar statutes, and we are invited upon the other hand to give weight to the fact that three times as many States, presumably as well informed and as anxious to promote the health and morals of their people, have refrained from enacting such legislation. These are all proper enough consideration for a legislative body, since their tendency is to establish the desirability or undesirability of the legislation; but they reflect no legitimate light upon the question of its validity, and that is what we are called upon to decide. The elucidation of that question cannot be aided by counting heads.

"Freedom of contract is the general rule," Sutherland commented in setting aside the wage law, "restraint the exception." The wage and price feature of a contract seemed to enjoy special constitutional sanctity in the eyes of the conservative majority.

Sutherland believed with Thomas M. Cooley that no "right to fix the price of commodities or limit the charge of services can exist as a part of any system of free government." But the Constitution says nothing of freedom of contract, nor of the general rule or exceptions to it. And one looks in vain to the Constitution itself for Sutherland's principle of special sanctity for wage-fixing and price-fixing. "Contract is not specifically mentioned in the text that we have to construe," Holmes said in dissent. "It is merely an example of doing what you want to do, embodied in the word liberty." "But," he continued, "pretty much all law consists in forbidding men to do some things that they want to do and contract is no more exempt from law than other acts." Chief Justice Taft, like Justice Holmes, had supposed "that *Lochner* v. *New York* . . . would be allowed a deserved repose." "It is not the function of this Court," the Chief Justice pointedly observed, "to hold congressional acts invalid simply because they are passed to carry out economic views the Court believes to be unwise or unsound."

In 1923 the Court also narrowed the scope of the concept "business affected with a public interest," a phrase the Justices had found useful in rationalizing rather extreme forms of state regulation. Chief Justice Taft, speaking for the majority in *Wolff Packing Co.* v. *Court of Industrial Relations* (262 U.S. 522, 1923) said that the legislature's declaration of the fact was not conclusive.

The case involved a Kansas statute, establishing a Court of Industrial Relations empowered to fix wages and other terms of employment in a number of vital industries declared to be "affected with a public interest." By sharply defining the formula, Taft limited its applicability. Such businesses fell into three categories: public utilities carried on under the authority of a public grant of privileges; businesses traditionally regulated, such as inns and grist mills; businesses which, though not "public" at their inception, may fairly be said to have become so through changed conditions. These categories had all but crystallized, except for the third. It presented a slight possibility of expansion—a majority of the Supreme Court so willing. The matter of determining the existence of a "public interest" the Chief Justice said, had always been "a subject of judicial inquiry."

Taft's contempt for whatever facts Kansas might produce to justify price regulation of butchering and other activities was expressed in the sweeping statement: "It has never been supposed, since the adoption of the Constitution, that the business of the butcher, or the baker, the tailor, the wood chopper, the mining operator or the miner was clothed with such a public interest that the price of his product or his wages could be fixed by state regulation." Yet the Justices three years earlier (*Green* v. *Frazier*, 253 U.S. 233, 1920) had upheld a series of North Dakota acts setting up a comprehensive scheme of public ownership of utilities and industries against the charge that taxation for these purposes was not a "public purpose" and therefore violated due process. Speaking through Justice Day, the Court took the position that the due process clause did not empower the Supreme Court to interfere with a declaration of the "people, the legislature, and the highest court of the state" that the purpose was of a "public nature."

In later cases, notably *Jay Burns & Co.* v. *Bryan* (264 U.S. 504, 1924), facts proved to be a double-edged sword. In this case, involving a Nebraska statute fixing the weight of loaves of bread to prevent fraud, each side confronted the Court with equally competent experts. Before the case was disposed of, the Justices themselves had achieved considerable competence in the science (or art) of bread-making. The seven Justices of the majority who denied the validity of the law, were able to cite facts as glibly as Brandeis in dissent.

This experience may have shaken Brandeis' reliance on facts in the judicial process. Six years before, the Court's decision outlawing state regulation of employment agencies had evoked from him the view that, "Whether a measure relating to the public welfare is arbitrary or unreasonable, whether it has no substantial relation to the end proposed is obviously not to be determined by assumptions or by *a priori* reasoning. The judgment should be based upon a consideration of relevant facts, actual or possible—*Ex facto juris oritur.* That ancient rule must prevail in order that we may have a system of living law." (*Adams* v. *Tanner*, 244 U.S. 590, 1917.) Similarly in the Jay Burns Baking case, he began by pointing out that the legislation under review had been passed after "prolonged discussion." "Facts" tended to show that the legislators had not been unreasonable in believing that prohibition of excess weights was necessary to protect buyers of bread from imposition and honest dealers from unfair competition. At this point the Justice appears to take the position stated by Holmes in his classic Lochner dissent:

> With this conflicting evidence, we have no concern. It is not our province to weight evidence. Put at its highest, our function is to determine, in the light of all facts which may enrich our knowledge and enlarge our understanding, whether the measure, enacted in the exercise of an unquestioned police power and of a character inherently unobjectionable, transcends the bounds of reason. That is, whether the provision as applied is so clearly arbitrary or capricious that legislators acting reasonably could not have believed it to be necessary or appropriate for the public welfare.

To decide, as a fact, that the prohibition of excess weights "is not necessary for the protection of the purchasers against imposition and fraud by short weights," that is "is not calculated to effectuate that purpose"; and that it "subjects bakers and sellers of bread" to heavy burdens, is, in my opinion, an excise of the powers of a super-legislature—not the performance of the constitutional function of judicial review.

Those inclined to cite Brandeis as authority for the Court's reliance on extra-legal data, as in the Segregation decisions of 1954, may have less support in his constitutional jurisprudence than is usually supposed. In the decision-making process facts are important. He would therefore open "the priestly ears" to the call of extra-legal voices, and doubtless would have concurred in Stone's judgment of 1936 as to the need for "an economic service—a small group of men, who have had some training as economists and statisticians, who would be qualified to assemble material for use of the Court." But in man's eternal pursuit of the more exact, there are facts and facts. As a Supreme Court Justice he was content, except in dissent, to follow "traditional policy"—"to presume in favor of constitutionality until violation of the Constitution is proved beyond all reasonable doubt." Burden of proof to the contrary was thus thrown on the defendant.

All this suggests the limitations of facts as a measure of due process. Social and economic data rarely exhibit the convincing proof usually afforded by scientific demonstrations in a laboratory. One can never be sure that all the facts are assembled; and even a full set of facts rarely points to only one conclusion. Brandeis himself realized this when asked by a friend, "How can you be so sure that a particular course of action is the right one?" Brandeis replied, "When you are 51 per cent sure, then go ahead." In other words, a government that had to possess the certainty of the physical scientist before taking action would be paralyzed.

Once the point of John Stuart Mill's truism that "facts do not speak for themselves, they must be interpreted" became apparent, once judges began to select their own facts as preference dictated, it was clear that when facts, however voluminous, are confronted with a "stubborn theory," it is the latter that usually wins. When dogmas and doctrines control a judge's thought, a formidable block is set against the entrance of facts into his mind. "Facts," as Professor Morris R. Cohen has said, "are more pliable than stubborn theories.

Facts can be ignored, explained away, or denied. But theories are mental habits which cannot be changed at will." In law, as in other fields, facts are moulded by the theories into which they have to fit.

On the altar of stubborn theory, and in the face of its own settled principle of "presumption of constitutionality," the Court had fashioned the paralyzing rule that "freedom is the rule, regulation is the exception." By a narrow margin the Justices singled out the price and wage feature of a contract as its "heart," and therefore entitled to special constitutional immunity. That category of business which, by changed circumstances, became "affected with a public interest" was by 1923 for all practical purposes closed. Various state statutes—a New York act designed to protect the public against theatre ticket scalpers (*Tyson* v. *Banton*, 273 U.S. 418, 1927), a New Jersey statute to protect employees from the rascality of private employment agencies (*Ribnik* v. *McBride*, 277 U.S. 350, 1928)—fell under the ban of one or the other of these judge-made formulas. Justice Holmes, supported by Justices Brandeis and Stone, reacted strongly to all such judicial obtuseness.

"To say that only those businesses affected with a public interest may be regulated," Stone commented, "is but another way of stating that all those businesses which may be regulated are affected with a public interest." Hence to use this formula as a basis of judicial decision was only to beg the question to be decided. Probing more deeply into what lay back of the majority's intransigence, Holmes observed:

> We fear to grant power and are unwilling to recognize it when it exists. . . . The police power often is used in a wide sense to cover and . . . apologize for the general power of the Legislature to make a part of the community uncomfortable by a change.
>
> I do not believe in such apologies. I think the proper course is to recognize that a State Legislature can do whatever it sees fit to do unless it is restrained by some express prohibition in the Constitution of the United States or of the State, and that Courts should be careful not to extend such prohibitions beyond their obvious meaning by reading into them conceptions of public policy that the peculiar Court may happen to entertain. . . . The truth seems to me to be that, subject to compensation when compensation is due, the Legislature may forbid or restrict any business when it has a sufficient force of public opinion behind it. [*Tyson* v. *Banton*, 273 U.S. 418, 1927.]

The majority was of a different persuasion. In 1932, Justice Sutherland led the Court in setting aside an Oklahoma statute designed to prevent entrepreneurs during economic depression—an "emergency more serious than war"—from entering an already hopelessly crowded ice business. Against this decision, Brandeis, again joined by Holmes and Stone, was moved to exclaim, "If we would guide by the light of reason, we must let our minds be bold" (*New State Ice Co.* v. *Liebmann*, 285 U.S. 262). To the dissenters, the most hopeful way to make the Constitution a workable instrument of government was that charted by Chief Justice Morrison W. Waite in the Munn opinion of 1877.

THE DECLINE OF SUBSTANTIVE DUE PROCESS

Two cases decided in 1934 indicated a return to that position. The Blaisdell case (*Home Building and Loan Assn.* v. *Blaisdell*, 290 U.S. 398), upholding a Minnesota emergency statute, postponing the foreclosure of farm loans, has already been considered. In *Nebbia* v. *New York* (291 U.S. 502), the Court sustained a New York statute fixing minimum and maximum milk prices. Justice Roberts, rejecting the old "business affected with a public interest" concept as a limitation on state action, observed: "There is no closed class or category of businesses affected with a public interest. The function of the Court . . . is to determine in each case whether circumstances vindicate the challenged regulation as a reasonable exertion of governmental authority or condemn it as arbitrary or discriminatory." Concerning the high barrier Justice Sutherland had erected about wages and prices, Roberts observed: "The due process clause makes no mention of sales or of prices any more than it speaks of business or contract. . . . The thought seems nevertheless to have persisted that there is something peculiarly sacrosanct about the price one may charge for what he makes or sells." Declaring that "the power to promote the general welfare is inherent in government," the majority upheld price regulation, quite apart from the emergency.

But Justice McReynolds in dissent seemed to think that the legislation somehow gained support as an emergency measure. Sounding the usual stoicism in the face of economic hardship, he said:

The exigency is of the kind which inevitably arises when one set of men continue to produce more than all others can buy. The distressing result to the producer followed his ill-advised but voluntary effort. . . . If here we have an emergency sufficient to empower the legislature to fix sales prices, then whenever there is too much or too little of an essential thing—whether of milk or grain or pork or coal or shoes or clothes—constitutional provisions may be declared inoperative. . . . If now liberty or property may be struck down because of difficult circumstance, we must expect that hereafter every right must yield to the voice of an impatient majority when stirred by distressful exigency. . . . Certain fundamentals have been set beyond experimentation; the Constitution has released them from control by the State.

"With the wisdom of the policy adopted," Justice Roberts had said, "the Courts are both incompetent and unauthorized to deal." "But plainly," Justice McReynolds retorted, "I think this Court must have regard to the wisdom of the enactment."

Both the Blaisdell and Nebbia cases were decided by vote of 5 to 4, and in 1936 (*Morehead* v. *New York ex rel. Tipaldo*, 298 U.S. 587) the Justices returned, in the face of these more recent rulings, virtually to the discredited Adkins precedent of 1923. Nevertheless, it was soon evident that the Nebbia decision had marked the beginning of the end of "due process" as a substantive limitation on legislation affecting economic rights. The death blow came in *West Coast Hotel Co* v. *Parrish* (300 U.S. 379, 1937) which sustained a Washington state statute fixing minimum wages for women and minors.

It had been a long, hard struggle. New York had tried to correct the error Justice Sutherland found in the District of Columbia statute declared invalid in 1923, but the effort proved in vain. In *Morehead* v. *Tipaldo* (298 U.S. 587, 1936) the Court set aside the New York Act on the authority of the Adkins case. Chief Justice Hughes, more generous than the majority in his estimate of New York's effort to avoid the pitfall of unconstitutionality, dissented, but only because there were, he said, "material differences" in the Adkins and Tipaldo cases. Taking exception to the narrow basis of Hughes's dissent, Stone wrote in a separate opinion:

> While I agree with all the Chief Justice has said, I would not make the differences between the present statute and that involved in the Adkins case the sole basis of decision. I attach little importance to

the fact that the earlier statute was aimed only at a starvation wage
and that the present one does not prohibit such a wage unless
it is also less than the reasonable value of the service. Since neither
statute compels employment at any wage, I do not assume that
employers in one case, more than in the other, would pay the
minimum wage if the service were worth less.

In words directed to Hughes's dissent quite as much as to the
majority, Stone continued:

> The vague and general pronouncement of the Fourteenth Amend-
> ment against deprivation of liberty without due process of law is a
> limitation of legislative power, not a formula for its exercise. It does
> not purport to say in what particular manner that power shall be
> exerted. It makes no fine spun distinctions between methods which
> the legislature may, and which it may not, choose to resolve a
> particular problem of government. Unless we are now to construe
> and apply the Fourteenth Amendment without regard to our
> decisions since the Adkins case, we could not rightly avoid its re-
> consideration even if it were not asked. We should follow our
> decision in the Nebbia case and leave the selection and the method
> of solution of the problems to which the statute is addressed where,
> it seems to me, the Constitution has left them, to the legislative
> branch of the government.

In the West Coast Hotel case Hughes took the broader position
Stone had advocated in the Tipaldo case. The Chief Justice discovered (this was after the President had introduced his Court-
packing proposal) that the Constitution does not speak of "liberty
of contract." His discovery marked a break with Justice Sutherland
that had not been recognizable in the Tipaldo case. "To sustain the
individual freedom of action contemplated by the Constitution,"
Justice Sutherland had observed in the Adkins case, "is not to strike
down the common good but to exalt it." In no other way could the
"good of society as a whole" be served. After having by inference
sanctioned Sutherland's view only a year earlier, Chief Justice
Hughes now interpreted the "freedom" guaranteed by the Constitution as "*liberty in a social organization* which requires the protection of law against the evils which menace the health, safety,
morals and welfare of the people." This broad concept of liberty
suggests that the right guaranteed by the Constitution can be infringed by forces other than government, and that government may
properly intervene to safeguard the individual against them.

The theory on which the Adkins case rested was finally expressly discredited. Thereafter a long list of precedents were ignored, overruled, or whittled away. In treating the complex subject of rate regulation the Court adopted a more generous attitude toward the actions of state and national officials. "The Constitution does not bind rate-making bodies to the service of any single formula or combination of formulas," the Court concluded in 1942 (*Federal Power Commission* v. *Natural Gas Pipeline Co.*, 315 U.S. 575). "If the total effect of the rate order cannot be said to be unjust and unreasonable, judicial inquiry . . . is at an end." In 1944 the Court abandoned the confused but stringent standards set forth in *Smyth* v. *Ames* (169 U.S. 466, 1898), and agreed to accept administratively determined rates (*Federal Power Commission* v. *Hope Natural Gas Co.*, 320 U.S. 591). Where former due process decisions had balked state and national regulation of social and economic matters, the reconstituted Court made it clear that a different judicial philosophy was to prevail. Thus, when Justice Frankfurter, dissenting from the Court's opinion in the Hope Natural Gas case, declared that "congressional acquiescence to date in the doctrine of *Chicago, Milwaukee and St. Paul Railroad* v. *Minn.* . . . may fairly be claimed," Justices Black and Murphy wrote a brief opinion solely to take exception "to what is patently a wholly gratuitous assertion as to constitutional law in the dissent of Mr. Justice Frankfurter." "That was the case," Black said of the Chicago, Milwaukee decision, "in which the majority of this Court was finally induced to expand the meaning of 'due process' so as to give courts power to block efforts of the state and national governments to regulate economic affairs." Castigating Frankfurter for ignoring his oft-professed judicial self-restraint, Black and Murphy declared that the Court had "not always fully embraced that principle [of broad review as established in the Minnesota Rate case] and we have never acquiesced in it, and do not now."

Speaking for the Court five years later, Justice Black declared that "due process" as a substantive limitation was rejected "at least as early as 1934, when the Nebbia case was decided." Since then the Court had "consciously returned closer and closer to the earlier constitutional principle" that the states may regulate injurious practices, so long as specific constitutional provisions or federal laws are not thereby violated. "Under this constitutional doctrine," Black observed, "the due process clause is no longer to be so broadly construed that the Congress and state legislatures are put in a strait jacket when they attempt to suppress business and industrial conditions which they regard as offensive to the public welfare" (*Lincoln Federal Labor Union* v. *Northwestern Iron and Metal Co.*, 335 U.S. 525 1949, pp. 536-37).

In the process of achieving this result, the Court had to uproot several well-established precedents. *Olsen* v. *Nebraska* (313 U.S. 236, 1941) overruled *Ribnik* v. *McBride* (277 U.S. 350, 1928). The earlier cases of *Adair* v. *United States* (203 U.S. 161, 1908) and *Coppage* v. *Kansas* (236 U.S. 1, 1915) where the Court had invalidated laws outlawing "yellow-dog" clauses in employment contracts (clauses by which employees agreed either to withdraw from or not to join labor unions), were overturned by *Phelps Dodge* v. *N.L.R.B.* (313 U.S. 177, 1941). *State Tax Commission of Utah* v. *Aldrich* (316 U.S. 174, 1942) ended the use of due process to frustrate double taxation by the states of intangible property (*First National Bank of Boston* v. *Maine*, 284 U.S. 312, 1932).

It would be extreme to say that the Court has completely abandoned its supervisory role. Even judges most tolerant of commercial regulations have discovered a point beyond which regulation becomes the taking of property without "due process." (See Justice Holmes in *Pennsylvania Coal Co.* v. *Mahon*, 260 U.S. 393, 1922, and Justice Brandeis in *Thompson* v. *Consolidated Gas Utilities Corp.*, 300 U.S. 55, 1937.) But recent decisions point strongly toward the hands-off position long advocated by Holmes, Brandeis and Stone. In upholding for a unanimous Court a congressional act authorizing a land redevelopment program for the District of Columbia, Justice Douglas wrote:

We deal . . . with what traditionally has been known as the police power. An attempt to define its reach or trace its outer limits is fruitless, for each case must turn on its own facts. The definition is essentially the product of legislative determinations addressed to the purposes of government, purposes neither abstractly or historically capable of complete definition. Subject to specific constitutional limitations, when the legislature has spoken, the public interest has been declared in terms well-nigh conclusive. In such cases the legislature, not the judiciary, is the main guardian of the public needs to be served by social legislation, whether it be congress legislating concerning the District of Columbia or the states legislating concerning local affairs. . . . The concept of the public wel-

fare is broad and inclusive. . . . The values it represents are spiritual as well as physical, aesthetic as well as monetary. It is within
the power of the legislature to determine that the community
should be beautiful as well as healthy, spacious as well as clean,
well-balanced as well as carefully patrolled. [*Berman* v. *Parker*, 348
U.S. 28, 1954, p. 32].

The District Court rebelled against an Oklahoma act designed to
raise professional standards by prohibiting anyone from fitting lenses
to a face, or duplicating or replacing into frames, lenses or other
optical appliances, except on a doctor's written prescription. The
Supreme Court reacted more tolerantly:

> The Oklahoma law may exact a needless, wasteful, requirement
> in many cases. But it is for the legislature not the courts, to balance
> the advantages and disadvantages of the new requirement. . . . The
> legislature might have concluded that the frequency of occasions
> when a prescription is necessary was sufficient to justify this regu-
> lation of fitting of eyeglasses. . . . The law need not be in every
> respect logically consistent with its aims to be constitutional. It is
> enough that there is an evil at hand for correction, and that it
> might be thought that the particular legislative measure was a
> rational way to correct it. [*Williamson* v. *Lee Optical Co.*, 348
> U.S. 482, 1954, p. 485. To the same effect, see *Day-Brite Lighting,
> Inc.* v. *Missouri*, 342, U.S. 421, 1952].

Justice Frankfurter made short shrift of the constitutional objections to a Michigan law forbidding female bartenders unless "she
be the wife or daughter of the male owner of such an establishment." "Beguiling as the subject is," Frankfurter commented, "it
need not detain us long. . . . To ask the question is to answer it.
. . . Michigan could beyond question forbid all women from
working behind bars." The Justice conceded that times have
changed; women have now achieved "virtues" that men long claimed
as their "prerogatives." They now indulge in the vices men have
long practiced, but "The constitution does not require legislatures
to reflect sociological insight or shifting social standards, any more
than it requires them to keep abreast of the latest scientific standards." (*Goesaert* v. *Cleary*, 335 U.S. 464, 1948, p. 466.)

It had been clear since 1943 as Justice Jackson then said, that
"The laissez-faire concept or principle of noninterference has
withered at least as to economic affairs, and social advancements
are increasingly sought through closer integration of society and

through expanded and strengthened governmental controls." Nor is laissez-faire the only dogma to pass into judicial limbo. "It is equally immaterial," the Court ruled in 1939, "that such state action may run counter to the economic wisdom either of Adam Smith or of J. Maynard Keynes, or may be ultimately mischievous even from the point of view of avowed state policy" (*Osborn* v. *Ozlin*, 310 U.S. 53, 1939, p. 62). "It may commend itself to a state," the Court said on another occasion, "to encourage a pastoral instead of an industrial society. That is its concern and its privilege" (*Freeman* v. *Hewitt*, 329 U.S. 249, 1946, p. 242).

Justice Stone had expressed the new approach. Speaking for the Court in *United States* v. *Carolene Products Co.* (304 U.S. 144, 1938), where an act of Congress prohibiting the shipment of filled milk was upheld against due process, as well as against other objections, he said: "The existence of facts supporting the legislative judgment is to be presumed, for regulatory legislation affecting ordinary commercial transactions is not to be pronounced unconstitutional unless in the light of the facts made known or generally assumed it is of such a character as to preclude the assumption that it rests upon some rational basis within the knowledge and experience of the legislators." In contrast to this expression of extreme judicial tolerance, Stone added in a footnote, "There may be narrower scope for operation of the presumption of constitutionality when legislation appears on its face to be within a specific prohibition of the Constitution, such as those of the first ten amendments, which are deemed equally specific when held to be embraced within the Fourteenth." This shift in constitutional theory had been preceded by a change in political theory. In the future, as we shall see, due process was to be primarily a limitation on state legislation affecting the great individual freedoms of press, of religion, and of speech, and the measure of proper legal procedure.

XII

EQUAL PROTECTION
OF LAWS

I N 1937-41, WHEN THE RECON-
stituted Supreme Court minimized due process as a substantive
safeguard for property rights, "equal protection" entered a period
of tremendous growth, climaxed in 1954 by the Court's decision
abolishing segregation in public school systems. There was little in
the Court's interpretation of the clause in its first 70 years to suggest this dramatic development, attributable both to vastly changed
circumstances and a more progressive judicial view of the rights of
minorities.

One of the most persistent ideas attending the proposal and ratification of the Fourteenth Amendment was that the states defeated
in war should be deprived constitutionally of their power to discriminate against the emancipated Negroes and their white pro-
tectors. From first draft to last, all legislative formulations of the
Amendment contained a clause embodying the concept of equal
protection. Its advocates viewed the clause as an answer to those
persons, including President Johnson, who had expressed serious

doubts concerning the constitutionality of the Civil Rights Bill of 1866, which, with its successors of 1870 and 1875, attempted to give Negroes the same protection of civil rights as white persons enjoyed. (The acts of 1866 and 1870 guaranteed equality of legal status and voting rights against state action; the act of 1875 placed the right to equal enjoyment of public inns, conveyances, and amusements, regardless of race, within the protection of federal law.) "Equal protection" expressed the desire, as Congressman Garfield, later President, put it, to "lift that great and good law [Civil Rights Act of 1866] above the reach of political strife" (*Globe*, p. 2462). "Whatever law punishes a white man for a crime," Congressman Stevens declared, "shall punish the black man precisely in the same way and to the same degree. Whatever law protects the white man shall afford 'equal' protection to the black man" (*Globe*, p. 2459). In the Senate, Howard of Michigan, one of the Amendment's sponsors, explained: "This abolishes all class legislation in the states and does away with the injustice of subjecting one caste of persons to a code not applicable to another" (*Globe*, p. 2766).

Yet, even before enactment of the 1875 Civil Rights Act the Supreme Court had refused to construe the Fourteenth Amendment as altering the existing design of federalism (*Slaughterhouse Cases*, 16 Wall. 36, 1873). Certain rights were attributable solely to state citizenship, and were not transformed by the adoption of the post-Civil War Amendments. Nevertheless, while denying the application of the equal protection clause to the Louisiana butchering monopoly, Justice Miller stated that the "pervading purpose" of the Civil War amendments was to achieve the "freedom of the slave race, the security and firm establishment of that freedom, and the protection of the newly-made freeman and citizen from the oppressions of those who had formerly exercised unlimited dominion over him." Miller doubted that the equal protection clause could have any application except in cases involving the rights of Negroes.

But when in 1883 the Court was confronted with Congressional legislation designed to guarantee equal protection of the laws to Negroes by making it a misdemeanor to deny any person equal rights and privileges in inns, theaters and on transportation facilities, it balked at giving the clause a positive meaning (*Civil Rights Cases*, 109 U.S. 3). By reading the first and fifth sections of the Fourteenth

256

Amendment to mean merely that Congress could pass legislation to supersede discriminatory state legislation and official acts (a power similar to that of judicial review), and could not legislate against private acts of a discriminatory character, it preserved the existing federal system at the expense of implementing the principle of equal protection of laws. Bradley's opinion for the Court seemed to assume that the then existing laws of all states required innkeepers and public carriers to furnish accommodations to all unobjectionable persons who applied for them, and further, that anyone refused accommodations had an adequate remedy under state law. Harlan, dissenting, treated the right to such accommodations as "legal" rather than "social," and argued realistically that this decision meant in practice the continuation of discrimination under the tolerant eyes of the state.

"SEPARATE BUT EQUAL"

It was essential, however, for the states to have an acceptable legal principle to support the policy of holding Negroes in their former status. The answer was soon found in laws requiring segregation of the white and colored races under the formula "separate but equal." An early Supreme Court decision had invalidated a state statute forbidding segregation on steamboats and other common carriers on the ground that interstate commerce required a uniform rule (*Hall* v. *DeCuir*, 95 U.S. 485, 1878). But the Court now accepted laws requiring segregation on common carriers within a state on the theory that they were police power regulations affecting purely intrastate commerce and did not burden interstate commerce unreasonably (*Louisville N.O. & T.R. Co.* v. *Mississippi*, 133 U.S. 587, 1890). Justice Harlan again dissented, contending that *Hall* v. *DeCuir* made such segregation on carriers invalid. "Separate but equal" received the Supreme Court's formal approval in *Plessy* v. *Ferguson* (163 U.S. 537, 1896). Here a Louisiana statute requiring separate but equal accommodations on railroads was upheld under the police power as a measure designed to preserve public peace and good order.

In an utterance rarely equaled for irony, Justice Brown asserted in his Plessy opinion for the Court that the fallacy of the (Negro) plaintiff's argument consisted in his "assumption that the enforced separation of the two races stamps the colored race with a badge of inferiority. If this be so, it is not by reason of anything found in the act, but solely because the colored race chooses to put that construction upon it." To Brown it was clear that although the object of the Fourteenth Amendment was undoubtedly to enforce the absolute equality of the two races before the law "in the nature of things it could not have been intended to abolish distinctions based upon color, or to enforce social, as distinguished from political equality, or a commingling of the two races upon terms unsatisfactory to either." This failed to satisfy Harlan, who, dissenting alone, insisted that the "thin disguise of 'equal' accommodations" misled no one.

Moreover, in spite of its willingness expressed ten years earlier in *Yick Wo* v. *Hopkins* (118 U.S. 356, 1886) to look behind the law and examine its practical administration (the Yick Wo case resulted in the invalidation of a San Francisco laundry building ordinance that appeared designed to eliminate Chinese owners from the laundry business), the Supreme Court was unwilling or unprepared to examine the factual basis of lower federal or state court findings that separate facilities for Negroes were in fact "equal."

As a result "separate but equal," came to mean in practice "separate but unequal," as Southern states assumed the uneconomic burden of providing duplicate facilities for education and other public services, and private organizations and enterprises, operating under laws requiring segregation, either excluded Negroes entirely, or accepted them on a separate basis. In virtually all instances, the assumption of the racial inferiority of the Negro that underlay both public and private action, as well as the higher cost of truly equal treatment, meant that schools, inns, train coaches, and recreation facilities for whites were superior in quality to those for Negroes.

It was not until the late 1930's that the Court began to give serious attention to the "equality" requirement. In 1938 the Court invalidated a law under which Lloyd Gaines, a Negro applicant, was refused admission to the School of Law of the State University of Missouri (*Missouri ex rel. Gaines* v. *Canada*, 305 U.S. 337, 1938). Missouri made funds available to Gaines and other qualified Negro applicants to finance their legal education in schools of adjacent states that offered unsegregated educational facilities, and argued that by this action it was meeting the "separate but equal" requirement. Chief Justice Hughes, for the majority of seven, disposed of the state's contention very briefly:

> The basic consideration is not as to what sort of opportunities other States provide, or whether they are as good as those in Missouri, but as to what opportunities Missouri itself furnishes to white students and denies to negroes solely upon the ground of color. The admissibility of laws separating the races in the enjoyment of privileges afforded by the State rests wholly upon the equality of the privileges which the laws give to the separated groups within the State. The question here is not of a duty of the State to supply legal training, or of the quality of the training which it does supply, but of its duty when it provides such training to furnish it to the residents of the State upon the basis of an equality of right. By the operation of the laws of Missouri a privilege has been created for white law students which is denied to negroes by reason of their race. The white resident is afforded legal education within the State; the negro resident having the same qualifications is refused it there and must go outside the State to obtain it. That is a denial of the equality of legal right to the enjoyment of the privilege which the State has set up, and the provision for the payment of tuition fees in another State does not remove the discrimination. . . .
>
> Manifestly, the obligation of the State to give the protection of equal laws can be performed only where its laws operate, that is, within its own jurisdiction. It is there that the equality of legal right must be maintained. That obligation is imposed by the Constitution upon the States severally as governmental entities,—each responsible for its own laws establishing the rights and duties of persons within its borders. It is an obligation the burden of which cannot be cast by one State upon another, and no State can be excused from performance by what another State may do or fail to do. That separate resonsibility of each State within its own sphere is of the essence of statehood maintained under our dual system. . . .
>
> Here, petitioner's right was a personal one. It was as an individual that he was entitled to the equal protection of the laws, and the State was bound to furnish him within its borders facilities for legal education substantially equal to those which the State there afforded for persons of the white race, whether or not other negroes sought the same opportunity.

In the 1941 case of *Mitchell* v. *United States* (313 U.S. 80) the Court refused to sanction the railroad practice of furnishing accommodations of different quality to white and Negro first-class passengers, which practice the railroads had sought to justify on the basis of the slight demand by Negroes for the more costly accommodations.

A cluster of cases between 1948 and 1950 indicated that the "separate but equal" doctrine would be increasingly difficult to apply in practice. *Sipuel* v. *University of Oklahoma* (332 U.S. 631, 1948) held that qualified Negroes must be admitted to a state law school or be furnished equivalent professional education within the state, a highly costly undertaking if feasible. *McLaurin* v. *Oklahoma State Regents* (339 U.S. 637, 1950) nullified state efforts to segregate the scholastic activities of a Negro student who had been admitted to the graduate school of the University of Oklahoma, pursuant to a federal court order. At that time the Governor of Oklahoma estimated that it would cost $10 million initially and $500,000 a year to provide equal separate facilities for McLaurin and other Negro graduate students. Finally, a direct challenge to the continuance of segregated education was presented to the Court in *Sweatt* v. *Painter* (339 U.S. 629, 1950), where an applicant who had been denied admission to the University of Texas Law School solely on the basis of color, claimed that the instruction available in the newly established state law school for Negroes was markedly inferior to the instruction at the University, and that equal protection of laws was thus denied.

Supported by an expertly drawn *amicus curiae* brief, prepared by a committee of outstanding law teachers, and by the testimony of law school administrators and professors that the quality of a student body and various other intangible characteristics of a law school were at least as important as physical facilities, Sweatt was able to convince the Supreme Court that the Negro law school was grossly inadequate. "The University of Texas Law School," the Court said, "possesses to a far greater degree those qualities which are incapable of objective measurement but which make for greatness in a law school." In a unanimous decision the Supreme Court ordered his admission to the white school, indicating that it was virtually impossible in practice, at least in professional education, for a state to comply with the separate-but-equal formula.

Following the decision in the Sweatt case, the National Association for the Advancement of Colored People and other organizations pressed the fight against segregation in public schools. Would the

260

Court expressly retract the principle of "separate but equal," or, alternatively, would it retain it and construe the requirement of "equality" so strictly that segregation in practice would be constitutionally impossible? After hearing argument in a group of public school segregation cases presented at the 1952 term, the Justices were unable to reach a decision. In setting the cases for reargument during the 1953 term, the Court took the unusual step of requesting counsel to provide answers to the following questions:

1. What evidence is there that the Congress which submitted and the State legislatures and conventions which ratified the Fourteenth Amendment contemplated or did not contemplate, understood or did not understand, that it would abolish segregation in public schools?

2. If neither the Congress in submitting nor the States in ratifying the Fourteenth Amendment understood that compliance with it would require the immediate abolition of segregation in public schools, was it nevertheless the understanding of the framers of the Amendment
    (a) that future Congresses might, in the exercise of their power under section 5 of the Amendment, abolish such segregation, or
    (b) that it would be within the judicial power, in light of future conditions, to construe the Amendment as abolishing such segregation of its own force?

3. On the assumption that the answers to questions 2 (a) and (b) do not dispose of the issue, is it within the judicial power, in construing the Amendment, to abolish segregation in public schools?

4. Assuming it is decided that segregation in public schools violates the Fourteenth Amendment
    (a) would a decree necessarily follow providing that, within the limits set by normal geographic school districting, Negro children should forthwith be admitted to schools of their choice, or
    (b) may this Court, in the exercise of its equity powers, permit an effective gradual adjustment to be brought about from existing segregated systems to a system not based on color distinctions?

5. On the assumption on which questions 4 (a) and (b) are based, and assuming further that this Court will exercise its equity powers to the end described in question 4 (b),
    (a) should this Court formulate detailed decrees in these cases;
    (b) if so what specific issues should the decrees reach;
    (c) should this Court appoint a special master to hear evidence with a view to recommending specific terms for such decrees;

    (d) should this Court remand to the courts of first instance with directions to frame decrees in these cases, and if so, what general directions should the decrees of this Court include and what procedures should the courts of first instance follow in arriving at the specific terms of more detailed decrees?

The Court's cautious procedure, though unusual, was understandable. Its decision would affect the school systems of seventeen states and the District of Columbia where segregation was required by law, and four states where segregation was permitted by local option. The pattern of education for more than 8 million white children and 2.5 million colored children, representing 40 per cent of the nation's public school enrollment, would be drastically changed if segregation practices were found unconstitutional. Even greater issues were involved, for if segregation in public schools were deemed a denial of equal protection of the laws it would be difficult, if not impossible, to defend segregation in other sectors of public life. The legal underpinnings of the social structure of a great part of the nation were under attack.

Eminent counsel, headed by John W. Davis, appeared for the states, and argued that *Plessy* v. *Ferguson* (163 U.S. 537, 1896) with its "separate but equal" doctrine embodied a rule no longer open to question. Historical data were cited to show that segregated school systems were in existence when the Fourteenth Amendment was adopted, and that advocates of the Amendment had not questioned their constitutionality.

Thurgood Marshall, the noted Negro spokesman, urged the Supreme Court to meet the "separate but equal" doctrine squarely, and reject it as "a faulty conception of an era dominated by provincialism." Marshall and his co-counsel also produced historical evidence of the intentions of the proponents of the Fourteenth Amendment, evidence from which they drew conclusions diametrically opposed to those of the states' supporters.

On May 17, 1954 the Court handed down its decision. Speaking for a unanimous Court, Chief Justice Warren declared in *Brown* v. *Topeka* (347 U.S. 483) that "in the field of public education the doctrine of 'separate but equal' has no place. Separate educational facilities are inherently unequal." The opinion is remarkable not only for its extreme brevity, but for its emphasis on sociological and psychological factors. The historical evidence that the Court had sought through additional briefs of counsel apparently had little positive influence on the decision. "In approaching this problem," said the Chief Justice, "we cannot turn the clock back to 1868, when the Amendment was adopted, or even to 1896, when *Plessy* v. *Ferguson* was written. We must consider public education in the light of its full development and its present place in American life throughout the nation."

In the case involving the public schools of the District of Columbia the Court came to a similar conclusion, using the due process clause of the Fifth Amendment since the equal protection clause of the Fourteenth Amendment was inapplicable. "Segregation in public education . . ." said the court, "imposes on Negro children of the District of Columbia a burden that constitutes an arbitrary deprivation of their liberty in violation of the Due Process Clause." In 1955 the Court entrusted to federal district courts responsibility for ordering desegregation of public schools, and advised them to proceed "with all deliberate speed" toward that objective.

This dramatic decision not only was a complete reversal of the Court's position of 60 years earlier (an about-face foreshowed in the Gaines and Sweatt decisions), but vindicated the judgment of Justice Harlan, the lone dissenter in *Plessy* v. *Ferguson*. Harlan had insisted that "our Constitution is color-blind, and neither knows nor tolerates classes among citizens"; "in my opinion," he had declared prophetically, "the judgment this day rendered will, in time, prove to be quite as pernicious as the decision made . . . in the Dred Scott Case."

After May 1955, substantial steps toward desegregation were taken by a number of states and local communities. As the Court had foreseen, stubborn resistance occurred in many of the states and local communities where the tradition of segregation was deep rooted. A flood of court suits pressed on District Court judges, confronting them with the difficult and delicate task of shaping decrees to accomplish integration without at the same time disrupting orderly community life. By 1958 it was apparent that the lower federal courts were not to be dissuaded by local opinion from implementing the Supreme Court order. Where in some instances a district court assumed a casual attitude toward public school integration, the courts of appeals reversed, and indicated that more vigorous action was required (*Clemons* v. *Hillsboro*, 228

F. 2d 853, 1956; *Jackson* v. *Rawdon*, 235 F. 2d 93, CA (5) 1956).
The Supreme Court refused to give a second review to a Florida
judgment requiring the prompt admission of a Negro to a graduate
professional school of the state university (*Florida ex rel. Hawkins*
v. *Board of Control*, 350 U.S. 413, 1956), holding that while the
principles of the first Brown decision are applicable to all levels
of education, the delay permitted in achieving integration in ele-
mentary and secondary school education was not tolerable in higher
education. Other decisions affirmed lower court decrees ordering
admission of Negro college applicants in North Carolina (*North
Carolina* v. *Frasier*, 350 U.S. 979, 1956) and Tennessee (*Booker* v.
Tennessee, 351 U.S. 948, 1956).

At the end of lengthy litigation, the Supreme Court held the
principle of the Brown decision applicable to an educational trust,
created by the will of Stephen Girard, and administered as Girard
provided by city officials of Philadelphia, insofar as admission to
otherwise "private" Girard College, supported by the trust, was
restricted to "poor white male orphans." (*Pennsylvania* v. *City of
Philadelphia*, 353 U.S. 793, 1957).

Once "separate but equal" was discarded as constitutional doctrine
in public education, it was inevitable that the courts would rule it
inapplicable in other fields. In an earlier decision, *Henderson* v.
United States (339 U.S. 816, 1950) the Court had held that adequate
dining facilities must be provided on all passenger trains and that
limited demand by Negro passengers did not justify limited facilities
for their use. Following the Brown decision, the Interstate Commerce Commission late in 1955 ordered several railroads to "ter-
minate their rules and practices maintaining segregation." (*ICC* v. *St.
Louis-San Francisco Railroad*, ICC no. 31423, Nov. 7, 1955). Late
in 1956, the Supreme Court affirmed without opinion a lower court
decree ordering the end of segregation in purely local bus transportation, thus rendering invalid all forms of segregation in public
transportation. (*Gayle* v. *Browder*, 352 U.S. 903).

Other activities were similarly affected. The right of Negroes
to admission on the same basis as white persons to a municipal golf
course was upheld by affirmance of a lower court decision without
opinion (*Holmes* v. *Atlanta*, 350 U.S. 879, 1955). Similarly, the right
to use public bathing facilities was asserted (*Dawson* v. *Baltimore*,
350 U.S. 877, 1955). The same rulings by lower courts have been

made with respect to parks, public housing, and other public facilities.

It should not be assumed that these legal solutions have meant the abolition of segregated schools and other public facilities throughout the South. A variety of state laws and constitutional amendments have been enacted in an attempt to find ways of evading the impact of the Supreme Court decision. The growth of White Citizens Councils and the use of various legal and informal devices to outlaw, or diminish the effectiveness of, the NAACP shows that southern states are loath to accept a change in their social system. In May 1956 a "Declaration of Constitutional Principles" issued by 19 United States Senators and 176 Representatives commended the use of all "lawful means" to resist integration. By 1957 it was estimated that no more than 189,000 of the 2,805,473 Negro students who traditionally attended segregated schools were actually enrolled in mixed schools. In six states in the Deep South—Alabama, Florida, Georgia, Louisiana, Mississippi, and South Carolina—no Negroes attended public school with white students. A similar situation prevails in Virginia and North Carolina under their "Pupil Placement Laws." Five districts in Arkansas and one in Tennessee had desegregated by mid-1957. In contrast, the President stationed federal troops at Little Rock, Arkansas from September 24, 1957 to May 8, 1958 to enforce a district court desegregation order there.

In its decision of September 12, 1958 (*Cooper* v. *Aaron*, 78 S. Ct. 1937) and in its opinion of September 29, 1958, the Supreme Court made it clear that, if there is state participation through "any arrangement, management, funds or property," no scheme of racial discrimination against Negroes attending schools can be squared with the equal protection clause of the Fourteenth Amendment. Turning down the Little Rock School Board's plea for a delay of two and a half years in effecting its integration program, and reviewing the record, the Court found that the violence attending integration in Little Rock was "directly traceable to the actions of legislators and executive officials of the State of Arkansas . . . which reflect their own determination to resist the Court's [desegregation] decision." In the face of such defiance, the Court's answer was firm and unequivocal: "The constitutional rights [of the students] are not to be sacrificed or yielded to the violence and disorder which have followed upon the actions of the Governor and Legisla-

ture. . . . Law and order are not . . . to be preserved by depriving Negro children of their constitutional rights." The Court went
on to cast the constitutional net more widely, castigating any and
all integration-dodging laws. "State legislators, or state executive or
judicial officers" cannot nullify "the constitutional rights of children not to be discriminated against in school admission on grounds
of race or color" openly and directly or "through evasive schemes
for segregation, whether attempted ingeniously or ingenuously."

In announcing the Court's unanimous judgment, Chief Justice
Warren declared that all nine members of the Court were joint
authors of it, and to underscore the point he looked at each of the
Justices as he read their names. He went further and declared that
"three new Justices [Harlan, Brennan and Whittaker] have come
to the Court" since the 1954 decision came down, and "they are
at one with the Justices still on the Court who participated in that
basic decision. . . ."

The gap between the law concerning desegregation as declared
by the Supreme Court and "the law" in action is obviously wide
and deep. American jurisprudence has been confronted with few
challenges of comparable magnitude and difficulty.

STATE DISCRIMINATORY ACTION

After the Civil War national legislation implementing the Fourteenth Amendment was invoked successfully to protect Negro
efforts to vote in congressional elections (*United States* v. *Cruik-
shank*, 92 U.S. 542, 1876; *Ex parte Yarbrough*, 110 U.S. 651, 1884).
In *Guinn* v. *United States* (238 U.S. 347, 1915) the Court invalidated
state efforts to use a "Grandfather clause," exempting from a literacy
test for voting all persons and their lineal descendants who had
voted on or before January 1, 1866. These decisions were not, however, disastrous to states intent on disfranchising the Negro. For one
thing, the Supreme Court held in *Newberry* v. *United States* (256
U.S. 232, 1921) that primaries were not "elections" in the constitutional sense. Clearly, if Negroes could be excluded from participation in primaries in one-party states, their political influence would
be destroyed. Nevertheless, the equal protection clause was successfully invoked both against a state law forbidding Negro participation

in the Texas Democratic Party primary (*Nixon* v. *Herndon*, 273 U.S. 536, 1927), and against a similar resolution by the Democratic State Executive Committee acting under authority of statute (*Nixon* v. *Condon*, 286 U.S. 73, 1932). But in *Grovey* v. *Townsend* (295 U.S. 45, 1935) a resolution forbidding Negro participation in the Party primary, adopted by the state convention of the Democratic Party was held to be private action, and therefore not within the protective range of "equal protection."

The story was not, however, to end on this note. In 1941 the Court held that the right to vote in a primary election in a one-party state, in this instance Louisiana, where the primary was a step in the election of members of Congress, was a right or privilege secured by the Constitution (Art. I, Secs. 2 and 4). Hence, the failure of state officials, acting under "color" of state law, to count ballots properly was held a violation of the provisions of the United States Criminal Code that prohibited acts or conspiracies that denied the right or privilege of a citizen of the United States (*United States* v. *Classic* 313 U.S. 299). In *Smith* v. *Allwright* (321 U.S. 649, 1944), the Court directly overruled *Grovey* v. *Townsend* and held that the right to vote guaranteed by the Fifteenth Amendment applied to primaries as well as general elections.

In 1955 a Court of Appeals decision invalidating an Oklahoma statute that required the notation "white" or "Negro" after the name of political candidates was upheld in effect by the Supreme Court denial of certiorari (*McDonald* v. *Key*, 224 F. 2d. 609; cert. den. *Key* v. *McDonald*, 350 U.S. 895), and in a number of cases lower court decisions have ordered election boards to register Negro voters.

In other areas, discriminatory state action against Negroes had been held contrary to the equal protection clause. Beginning with *Strauder* v. *West Virginia* (100 U.S. 303, 1880), the Court has been faced with numerous claims that Negroes were denied the privilege of serving on grand and petit juries. The law involved in the Strauder case expressly excluded Negroes, but in *Norris* v. *Alabama* (294 U.S. 587, 1935) and *Patterson* v. *Alabama* (294 U.S. 600, 1935) the petitioners were allowed to prove an administrative practice of excluding Negroes from both grand and petit juries. On the other hand, there is no right to have members of a specific race on any particular jury (*Cassell* v. *Texas*, 339 U.S. 282, 1950).

In *Shelley* v. *Kraemer* (334 U.S. 1, 1948), the Court unanimously held that state court action enforcing restrictive racial covenants in property deeds was in violation of the equal protection of laws. When combined with the earlier case of *Buchanan* v. *Warley* (245 U.S. 60, 1917), where the Court invalidated a local ordinance imposing residential restrictions based on color, this decision seems to rule out any state action or assistance to private efforts to enforce property restrictions. On the other hand, the Supreme Court subsequently refused to review a New York decision holding that a private corporation could exclude Negroes from a housing project constructed with the aid of the state's power of eminent domain and city tax exemption for 25 years (*Dorsey* v. *Stuyvesant Town*, 299 N.Y. 512, 1949, cert. den. 339 U.S. 981, 1950).

PROTECTION OF ALIENS

In *Truax* v. *Raich* (239 U.S. 33, 1915), the Court invalidated, as a denial of equal protection, an Arizona law that discriminated against aliens in employment by requiring that 80% of any firm's employees had to be citizens. A similar result was obtained in *Yick Wo* v. *Hopkins* (*supra*), where Chinese laundrymen were the victims of discriminatory administration of a local ordinance requiring permits for all wooden buildings used for laundry purposes. However, the Supreme Court has often upheld state laws denying to aliens the privilege of fishing (*Bayside Fish Flour Co.* v. *Gentry*, 297 U.S. 422, 1936), hunting (*Patsone* v. *Pennsylvania*, 232 U.S. 138, 1914), or owning land within state boundaries (*Terrace* v. *Thompson*, 263 U.S. 197, 1923). These decisions rest primarily on the proprietary relationship between the state and all forms of real property and natural life within its jurisdiction. They may be distinguished from the *Raich* case, where the "right to employment" was considered fundamental. The same distinction may be used to explain *Takahashi* v. *Fish and Game Commission* (334 U.S. 410, 1948), where the Court held that anyone admitted to this country, even though ineligible for citizenship, could not be denied a commercial fishing license because of such ineligibility. Equal protection, said the Court, required that anyone admitted to a state must have the right to work.

It may well be that the Court is prepared to take a less generous attitude toward state laws discriminating against aliens, even where the state has claimed to act in its capacity as sovereign. *Oyama* v. *California* (332 U.S. 633, 1948) invalidated a provision of the California Alien Land Law that made payment by an alien for the transfer of land to a third person *prima facie* evidence of intent to evade the statute. Four Justices held the Alien Land Law unconstitutional. The provision was an essential part of the law banning ownership of agricultural land by aliens ineligible to acquire citizenship.

The Court, following its decisions where discrimination against Negroes in jury selection caused new trials, has extended the principle to aliens. Hernandez, a person of Mexican descent, sought reversal of his murder conviction on the ground that he had been denied equal protection of the laws, persons of Mexican ancestry having been systematically excluded from service as jurymen. The state court affirmed the conviction, but Chief Justice Warren, speaking for a unanimous court, reversed the decision (*Hernandez* v. *Texas*, 347 U.S. 475, 1954). The Fourteenth Amendment, the Court ruled, contemplates not only discrimination affecting whites and Negroes, but also all other racial discrimination.

It appears that the absence of the equal protection clause in the Bill of Rights was helpful to the United States government in defending the World War II Japanese exclusion order. "The Fifth Amendment," Chief Justice Stone commented in *Hirabayshi* v. *United States* (320 U.S. 81, 1943), "contains no equal protection clause and it restrains only such discriminatory legislation by Congress as amounts to a denial of due process." The implication is that the standard of reasonableness required under the equal protection clause is higher than that of due process.

EQUAL PROTECTION IN CLASSIFICATION

Since virtually all legislation involves classification, it is not surprising that the equal protection clause should be frequently invoked by those challenging state acts under the police power. In *Barbier* v. *Connolly* (113 U.S. 27, 1885), upholding a San Francisco ordinance limiting the hours during which laundries might operate, Justice

Field tried to distinguish between acts with schemes of classification within the ban of the equal protection clause and acts with classification schemes not covered by the clause: "Class legislation, discriminating against some and favoring others, is prohibited but legislation which, in carrying out a public purpose, is limited in its application, if within the sphere of its operation it affects all persons similarly situated, is not within the amendment." Justice Field merely restated the problem, namely, what "classes" may be created for legislative purposes, and what are the limits of legislative actions affecting a class once defined?

Justice Holmes, in upholding a Pennsylvania statute prohibiting aliens from owning or possessing shotguns or rifles, suggested this approach: "We start with the general consideration that a state may classify with reference to the evil to be prevented, and that if the class discriminated against is or reasonably might be considered to define those from whom the evil mainly is to be feared, it properly may be picked out. The question is a practical one, dependent on experience." In this case it was found that aliens could be singled out as the source of danger to Pennsylvania's wild life. Nor need the classification be perfect: "It is not enough to invalidate the law that others may do the same thing and go unpunished"; nor was it essential that the state cover "the whole field of possible abuses."

In *Truax* v. *Corrigan* (257 U.S. 312, 1921), however, where the Justices voted 5 to 4 to invalidate an Arizona statute withdrawing the right of an employer to obtain an injunction against peaceful picketing in labor disputes, the invalidation was specifically on the ground that employers as a class were deprived of a remedy available to others. The dissenting Justices took the position that in view of the realities of labor-management relations and the then widespread use (and abuse) of court injunctions in labor disputes, such a classification was permissible.

Similarly in tax cases, an inevitable issue is that the classification singling out the appellant and similar persons for taxation is arbitrary. In *State Board of Tax Commissioners* v. *Jackson* (283 U.S. 527, 1931), a progressively higher license fee for chain stores was upheld on the ground "that a reasonable basis existed for the tax discrimination employed." But in *Liggett* v. *Lee* (288 U.S. 517, 1933), a majority invalidated a higher tax rate designed to apply if the chain stores were located in two or more counties. In an elaborate dissent, Brandeis tried to show the reasonableness of such a classification.

Statutes that affect bodily security or freedom must have a reasonable basis. A statute that provided for sterilization of mental defectives was upheld (*Buck* v. *Bell*, 274 U.S. 200, 1927); but similar treatment of those convicted three times of felonies involving moral turpitude was invalidated as a denial of equal protection, because the state classification of crimes involving moral turpitude was plainly arbitrary (*Skinner* v. *Oklahoma*, 316 U.S. 535, 1942). In numerous instances involving less drastic penalties or consequences the Court has deferred to the legislative judgment on classification.

This brief review is enough to indicate the problems that plague the Justices in applying the equal protection clause. Even if the present issues surrounding racial discrimination should largely disappear, the increasingly complex positive legislation of the modern state will inevitably affect certain individuals and groups more than others, and these in turn will continue to raise the question of equal protection. There is an enduring source of conflict between the notion of "one law for all" and the obvious necessity government faces of operating through law on certain classes of persons or types of action because the public interest requires such action. "Equal protection of law," thus becomes an almost commonplace plea of petitioners before the Court, so much so that Justice Holmes termed it the "last refuge of constitutional arguments." Nevertheless, it requires no gift of prophecy to see that the equal protection clause is just coming into its own as a limitation on alleged discriminatory state action, and on private action sanctioned by the state. With increased Supreme Court recognition of the principle that no persistent discrimination of general importance can take place without the assistance of a state's enforcement powers the equal protection clause is likely to find more and more use as a weapon to create equal treatment of all persons. In time, the high purpose of the equal protection clause, as envisaged by Justice Harlan over 60 years ago in the Civil Rights cases and *Plessy* v. *Ferguson*, may become a constitutional reality.

XIII

CIVIL LIBERTIES—
CRIMINAL PROCEDURE

STATE CONSTITUTIONS ADOPTED
in 1776 and in subsequent years invariably contained either a separate
bill of rights or other provisions that achieved the same objective.
The delegates at the Constitutional Convention of 1787, however,
preoccupied with the difficult task of infusing power into the new
government, thought the inclusion of a bill of rights both unwise
and unnecessary. In *The Federalist*, No. 84, Hamilton summarized
two arguments that Madison, Charles Pinckney, James Wilson, and
other supporters of the Constitution had repeated endlessly: first,
because the new government's powers were enumerated, no need
existed for reciting prohibitions; second, any attempt to list rights
was dangerous since omissions might seem deliberate. To Hamilton, "the Constitution is itself, in every rational sense, and to every
useful purpose, a Bill of Rights." Madison stated an additional reason for opposing a bill of rights: the fear that the force of contemporary public opinion would compel an excessively narrow
definition of religious and other freedoms.

Jefferson, in a letter to Madison from France, took a different view: "A bill of rights is what the people are entitled to against every government on earth . . . and what no just government should refuse."

When the arguments of the Constitution's supporters proved unavailing against the insistent demands of majorities in six ratifying state conventions and highly vocal minorities in two others, they readily agreed to the addition of the Bill of Rights, thus ensuring ratification.

THE BILL OF RIGHTS

In the first Congress, Madison, as majority leader, drew up and pressed through both Houses twelve amendments. Some were included because most states had requested them; others, because Madison favored them personally. After a two-year delay, ten of the proposed amendments were ratified.

The first eight amendments, singling out specific rights for protection, may be conveniently divided into three groups. The substantive rights of speech, press, religion, and assembly, mentioned in the First Amendment, will be discussed in the following chapter. The Second Amendment, guaranteeing the right to bear arms, and the Third, against the quartering of troops, have not been significant in our constitutional history. The quartering problem has not recurred since colonial days, and the Court has upheld reasonable regulation of the right of private citizens to bear arms (*Presser* v. *Illinois*, 116 U.S. 252, 1886; *United States* v. *Miller*, 307 U.S. 174, 1939).

Other rights, mainly procedural, are designed to protect the citizen against arbitrary police action, and to ensure fair judicial procedures in any official action by which a person might lose his liberty or property. This chapter considers these important rights.

It was not until 1833 that the Supreme Court answered the question whether the first eight amendments limited state as well as national action. To Marshall this was a question "of great importance, but not of much difficulty" (*Barron* v. *Baltimore*, 7 Pet. 243). The City of Baltimore, under acts of the Maryland legislature, had diverted the flow of several streams. As a result of the changes, silt was deposited around Barron's wharf, making it unfit for shipping and, in Barron's opinion, depriving him of property without just compensation. Denying the Supreme Court's jurisdiction to declare the state acts repugnant to the Constitution, Marshall observed: "We are of the opinion, that, the provision in the Fifth Amendment to the Constitution, declaring that private property shall not be taken for public use without just compensation is intended solely as a limitation on the power of the United States, and is not applicable to the legislation of the states." In support of this conclusion, the Chief Justice pointed out that the limitations set forth in the Constitution in general terms, as well as the powers conferred, applied to the "government created by the instrument." In addition, he cited proceedings in the state ratifying conventions culminating in the demand for a bill of rights to furnish "security against the apprehended encroachments of the general government."

CRIMINAL PROCEDURES AND THE NATIONAL GOVERNMENT

On the whole, the national government has been more concerned than most of the states with safeguarding procedural rights. Men convicted of serious crimes (there were approximately 11,000 convictions in FBI prosecuted crimes alone in 1956; in New Jersey alone there was an equal number of convictions for serious offenses in 1956) have little to lose by attempting to convince an appellate court that the trial court or law enforcement officials committed an error of constitutional significance. Trial judges faced with questions involving the admissibility of evidence obtained in unique ways may rule incorrectly. Zealous federal law enforcement officials may exceed constitutional limits in their efforts to obtain convictions, although they are much less prone to err in this respect than their state counterparts.

Many national and state officials and a large part of the public look upon certain of these constitutional guarantees as socially undesirable. Newspaper editors are prone to flail away at what are termed "technicalities" of the law, by which improperly seized evidence is held inadmissible or an improperly admitted confession produced by coercive police methods is the cause of reversal by an appellate court. The frequent use by witnesses before grand juries and legislative investigation committees of the self-incrimination clause of the Fifth Amendment has resulted in a public clamor that the scope of the right should be narrowed. Since the numerous instances in which these guarantees have been invoked by persons later proved innocent have received virtually no publicity, there is fostered in the public mind the picture of large numbers of guilty persons escaping punishment through constitutionally created loopholes in the law.

Another line of reasoning, taking an historical approach, concludes that the democratic character of American institutions obviates the need for devices that admittedly fulfilled a valuable function as a check on the absolutist tendencies of English monarchs. This argument is easily answered: there are thousands of cases on record in which American officials, either from zeal to enforce the law or solve a crime, or from a basic dislike of members of certain minority groups, have committed acts that no civilized nation can permit. Little imagination is required to picture the dangers to personal liberties that would follow an abandonment of these constitutional guarantees.

The clash of interests in the cases to be reviewed is frequently stated in highly misleading terms. What is involved is not the relative merits of individual freedom when compared with security of the community, a conflict that inevitably results in the dominance of the latter. Rather, it is the subtle, complex task of determining *how much* protection can be given to each individual citizen, without unduly hampering the efforts of government to maintain the peace and order without which freedom is meaningless. The difficulty of this task helps to explain the attention given in our national and state constitutions to procedural rights. Far from demonstrating a fondness for mere technical rules, this emphasis on procedural guarantees reflects thoughtful conclusions on the dangers to freedom posed by governmental activity. As Justice Frankfurter has remarked "the history of American freedom is, in no small measure, the history of procedure" (*Malinski* v. *New York*, 324 U.S. 401, 419, 1945).

Decisions of the Supreme Court have tended, on the whole, to impose high standards of behavior upon federal officials and federal trial courts. This has been the result not only of the Court's application of Constitutional rules, but has been due in part to the

Supreme Court's position as supervisor of the federal judicial system. The danger of unreasonable searches and seizures, for example, has been minimized by the Court's ruling that evidence so obtained is not admissible in federal court, it being the Court's theory that the Fourth Amendment right should be joined with the Fifth Amendment "self-incrimination" clause in order to effectuate the purposes of both provisions (*Boyd* v. *United States*, 116 U.S. 616, 1886; and *Weeks* v. *United States*, 232 U.S. 383, 1914). This rule— of excluding evidence illegally obtained—is a departure from the common law rule, and is not followed in England today. An apparent exception to the Court's vigorous assertion of this right was its refusal to exclude evidence obtained by wire-tapping in *Olmstead* v. *United States* (277 U.S. 438, 1928) largely on the ground that a wire-tap was not a search and seizure in the traditional sense. Brandeis, dissenting, made an eloquent argument in support of a "right to privacy" obviously invaded by wire-tapping or other electronic intrusions. The *Olmstead* decision was severely criticized and finally overcome by amending the Federal Communications Act in such a way as to penalize the divulging of intercepted messages. That the problem of searches and seizures incident to arrest continues to plague the Court is shown by the *Rabinowitz* case (339 U.S. 56, 1950), only one in a series of similar decisions in the post World War II period. In this case the Court held that an arrest with warrant justified a search of the one-room office in which the defendant conducted his business as a stamp dealer, so that allegedly altered postal stamps found in the search were admissible. In 1957 the Court held that the seizure and removal of the entire contents of a house even where lawful arrest warrants were used exceeded the constitutional requirement against "unreasonable" seizures (*Kremen* v. *United States*, 353 U.S. 346).

The self-incrimination clause of the Fifth Amendment has also presented difficult questions. Although the phrase "in any criminal case" seemingly limits the application of this guarantee, its protection may be claimed by a witness to justify refusal to testify before a grand jury, jury, or legislative committee, or to prevent being compelled to produce papers or other evidence (*Counselman* v. *Hitchcock*, 142 U.S. 547, 1892). The clause has been invoked with such frequency before grand juries and Congressional investigating committees by witnesses who refuse to say whether they are now or ever have been members of the Communist Party (see *Blau* v. *United States*, 340 U.S. 159, 1950), that the public has tended to identify the "Fifth Amendment" with this one clause.

In an effort to overcome the handicap thus imposed on the grand jury investigators in national security and defense cases, Congress passed the Immunity Act of 1954, giving witnesses who otherwise would refuse to testify immunity against prosecution with respect to any matter raised by the testimony through a District Court order, obtained by application of a United States attorney, with the approval of the Attorney General. By 7-2 the Court upheld the act stating that the immunity granted by the statute extended to state prosecutions as well as those in federal courts (*Ullman* v. *United States*, 350 U.S. 422, 1956). The self-incrimination clause also protects a defendant against the admission in evidence of coerced confessions (*McNabb* v. *United States*, 318 U.S. 332, 1943). The "coercion" need not be physical but, as in the McNabb case, may arise from prolonged questioning of an accused. Federal law enforcement officials are expected to adhere closely to procedural rules laid down by Congress. The failure of officials to bring an arrested person before a federal commissioner "without unnecessary delay" for arraignment, as required by the Federal Code of Criminal Procedure, invalidates even a voluntary confession made before such arraignment (*Mallory* v. *United States*, 354 U.S. 449, 1957).

Once the meaning of double jeopardy was spelled out to mean protection against a second trial after acquittal, the other specific rights of the Fifth Amendment caused no real difficulty (*Kepner* v. *United States*, 195 U.S. 100, 1904). Invoking its authority as the supervising head of the federal court system, the Court has held that, although not required by any constitutional provision, FBI and other governmental files must be open to the defense in criminal cases, where there are reports and data in the file that have been the subject of oral testimony (*Jencks* v. *United States*, 353 U.S. 657, 1957).

Grand jury indictment is a regular part of federal criminal proceedings, and the Fifth Amendment due process requirement, although a significant limitation on national legislative power at an earlier period, now serves no important role as a procedural limitation. It is simply a general guarantee of fairness and need not be relied on as frequently in federal courts, with their numerous specific procedural safeguards for the accused, as in state proceedings.

The Sixth Amendment guarantee of the right to the assistance of counsel has been construed as a mandate that every indigent defendant in federal criminal trials be offered counsel (*Johnson* v. *Zerbst*, 304 U.S. 458, 1938). The requirement of trial by jury has been held to permit the defendant to waive jury trial with the prosecutor's acquiescence (*Patton* v. *United States*, 281 U.S. 276, 1930). The other rights of the Sixth Amendment have occasioned no serious difficulties.

Issues concerning several of these rights arise in connection with trials by military commissions. In the famous case of *Ex parte Milligan* (4 Wall 2, 1886), the Court held that military commissions could not displace the civil courts as long as these courts were sitting and able to function. A modern application of this rule occurred in *Duncan* v. *Kahanamoku* (327 U.S. 304, 1946), where the Court held that the threatened invasion of Hawaii did not justify use of military commissions to try civil offenders as long as the civil courts were available for trials.

Interesting constitutional issues arose as the result of the new international role of the United States after 1945 when members of the armed forces and their dependents in large numbers were stationed abroad. After deciding in 1956 that civilians accompanying the armed forces were subject to trial by a court-martial as provided in the Code of Military Justice enacted by Congress (*Kinsella* v. *Krueger*, 351 U.S. 470), the Court granted a rehearing and reversed itself in the very next session, concluding that constitutional guarantees could be denied only as to Military personnel (*Reid* v. *Covert*, 354 U.S. 1, 1957).

A unique problem was presented at the end of World War II hostilities, when the Court was asked by the Japanese General Yamashita and other Japanese war leaders to review their trials by military commissions for violations of the laws of war. The Court decided that the findings of a military commission are not reviewable, thus in effect permitting these tribunals to follow rules that depart sharply from those required in the regular trial courts. Murphy and Rutledge, dissenting, pointed out that the Court's decision meant that minimal standards of fairness need not be followed by military commissions, and that such commissions are thus effectively placed beyond the "rule of law" (*In re Yamashita*, 327 U.S. 1: 1946). The proceedings of military courts are similarly free from the restrictions of judicial rules and standards of due process. On habeas corpus, the sole method of obtaining civil court review of military courts' findings, the only question open for review is whether the military court had "jurisdiction" (*Hiatt* v. *Brown*, 339 U.S. 103, 1950).

A question concerning the authority of the United States to relinquish jurisdiction over its service personnel stationed in foreign countries, arose in 1957. In accordance with a Status of Forces Agreement signed in 1952 by representatives of Japan and the United States, pursuant to a treaty between these two countries, the United States yielded to Japanese demands that an American soldier, William Girard, be tried by their courts for killing a Japanese civilian. The terms of the Agreement were that offenses committed while "off-duty" and those committed "on-duty" if not part of officially required conduct, were triable by the Japanese courts; all "official" offenses were triable by United States military courts. In this instance the soldier, while guarding military equipment, allegedly fired a shell casing at a woman scavenging scrap metal. A federal district judge enjoined the United States authorities from relinquishing Girard to the Japanese when the decision to yield Girard to them was announced. But in a short, unanimous decision, his action was reversed by the Supreme Court, holding that there was no constitutional or statutory barrier to such agreements, and none prohibited its administration as in this case (*Wilson* v. *Girard*, 354 U.S. 524, 1957). As the Court viewed the problem, the wisdom of the particular action in this and similar service cases was a matter of executive or Congressional, rather than judicial concern.

This brief survey of some of the leading cases indicates substantial compliance by the national government with the commands of the amendments guaranteeing procedural rights. In response to the oft-voiced complaint that ancient modes of procedure are ill-suited to modern conditions, it can be shown that efficient federal personnel with a will to act within the Constitution have rarely been frustrated in their law enforcement efforts.

STATE CRIMINAL PROCEDURE

Shortly after the end of the Civil War, the Court was confronted with a question of highest importance to our federal system: did the Fourteenth Amendment have the effect of incorporating the Bill of Rights, either through the privileges and immunities clause, or by virtue of the due process clause? A 5-4 decision in the *Slaughterhouse Cases* (16 Wall 36, 1873) held that the doctrine of *Barron* v. *Baltimore* was still in effect.

Nevertheless, suitors continued to press upon the Court arguments showing that one or more of the rights mentioned in the Bill of Rights was included in the phrase "due process of law" protected by the Fourteenth Amendment against state action. The Supreme Court eventually displayed willingness to incorporate the First Amendment rights in the Fourteenth Amendment; but this concession was not destined to extend to all other provisions of the Bill of Rights. Instead it has adopted the principle that if one or more of the procedural guarantees is effective against state action it is because the due process clause of the Fourteenth Amendment requires it.

In the 1884 case of *Hurtado* v. *California* (110 U.S. 516) the Court refused to hold that the due process clause of the Fourteenth Amendment prevented the substitution by a state of a prosecutor's affidavit (information) for grand jury indictment in criminal cases. Later, the Court cast doubt on its adherence to the Hurtado doctrine by holding that the due process clause limited state action that had the effect of taking property without just compensation (*Chicago, Milwaukee & St. Paul Railway Co.* v. *Minnesota*, 134 U.S. 418, 1890). But, with this exception in favor of property rights, the Court was unwilling to depart from its basic position that due process—being enumerated in the Fifth Amendment as a separate right, distinct from the various other procedural rights of the Bill of Rights—could not be treated as a shorthand expression of all procedural rights required of the states by the Fourteenth Amendment.

Thus, states were allowed to weaken the protection against self-incrimination by allowing judicial comment on the failure of a defendant to testify in his defense (*Twining* v. *New Jersey*, 211 U.S. 78, 1908), and to alter the common-law trial by jury, meaning a trial by a jury of twelve persons (*Maxwell* v. *Dow*, 176 U.S. 581, 1900). By 1937, long after the Court had agreed that the "liberty" protected by the Fourteenth Amendment included some of the First Amendment freedoms, the Supreme Court, speaking through Justice Cardozo in *Palko* v. *Connecticut* (302 U.S. 319), reaffirmed its long-held view that the entire Bill of Rights was not incorporated in the Fourteenth Amendment and attempted to justify its selective process:

> There emerges the perception of a rationalizing principle which gives to discrete instances a proper order and coherence. The right to trial by jury and the immunity from prosecution except as the result of an indictment may have value and importance. Even so, they are not of the very essence of a scheme of ordered liberty. To abolish them is not to violate a "principle of justice so rooted in the traditions and conscience of our people as to be ranked as fundamental. . . ."
> We reach a different plane of social and moral values when we pass to the privileges and immunities that have been taken over from the earlier articles of the Federal Bill of Rights [First Amendment] and brought within the Fourteenth Amendment by a process of absorption. These in their origin were effective against the federal government alone. If the Fourteenth Amendment has absorbed them, the process of absorption has had its source in the belief that neither liberty nor justice would exist if they were sacrificed.

This "natural law" method of selecting and discarding rights has not gone unchallenged. From 1873 to the present time, various Justices have argued that the entire Bill of Rights should be incorporated in the Fourteenth Amendment. Consider Justice Black's dissenting opinion in *Adamson* v. *California* (332 U.S. 46, 1947):

> My study of the historical events that culminated in the Fourteenth Amendment, and the expressions of those who sponsored and favored, as well as those who opposed its submission and passage, persuades me that one of the chief objects that the provision of the Amendment's first section, separated, and as a whole were intended to accomplish, was to make the Bill of Rights applicable to the states. . . . The "natural law" formula should be abandoned as an incongruous excrescence on our Constitution. I believe that formula to be itself a violation of our Constitution, in that it subtly conveys to courts, at the expense of legislatures, ultimate power over public policies in fields where no specific provision of the Constitution

limits legislative power. . . . I fear to see the consequences of the Court's practice of substituting its own concepts of decency and fundamental justice for the language of the Bill of Rights as its point of departure in interpreting and enforcing that Bill of Rights.

Justice Frankfurter's reading of history led him to exactly the opposite conclusion. In the 70 years following adoption of the Fourteenth Amendment, he reports, its scope was passed upon by 53 judges. Only one of these—an eccentric exception at that (Justice Harlan)—ever indicated that the Fourteenth Amendment was a "shorthand summary" of the first eight amendments.

Justice Black's strictures on the Court's use of the "natural law" formula as an instrument of judicial decision recall Justice Iredell's misgivings in *Calder* v. *Bull*. Similarly, Justice Field's inclination in the Granger decision and other cases to invoke "the structure and spirit of our institutions" as a bar to legislative action regulating rights of property provoked critical comment from both within and without the Court. After extensive research Professor Charles Fairman concluded that "the record of history is against him [Black]." Fairman describes the evidence against the Justice as "a high mountain" and the evidence supporting him as "a few pebbles and stones." It is Fairman's belief that the Amendment is best interpreted according to Cardozo's selective natural law principle as set forth in the *Palko* case.

THE FAIR TRIAL RULE

In spite of the Court's refusal to incorporate the entire Bill of Rights in the due process clause, many limitations on state criminal procedure have emerged from the Court's direct application of due process. Some of these are similar in scope to certain of the specific guarantees of the Fourth, Fifth, and Sixth Amendments. Although the Court's analysis has not always been clear, the rule is that minimal standards of "fairness" must characterize state trial and pre-trial procedures vitally affecting the trial in order to meet due process requirements. This is the so-called "fair trial rule."

This scrutiny of state court proceedings commenced in the period following World War I. Before that time the Supreme Court had been willing to review state criminal trials only to the extent necessary to ascertain whether the state court had exercised jurisdiction properly (*Frank* v. *Mangum*, 237 U.S. 309, 1915) as it does in reviewing military court proceedings today. But in *Moore* v. *Dempsey* (261 U.S. 86, 1923), the Court, speaking through Justice Holmes, held that the allegation that a state trial had been dominated by a mob marked so serious a departure from the due process guaranteed by the Fourteenth Amendment as to require a remand to a federal district court for a hearing on the facts. The picture of lawless state police action set forth in the Report of the Wickersham Commission in 1931 indicates that the Court's willingness to review state criminal cases came just in time.

The cases, however, reveal a confusing inconsistency of attitude on the part of the judges. At least in capital cases the state must furnish counsel to indigent defendants (*Powell* v. *Alabama*, 287 U.S. 45, 1932); in some cases the absence of counsel will render a confession made during confinement inadmissible at the trial (*Haley* v. *Ohio*, 332 U.S. 596 1948). The Court has not recognized that a person detained by the police has a right to phone his own lawyer (*Crooker* v. *California*), 78 S. Ct. 1287, 1958) or see his own lawyer waiting outside the room where interrogation is taking place (*Cicenia* v. *LaGay*, 78 S. Ct. 1297, 1958). But the Court has been willing to scrutinize with some care the circumstances surrounding confessions produced by intensive police interrogation, and has invalidated convictions where coercion was shown (*Brown* v. *Mississippi*, 297 U.S. 278, 1936; *Chambers* v. *Florida* (p. 531); *Ashcraft* v. *Tennessee*, 332 U.S. 143, 1944; *Watts* v. *Indiana*, 338 U.S. 49, 1949; *Fikes* v. *Alabama*, 352 U.S. 191, 1957). The Justices have been especially sympathetic where defendants are youthful, inexperienced, ignorant, or members of minority groups. In many of the cases, a denial of due process has been found in the combination of two or more illegal features, rather than any one. Refusal to allow communication by defendant with friends or family, failure to arraign promptly, long periods of questioning, lack of advice as to his rights, and other deficiencies are frequently found in the same case. The important distinction between review of federal and state cases by the Supreme Court is that any one of the illegal official actions would normally upset a federal conviction. But more is needed to prove a lack of due process in state cases. Sometimes the Court reverses where state action appears extreme. In *Rochin* v. *California* (342

U.S. 165, 1952), it was found that evidence obtained by the use of a stomach pump on an unwilling prisoner was inadmissible, on the ground that the police conduct was offensive to "a sense of justice." Yet, in *Breithaupt* v. *Abram* (1 L. ed. 2d 448, 1957) the Court upheld by 6-3 an involuntary manslaughter conviction where an unconscious driver suspected of being intoxicated was given a blood test, the results of which were admitted in evidence at his trial. Chief Justice Warren, joined by Black and Douglas, thought the facts were sufficiently similar to those in the Rochin case as to require the same result.

The fair trial rule has been applied in such a way as to permit states to refuse to appoint counsel for mature criminal defendants (*Betts* v. *Brady*, 316 U.S. 455, 1942) in simple, noncapital cases. But if a defendant is young, ignorant or inexperienced or the case is complex, the state must offer to appoint counsel. State acts may permit comment by the judge to the jury on defendant's failure to testify in his own defense (*Adamson* v. *California*, 332 U.S. 46, 1947, adhering to *Twining* v. *New Jersey*, 211 U.S. 78, 1908); and state tribunals are free to admit evidence that in federal trials would be excluded for being in violation of the searches and seizures provision of the Fourth Amendment (*Wolf* v. *Colorado*, 338 U.S. 25, 1949). In the Wolf case, the Court takes the position that the state action may violate the Fourth Amendment, but that the "exclusionary rule" used in federal courts to discourage such violations does not apply to state action. The Court seemed satisfied because damage suits and criminal prosecution served at least in theory as remedies against illegal state searches and seizures. The Court has also found a denial of due process in the summary dismissal of a New York City employee on the sole ground that he violated a City Charter provision by invoking the Fifth Amendment privilege (*Slochhower* v. *Board of Education*, 350 U.S. 551, 1956).

Well aware of the dangers to the federal principle posed by over-zealous review of state court decision, the Court has firmly resisted any suggestion that the fair trial rule should be replaced by one requiring adherence to the Bill of Rights, and imposing higher standards on state criminal procedures. As Justice Burton said in *Bute* v. *Illinois:* "There is nothing in the Fourteenth Amendment specifically stating that the long recognized and then existing power of the states over the procedures of their own courts in criminal cases was to be prohibited or even limited" (333 U.S. 640, 1948). In *Malinski* v. *New York* (324 U.S. 401, 1945), Justice Frankfurter urged "an alert deference to the judgment of the state court under review," an attitude that has increasingly characterized decisions reviewing state criminal cases since the death of Justices Murphy and Rutledge in 1949.

Regardless of the deference or lack of it shown state criminal judgments, the one certain result of Supreme Court review using a "fair trial" rule is to bring about a substantial increase in petitions for review. The flood of state cases in which Supreme Court review is sought in recent decades has been an inevitable result of this case-by-case, fact-situation-by-fact-situation approach of the Court in applying due process. To a convicted defendant any slight chance to obtain his freedom is worth seizing. With changes in Court personnel lawyers know that the 5-4 or 6-3 adverse decision of yesteryear may well be reversed, especially since the Court may justify its new decision by concentrating on the particular fact-situation presented. And although the lack of clear rules has bred confusion in the minds of state officials, the Court's review and disapproval of many deplorable state practices has tended to raise state standards at least somewhat toward the ideal of criminal justice envisioned by Justice Murphy in *Malinski* v. *New York*: "Those clothed with authority in the courtrooms of this nation have the duty to conduct and supervise proceedings so that an accused person may be adjudged solely according to the dictates of justice and reason."

Whether this goal might be attained more readily by reading into "due process" more precise rules (which admittedly might be changed as succeeding generations elevate their standards of justice) is a question that has not seriously engaged the attention of the Court. Yet, it would seem that between the extremes of the doctrine of full incorporation of the Bill of Rights (strait-jacketing state procedures) and the present case-by-case method, with its tendency to increase undesirably the review function of the Court in criminal cases, there must lie a middle ground that would retain the historic purpose of due process and at the same time promote more efficient administration of justice.

XIV

FIRST AMENDMENT
FREEDOMS

DURING THE LONG PERIOD BE-
tween 1787 and World War I, the First Amendment served as
little more than a historical reminder of the lively concern for
personal freedom expressed during the formative years of the nation. Since the Court revolution of 1937, however, the First Amendment has been the focal point of our constitutional jurisprudence.

At the very inception of our national government, the federalists
had, it is true, thought it necessary to curb the speech of their
political opponents. Under the Alien and Sedition Acts scandalous
criticism of the President or Congress with intent to bring them
into disrepute was proscribed in sweeping terms. These laws, generally considered unconstitutional, were never tested because Jefferson and the Republicans feared that the federalist Supreme Court
would declare the laws valid, thus establishing an unfortunate
precedent. It is noteworthy that the federalist proponents of these
laws, many of whom had played leading roles in the drama of Con-
stitution-making, used an argument that has become familiar as a

defense of this type of limitation on free speech. Threats to national security, they argued, made curbs on speech absolutely necessary; preservation of the Constitution was more important than protection of any one right it guaranteed. Obviously, this logic could be used to justify destruction of all Constitutional rights, if the rights are attacked one by one.

Barring Lincoln's unofficial suppression of Northern critics of governmental policies during the Civil War, no national government action raising free speech issues occurred until World War I. In 1917 and 1918 Congress passed two laws that resulted in extensive litigation, and focused public attention on basic issues of freedom of speech in wartime. The so-called Espionage Act of 1917 prohibited and punished interferences with recruitment or the draft, or acts adversely affecting military morale, and made the intent of the actor or speaker an essential element of the offense. This latter requirement made application of the law difficult. Only two cases require mention. In each of these the Court fashioned certain tests or standards to decide whether the law as applied to words or writings had encroached on free speech.

In *Schenck* v. *United States* (249 U.S. 47, 1919), Justice Holmes, in upholding the 1917 act as applied to antidraft leaflets, suggested the now famous "clear and present danger" test: "The question in every case is whether the words used are used in such circumstances and are of such a nature as to create a clear and present danger that they will bring about the substantive evils that Congress has a right to prevent." Holmes's test invited more questions than it answered. Enmeshed with highly complex issues of proximity, degree, and content, it nevertheless displayed a preference for a wide latitude of speech. Dissenting in *Gitlow* v. *New York* (268 U.S. 652, 673, 1925) Holmes said: "If in the long run the beliefs expressed in proletarian dictatorship are destined to be accepted by the dominant forces of the community, the only meaning of free speech is that they should be given their chance, and have their way."

Shortly after Holmes announced this "clear and present danger" test, the Court indicated that it was not convinced of its virtues. In *Pierce* v. *United States* (252 U.S. 239, 1920), the Court adopted the "bad tendency" doctrine, a test less generous to the speaker.

Here a Socialist antiwar pamphlet was held within the 1917 law as having "a tendency to cause insubordination, disloyalty, and refusal of duty." Holmes and Brandeis opposed the new rule because it eliminated both the speaker's intent and the likelihood of danger as relevant elements.

A Sedition Law of 1918 went far beyond the 1917 act, making punishable speech that in World War II would have been deemed mere political comment. It singled out for punishment any "disloyal, profane, scurrilous, or abusive language about the form of government, the Constitution, soldiers and sailors, flag or uniform of the armed forces," and in addition made unlawful any "word or act [favoring] the cause of the German Empire . . . or [opposing] the cause of the United States." This law was upheld. In *Abrams* v. *United States* (250 U.S. 616, 1919), distribution of pamphlets opposing the Allied (and American) intervention in Russia after the revolution were held to be within its terms. Holmes, dissenting, thought that the majority had inferred an intent not shown by evidence and that, in any event, no threat of clear and present danger to our war effort had been shown. The effect of this postwar litigation was to enlarge the importance of the free speech guarantee, although it should be emphasized that the cases involved the proper application of federal statutes to specific forms of speech or writing rather than serious questions concerning the constitutionality of the statutes themselves. When this flurry of cases subsided, issues involving federal action affecting First Amendment rights virtually disappeared until the era of World War II.

THE NATIONALIZATION OF THE FIRST AMENDMENT

One of the most spectacular developments in American constitutional law has been the Supreme Court's expansion of the due process clause in the Fourteenth Amendment to include the First Amendment freedoms. At the outset there was little hint of this development, except for the powerful dissenting opinions in the *Slaughterhouse Cases* (16 Wall. 36, 1873). Here the majority narrowed the scope of the privileges and immunities clause and, in passing, ridiculed the argument that due process possessed more than a procedural meaning.

Similarly, due process was held in *Davidson* v. *New Orleans* (96 U.S. 97, 1878) to require only that a state grant an "appropriate hearing." Justice Bradley's concurring opinion in the Davidson case, however, proved prophetic. Due process, he said, was a standard by which the Court should examine the "reasonableness" of state legislation.

The Justices were not yet willing to become the censors of state legislation. In *Hurtado* v. *California* (110 U.S. 516, 1884), they denied that anything in the due process clause prevented a state from substituting information (affidavit by the prosecutor) for grand jury indictment. Speaking for the Court, Justice Matthews argued that since the Fifth Amendment contained a due process clause as one of many rights in the Bill of Rights, the same provision in the Fourteenth Amendment could not logically be held to include other specific Bill of Rights provisions. Due process, he said, was the "law of the land in each state . . . exerted within the limits of those fundamental principles of liberty and justice which lie at the base of all our civil and political institutions." These rights, according to Matthews, were best protected by the ballot box and the state legislatures. Justice Matthews' vague and sweeping "natural law" language provided a crude but effective basis of review for later judges less hesitant to reverse the legislative judgment.

Justice Moody, in the *Twining* case (211 U.S. 78, 1908), indicated a new trend in judicial thinking: "It is possible that some of the personal rights safeguarded by the first eight amendments against national action may also be safeguarded against state action because a denial of them would be a denial of due process of law." Though Moody struggled vainly to define such rights by references to "fundamental principles," "arbitrary action," "inalienable rights of mankind," and "immutable principles of justice," the precise meaning of "due process" eluded him. Justice Harlan dissented, as he had throughout this period, insisting that the Bill of Rights in its entirety had been nationalized by the Fourteenth Amendment.

From 1890 on, as has already been shown, the Supreme Court displayed remarkable willingness to employ due process as a protective shield against state action affecting property rights. "Liberty"

became a highly meaningful concept as applied, for example, to
the liberty of employer and employee to enter into contracts free
from state interference (*Lochner* v. *New York* 198 U.S. 45, 1905).
At the same time, the Justices refused to expand the meaning of the
due process clause where personal freedoms were at stake.

This illogical position could not long endure. The change began
when Justice McKenna, in *Gilbert* v. *Minnesota* (254 U.S. 325,
1920), assumed for the sake of argument that the freedom of speech
guarantee in the First Amendment was applicable to state action,
although on the merits the state sedition law as applied to anti-war
writings was upheld. Brandeis in dissent was more forthright, "I
cannot believe," he declared, after citing a number of cases in which
due process had been used to protect property rights, "that the
liberty guaranteed by the Fourteenth Amendment includes only
liberty to acquire and enjoy property." Three years later, *Meyer* v.
Nebraska (262 U.S. 390, 1923), proclaimed a broader meaning of
the "liberty" that could not be denied without due process. Here
the Court agreed that it protected both the right of teachers of the
German language to follow their calling and the right of parents to
control the education of their children against state legislation forbidding German language instruction.

The judicial about-face was completed in 1925 in *Gitlow* v. *New
York* (268 U.S. 652). Gitlow had been convicted under the New
York Criminal Anarchy Act of 1902, prohibiting advocacy of the
overthrow of government by force or violence, of circulating
pamphlets urging workers to revolutionary mass action to establish
a "dictatorship of the proletariat." In Gitlow's defense his counsel
argued that the New York statute deprived him of "liberty" without due process of law. Though the Court ruled that the 1902 Act,
as applied to Gitlow, did not unduly restrict freedom of speech or
press, it accepted the view that the freedoms guaranteed in the First
Amendment are safeguarded by the due process clause of the
Fourteenth Amendment. "For present purposes," the Court observed,
"we may and do assume that freedom of speech, and of the press—
which are protected by the First Amendment from abridgement
by Congress—are among the fundamental personal rights and
'liberties' protected by the due process clause of the Fourteenth
Amendment from impairment by the states." Rejecting Holmes's
"clear and present danger" test, the majority ruled that even though

speeches and publications themselves create no immediate danger, the state may, under its police power, validly forbid them as having a "bad tendency"—that is, a tendency to bring about results dangerous to public security. Two years later, in *Fiske* v. *Kansas* (274 U.S. 380) the Court invalidated a similar state criminal syndicalism act as applied to an organization not shown to have advocated violence, because it violated the due process clause of the Fourteenth Amendment.

The incorporation of the other First Amendment rights followed. In 1931, confronted with a Minnesota law allowing the suppression of any "scandalous" newspaper as a "public nuisance," the Supreme Court held that freedom of the press is within the protection of the "liberty" guaranteed in the Fourteenth Amendment, and that it had been infringed in this case (*Near* v. *Minnesota*, 283 U.S. 697). In 1937 the right of peaceable assembly was included (*DeJonge* v. *Oregon*, 299 U.S. 353).

In 1940 the freedom of religion clause was used to invalidate the conviction of Jehovah Witnesses under Connecticut law. The state required every solicitor for a religious or charitable cause to obtain a permit from the secretary of the state public welfare council who determined whether a cause was "religious" or "charitable." Cantwell had violated the law by not obtaining this permit. In addition, he and other Witnesses were convicted of a "breach of the peace" for playing phonograph records on the sidewalk near a Catholic church, attacking all organized religions but singling out the Roman Catholic Church for particular censure. While some passers-by were angered, no violence had occurred. The Supreme Court found state action invalid on both counts (*Cantwell* v. *Connecticut*, 310 U.S. 296, 1940).

Finally, in 1947, the Court, while upholding 5 to 4 a New Jersey municipal ordinance providing bus service to all children attending public and parochial schools, served notice that the First Amendment provision denying to Congress the power to pass laws respecting an establishment of religion was within the scope of the Fourteenth Amendment, and was intended to create a "wall of separation" between church and state (*Everson* v. *Board of Education*, 330 U.S. 1, 1947). In *McCollum* v. *Board of Education* (333 U.S. 203, 1948), a public school released-time program for religious training, under which denominational teachers gave religious instruction in classrooms during school hours, was invalidated because, in the Court's view, it breached the "wall of separation." In a later case, a New York released-time plan, similar to that invalidated in the McCollum case, except that the teaching took place outside the school, was held constitutional (*Zorach* v. *Clauson*, 343 U.S. 306, 1952). As in so many other areas of constitutional controversy, both proponents and opponents of released-time programs could cite historical data in support of their views.

As a result of these and other cases of similar import, all the rights of the First Amendment have been absorbed into the due process clause of the Fourteenth, and now receive protection in federal courts against adverse action by state or national government.

THE TESTS OF FREEDOM

When the Supreme Court is presented with a case involving a First Amendment freedom, a task of the highest difficulty is involved, one that is not present in all cases of judicial review. Where enumerated powers of Congress or the President are subject to interpretation, the Court's function is at an end when the action taken is found to be within the limits of constitutionally granted power. In reaching such a conclusion the Court is immeasurably aided by the well-established presumption of constitutionality that accompanies most legislative and executive actions.

In cases involving freedom of speech, of press, or of religion, however, the Court must interpret and apply a grant of power— frequently the "reserved" police power of the state—while at the same time it must interpret and apply a constitutional limitation on governmental power. Governments have police power to maintain themselves against attacks from within, just as military power is needed to resist attacks from without. Police power, meaning in this context the power necessary to maintain a peaceful and orderly society, is a primary requisite of government. For obvious reasons decisions concerning the values to be upheld and the freedoms to be protected cannot rest in private hands. The Court is equally aware that the American political tradition has opposed unlimited governmental power, and that the Bill of Rights represents one of the "auxiliary precautions" against its emergence. More specifically, it is generally recognized that the political guarantees of the First Amendment are fundamental in a democratic society—free speech, a free press, and the right of assembly make possible a continuing debate on issues large and small, without which the electoral process becomes an empty ritual. The other First Amendment rights—free exercise of religion and the separation of church and state—represent the American solution to one of the basic issues in the Western political tradition—the proper relation of state and church, of man to his God and his government.

It is apparent, then, that the easy path to constitutional decision by way of the presumption of constitutionality of legislative or administrative action is not readily available in this field. Rather the Court has been forced to invent tests and create other presumptions. Whatever tests are employed, answers must depend ultimately on the Justices' view of correct social policy and their conception of the role of the judiciary in achieving balance between freedom and order. By 1925 the Court possessed two tests for First Amendment cases—"clear and present danger," a test that seemed to express a preference for free speech and "bad tendency," a test more favorable to restrictive action.

FREEDOM AND STATE ACTION

State cases since 1925 featured a continuous battle between these two tests. In 1927, in *Whitney* v. *California* (274 U.S. 357) the majority upheld a conviction under a state criminal syndicalism law, primarily because a criminal conspiracy was not within the bounds of free speech, a position echoed in Justice Jackson's concurring opinion in the Dennis case. In concurring, Brandeis reasserted the merits of the clear-and-present-danger test. In 1931 (*Stromberg* v. *California*, 283 U.S. 359) the Court, invalidating for vagueness a state statute prohibiting the display of a red flag as a symbol of opposition to organized government, placed its decision squarely under the freedom-of-speech provision.

By 1937 the Court was prepared to use the clear-and-present-danger test to pass on the legality of speeches and material disseminated by a Communist Party organizer, contrary to a general Criminal Syndicalist law of Georgia (*Herndon* v. *Lowry*, 301 U.S. 242). "The legislature of Georgia has not," the Court ruled, "made membership in the Communist Party unlawful by reason of its supposed dangerous tendency even in the remote future." Justice Roberts, speaking for the Court, found the act defective as applied because the judge and jury had not determined that the defendant's utterances constituted "a clear and present danger of forcible obstruction of a particular state function."

In 1940 peaceful picketing in labor disputes was brought under the protection of freedom of speech (*Thornhill* v. *Alabama*, 310 U.S. 88). In setting aside an Alabama statute, Justice Murphy declared that abridgment of liberty of discussing issues involved in labor disputes was permissible "only where the clear danger of substantive evils arises under circumstances affording no opportunity to test the merits of ideas by competition for acceptance in the market of public opinion."

In that same year, however, the Court departed sharply from the clear-and-present-danger test. With only Chief Justice Stone dissenting, it sustained a state act requiring all school children to salute the flag, against the religious convictions of the Jehovah's Witnesses, whose religious tenets forbade participation in such ceremonies (*Minersville* v. *Gobitis*, 310 U.S. 586). In 1943 the Court reversed its 1940 flag-salute decision and held state action coercive in a similar situation (*West Virginia School Board v. Barnette*, 319 U.S. 629). Here Justice Jackson stated that First Amendment freedoms might be restricted "only to prevent grave and immediate dangers."

In *Thomas* v. *Collins* (323 U.S. 516, 1945), a Texas statute requiring union organizers to obtain a permit before soliciting members for their organization was invalidated in a 5 to 4 decision. "Lawful public assemblies," Justice Rutledge observed, "involving no element of grave and immediate danger to an interest the state is entitled to protect, are not instruments of harm which require previous identification of the speaker." This perhaps was the high water mark in the use of the clear-and-present-danger test, which had gradually become the touchstone of constitutionality in all cases involving freedom of expression. A year later it was invoked as it had been in the earlier case of *Bridges* v. *California* (314 U.S.

252, 1941), to reverse a contempt of court conviction on the ground that no clear and immediate danger to the administration of justice had been shown (*Pennekamp* v. *Florida*, 328 U.S. 331, 1946).

During the period that began with the "cold war" in 1947, the Court seemed to move more cautiously in applying the clear-and-present-danger test, First Amendment cases being resolved without specific mention of any standard or criterion. In no case, however, has the Court signified flat rejection of the clear and present danger test. In *Kovacs* v. *Cooper* (336 U.S. 77, 1949), the Court upheld a Trenton, New Jersey ordinance prohibiting sound trucks from emitting "loud and raucous noises." Said Justice Reed: "The preferred position of freedom of speech in a society that cherished liberty for all does not require legislators to be insensible to claims by citizens to comfort and convenience."

Still other cases indicate the range of municipal "free speech" infringements that will continue to trouble the Court. In *Terminiello* v. *Chicago* (337 U.S. 1, 1949) the Court divided 5 to 4 in reversing the conviction of a speaker for a "breach of peace" where the extreme "rightest" utterances of the speaker in a private hall brought on attacks by extreme "leftist" opponents. Though the majority referred to the clear-and-present-danger test it based its decision on the broad charge of the trial judge. As Justice Jackson's dissenting opinion makes clear, this case raised fundamental issues concerning the maintenance of public order where speech threatens to disturb it.

In *Kunz* v. *New York* (340 U.S. 290, 1951), the Court, by a vote of 4 to 3, reversed the disorderly-conduct conviction of a religious speaker who had held an outdoor meeting in New York City without a permit, which he had sought and been refused. The ground for denying Kunz's permit application, however, was that the records showed a revocation, after a hearing, of a previous permit to Kunz to conduct street meetings—on the ground that he had consistently ridiculed and denounced the religious beliefs of others. Chief Justice Vinson's opinion for the Court seems to hold that the standards set by the city ordinance for guidance of officials were not clear and constituted unlawful prior restraint. The Chief Justice avoided the question whether prior restraint would be permissible under a more narrowly drawn ordinance, and whether improper conduct by Kunz might be punishable.

In the third case, *Feiner* v. *New York* (340 U.S. 315, 1951), the Court denied the free speech claim of a sidewalk orator who had used derogatory language about public officials (including the President) and the American Legion to a small crowd clustered around him. Unrest and threatening movements among the crowd prompted a policeman to order the speaker to stop, and to arrest him when he refused. The Supreme Court, with three vehement dissenters, upheld the speaker's conviction. Citing with approval a statement in the Cantwell case, Chief Justice Vinson declared: "When clear and present danger of riot, disorder, interference with traffic upon the public streets, or other immediate threats to public safety, peace, or order, appears, the power of the state to prevent or punish is obvious." In this and similar cases, the confusion of facts that usually surrounds the allegedly illegal speech makes effective review by an appellate court extremely difficult, if not impossible. The trial court, by accepting the official version of the incidents involved, severely handicaps a speaker who wants to appeal his conviction.

It has usually been true that only where the Supreme Court is willing to review the facts in a civil liberties case will an appellant from a state conviction succeed in reversing that conviction. "Many times in the past," Justice Black commented in dissent in the Feiner case, "this Court has said that despite findings below, we will examine the evidence for ourselves to ascertain whether federally protected rights have been denied. . . . Even a partial abandonment of this rule makes a dark day for civil liberties in our nation. But," he continued, "still more has been lost today. . . . In my judgment, today's holding means that as a practical matter, minority speakers can be silenced in any city. Hereafter, despite the First and Fourteenth Amendments, the policeman's club can take heavy toll of a current administration's public critics. Criticism of public officials will be too dangerous for all but the most courageous."

Later cases, involving other forms of free speech, did not present clear opportunities for the Court to reveal its position. In *Beauharnais* v. *Illinois* (343 U.S. 250, 1952), Justice Frankfurter dealt with a state law prohibiting libels of racial or other groups solely in terms of the law's reasonableness in classifying certain printed matter as "criminal libel." *Burstyn* v. *Wilson* (343 U.S. 495, 1952), held that movies were protected by the First Amendment against prior state censorship, at least when the standard used by censors was the excessively indefinite word "sacrilegious." Because of slight use of the clear-and-present-danger test in such cases as these, the future of the test as a measuring stick in First Amendment cases remains in doubt.

FREEDOM AND FEDERAL ACTION

The most serious blot on the national government's otherwise good civil liberties record during World War II occurred when Japanese-Americans, in spite of their American citizenship and a lack of any evidence to show their disloyalty, were excluded from designated West Coast areas and either detained in prison camps or, if released, were not permitted to return to their old homes. This program was authorized by Presidential orders and Congressional acts. In *Korematsu* v. *United States* (323 U.S. 214, 1944), the Court upheld the exclusion order, primarily on the ground that the war power gave military judgment wide latitude, the loss of individual rights being considered one of the inevitable hardships of war. The curfew features of the program had previously been upheld in *Hirabayashi* v. *United States* (320 U.S. 81, 1943). In *Ex parte Endo* (323 U.S. 283, 1944), decided on the same day as the *Korematsu* case, the Court agreed that once the loyalty of an internee had been established, continued restraint was illegal. The Justices' refusal to pass upon the constitutionality of the confinement program in its entirety was interpreted as unwillingness to set its judgment of reasonableness against that of the nation's military leaders. This apparent concession to the military of the power to define the content of civil liberties had the over-all effect of establishing the principle that in wartime certain portions of the Constitution may, in effect, be suspended. In the context of war, stringent action by the government can readily be defended under the clear-and-present-danger test.

A unique case, questioning the extent to which Congress may exercise its power to regulate and protect interstate commerce where such regulation affects the right of free speech, was resolved in favor of the government in *American Communications Association* v. *Douds* (339 U.S. 382, 1950). In this case the requirement of the Taft-Hartley Act of 1947 that labor leaders sign a non-Communist oath in order to qualify their union for participation and benefits under the act was held not to violate the First Amendment rights of nonsigners. The dissenters tried in vain to invoke the clear-and-present-danger test.

It was not until the Court was confronted with a case testing the Smith Act of 1940, Section 1 of which made it a felony to advocate the violent overthrow of the government of the United States, or to conspire to organize a group advocating such violence, that the clear-and-present-danger test "bowed out." In upholding the Act as applied to eleven leaders of the American Communist Party (*Dennis* v. *United States* 341 U.S. 494, 1951) the Supreme Court applied a standard suggested by Judge Learned Hand in his Second Circuit Court of Appeals opinion: "In each case Courts must ask whether the gravity of the 'evil,' discounted by its improbability, justifies such invasion of free speech as is necessary to avoid the danger." To Chief Justice Vinson, spokesman for the Court, the clear-and-present-danger test, while applicable to the isolated speech of individuals or small groups, was inappropriate for testing words associated with a large-scale conspiratorial movement: "The situation with which Justices Holmes and Brandeis were concerned in Gitlow was a comparatively isolated event, bearing little relation in their minds to any substantial threat to the safety of the community." At another point in the same opinion, however, the Chief Justice stated flatly: "In this case we are squarely presented with the application of the 'clear-and-present-danger' test, and must decide what that test imports."

Apparently Vinson approved the trial judge's holding as a matter of law that defendants' alleged activities presented "a sufficient danger of a substantive evil" to justify the application of the statute under the First Amendment. But the Chief Justice's attempt to square Judge Hand's formula with the clear-and-present-danger test is unconvincing. The Court's decision in the Dennis case is highly reminiscent of the decisions obtained earlier by application of the "bad tendency" test.

Numerous convictions of lesser Communist Party leaders followed, without giving rise to constitutional issues. Then in 1957 the Warren Court passed on the convictions of fourteen West Coast Communist Party leaders, reversing and ordering new trials in the case of nine, and taking the unprecedented step of directing acquittals in the other five cases (*Yates* v. *United States*, 354 U.S. 298, 1957). The opinion of Justice Harlan for the Court turns on rather fine distinctions difficult to convey by brief summary. While he does not rely on the clear-and-present-danger test, he seemingly moved away from the rigidity of the Dennis decision.

The two chief grounds for reversal were: first, the error of the government and trial court in construing the term "organize" in the Smith Act to mean continuing actions on behalf of the Communist Party, rather than original actions to organize the Party in 1945, when the Communist Party was re-constituted in the United States. Since these indictments were brought in 1951, the three year statute of limitations barred prosecution. Second, the charge of the trial judge was deemed defective, in that he refused a charge requested by defendants that in order to convict the jury must find that the advocacy, which the defendants conspired to promote, was of a kind calculated to "incite" persons to action for the forcible overthrow of the government. Harlan thought the charge actually given ignored the quality of the words used in advocacy, and would permit conviction for "advocacy and teaching of forcible overthrow divorced from any effort to instigate action to that end." Black and Douglas reiterated their views expressed in the Dennis decision, that any restriction of speech on public affairs violated the First Amendment. Justice Clark, with some justification, expressed perplexity with the "artillery of words." In his view the majority opinion, was not calculated to enlighten trial judges. These cases, he believed, should have been disposed of on the same basis as the Dennis case.

Perhaps the viewpoint expressed in the Court's opinion is more significant than the actual decision. The tone is hostile to the theory of the prosecution. Reference is made to "the equivocal character of the evidence in this record." "Instances of speech that could be considered to amount to 'advocacy of action' are so few and far between as to be almost completely over-shadowed by the hundreds of instances in the record in which overthrow, if mentioned at all, occurs in the course of doctrinal disputation so remote from action as to be almost wholly lacking in probative value." The government's policy of lumping the "innocent," "abstract" speech-making of the Party together with a few more explicit acts to spell out "conspiracy is criticized." It would appear that in the absence of proof of explicit "organizing" activities, such as were present in the Dennis case, the above-ground activities of Communist Party leaders would seem far less vulnerable to Smith Act prosecution in the future.

Even more serious issues may arise in the future from the application of the so-called McCarran Act of 1950 (50 U.S.C.A. 813), which provided, among other measures, for the registration of certain organizations and the detention during a presidentially declared "emergency" of persons concerning whom there are reasonable grounds for believing that they would probably engage in sabotage or espionage. Although the Act provided for a hearing and review of administrative findings, it seemed to strain the traditional common-law doctrine of presumed innocence and suggested ugly parallels with the concentration camp. To justify such extreme measures, its supporters stressed the increased dangers of subversive activity in future wars. They recognize too that past challenges to such measures in the context of war have had little success.

ARE THERE PREFERRED FREEDOMS?

This summary revealing the Court's willingness to review state action affecting First Amendment freedoms, contrasts with its generally more tolerant attitude in reviewing state criminal procedures, and suggests that the freedoms of the First Amendment enjoy a status superior to that of the other rights in the first eight amendments. But a further question remains: in reviewing state or national action affecting speech, press, and religion does the Court employ assumptions and presumptions different from those it relies upon in other cases where the question of constitutionality is raised? In other words, does the Court envision a hierarchy of Constitution-protected values, with the First Amendment freedoms at the apex and property rights placed further down?

The clear-and-present-danger test itself, evolved as it was by Justice Holmes, who ordinarily presumed the constitutionality of legislation under scrutiny, indicates at the very least a preference for a wide latitude of speech. Holmes never spelled out the principle, and later on certain Justices began consciously to reveal a preference for First Amendment freedoms. In a now famous footnote to his opinion in *United States* v. *Carolene Products Co.* (304 U.S. 144, 1938), Justice Stone commented, "There may be narrower scope for operation of the presumption of constitutionality when legislation appears on its face to be within a specific prohibition of the Constitution, such as those of the first ten amendments, which are deemed equally specific when held to be embraced within the Fourteenth." He then suggested that there might be more careful judicial scrutiny of legislation or administrative action limiting political activity or adversely affecting minorities. Justices Black, Douglas, and Murphy adopted this position with alacrity, although they would have extended this preferred position not only to First Amendment rights, as Stone suggested, but to all rights listed in the first eight amendments (*FPC* v. *Natural Gas*, 315 U.S. 575, 1942).

Justice Jackson, in the second "flag-salute" case, *West Virginia School Board* v. *Barnette* (319 U.S. 624) argued that more than a rational basis must support restrictions on freedoms of speech, press, assembly, and worship because "the very purpose of a Bill of Rights was to withdraw certain subjects from the vicissitudes of political controversy, to place them beyond the reach of majorities." In 1945, Justice Rutledge stated the doctrine most clearly in *Thomas* v. *Collins* (323 U.S. 516): "The case confronts us again with the duty our system places on this Court to say where the individual's freedom ends and the state's power begins. Choice on that border, now as always delicate, is perhaps more so where the usual presumption supporting legislation [that it is constitutional] is balanced by the preferred place given in our scheme to the great, the indispensable democratic freedoms secured by the First Amendment." In 1952 Justice Clark, speaking for the Court, said that freedom of expression was "the rule" in invalidating a provision of the New York state censorship law (*Burstyn* v. *Wilson*, 343 U.S. 495).

Justice Frankfurter has on many occasions criticized any and all efforts to create a preferred status for First Amendment rights. In *Kovacs* v. *Cooper* (336 U.S. 77, 1949), he opposed Justice Reed's use of the "preferred position" concept, stating, "This is a phrase that has uncritically crept into some recent opinions of this Court. I deem it a mischievous phrase, if it carries the thought, which it may safely imply, that any law touching communication is infected with presumptive invalidity."

Frankfurter, joined by the majority of his colleagues in most cases after 1949, prefers to examine all legislative and official action against the standard of "reasonableness," with the presumption of validity applying in freedom cases as in all others, although in church-state controversies he seems more suspicious of official action. Justices Black and Douglas, voting together in most instances, have waged a rear-guard action in support of the preferred-freedoms doctrine. In the tense atmosphere of a "cold war" world it appeared that the protection of individual freedom rested less and less in the hands of the Supreme Court and more and more in the hands of citizens acting through their legislative representatives.

To many observers the Vinson Court inevitably preferred authority when the people's government took steps that limited the people's freedom. With the death of Chief Justice Vinson in 1953 and the replacement of Reed, Minton, and Jackson by Harlan, Brennan, and Whittaker, the Court under the leadership of Chief Justice Earl Warren began to take a more favorable attitude toward personal freedoms. Several opinions handed down toward the end of the October, 1956 term suggested that such a change might be underway. Several of the cases involved Communists, or alleged Communists, successors to the Jehovah Witnesses as prolific breeders of constitutional litigation.

Beneath the seemingly technical argument there is considerable evidence that the Warren Court is opposed to Smith Act convictions based on evidence of little more than abstract discussion. It has ruled that two men, denied licenses to practice law by state examiners because of one-time membership in the Communist Party, could not be barred on that ground (*Konigsberg* v. *State Bar of California*, 353 U.S. 252, 1957; *Schware* v. *Board of Examiners of New Mexico*, 353 U.S. 232, 1957). It ordered a new trial where "tainted" evidence had been used by the government in convicting four Communist Party leaders (*Mesarosh* v. *United States*, 352 U.S. 1, 1956). It took similar action where a government investigator had questioned members of a jury sitting in a prosecution of a labor leader for falsely signing a non-Communist oath under the Taft-Hartley Act (*Gold* v. *United States*, 352 U.S. 985, 1957).

The Court also showed fresh interest in protecting witnesses in Congressional investigations. In the controversial Watkins case (*Watkins* v. *United States*, 354 U.S. 178, 1957) it reversed the contempt conviction of a witness at a Congressional hearing because of the failure of the committee to show the pertinence of its questions to any legitimate legislative purpose, and took a similar view in a case involving a state investigation, where a New Hempshire college professor had been convicted of contempt (*Sweezy* v. *New Hampshire*, 354 U.S. 234, 1957). The Court upheld the claim of John S. Service that Secretary of State Dulles in discharging him as a "security risk" had failed to follow required administrative procedures (*Service* v. *Dulles*, 354 U.S. 363, 1957).

In the 1957-58 term the same tendencies were evident, although many of the decisions turned on points that blunt the freedom issue. In what may be the most significant of the decisions, because it was based solely on constitutional grounds, the Court held that a lawful association may maintain the secrecy of membership lists, and may protect the right of its members to associate by taking legal action on their behalf (*NAACP* v. *Alabama ex rel. Patterson*, 357 U.S. 449, 1958). In the present less individualistic age, in which constitutional rights are more and more frequently asserted by and on behalf of groups and associations, which in turn provide legal and financial support of the constitutional claims of their members, the Court's position is highly realistic.

In less striking fashion, the Court invalidated a California oath requirement, based on a state constitutional provision, as a condition for receiving state tax exemption (*Speiser* v. *Randall*, 357 U.S. 513; *First Unitarian Church* v. *Los Angeles*, 357 U.S. 545, 1958). Individual taxpayers and two Unitarian churches refused to submit an oath asserting that they did not "advocate the overthrow of the government, etc." Justice Brennan, for the Court, with only Clark dissenting, held that the burden of proof had been improperly placed on petitioners for tax exemption under the California scheme, insofar as it deters freedom of political belief and action, and thus denies due process of law. Brennan "assumed" that California had the constitutional power to deny tax exemption to persons who engaged in proscribed speech for which they might be fined or imprisoned. Presumably California must place on its tax assessor the duty of determining those ineligible for tax exemption.

The right to travel was proclaimed "part of the liberty of which the citizen cannot be deprived without due process of law," (in

Kent v. *Dulles*, 357 U.S. 116, 1958 and companion cases). But the actual decision turns on the limits under congressional acts of the Secretary of State's power to issue passports—his power to deny them to Communists and others whose travel abroad is not in the national interest. Beginning in 1856 Congress had delegated the power to issue passports to the Secretary of State in sweeping terms. "The Secretary of State may grant and issue passports . . . under such rules as the President shall designate and prescribe for and on behalf of the United States, and no other person shall grant, issue, or verify such passports." Douglas argued that this provision, codified in 1926, and presently in effect, should not be interpreted expansively because of the important constitutional right involved, but rather should be construed as embodying the administrative practice of the Secretary of State up to 1926. Douglas found that in administrative practice up to that time passports were denied only to those lacking allegiance to the United States and those participating in illegal conduct. He assumed that Congress intended that only on such grounds were passports to be denied. Justice Clark's dissent, joined by Burton, Harlan, and Whittaker, provides numerous examples of departures by the State Department from this administrative "practice." About all that one can say is that Congress must make its intentions clearer (as attempted by an administration bill introduced immediately after the decision proposes), leaving to a future case a determination of the scope of the Constitutional "right to travel."

This is an impressive list of pro-civil liberties decisions but it does not signify that the Court is prepared to go beyond its demand for more careful Congressional definition of its intentions, and more scrupulous adherence by administrative officials to principles of fairness. Many of these cases it should be noted turned on rather fine distinctions in the interpretation and application of law and did not come to grips with legislative policy, suggesting the likelihood that broad generalizations in many of the opinions will prove less meaningful in application to different fact situations in future cases. Finally, it is not yet clear whether Congress will complacently accept all the Court's holdings. Hardly had certain of the decisions been announced when Congressional proposals were advanced to whittle down the breadth of Court holdings. A bill was passed to limit the scope of the decision in the Jencks case, opening FBI and other government files to defendants. Other legislative proposals sought to reverse the Watkins decision, thought by some Congressional leaders to be a serious barrier to effective investigations. These decisions have evoked criticism rivaling the bitter attacks on the Court following the desegregation decisions.

As though to blunt the criticism of its congressional critics, the Court substantially modified some of the broad principles set forth in the Watkins decision by its June 8, 1959 holding in *Barenblatt* v. *United States*. In that case it upheld the power of the same committee of Congress to question a college instructor concerning his alleged communist party activities and associates. At the same time it narrowed some of the implications of *Pennsylvania* v. *Nelson* that had disquieted supporters of states rights by sanctioning the efforts of the New Hampshire Attorney General to obtain information about subversive activities within the state (*Uphaus* v. *New Hampshire*). Both decisions were 5-4, with sharp, vigorous dissents, but both have the natural effect of disarming critics.

Few believe the Court is in serious danger, or will fail to weather one more storm in its long, sometimes turbulent, history. Most thoughtful Americans realize that the Court has not resisted persistent democratic pressures to limit freedom when such limitation seemed to serve the national interest. The list of legislative acts restricting freedom held contrary to the Constitution is small. What the Court had done is to moderate the enforcement process, and limit irrational official actions. Few, except extremists at both edges of the political spectrum, would deny the long term value of this modest judicial role.

XV

TOWARD POSITIVE
RESPONSIBILITY

AMERICANS HAVE BECOME SO
accustomed to judicial review that they take it for granted. Whenever government enters any new domain the natural and inevitable
question is whether the steps taken are constitutionally valid. Since
1937 responsible observers, including the late Justice Owen J.
Roberts, have wondered whether a government so circumscribed
can survive in an age which calls for power and more power—
power to deal with domestic problems of ever-increasing complexity, power to cope with the most baffling international issues.
These pressures may help explain why, during the years since 1937,
the principle of constitutional limitations has been in eclipse. Americans are still accustomed, nevertheless, to think in terms of the
constitutionality of governmental action rather than of its wisdom.

Long before he became a Supreme Court Justice, Professor
Felix Frankfurter began to query America's "constant preoccupa-
tion with the constitutionality of legislation." This tends, he said,
to make us think "a law is all right if it is constitutional." Frankfurter is convinced now, as he was before donning judicial robes,

that "much that should be rejected as illiberal, because repressive and envenoming, may well be not unconstitutional. The ultimate reliance for the deepest needs of civilization must be found outside of their vindication under the guarantees of the Constitution." (*Dennis* v. *United States*, 341 U.S. 494, 556, and *New Republic*, Jan. 17, 1925.)

Justice Frankfurter's concern is less relevant in 1959 than it was in 1925. For judicial review of acts of Congress and of state regulation of the economy has now become an inconspicuous feature of the judicial process. The Court has not surrendered its power, as the current attack on it clearly indicates, but the bars against government action are seldom found in the Constitution. So one may ask whether this most distinctive aspect of the political process—constitutional limitations—can survive in a world constantly faced with the possibility of paralyzing economic crisis and/or devastating atomic war.

The answer may be suggested by consideration of what has happened in the last two decades to three of our most important power-delimiting principles: separation of power, dual federalism, and due process of law. In comparatively recent years—down to 1936—all these principles had been invoked by the Supreme Court. Since 1937 all have been eroded in the face of the insistent demand for the power to govern.

Consider the principle of separation of powers. It finds no specific authorization in the Constitution. Rather it is implicit in the structure and organization of the document. The Constitution does not, in any event, preclude all blending of powers. This is fortunate, since modern government tends to be largely administrative, involving fusion of legislative, executive and judicial powers, all relatively free from judicial control. Writing in 1958, Justice William O. Douglas observed:

Today the administrative agency is supreme in state and federal governments. Its functions are manifold and varied. . . . The agency is supreme because of its pervasive influence in American affairs. It is also supreme because, once launched in its orbit, there is often no real effective control over it . . . whether we think in terms of congressional action, executive supervision or judicial review. [*Columbia Law Alumni Bulletin*, Dec. 1958, p. 16.]

The viability of separation of powers has not, however, completely vanished. In 1952, the heyday of judicial quiescence under Chief Justice Vinson, President Truman, without statutory authorization, seized and operated the steel mills. The Supreme Court acted quickly. "In the framework of our Constitution," Justice Black observed, "the President's power to see that the laws are faithfully executed refutes the idea that he is to be a law maker." Justice Black's rejection of the claim of inherent power in the President to deal with the emergency as he pleased was rooted in the doctrine of separation of powers. Against an impressive background of unprecedented executive aggrandizement and with the banner of self-restraint still flying, the Court interposed its authority, making it quite clear that Presidential action is not immune to judicial review. Justice Douglas has called the Youngstown Steel decision "the most important one in our history concerning separation of powers between the President and Congress, and the role of the Court in enforcing the separation."

We turn now to the second working doctrine serving constitutional limitations, particularly after 1890—dual federalism. What has happened to it under the stress of economic emergency and war? The reciprocal operation of this doctrine is illustrated in national and state effort to deal with the liquor problem. When a state tried to prevent introduction of liquor into its borders it was blocked because the state's prohibition laws interfered with the power of Congress to regulate interstate commerce. When, on the other hand, Congress attempted to reach the same or similar evils, such as child labor, it was blocked as invading the domain of the states. The states could not effectively outlaw child labor because national commerce power is vested in Congress. In the face of emergency, this power-crippling doctrine has yielded. After veering away from Marshall's broad concept of the subject matter of commerce and equally broad view of the national commerce power, a unanimous Court came full circle. Returning in 1940 to Chief Justice Marshall's position, a unanimous Court held that Congress is in large measure the final judge of policy as well as of power. Like Marshall, Justice Stone ruled that Congress's powers to regulate commerce must be interpreted as if there were no states. Stone called the Tenth Amendment a "truism," merely another way of stating the substance of the supremacy clause. Commenting in 1951 on the increased scope accorded state and national power, Justice Roberts observed:

> Both a state and the nation may exercise the police power, the former without restriction, save as the authority granted to the federal government limits its action. . . . The exercise of the power of Congress to regulate can neither be enlarged or circumscribed by state action. Congress has the choice whether to prescribe that which supports state policy or that which runs counter to it.

On the effect of the Darby decision, Roberts said:

> Of course the effect of sustaining the act [Fair Labor Standards] was to place the whole matter of wages and hours of persons employed throughout the United States with slight exceptions under a single federal regulatory scheme, and in this way completely supercede state exercise of the police power in this field.

So just as the separation of powers principle has undergone considerable qualification in the face of over-hanging emergency and the demand for national authority to meet it (Youngstown Steel being perhaps the exception that proves the rule), so dual federalism melted under the same solvents. But dual federalism has not lost all its vitality. Within less than two years after Justice Stone had apparently pronounced its death knell, he made it clear that he did not endorse any implication that this principle was ended. In *Cloverleaf Butter Co.* v. *Patterson* (315 U.S. 148, 1942, 176) he deplored the majority opinion as precluding "a working harmonious federal-state relationship for the sake of a sterile and harmful insistence on exclusive federal power."

> It is one thing for Courts in interpreting an Act of Congress regulating matters beyond state control to construe its language with a view to carrying into effect a general though unexpressed Congressional purpose. It is quite another to infer a purpose, which Congress has not expressed, to deprive the states of authority which otherwise constitutionally belongs to them, over a subject which Congress has not undertaken to control. Due regard for the maintenance of our dual system of government demands that the courts do not diminish state power by extravagant inferences regarding what Congress might have intended if it had considered the matter, or by reference to their own conceptions of a policy which Congress has not expressed and is not plainly to be inferred from the legislation which it has enacted.

309 TOWARD POSITIVE RESPONSIBILITY

The decision was 5 to 4. In 1944 Justice Frankfurter, speaking for a unanimous Court, put the matter this way:

> The interpenetrations of modern society have not wiped out state lines. It is not for us to make inroads upon our federal system either by indifference to its maintenance or excessive regard for the unifying forces of modern technology. Scholastic reasoning may prove that no activity is isolated within the boundaries of a single state, but that cannot justify absorption of legislative power by the United States over every activity. [*Polish National Alliance* v. *NLRB*, 322 U.S. 643, 1943, p. 650.]

Concern for states' rights has mounted since Frankfurter voiced these sentiments, especially as a result of the segregation decisions and cases such as Steve Nelson (350 U.S. 497) and Konigsberg (353 U.S. 252, 1957). Justice Harlan, perhaps even to a greater extent than Justice Frankfurter, is sensitive to the federal-state dichotomy. In *Roth* v. *United States* (354 U.S. 476, 1957) Harlan suggested, in dissent, that a federal obscenity statute was too broad, and should therefore be invalidated. But, at the same time, he refused to strike down a state statute which he considered as broad as the federal act. His opinion makes it quite clear that in federal-state relations the Court still has an important and delicate function to perform.

> The Constitution differentiates between those areas of human conduct subject to the regulation of the states and those subject to the powers of the Federal Government. The substantive powers of the two governments, in many instances, are distinct. And in every case where we are called upon to balance the interests in free expression against other interests, it seems to me important that we should keep in the forefront the question of whether those other interests are state or federal. Since under our constitutional scheme the two are not necessarily equivalent, the balancing process must needs often produce different results. Whether a particular limitation on speech or press is to be upheld because it subserves a paramount governmental interest must, to a large extent, I think, depend on whether that government has, under the Constitution, a direct substantive interest, that is, the power to act, in the particular area involved.

Speaking in 1958, Chief Justice Warren conceded that Washington had at times become too deeply involved in matters that were the proper prerogatives of the states, but he went on to explain that the fault lies more often than not with the states themselves.

When the state governments fail to satisfy the needs of the people, the people appeal to the Federal Government. Whether the question is one of the advancement of human knowledge through research, of law and order or the right of all persons to equal protection of the law, the Federal Government need become involved only when the states fail to act.

We come finally to "due process"—that mighty constitutional barrier limiting both the national government and the states. From a somewhat technical procedural requirement affecting the exercise of legislative power, we have seen how the Court transformed this clause into a substance limitation on power at all levels. In due course the Justices extended the definition of liberty in the Fourteenth Amendment to cover "liberty of contract" and "freedom of competition." By the end of the 1920's these judicially created concepts had become virtually absolute barriers against government control and regulation of the economy. "Freedom is the rule, regulation the exception," Justice Sutherland announced in 1923. In a series of cases, the Court proceeded to enforce this dictum. In *Nebbia* v. *New York* of 1934, however, Justice Roberts indicated what had happened to substantive due process. "The power to promote the general welfare is inherent in government," he said, and the context makes clear Justice Roberts' purpose to include both national and state government.

After the Nebbia decision students of the Court saw the practical end of judicial review under the due process clause as a substantive limitation on the power to govern. In 1943, Justice Jackson declared that "the laissez-faire concept or principle of non-interference, at least as to economic affairs, has withered, and social advancements are increasingly sought through closer integration of society and through expanded and strengthened governmental controls." The Court had apparently accepted the collectivist theory of government. Social democracy could be achieved, in spite of the due process clause, within the four corners of the Constitution. On occasion certain Justices have hinted that this is not so but, as we have seen, such assertions have aroused vehement denials. In terms of constitutionality it is now immaterial whether state action runs counter "to the economic wisdom either of Adam Smith or of J. Maynard Keynes" (*Osborn* v. *Ozlin*, 310 U.S. 53, 1939, 62). If a state wishes to encourage a pastoral instead of an industrial society, "that is its concern and its privilege." (*Freeman* v. *Hewitt*, 329 U.S. 249, 1946, 252.) "The day is gone," Justice Douglas observed in a 1955 decision, "when this Court uses the Due Process Clause of the 14th Amendment to strike down state laws, regulating business and industrial conditions, because they may be unwise, improvident or out of harmony with a particular school of thought." (*Williamson* v. *Lee Optical Company*, 348 U.S. 483, 488.)

In the face of this remarkable development certain commentators are profoundly pessimistic. "Legislative independence and legislative wisdom," Frank J. Hogan complained in 1939, "are now America's sole reliance for the continuance of that security of the blessings of liberty for which the Constitution was framed and the government of the United States created." Justice Roberts, writing in 1951, several years after his retirement, dolefully commented:

> The Supreme Court has limited and surrendered the role the Constitution intended to confer on it. *Vox Populi, vox Dei* was not the theory on which the charter was drawn. The sharp divisions of power intended has become blurred . . . doctrines announced as corollaries to express grants of power to Congress have more and more circumscribed the pristine powers of the States, which were intended to be preserved to them by the Constitution, and that resistance to the expansion of those doctrines seems to have weakened as our nation has grown.

Mr. Hogan and Justice Roberts appear unduly alarmed. Political restraints are now, as they say, our primary dependence. But that is what the framers originally intended them to be. The judiciary had merely lost its self-acquired pre-eminence. Chief Justice Marshall had been content, as we have seen, to rely on the "wisdom and discretion of Congress," along with the usual political restraints. Half a century later, Chief Justice Waite emphatically told aggrieved litigants to "resort to the polls, not the courts," when seeking correction of alleged wrongs inflicted by a state legislature. Justice Bradley voiced these same convictions in 1890. By that time, however, judicial aggrandizement had reached such a pitch as compelled him to do so in dissent, and thus initiate a plaintive note which became a resounding refrain later on in dissenting opinions by Justices Holmes, Brandeis, and Stone. Substitution of judicial *supremacy* for judicial *review*, reversal of the subordinate position of judicial restraints in relation to political restraints created the impasse of 1937. The corrective was found in returning to the wisdom of the framers, to the judicial humility of Marshall, Waite, Holmes, Brandeis, and Stone.

Once political controls had been re-established as the primary check on government, it seemed logically to follow that the Court must shoulder a corresponding responsibility for the effective functioning of the political process. But cases involving such responsibility have evoked a variety of responses from the Justices. For certain of them, First Amendment freedoms are "preferred." More sacred than those of property and contract, these freedoms are protected from legislative encroachment not only by the due process requirement but also by the injunction that "Congress shall make *no* law . . . abridging the freedom of speech, or of the press; or the right of the people peaceably to assemble. . . ." The thought of the so-called activists (notably Justices Black and Douglas) seems to be that though the Constitution does not embody, as Holmes said, any particular *economic* philosophy, it does incorporate a particular political theory. Central to that theory are the freedoms listed in the First Amendment. As to these, judicial self-restraint does not mean that the Court is paralyzed. "It simply conserves its strength," as Attorney-General Jackson put it, "to strike more telling blows in the cause of a working democracy."

Except for occasional deviations, especially those occurring during Fred Vinson's Chief-Justiceship, the Court since 1937 has subjected legislative and administrative infringements on civil rights to more exacting scrutiny. When, in 1956, Justice Frankfurter observed, "as no constitutional guarantee enjoys preference, so none should suffer subordination or deletion." Justice Reed wrote a cryptic concurrence solely to take exception to Justice Frankfurter's statement that "no constitutional guarantee enjoys preference."

Evidence mounts that the "self-restraint" banner raised in 1937 has not blinded Chief Justice Warren's Court to certain positive responsibilities which his predecessors had, on occasion, shunned. His Court began to discharge these on May 17, 1954, that historic day when the Justices handed down their unanimous judgment in the school segregation cases. The anxiously awaited opinion was short and incisive. The Chief Justice found neither history nor precedent an adequate guide. Special studies of the intention of the framers of the Fourteenth Amendment were inconclusive. "In approaching this problem," the Chief Justice remarked, "we must consider public education in the light of its full development and its present place in American life throughout the Nation." Segregation, he said, may affect hearts and minds in a way unlikely ever to be undone.

Certain observers marked the case as statesmanship of the first order. For others the decision opened a veritable Pandora's box of criticism and recrimination, not only among Southerners but also among thoughtful people elsewhere. The Governor of Georgia naturally predicted "dark days ahead" and in his anguish, cried out, "Georgia belongs to Georgians—not to the U.S. Supreme Court and not to the NAACP." A sober student of constitutional law concluded that the Court had displayed a "missionary zeal in behalf of . . . underprivileged . . . Negroes," that "is not compatible with [the] true function of democratic leadership."

Nor is racial segregation the only field in which the Warren Court has responded to a larger responsibility. At a single sitting, June 17, 1957, the Justices shouldered other tasks in the civil rights orbit. In the *Yates* case the Court upheld the right of anyone to advocate overthrow of the government, so long as the preaching does not openly advocate specific action. In the *Watkins* case, it qualified the power of congressional committees to make investigations and require witnesses to testify. In *Sweezy* v. *New Hampshire*, it limited the state's power to require witnesses to testify in investigations authorized by state law. In the *Jencks* case earlier in the term, the Justices held that the F.B.I. and other government agency reports must be made available to defendants in criminal trials if the persons who made the report are called as witnesses. In *Trop* v. *Dulles*, decided in 1958, the Court declared unconstitutional a section of the Nationality Act of 1941 which expatriates the wartime deserter dishonorably discharged after conviction by court-martial. In all these cases the Court took the position that government action restricting or taking away fundamental rights of citizenship should be examined with special diligence, that "the Judiciary has the duty of implementing the constitutional safeguards that protect individual rights."

"We cannot simply assume," Chief Justice Warren commented in the *Watkins* case, "that every congressional investigation is justified by a public need that overbalances any private rights affected.

To do so would be to abdicate the responsibility placed by the Constitution upon the judiciary to insure that the Congress does not unjustifiably encroach upon an individual's right of privacy nor abridge his liberty of speech, press, religion or assembly." Even Justice Frankfurter, the most persistent exponent of judicial laissez-faire, regardless of the area involved, now recognizes that the Court must balance the contending claims of a citizen to political privacy and the right of the state to self-protection. "This is the inescapable judicial task," Frankfurter wrote, concurring in the *Sweezy* decision, "and it is a task ultimately committed to this Court."

Because of these decisions and of others in this genre, the Warren Court finds itself the focus of public controversy. Are its troubles like those in which the Hughes Court was embroiled?

The adverse criticism directed against Warren and his Court comes mainly from outsiders, many of them lawyers. The most telling blasts against the Hughes Court of 1935-36 came from the Justices themselves. Dissenting opinions in the Warren Court are less significant both quantitatively and qualitatively than those directed against the majority on Hughes's Bench. The segregation decision was unanimous. The *Yates* decision was six to one, *Jencks*, seven to one, *Sweezy*, six to two, *Watkins*, six to one. In quality, the dissents tend to drop to the level of Justice Clark's outburst in the *Jencks* case, that the majority had opened F.B.I. files "to the criminal and thus afforded him a Roman holiday for rummaging through confidential information as well as vital national secrets." Justice Clark's complaint is reminiscent of McReynold's frenzied outcry in the Gold Clause case of 1935—"The Constitution is gone"—rather than of Stone's trenchant analysis of the majority opinion in the AAA case. Though certain of the Warren Court's decisions are open to valid criticism and may be in for trimming (some has already occurred), one finds little in the dissents likely to qualify them as future majority opinions.

The Warren Court, while responding to the positive responsibility committed to it by the Constitution, has not been unmindful of the bounds set by the principle of judicial self-restraint. Since 1937, the Constitution has been seldom invoked as a barrier against congressional action. Statutory interpretation rather than constitutional interpretation is involved. Here contrast with the Hughes

Court is sharp. The Justices of 1935-36 met the constitutional issue with alacrity. The Hughes Court vitalized old constitutional barriers and refashioned new ones against the power to govern. Even the well-worn principle of presumption of constitutionality was sometimes ignored. This flouting of judicial self-restraint, this destruction of a national legislative program having strong popular support meant the raising of bars that could be removed only by constitutional amendment, or by reversal of judicial decisions. The Warren Court, on the other hand, has achieved libertarian objectives largely by statutory interpretation. Thus the ill-effects and shortcomings of momentous decisions like *Yates, Watkins* and *Jencks,* can be removed by an act of Congress, or by the Justices themselves. It thus seems improbable that some future commentator will be able to write as an epitaph on Warren's Chief-Justiceship the words Samuel Hendel used to describe Hughes's strategy in 1937.

> When the pressure for innovation became great, and the risks to the nation and to the Court itself apparent, reluctantly at first, but increasingly he went along with change. Having sedulously sought to protect the precedents of the Court, sometimes at the risk of offending logic, he witnessed and often participated in the shattering of one precedent after another. He stood thus as a kind of heroic and in a sense, tragic figure, torn between the old and the new, seeking at first to stem the tide, but then ruthlessly caught up and moving with it.

The Hughes Court precipitated a crisis by blocking legislation which the Constitution itself did not enjoin. The Warren Court is under attack in responding to popular aspirations, perhaps in moving ahead of them, as in the segregation decisions. In repudiating the separate but equal doctrine and thus bringing the law of the American Constitution into line with the social conscience of the world, it has aroused strong protest in certain Southern states. The Court has also evoked criticism from less localized quarters. By curbing legislation designed to achieve national security in a time of unprecedented peril, it finds itself in the awkward posture of frustrating government effort to stave off the Communist threat. Little wonder the Court is under fire. Like that headed by John Marshall, the Warren Court is damming a powerful current in our politics. Just as Marshall's fervent nationalism stirred violent criticism among Democratic Republicans, so the Warren Court's defense

of our basic freedoms rouses bitter denunciation from those inclined
to equate security with repression.

Can a rationale be fashioned justifying greater judicial alertness
to infringements on civil liberties than to legislation regulating the
economy? The Justices, in attempting to supply it, have reached
different results. There is, for example, the doctrinaire formula of
Justices Black and Douglas, which elevates First Amendment freedoms practically to an absolute. There is the more restrained position
of Justice Stone which suggests that legislation infringing speech,
thought and religion, and legislation so restrictive of the political
process as to make it impossible for minorities to resort to it effectively, must be subjected to more careful judicial scrutiny. In applying Stone's formula, the Warren Court has the sanction of tradition,
as well as the support of such eminent jurists as Brandeis, Cardozo,
Holmes, and Hughes.

Those who won our independence and framed the Constitution
believed that the only security worth having is built on freedom.
By 1790, American society had already reached a degree of stability
sufficient to prompt the first Congress to write into the Constitution
provisions protecting the right of political disagreement. In piloting
the bill of rights through the first Congress, Madison observed:

> The prescriptions in favor of liberty ought to be levelled against
> that quarter where the greatest danger lies, namely, that which
> possesses the highest prerogative of power. But this is not found in
> either the Executive or Legislative departments of Government, but
> in the body of the people, operating by the majority against the
> minority. . . . If they [the bill of rights] are incorporated into the
> Constitution, independent tribunals of justice will consider them-
> selves in a peculiar manner the guardians of those rights; they will
> be an impenetrable bulwark against every assumption of power in
> the Legislative or Executive; they will be naturally led to resist
> every encroachment upon rights, expressly stipulated for in the
> Constitution by the declaration of rights.

A century and a half later the late Justice Robert H. Jackson
echoed Madison's sentiments:

> There is nothing covert or conflicting in the recent judgments of
> the Court on social legislation and on legislative repressions of civil
> rights. The presumption of validity which attaches in general to
> legislative acts is frankly reversed in the case of interferences with
> free speech and free assembly, and for a perfectly cogent reason.

Ordinarily, legislation whose basis in economic wisdom is uncertain can be redressed by the processes of the ballot box or the pressures of opinion. But when the channels of opinion or of peaceful persuasion are corrupted or clogged, these political correctives can no longer be relied on, and the democratic system is threatened at its most vital point. In that event the Court, by intervening, restores the processes of democratic government; it does not disrupt them.

Despite the apparent strength of the Warren Court's position, its defenders are small in number compared to the host that rallied around Hughes's when F.D.R. launched his abortive crusade to "reform" the Court. The 1937 crisis represented a conflict between the Court and the President. The current battle is between the Court and Congress, the President being a somewhat confused spectator. Among the Warren Court's most vigorous defenders are the Justices themselves. On November 8, 1958, Justice Douglas bluntly announced that the Court would not "take a back seat." "The courts as an institution are too deeply fixed in our society," he said. "There is no sturdier element in our democratic system than an independent judiciary." On November 25, Justice Harlan, mindful of the poison in the Butler-Jenner bill limiting the Supreme Court's appellate jurisdiction in a wide assortment of cases involving civil rights, stressed the seriousness of the attack. At the peak of his power F.D.R. could muster the support of only 30 Senators in favor of Court packing. The Butler-Jenner bill went down in the Senate by the narrow margin of 49 to 41. F.D.R. proposed to increase the Court's membership, leaving its power untouched. The Butler-Jenner bill went far beyond these bounds. By withdrawing appellate jurisdiction in an important group of national security cases, it made the Court, in this extremely crucial area, something less than supreme.

Why should defense of the Court against F.D.R.'s attempt to pack it have been so spontaneous, and the Warren Court's outside support, including that of President Eisenhower, have been so ambiguous? There are, of course, various possible reasons; one may be the inroads which the Warren Bench has made on the Court as a powerless symbol of justice. Four short years have witnessed the shattering of judicial axioms of the most sacred character. The legal profession's mighty principle of stare decisis has been rudely shaken; the notion that sociological and other extra-legal data are meet for the legislature but not for courts has been ignored; the venerable fiction that courts exercise judgment and not will, always tenuous, has been honored only in the breach. Chief Justice Warren himself has slighted the symbolic aspects of our jurisprudence. "Our judges are not monks or scientists," the Chief Justice wrote in 1955, "but participants in the living stream of our national life, steering the law between the dangers of rigidity on the one hand and formlessness on the other. . . ." As Thurman Arnold has observed, the Court under Chief Justice Warren, is becoming "unified," "a Court of inspired choice and policy, . . . rather than a Court of law as we used to know it."

Though the Court in playing a positive role in support of civil liberties may not have inflicted any major wound on itself, it has on occasion, as in *Jencks* and *Watkins*, been guilty of something less than good craftsmanship. "The real concern," Paul Freund has observed, "is with the Court's tendency to make broad principles do service for specific problems that call for differentiation." In preparing an exhaustive treatise on Administrative Law, Kenneth Culp Davis was prompted to make five "constructive suggestions."

> (1) The Court probably should write fewer general essays in its opinions and it should give more meticulous care to the ones it does write. (2) The Court should take greater advantage of the values of case-to-case development of law. (3) The Court should make further effort to reduce the frequency of contradictory holdings, and it should check its apparently growing tendency to indulge in easy generalizations that are misleading if read literally. (4) The Court should have greater respect for its own holdings and for its own opinions; without restricting its freedom to overrule, it should restrict its freedom to violate its own doctrine. (5) The Court should inquire whether it is often too lighthearted about the manipulation of technical doctrine in order to produce desired substantive results in particular cases.

Professor Davis left open the question whether these suggestions would apply to other fields of law, but students of the Court will perhaps find little difficulty in citing recent Supreme Court cases illustrative of the points he finds applicable in Administrative Law.

It is still relevant to ask whether a politically irresponsible body, such as the Supreme Court, can block the will of the majority in the name of minorities and still remain a democratic institution. When the minority rights protected are those of property, the answer is probably "no." Between 1890 and 1937, the Supreme Court actually retarded the growth of democracy. When, on the other hand, judicial review serves to give a minority, otherwise barred, access to the political process, it implements rather than limits free government. The Court's function is not to determine what decisions can be made by political processes, but to prevent the mechanism from breaking down. Under this theory the legislature can control the wages and hours of workers; it cannot limit the right to vote with respect to race or color. Congress can regulate agricultural production; it cannot control the content of newspapers. The state can demand that children attend school; it cannot compel them to participate in ceremonies that violate their religious convictions. Judicial hands-off in economic matters is perfectly consistent with judicial activism to preserve the integrity and effective operation of the political process.

An appointive body, such as the Supreme Court, exercising political control in a system of government whose powers are supposed to derive from the people, has, as we have seen, sometimes been considered an alien offshoot from an otherwise democratic polity. The dilemma was once resolved by invoking the fiction that the Court had no power—that it merely applied the Constitution which, in some mystical way, is always the highest expression of the people's will. Though this ancient theory still shows signs of vitality, it is not altogether satisfying. The real problem is to protect individuals and minorities without thereby destroying capacity in the majority to govern. Majorities—and this is the key point of democratic theory—are always in flux. Tomorrow's majority may have a different composition as well as different goals. Defense of the political rights of minorities thus becomes, not the antithesis of majority rule, but its very foundation. The Supreme Court can contribute toward realization of free government by guaranteeing all minority groups free access to the political process and the instruments of political change, while at the same time, allowing the majority government—as long as the political process is open and untrammeled—to rule.

In a free society, no organ of government can be defended solely in terms of its symbolic value. The Supreme Court is but one among several agencies empowered, within limits, to govern. The suggestion that any organ of government is beyond public scrutiny, more particularly that the judiciary should enjoy freedom from critical examination greater than any other agency can claim is to be deplored. Nothing of the sort was envisioned by the framers of the Constitution. Implicit in the system of government they established is the basic premise that unchecked power in any hands whatsoever is intolerable. The freedom the judiciary has from political responsibility and control makes its processes more rather than less appropriate for critical exploration. To the recently expressed notion that "the judicial process requires a degree of privacy incomparably stricter than is fitting in the legislative or executive process," Justice Frankfurter has retorted:

> Judges as persons, or courts as institutions, are entitled to no greater immunity from criticism than other persons or institutions. Just because the holders of judicial office are identified with interests of justice they may forget their common human frailties and fallibilities. There have sometimes been martinets upon the bench as there have also been pompous wielders of authority who have used the paraphernalia of power in support of what they call their dignity. Therefore, judges must be kept mindful of their limitations and of their ultimate public responsibility by a vigorous stream of criticism expressed with candor however blunt. [Dissenting in *Bridges* v. *California*, 314 U.S. 252, 289, 1941.]

The Supreme Court is a forum. Its contribution consists in what it does, in the deliberative process that precedes judgment. An act of judgment based on reason can have a moral force far exceeding that of the purse or sword. Thus the Court's worth consists not only in its restraining power, but also in the part it plays in making vocal and audible the ideals and values that might otherwise be silenced. The Court explores and passes judgment on living issues, on complexities which are at any given moment puzzling and dividing us. By precept and example the Court now, as in the past, is showing us what free government means.

XVI

THE WARREN COURT:
IN THE VANGUARD

*E*IGHT YEARS HAVE PASSED SINCE
the original publication of this book. The Warren Court (some call
it the "Warren Revolution"), now entering its fourteenth year,
continues unabated its myth-shattering, precedent-breaking course.
Hamilton's relaxed portrayal of the Judiciary as a weakling, along
with Chief Justice Marshall's description of the judicial function as
involving only judgment, not will, are revealed once again as gross
misrepresentations. Jefferson and Madison envisaged a more positive
role for the Judiciary, anticipating with warm approval that it would
participate creatively in the enforcement of the Bill of Rights. Fulfilled
is Governor Warren's dictum of 1947: "The heart of any constitution
consists of its Bill of Rights."

If there is any single characteristic of the past eight years, it is the
Court's willingness to speak forthrightly and with greater confidence
on the delicate issues of individual and group freedom. The Court, a
supposedly unrepresentative body, seeming to grasp the implications
of revolutionary demands for freedom and equality at home and in
the world, is attempting to make American life accord with the noble

ideals we Americans profess. Judicial action keeps "revolution" within constitutional bounds, and therein lies its strength. But change, no matter how benign, disturbs many individuals and groups in our society. Actions, perceived as threats to the status quo, are resisted. The Court, like any political institution, must be alert to criticisms so that its actions appear legitimate, not inconsistent with the purposes and procedures as originally conceived and modified through the years.

Judicial history is repeating itself, but not precisely. The Warren Court's dramatic intervention in the governing process echoes the 1920–1936 period in boldness. But in the ends served there is no parallel. More illuminating antecedents may be found in the constitutional jurisprudence of John Marshall. Like the bench Chief Justice Marshall headed (1803–1835), the Warren Court is stirring powerful currents in our politics. Just as Marshall's fervent nationalism evoked criticism among Democratic-Republicans, so the Warren Court's defense of basic freedoms rouses bitter denunciation among those inclined to equate security with repression. Under Earl Warren, as during John Marshall's long regime, the Supreme Court has become a creative force in American life.

Triumph of the positive approach to constitutional interpretation under Chief Justice Warren reflects changes in judicial personnel. In 1959 the Court consisted of Chief Justice Warren and Associate Justices Black, Frankfurter, Brennan, Douglas, Clark, Whittaker, Stewart, and Harlan. Two changes occurred in 1962: Justice Goldberg replaced Justice Frankfurter, and Justice White succeeded Justice Whittaker. In 1965 Justice Fortas took the place of Justice Goldberg, who resigned to accept appointment as United States Ambassador to the United Nations. The effect of these changes was significant. Four Justices—Black, Douglas, Brennan, and Chief Justice Warren, frequently in dissent before 1962, were joined by Justice Goldberg, making a majority in favor of freedom claims. The 1965–66 term decisions, though hardly conclusive, suggest that Justice Fortas is inclined to follow in the footsteps of his predecessor, Justice Goldberg.

It would be a serious mistake, however, to view the Court as divided into two rigid blocs. As the voting in leading cases shows, the specific issue or clash of issues may cause one or more members of each of the major blocs to shift ground. Tom Clark's successor, Thurgood Marshall (the first Negro to sit on the Supreme Court) may shift the alignment solidly to the activist side.

ONE MAN, ONE VOTE

In 1946 the Supreme Court, voting 4 to 3, held that wide disparity in the population of Illinois Congressional districts (8 to 1 in the extreme) did not present a justiciable issue (*Colegrove* v. *Green*, 328 U.S. 549). "Courts ought not to enter this political thicket," the Court's spokesman Justice Frankfurter warned. "The remedy for unfairness in districting is to secure State legislatures that will apportion properly, or to invite the ample powers of Congress." Rarely have the Justices displayed so little realism. Between 1872 and 1929, when Congressional apportionment acts had required districts to contain "as nearly as practicable an equal number of inhabitants," neither Congress nor state legislatures had made a serious effort to comply. To expect members of Congress and state legislatures, the beneficiaries of malapportionment, to destroy voluntarily their own political advantage was to expect too much of ordinary mortals. But whatever the inequities in apportionment of state legislatures and Congress over the past century, the problem seemed less acute when the United States was still predominantly agricultural. In the period after World War II, however, when urban concentration and problems of urban life loomed ever larger, distortion of the representative process had such obvious adverse consequences for the urban majority that increasing efforts were made to obtain judicial intervention, the only practical source of reform. In *Baker* v. *Carr* (369 U.S. 186, 1962) the Court responded, holding 6 to 2, that state legislative apportionment presented a judicial question.

Opposition was vehement. The Council of State Governments proposed a constitutional amendment to overcome the decision. On the other hand, the National Municipal League hailed the decision and its promise of fairly apportioned legislatures, which, hopefully, would show more concern for the cities represented by the League. *Wesberry* v. *Sanders* (376 U.S. 1) completed the "revolution," ruling that Congressional districts must be equal. The Court, speaking through Justice Black, relied on Article I, declaring that the "House of Representatives shall be composed of members chosen every second year by the People of the several states . . ." Justice Harlan, dissenting, fiercely attacked the majority's reading of the Constitution and its interpretation of supporting historical evidence.

Having plunged into the "political thicket," the Justices went on to complete their work. In six state apportionment cases decided the same day as *Wesberry*, it was held that population was the only permissible basis of representation in either house of state legislatures *(Reynolds* v. *Sims*, 377 U.S. 533). Chief Justice Warren found the attempted analogy of state upper houses to the Senate of the United States unconvincing. The unrepresentative composition of the United States Senate, in his view, represented a political bargain without which the convention delegates assembled in Philadelphia might have dissolved. Application of the equal protection of the laws clause to only one house of state legislatures was meaningless. In practice, a malapportioned upper house could frustrate majority will just as effectively as two unrepresentative bodies.

A somewhat surprising reaction to these decisions has been the alacrity with which states have sought to comply with the Court's rulings. Although the two major political parties struggle to obtain favorable state districting, and the state or federal courts have had to intervene when a legislative districting scheme has been challenged, there has been virtually no attempt to flout the principle of equal representation. In a political system professing to be democratic there appears to be nothing inherently wrong with the principle of "one man, one vote." "Legislators represent people, not trees or acres," Chief Justice Warren declared. "Legislators are elected by voters, not farms or cities or economic interests." Apart from the significance of the reapportionment decisions for the electoral system itself, judicial willingness to initiate solution of a problem where adequate alternative means of correction are lacking marks a long step toward assumption of positive judicial responsibility for the equitable functioning of the governing process.

EQUALITY IN LAW AND IN FACT

The momentous 1954 and 1955 decisions *(Brown* v. *Board of Education*, 347 U.S. 483; 349 U.S. 294), outlawing segregation in public education, left several questions unanswered. Would the Court extend the principle of the school decisions into other areas where state and state-influenced racial discrimination are evident? Would it insist on strict compliance with its mandates, or would the lower courts be allowed to determine the pace of desegregation? Would state officials try to circumvent the rulings, and, if they did, how would the courts respond? Finally, what were to be the roles of President and Congress in implementing the Court's rulings? Brief answers to these questions must suffice here.

The Court has continued to apply the principle of *Brown* to all state activity—to public swimming pools, beaches, parks, housing. In addition, the concept of "state action" has broadened to include discriminatory treatment by private persons who have a special relationship to state government, or whose seemingly private action can be attributed to a state action. In a 1961 case, *Burton* v. *Wilmington Parking Authority* (365 U.S. 715), the discriminatory act was refusal of a privately owned coffee shop to serve a Negro. The shop leased space in a building owned and operated by the Wilmington, Delaware, Parking Authority, a state agency. By a vote of 6 to 3, the Justices held that this was discriminatory state action, since operation of the coffee shop was an integral part of the state-owned facility. Nor would the Court permit public facilities to be transformed into private undertakings, thus freeing themselves from constitutional restrictions. In 1966 *Evans* v. *Newton* (382 U.S. 296) held that a city which had operated a park, a "public function," as trustee under a will restricting use to white persons, could not resign its trusteeship and permit substitution of private trustees. Justice Black, dissenting, thought that the city had a right to abandon its trusteeship under state law, and could find no constitutional obstacle to that action. Justice Harlan's dissent, concurred in by Justice Stewart, argued that the principle of the Court's holding could be extended to numerous other private enterprises that perform a "public function," such as private schools and colleges, thus wiping out the traditional distinction between governmental and private action.

The most dramatic issues involving the nature of state action arose from "sit-ins," protesting refusals of service at Southern lunch counters and other places where Negroes had traditionally been denied equal treatment. The arrests and convictions for disturbing the peace, criminal trespass, or disorderly conduct in violation of local ordinances raised freedom-of-expression issues, as well as denial of equal protection of the laws. In the first set of cases (*Garner* v. *Louisiana*, 368 U.S. 157, 1961), state convictions of students for disturbing the peace were reversed unanimously, on the ground that peacefully sitting at a lunch counter was not "disturbing the peace" as that term had been interpreted in other Louisiana cases. In other sit-in cases (*Peterson* v. *Greenville*, 373 U.S. 244, 1963), local ordinances or official statements commanding segregation were cited in overturning the convictions. But in 1964 a conviction for criminal trespass, where a restaurant owner ordered prospective Negro customers to leave the premises, and, when they refused, had them arrested, presented a more difficult problem. In *Bell* v. *Maryland* (378 U.S. 226), the Justices evaded the constitutional issue, holding that state laws enacted after the conviction, but before Supreme Court review, had outlawed segregation in places of public accommodation. The importance of *Bell* arises from the marked division among the Justices as to the boundary lines of "private" and "state" action. Justice Goldberg, joined by Chief Justice Warren and Justice Douglas, argued in a concurring opinion that equality of access to public accommodations was a civil right protected by the Civil War Amendments. Justice Douglas, in a separate concurrence, directly attacked the conception that a privately owned restaurant or store should be treated in law as though an owner's rights in his private home were at stake. A place of public accommodation, he asserted, was dedicated to public use, and the right of all orderly persons to enjoy such use was protected by the Constitution. When the state used its authority to support the private owner's policy of segregation, it violated the Fourteenth Amendment. In a strong dissent, Justice Black insisted that there was nothing in the Constitution to prevent a storekeeper or restaurant owner from choosing his customers. Nor did a claim to freedom of expression justify a sit-in, an improper locale for disseminating ideas. Justice Black, with the concurrence of Harlan and White, seemed much disturbed by the possibility of disorder if dissenting groups chose to act directly against private persons whose behavior they disliked. Justice Black was able to speak for a five-man majority of the Court in a later case upholding the conviction of civil rights demonstrators for trespassing on the grounds of a county jail *(Adderly* v. *Florida*, 17 L. ed. 2d 149, 1966), but it should be recognized that although a public facility was the demonstration site, a jail is usually viewed as a poor locale for claiming freedom of expression.

The enactment of the Civil Rights Act of 1964, which entitles all persons to equal treatment in places of public accommodation, obviously ruled out future prosecutions in the type of situation described above. In cases reviewed after passage of the Act, the Court held, 5 to 4, that the prosecutions be abated, even though a federal statute seems to hold to the contrary *(Hamm* v. *Rocky Hill*, 379 U.S. 306, 1964).

Apart from the effort to define "state action," the Supreme Court has struggled to implement *Brown* v. *Board of Education* and its progeny, reversing lower court decisions contrary to the command to desegregate and upholding those that were consistent with its spirit. But the burden has remained where the decision of 1955 placed it—on the lower federal courts. In the absence of specific rules set by the Supreme Court, each litigant seeking to desegregate public schools or other public facilities has had to convince federal district and courts of appeals judges that what he sought was not only constitutionally required but was reasonable and equitable in light of all the circumstances. "With all deliberate speed"—used in the second *Brown* opinion as a touchstone for determining the pace of integration—has meant in practice that only 2 per cent of the Negro children in eleven Southern states attended desegregated schools ten years after the original *School Segregation* cases. Through adroit use of "pupil placement" and "open enrollment" schemes, officials in many states have found ways of preventing desegregation on a substantial scale.

The desegregation problem that increasingly confronts the courts and the American people, both North and South, is not that arising from legally imposed desegregation but that of *de facto* segregation resulting from segregated patterns of housing. Nor has the Court attempted to provide guidelines, and it is doubtful, except in unusual cases of discrimination in the drawing of school districts, whether any court will undertake a social transformation that more appropriately belongs to elected representatives.

The role of Congress became more significant as the need for legislative definition of rights mounted in step with positive judicial action and the increasing vigor of Negro protests. In 1957 and 1960 Congress passed modest civil rights acts designed to win the right of Negroes to register and vote. In 1963 President Kennedy sent a sweeping Civil Rights Act to Congress, the principal provisions of which prohibited discrimination in places of public accommodation, authorized the Attorney General to initiate school integration suits, set up a federal commission to investigate discrimination in hiring, sought to protect the voting rights of Negroes, and outlawed discrimination in federally financed state programs. The public accommodation provision of the Act, passed in 1964, was upheld under the commerce power in *Heart of Atlanta Motel* v. *United States* (379 U.S. 241) and in *Katzenbach* v. *McClung* (379 U.S. 294). The more difficult case was *McClung* because the restaurant involved was local and was covered by the Act on the ground that "a substantial portion" of the food sold had "moved in commerce." Justices Goldberg and Douglas would have preferred reliance on the Fourteenth Amendment, in which Congress was given power to enforce the equal protection of the laws. The obvious advantage of Congressional legislation is clear. Not only can it reach discriminatory acts by state law or officials but also private actions having a significant adverse impact on minority rights. Senator Dirksen's opposition to the open housing section of the proposed 1966 Civil Rights Act, based on constitutional grounds, seems seriously undermined by two cases, *Katzenbach* v. *Morgan* (384 U.S. 681, 1966) and *United States* v. *Guest* (383 U.S. 745, 1966), in which six Justices indicated that Congress, apart from the commerce clause, has power to deal with private actions which interfere with the enforcement of rights guaranteed by the Fourteenth Amendment.

No matter how clearly the Court may speak, the apparatus of federal law enforcement moves vigorously only in response to executive orders. From 1954 to 1960 President Eisenhower displayed little interest in desegregation. Refusing to comment on the merits of the *Brown* decision, he reiterated that he would continue to enforce "the law." Education was needed, he insisted, to change human attitudes. When rioting broke out, following the admission of a Negro student to the University of Alabama by federal court order in 1956, the President took a hands-off position. In 1957, however, after originally failing to act, he was forced to send troops to Little Rock, Arkansas, to prevent the Governor and mobs from completely frustrating enforcement of federal court orders to admit Negro students to a previously all-white high school. The strong means taken found justification in *Cooper* v. *Aaron* (338 U.S. 1, 1959). Attorney-General Herbert Brownell, Jr. (along with Senate leader Lyndon Johnson) helped achieve passage of the 1957 and 1960 civil rights acts with little help from President Eisenhower. President Kennedy's avowed support of civil rights resulted in increased participation by the Attorney General and the Department of Justice in desegregation suits, as well as use of executive orders to eliminate discrimination in federally assisted housing. Kennedy was more forthright in his dramatic confrontation with Governor Wallace of Alabama over the admission of Negroes to the state university. President Johnson's vigorous assertions of the fundamental correctness of the 1964 Civil Rights Act and bipartisan support in both houses ensured its passage.

The end of the stormy battle for civil rights is not in sight. As laid down by the Supreme Court and lower federal courts, the law is clearly on the side of those who seek equality. But many of those wielding power in local communities continue by legal and illegal stratagems to defend the status quo. The advance is piecemeal and painfully slow.

CRIMINAL JUSTICE

In 1958, when the Conference of State Chief Justices passed a resolution criticizing Supreme Court decisions affecting federal-state relations, one of the chief indictments was the high Court's growing tendency to reverse state criminal convictions, frequently by an independent examination of the facts. Although not all Justices favored its use, the Supreme Court's principal test was the "fair trial" rule. Under this rule the states were not bound by all the requirements of the Bill of Rights, but only those that appeared essential to a "fair trial" in the context of an actual case. Justice Black's elaborate plea of 1947 for incorporating all of the Bill of Rights in the Fourteenth Amendment due process clause fell on deaf ears. For Justice Frankfurter the issue was closed; the matter "no longer called for discussion" (*Adamson* v. *California*, 332 U.S. 46, 1947; *Wolf* v. *Colorado*, 338 U.S. 25, 1949). Frankfurter was wrong. During the 1959-1966 period an increasing number of Bill of Rights provisions were incorporated into the Fourteenth Amendment, thus precluding use of the "fair trial" rule.

One of the most significant advances in protecting an accused person is the requirement that every indigent defendant must have counsel provided by the state (*Gideon* v. *Wainwright*, 373 U.S. 335, 1963), thereby eliminating the previous judicial guessing-game in which the Court decided that a defendant in non-capital cases should have appointed counsel because, in retrospect, he had not received a "fair trial." Thus, the federal right to counsel is made applicable to the states.

In other "incorporating" decisions, the Court applied the federal rule excluding from trial evidence illegally obtained. In a technical sense the Fourth Amendment provision banning unreasonable searches and seizures had been held applicable to the states in the 1949 case of *Wolf* v. *Colorado* (338 U.S. 25), but the exclusionary rule, which puts teeth in the constitutional provision, was not imposed on state trials until *Mapp* v. *Ohio* (367 U.S. 643, 1961). Without a warrant, police had forced their way into an Ohio home in search of materials allegedly used to violate gambling laws. The homeowner subsequently was convicted of possessing obscene materials revealed by the search. But in Ohio and many other states, evidence otherwise admissible was not excludable because of the way it had been obtained. *Mapp* has changed this and made the state and federal rules identical. Mitigating the impact of this ruling was the later decision in *Linkletter* v. *Walker* (381 U.S. 16, 1965), holding that the application of *Mapp* was prospective.

In *Malloy* v. *Hogan* (378 U.S. 1, 1964) the Fifth Amendment rule against self-incrimination was held applicable to the states, reversing a contrary ruling of 1908 in *Twining* v. *New Jersey* (211 U.S. 78), whose "intrinsic authority" Justice Frankfurter had considered invulnerable (*Adamson* v. *California*, 332 U.S. 46, 1947, p. 59). *Malloy* involved the refusal of a witness to answer questions at a state inquiry into gambling activities. The privilege was extended in *Griffin* v. *California* (380 U.S. 609, 1965) to a defendant on trial whose refusal to testify was the subject of comment from the bench, a practice permitted under California law and previously upheld by the Supreme Court in both *Twining* and *Adamson* v. *California*. Here again the Supreme Court took the step unprecedented before *Linkletter* v. *Walker* of refusing to give the decision retrospective effect (*Tehan* v. *United States ex. rel. Shott*, 382 U.S. 406, 1966). The Court has continued and strengthened the application of federal standards of admissibility where confessions introduced in state trials were challenged as improperly induced (*Rogers* v. *Richmond*, 365 U.S. 534, 1961; *Lynum* v. *Illinois*, 372 U.S. 528, 1963).

Perhaps the most bitter controversy has centered on the Court's increasing concern about the circumstances surrounding the interrogation of the accused and the protections given him during this crucial period. In *Escobedo* v. *Illinois* (378 U.S. 478, 1964) the accused had been arrested and interrogated at police headquarters until he made a statement implicating himself in a murder. He was not advised of his right to remain silent, nor was he permitted, despite repeated requests, to consult with his lawyer. In a brief earlier contact his lawyer advised him to remain silent. For a majority of five, Justice Goldberg held that when an investigation focused on a particular suspect in custody, any statement obtained after failure to advise of his right to silence and refusal of access to counsel could not be used against the defendant at trial.

Escobedo produced a storm of criticism. Since it was unclear whether the ruling extended beyond the specific facts, various law enforcement representatives and associations began a drumfire of attack. It was alleged that the *Escobedo* doctrine would make interrogation virtually useless and would, as a result, prevent the solution of many crimes where interrogation was a vital necessity. On June 13, 1966, the Court elaborated the *Escobedo* doctrine, reversing convictions in a series of state cases where confessions had been obtained during interrogation. Combining the guarantees against self-incrimination and the right to counsel, the Court laid down a series of rules to protect the accused against the psychological pressure of questioning in the privacy of the police station. Now, the accused must be told of his right to remain silent, and be clearly informed of his right to consult with a lawyer and to have the lawyer with him during interrogation. If the accused wishes to have counsel, he must be permitted to obtain one before questioning can continue. If he is indigent, the state must furnish a lawyer. To prevent the police from encouraging suspects to waive their rights, the Court warned that, when a statement is made without counsel present, the state must assume the burden of showing voluntary waiver of the suspect's privilege against self-incrimination and his right to counsel.

In *Miranda* v. *Arizona, et al* (384 U.S. 436, 1966) the decision was 5 to 4. Dissenters, speaking through Justices Harlan and White (Justice Clark dissented separately), protested the rule, calling it "voluntariness" in "a utopian sense," "voluntariness with a vengeance." Viewed as a choice based on pure policy, Harlan wrote, "these new rules prove to be highly debatable if not one-sided appraisal of the competing interests, imposed over widespread objection, at the very time when judicial restraint is most called for by the circumstances." Recognizing the probable result of *Escobedo* and *Miranda*, opening prison doors for thousands of inmates, the Court announced a week later that both of these innovating decisions should take effect only in those trials which began after the date of the decisions (*Johnson* v. *New Jersey*, 384 U.S. 719, 1966).

Another unsolved problem arising in the more sensational criminal trials concerns freedom of the press to publish details before and during trial that may influence jurors (or a judge) in reaching a verdict. In *Estes* v. *Texas* (381 U.S. 532, 1965) a conviction was set aside because the state had permitted radio and television coverage of the pre-trial and trial proceedings in a notorious case. *Sheppard* v. *Maxwell* (384 U.S. 333, 1966) reversed a conviction in a widely reported Ohio murder case, where newspapers had engaged in a prolonged campaign to induce the authorities to charge the defendant with the murder of his wife. In addition, the inquest, held in a school gymnasium, was televised and the trial courtroom was jammed with representatives of the press and other media who came and went continuously, badgering jurors and other participants throughout the trial. With a hint of things to come, the Court admonished: "The Courts must take such steps by rule and regulation that will protect their processes from prejudicial outside interferences."

Not all decisions favor the accused. In *Schmerber* v. *California* (384 U.S. 757, 1966) the Court adhered to the earlier holding in *Breithaupt* v. *Abram* (352 U.S. 432, 1957), ruling that the taking of a blood sample from one suspected of driving an automobile under the influence of intoxicating liquor did not violate his privilege against self-incrimination. Justices Black, Douglas, Fortas, and Chief Justice Warren dissented. The key vote was that of Justice Brennan, whose majority opinion expressed the view that the privilege against self-incrimination barred only testimonial incrimination.

Nor has the Court ruled out police uses of electronic devices. In *Lopez* v. *United States* (373 U.S. 427, 1963) a federal revenue agent was offered a bribe by a nightclub owner to clear up a cabaret tax deficiency. After reporting the bribe attempt to his superiors, the agent secreted a recording device in his clothing, and evidence thus obtained was admitted to corroborate the agent's testimony. Chief Justice Warren concurred separately in upholding the conviction, emphasizing that he was prepared to overrule in a proper case the earlier holding in *On Lee* v. *United States* (343 U.S. 747, 1952) where, voting 5 to 4, the Court had sanctioned the admission of evidence secured by an informer equipped with a transmitting device, although the informer himself did not take the stand. No unfair police tactic was involved in *Lopez*, said the majority, nor was the trial use of the evidence unfair since the agent's own testimony was subject to cross examination. But four Justices dissented, Justice Brennan emphasizing the serious invasions of "privacy" resulting from government use of electronic surveillance.

Also favorable to the police was the decision in *Ker* v. *California* (374 U.S. 23, 1963), decided after *Mapp* v. *Ohio* (367 U.S. 643, 1961), which adopted the rule that evidence obtained through violation of the Fourth Amendment was inadmissible. By 5 to 4 (Justice Black voting with the majority), the Court ruled that the police, seeking to arrest the defendant, were entitled, without announcement and without warrant, to enter his apartment with a key and seize narcotics at the time of the arrest, on the ground that a demand of admission would probably result in destruction of the evidence.

Regardless of the actual holding, the cases reviewing criminal convictions make it clear that the Court is committed to supervision of state proceedings comparable to its careful screening of federal trials. Technical rules have been modified to increase the availability of habeas corpus in federal court to state prisoners who claim a federal right after failing to exhaust all state remedies (*Fay* v. *Noia*, 372 U.S. 391, 1963). In a 1965 case (*Dombrowski* v. *Pfister*, 380 U.S. 479) involving Negro defendants active in civil rights, a 5 to 2 majority took the unusual step of allowing a lower federal court to issue an injunction prohibiting a Louisiana prosecution under a law alleged to be invalid. At issue was a vague State Subversive Activities and Communist Control Law; perversion of normal legal processes seemed clear. Nevertheless, Justice Harlan, joined by Justice Clark, dissenting, noted that this decision marked a significant departure from the usual procedure of waiting until state proceedings have been exhausted before federal courts examine federal claims. In resisting changes in civil rights, a Southern state, ironically, further weakened "states rights."

SOME CONTINUING FREEDOM ISSUES

RELIGION AND THE STATE

The hubbub created by the decisions on prayers and Bible reading in public schools has not yet subsided; amendments designed to overturn them are still pending. In *Engel* v. *Vitale* (370 U.S. 421, 1962) the immediate issue was the validity of a short prayer recommended by the New York State Board of Regents as a suitable opening ceremony prayer if local boards chose to use one: "Almighty God, we acknowledge our dependence upon Thee, and we beg Thy blessings upon us, our parents, our teachers and our country." The School Board of New Hyde Park, one of the minority of school boards adopting the prayer, added a proviso that no student was compelled to take part. By 6 to 1 the Court held that this was a religious ceremony and the state, under the establishment clause, was prohibited from aiding religion. Although Justice Black's majority opinion stressed the fact that a state-composed prayer was involved, that element disappeared in two 1963 decisions. In *Abington* v. *Schempp* and *Murray* v. *Curlett* (374 U.S. 203) the Justices held 8 to 1 that school religious exercises, whether the reading of sections of the Bible or the use of the Lord's Prayer or any other prayer, violated the principle of separation of church and state. Justice Stewart again was the lone dissenter. Following each of these decisions, patriotic and religious groups protested that the Court was taking a stand against religion in opposition to the wishes of a great majority of parents, wanting to strengthen the religious impulses of their children. The opposition of scholars and religious leaders to constitutional amendment, however, seems likely to doom favorable action.

Yet, as both friends and critics of these decisions would agree, there is not, and never has been, complete separation of church and state. Chaplains in the armed services and in the Congress of the United States, inscriptions on coins, tax exemption for church activities, all testify to the existence of special attitudes toward religion. The line to be drawn between permissible and forbidden relationships is difficult to justify on rational grounds. Troublesome to non-Christians are laws requiring the closing of stores and other commercial enterprises on Sunday. Stores owned by orthodox Jews and Seventh Day Adventists, who observe a different Sabbath, must remain closed two days in every seven, while their competitors are closed only on Sunday. The Sunday-closing issue became acute only in the past decade, as large highway discount houses began to do a substantial Sunday business, prompting city competitors to demand enforcement of the ancient but frequently unenforced closing law. The decisions in two cases involving discount houses (*McGowan* v. *Maryland*, 366 U.S. 420; *Two Guys from Harrison-Allentown* v. *McGinley*, 366 U.S. 582) were resolved, 8 to 1, in favor of the respective state laws. A uniform day of rest was not unreasonable, the Court declared, and the original and perhaps continuing tendency to select a day of rest significant to the dominant Christian denominations did not alter the essential reasonableness of setting aside one day for rest and recreation.

The vote was closer in two other Sunday-closing cases. A 6 to 3 decision upheld closing laws against the attack of merchants who claimed that the statute discriminated against them because their religious beliefs and the closing law required them to be closed for two days each week *(Braunfeld* v. *Brown,* 366 U.S. 599; *Gallagher* v. *Crown Kosher Super Market,* 366 U.S. 617). There were several opinions, but the essence of the majority's reasoning was that, though the law imposed a burden on members of some religions, it was not purposefully discriminatory. Yet, when an individual suffered more drastically because of religious faith, as in the case of a Seventh Day Adventist denied state unemployment benefits because of her refusal to work on Saturdays, the Sabbath of her religion, the Court held, 7 to 2, the state action unconstitutional as a restriction on the free exercise of religion *(Sherbert* v. *Verner,* 374 U.S. 398, 1963). Nor could the State of Maryland constitutionally require a prospective office-holder to take an oath expressing a belief in God as a condition for taking office *(Torcasso* v. *Watkins,* 367 U.S. 488, 1961). The decision was unanimous.

Clearly the cases spell out increasing concern lest individuals suffer because of the nature of their religious beliefs or non-beliefs, and firm resolve to prevent state power and religious activities from becoming too closely enmeshed, to the possible detriment of both.

FREEDOM OF PRESS AND EXPRESSION

The most notable freedom of speech and press decision in recent years arose as a by-product of racial strife in Montgomery, Alabama. Four clergymen were charged with defaming the police commissioner of Montgomery in a paid advertisement, published in *The New York Times,* asserting that he had mistreated protesting Negro leaders and followers. The Alabama trial court held the publication libelous, since the defendants were unable to demonstrate the truth of several allegations. Under Alabama libel law (and that of most other states) actual malice on the part of the defendants need not be proved. Since the *Times* had refused a retraction, the plaintiff was able to claim punitive as well as compensatory damages; the $500,000 verdict suggests that the jury understood the concept of punitive damages. *New York Times* v. *Sullivan* (376 U.S. 254, 1964) reversed the Alabama decision, holding that freedom to discuss public issues is protected by the First Amendment. Comment about public officials and their acts is subject to libel suit only where there is proof of malice. Justice Brennan's majority opinion, citing the notorious Sedition Act of 1798, aligned the Court with a consensus that the Sedition Act was unconstitutional because of the central value of free political discussion. The need for full debate of state and national political matters, not the familiar balancing-of-interests or the clear and present danger tests, figured prominently in the Court's analysis. The doctrine applied in *Times* v. *Sullivan;* protection for those who criticized public officials from private suit was extended to prosecution for criminal libel in *Garrison* v. *Louisiana* (379 U.S. 64, 1964). In that case a district attorney made disparaging remarks about local judges, implying that they were excessively sympathetic to local vice operators and other criminal types. In separate concurrences, Justices Black, Goldberg, and Douglas argued, as they had in the *Times* case, in favor of an absolute privilege to criticize public officials.

While literary expression is protected by the First Amendment, pornographic writings do not come within the protected area (*Roth* v. *United States*, 354 U.S. 476, 1957). The 1957 case provided no definition of pornography that readily separated it from literature dealing with sexual themes realistically or artistically, or in such a way as to offend or outrage at least a large part of the public. "Whether the dominant appeal is to prurient interests," the test proposed in *Roth*, calls for judgment that rarely finds all men or all judges in agreement. In three cases decided in March, 1966, the Court apparently added a new dimension in the interpretation of obscenity statutes, upholding convictions in a federal case (*Ginzberg* v. *United States*, 383 U.S. 463) and in a state case (*Mishkin* v. *New York*, 383 U.S. 502), while reversing a state conviction in *Memoirs of a Woman of Pleasure* v. *Massachusetts* (383 U.S. 413). The new element emphasized the intentions and behavior of the seller or distributor of the publication. Ginzberg's conviction was justified because his advertising and promotional materials had the "leer of the sensualist," while Mishkin had given clear instructions to his stable of pulp writers to inject "sadistic" and "masochistic" themes throughout their works. The old and respected G. P. Putnam's Sons, publisher of the new edition of *Memoirs of a Woman of Pleasure*, or *Fanny Hill*, as it is commonly known, was more discreet and had the advantage of promoting a book written in the mid-eighteenth century, one which in the eyes of the Court was not utterly without redeeming social importance. The Justices split 5 to 4 in *Ginzberg*, and 6 to 3 in the other two cases. Justices Black, Douglas, Stewart, and Harlan dissented in *Ginzberg*, with all but Justice Harlan dissenting in *Mishkin*. Justice Harlan has consistently viewed state censorship actions more tolerantly than he has those of the federal government, while Justices Black and Douglas have taken a strong anti-censorship position. Justice

Stewart regards only "hard core" pornography as beyond the pale and does not consider the distributors' motives as constitutionally relevant. Apart from the confusion introduced by the new emphasis on the attitude of the seller, *Ginzberg* and *Mishkin* seem to portend a stiffening of the application of obscenity laws to purveyors of outright pornography or to those whose solicitations are indiscreet. The decision on *Fanny Hill* seems to offer continuing protection for most books that can be viewed as possessing a slight amount of social value.

COMMUNIST PARTY IN THE COURTS

The long-running battle between the Communist Party, U.S.A., and the federal government has witnessed a few more skirmishes in the years since 1959 and, on the whole, the Party has been victorious. In *Scales* v. *United States* (367 U.S. 203, 1961) the Court sustained, 5 to 4, a conviction of a Party member for violation of a provision of the Smith Act of 1940, which makes a felony the acquisition or holding of knowing membership in any organization that advocates the violent overthrow of government. Chief Justice Warren and Justices Black, Douglas, and Brennan dissented. The prosecution produced evidence that Scales was an active member, committed to Party objectives, who knew of the advocacy of violent overthrow by the Party leaders. In *Noto* v. *United States* (367 U.S. 290), however, the Court unanimously reversed, for a lack of evidence showing that the Party branch of which Noto was a member advocated violent overthrow of government. Consistent with this conception of the varying nature of Party membership was *United States* v. *Brown* (381 U.S. 437, 1965), where a provision of the Labor-Management Reporting and Disclosure Act of 1959 was held unconstitutional as a bill of attainder. In the provision under challenge, Congress had declared that no person who is or has been a member of the Communist Party may be an officer, director, trustee, or member of an executive board of any labor organization during or for five years after the determination of his membership. Four of the Justices, speaking through Justice White, dissented, arguing that reference to the Communist Party was, by this late date, a reasonable way of designating a set of characteristics that would make officers unfit for union leadership.

In another area of litigation the Communist Party first lost, then gained, a decisive victory. The 1950 Subversive Activities Control Act required the registration of "Communist action" and "Communist front" organizations. A Subversive Activities Control Board, created by the Act, was authorized to require registration of organizations that failed to sign up voluntarily. In *Communist Party* v. *S.A.C. Board* (367 U.S. 1, 1961) a 5 to 4 majority held that the Communist Party, as an organization under foreign control, could be compelled to register. The dissenters argued that the Act, in compelling individual members or officers of an organization to register upon failure of the organization to do so, infringed their privilege against self-incrimination. But to the majority, such a claim seemed premature. The privilege against self-incrimination was upheld in *Albertson* v. *S.A.C. Board* (382 U.S. 70, 1965), where the S.A.C. Board had ordered individual Party members to register, following the failure of the Party or its officers to comply with the statute. Thus the criticism voiced at the time the legislation was enacted—that those required to register under the 1950 Act would be forced to incriminate themselves as violators of the membership clause of the 1940 Smith Act—found acceptance by the Court.

LOSS OF CITIZENSHIP

The Court continued and broadened a line of decisions protecting individuals against loss of citizenship for causes declared by Congress. In *Perez* v. *Brownell* (356 U.S. 44, 1958) the power of Congress over foreign affairs was held, 5 to 4, as justifying expatriation where a citizen voted in a foreign election. But another 1958 case *Trop* v. *Dulles* (356 U.S. 86) invalidated, 5 to 4, a provision allowing divestment of citizenship of a man discharged dishonorably for desertion in wartime. In 1963 the Court invalidated a statute that expatriated one guilty of draft evasion *(Kennedy* v. *Mendoza-Martinez,* 372 U.S. 144). And in *Schneider* v. *Rusk* (377 U.S. 163, 1964) the Court, 5 to 3, Justice Brennan not participating, struck down a section of the Immigration and Nationality Act of 1952 which provided that a naturalized citizen would lose his nationality by three years of continuous residence in a foreign state. The majority seemed to hold that Congress could not discriminate by legislating only against naturalized citizens. Sufficiently substantial ground to justify this harsh treatment of citizens who resided abroad could not be found.

As these and other decisions show, the Court has deep concern for the rights of unpopular or politically weak persons and groups against the claims of government. Without specific reference to that doctrine, the Justices increasingly show a preference for First Amendment rights and other constitutional guarantees of individual freedom and

dignity. In the next section we examine some of the decisions involving new rights of constitutional stature.

THE DEVELOPMENT OF NEW
CONSTITUTIONAL RIGHTS

Most observers, especially the Court's critics, seem agreed that the
Justices have shown little reluctance toward extending the principle
of past decisions into areas that formerly appeared to be immune.
There has been increasing judicial intrusion in pre-trial criminal procedures, and the Court has checked Congress, which traditionally
has claimed omni-competence in dealing with aliens. Legislation depriving citizens of their status for certain kinds of misbehavior and
discriminatory action affecting Negroes and other minorities are
subjected to close scrutiny.

Still another dimension of the Court's work in the past decade indicates a willingness to find new freedoms that are either deducible for
the nature of a free society or inferable from rights specified in the
Constitution. To those who regard a constitution simply as a grander
example of a written contract, the Court's activism seems heretical
and dangerous. Critics emphasize the Court's unrepresentative nature
and cite baneful examples of past efforts to impose judicial conceptions on the good society, bringing the wrath of the nation upon the
judicial head, and, at least for a time, weakening its role in the governing process. In the face of fierce criticism, the Warren Court drives
ahead, and its innovations cover a wide area.

FREEDOM TO TRAVEL

In *Kent* v. *Dulles* (357 U.S. 116, 1958) the Justices held, 5 to 4, that
Congress, in its general grant of power to the Secretary of State to
issue passports, had not authorized him to withhold passports from
members of the Communist Party. "The right to travel is a part of the
'liberty' of which the citizen cannot be deprived without 'due process
of law under the Fifth Amendment.'" The dissenters did not attack
this proposition, which, indeed, had been conceded by the Solicitor
General, but thought that the action of the Secretary of State had been
authorized by Congress.

In a 1964 case, *Aptheker* v. *Secretary of State* (378 U.S. 500), the
Court applied a strict standard of review, invalidating a provision of
the Subversive Activities Control Act of 1950 that denied passports

to Communists after a final order of the Control Board directed registration of the Party. Noting that the right to travel abroad is an important aspect of the citizen's "liberty" protected by the Fifth Amendment, the Court found the statute overly broad and unconstitutional on its face, a fate usually reserved for First Amendment "preferred freedom" cases. In contrast to these decisions inhibiting restrictions on certain classes of applicants, the Court upheld area restrictions on the issuance of passports—specifically the Department of State's 1961 ban on travel to Cuba—in *Zemel* v. *Rusk* (381 U.S. 1, 1965). Justices Douglas, Goldberg, and Black dissented in separate opinions. The Court, on rather shaky evidence, assumed that Congress had in mind the practice of imposing area restrictions when it passed the 1926 and 1952 Acts regulating the issuance of passports, though no specific delegation of the power imposing area restrictions is contained in the Acts.

THE RIGHT OF ASSOCIATION

In a significant 1958 decision, the Court upheld a constitutional right of association, recognizing that advocacy of public and private points of view is enhanced by group association. "Freedom to engage in association for the advancement of beliefs and ideas is an inseparable aspect of the 'liberty' assured by the Due Process Clause of the Fourteenth Amendment, which embraces freedom of speech." (*NAACP* v. *Alabama*, 357 U.S. 449). In the Alabama case the state had tried to compel the NAACP to reveal its membership list as part of a proceeding to stop the Association from doing business in the state.

Two years later, a unanimous decision upheld the right of association against an Arkansas city ordinance requiring membership and contributor lists of all organizations, noting that protecting the privacy of association was essential in many instances to the protection of the right of association (*Bates* v. *Little Rock*, 361 U.S. 516, 1960). Privacy of association, in the Court's eye, should give way only when a very important state interest can be cited in justification, which Arkansas failed to supply.

A more difficult case arose in the 1963 case of *NAACP* v. *Button* (371 U.S. 415). Here, Virginia had amended a state statute barring the soliciting of legal business to include any organization which retained a lawyer to furnish legal services to others in cases where it was not a party. Obviously this was aimed at the NAACP, but, traditionally, states have had wide powers to prevent the stirring up of litigation regarded as socially undesirable. Speaking through Justice Brennan, the Court held, 6 to 3, that the activities of the Association are modes of expression protected by the First and Fourteenth Amendments, recognizing that a majority of the leading civil rights cases had been brought by organizations.

Not all associational activity is protected, as the Communist Party cases show. The Justices did not protect Willard Uphaus against the New Hampshire Attorney General's order compelling him to reveal the names of guests at a camp of World Fellowship, of which Uphaus was executive director and which was suspected of being a leftist organization. By 5 to 4 the Court held that the state legislature's interest in protecting the security of the state outweighed Uphaus' and the Association's interest in secrecy of membership (*Uphaus* v. *Wyman*, 360 U.S. 72, 1959 and 364 U.S. 388, 1966). Uphaus went to prison rather than reveal the desired information. Justices Black, Douglas, and Chief Justice Warren joined in a dissenting opinion, written by Justice Brennan, that stressed the lack of a meaningful legislative purpose in the New Hampshire investigation. Obviously, the search for subversives is viewed as a more plausible ground for obtaining membership lists. In *Gibson* v. *Florida Legislative Committee* (372 U.S. 539, 1963), the Court upheld, by a narrow 5 to 4 vote, the refusal of an NAACP official to yield his membership records to a legislative investigating committee. It is difficult to square this decision with *Uphaus* except by emphasizing factual differences that hardly seem to justify a different result.

ACADEMIC FREEDOM

The Constitution does not explicitly protect academic freedom, except to the extent that freedom of speech might be held to apply to exercises of free speech by students and instructors. Yet, six of the eight Justices who participated in *Sweezy* v. *New Hampshire* (354 U.S. 234, 1957) granted constitutional recognition to academic freedom. At issue was the power of a one-man legislative investigator to compel Professor Sweezy to reveal the contents of his lectures at the University of New Hampshire and his knowledge of Progressive Party supporters and activities. There is a limit on academic freedom, Justice Frankfurter observed, but the state may intrude only for reasons that are "exigent and obviously compelling." While Justice Frankfurter found sufficiently compelling reasons in *Shelton* v.

Tucker (364 U.S. 479, 1960), where Arkansas required public school and state college leaders to file a list of organizations of which they were members, five members of the Court thought that this requirement impaired a teacher's freedom of association. As Justice Stewart observed, "the vigilant protection of constitutional freedoms is nowhere more vital than in the community of American schools." Dissenting Justices thought a knowledge of his associational memberships was a legitimate part of a state's determination of a public school teacher's fitness to teach. Justice Frankfurter's dissenting opinion on this point suggests that, if an intelligent man sets out to find "reason" in a legislative act, he will usually accomplish his purpose. One of the evident limitations on academic freedom arises from legislative investigations, as shown in the 5 to 4 decision in *Barenblatt* v. *United States* (360 U.S. 109, 1959), upholding a contempt conviction of a college instructor who refused to answer questions about his membership in the Communist Party. The questions, said the majority, had a legitimate purpose and were not aimed at academic activities. Chief Justice Warren and Justices Black, Douglas, and Brennan dissented. The conclusion is that, with certain limitations, academic freedom is protected as though it were another right included in the First Amendment.

THE RIGHT TO PRIVACY

Potentially the most important of the "new" constitutional rights is the right to privacy. First suggested by Louis D. Brandeis, in the *Harvard Law Review* of 1890, as a private law right, it entered constitutional jurisprudence in *Olmstead* v. *United States*. Justice Brandeis' pleas that the Fourth Amendment protected a "right to be let alone," by which he meant a right to be free from all unjustifiable interferences or intrusions by the government, did not then command the support of a majority of the Court. In the years that followed, various opinion writers referred from time to time to a right of privacy in search and seizure cases. In *Wolf* v. *Colorado* (338 U.S. 25, 1947), for example, Justice Frankfurter observed that "the security of one's privacy against arbitrary intrusion by the police—which is at the core of the Fourth Amendment—is basic to a free society." In Court opinions and other writings, Justice Douglas has pressed for recognition of a very broad right to privacy, which to him includes several of the recognized constitutional rights and implies many others. As government undertakes programs that endanger human dignity and privacy, "the right to be let alone" assumes greater importance.

But recognition of a right to privacy was not forthcoming until 1965, in a case involving a Connecticut statute prohibiting the use of and the dissemination of advice concerning birth control devices. The Connecticut statute was challenged in 1961 when two married couples and a physician sought a declaratory judgment against enforcement of the birth control statute, which had not been the basis of prosecution since its enactment in 1879. But, in *Poe* v. *Ullman* (367 U.S. 497), five Justices held that there was no judiciable controversy, since the threat of prosecution was not clear. Two of the four dissenters, Justices Stewart and Harlan, thought a justiciable controversy existed. Justice Harlan went further and concluded that the statute was unconstitutional, as an invasion of privacy protected by the due process clause of the Fourteenth Amendment. His analysis echoed Brandeis' *Olmstead* dissent, emphasizing the dangers of new forms of government intrusion.

Invalidation of the Connecticut act *(Griswold* v. *Connecticut,* 381 U.S. 479, 1965) came as no surprise. The vote was 7 to 2, dissenters Justices Black and Stewart asserting that there was no constitutional right to privacy. Justice Goldberg, in a concurring opinion joined by Justice Brennan and Chief Justice Warren, placed heavy emphasis on the Ninth and Tenth Amendments as excluding the idea that only the Bill of Rights was to be included in the concept of "liberty" protected against state action by the Fourteenth Amendment. Justices Harlan and White assigned the right to privacy to the term "liberty" in the Fourteenth Amendment, with Justice Harlan advocating the use of the term as embodying basic values "implicit in the concept of ordered liberty," an approach favored by the late Justice Frankfurter. Justice Harlan also took the occasion to attack Black's argument that only by adhering closely to specific provisions of the Constitution could the Justices avoid reading into the document their own notions of right and wrong. He cited the reapportionment decisions as examples of political ideology enforced by the Constitution.

These decisions "reading in" a right to privacy, academic freedom, a right of association, and a right to travel can be viewed as a reasoned response to governmental actions not envisaged by the Founding Fathers. We know that Madison, in drawing up a list of rights which eventually became the first eight amendments, included those that seemed to him, in the context of that period, to be advantageous. He rejected many of those favored by the majority of the states and

adopted some that had few proponents. What he and the other advocates of a Bill of Rights sought to achieve was the elevation of the
rights of men through their incorporation in the Constitution itself,
which provided for the freest government yet known to the world.
In a Constitution "intended to endure for ages to come" it is hardly
unreasonable for the Court to recognize new claims to freedom in
response to new forms of governmental oppression. A majority of the
Justices of the present Court, at least, find no impediment, in our history or in the document itself, to carrying on their work in that spirit.
As in the past, popular acceptance or denial of this conception of the
Court's role will determine whether they will have a short-run or a
continuing impact on our constitutional jurisprudence.

THE COURT IN SEARCH OF A ROLE

The development unfolded in the above cases under Chief Justice
Warren's leadership did not come as a bolt from the blue. Certain
foundations were laid for it, as we have seen in the *Carolene Products*
footnote. The late Edward S. Corwin, dubbing the judicial "switch
in time" a *Constitutional Revolution Ltd.*, predicted that hereafter the
Justices would pay greater deference to the policy-forming organs
of government and be less concerned with the wisdom of social and
economic legislation. Corwin suggested that the Court, having abandoned guardianship of property, would still have plenty to do if it
intervened "on behalf of the helpless and oppressed": it would then
"be free, as it has not in many years, to support the humane values of
free thought, free utterance, and fair play." Surrender of its self-
acquired role as protector of economic privilege would allow the
Court "to give voice to the conscience of the country." These prophetic words, reminiscent of Jefferson's argument of 1788 in favor of
a Bill of Rights—the "legal check" it places in the hands of the
Judiciary—were written in 1940. Looking back as well as ahead,
Corwin noted in 1941: "Constitutional law has always a central
interest to guard."

The Warren Court's remarkable fulfillment of Corwin's prognosti-
cations has evoked fierce criticism in both the Court and the country.
Among the Justices battle rages over basic constitutional verities —
federalism and the Bill of Rights—and the Court's responsibility
toward them. Upholding the values long identified with the late
Justice Frankfurter, and in the face of his grandfather's assertion of

affirmative Congressional authority in the civil rights cases and of judicial duty in *Hurtado*, Justice Harlan deplores what he considers the majority's mad rush to bring an ever-increasing number of Bill of Rights provisions under the equal protection and due process clauses of the Fourteenth Amendment—at the expense of federalism and separation of powers—the values which, he insists, "lie at the root of our constitutional system."

"We are accustomed," Justice Harlan observes, "to speak of the Bill of Rights and the Fourteenth Amendment as the principal guarantees of personal liberty. Yet it would surely be shallow not to recognize that the structure of our political system accounts no less for the free society we have." The Founding Fathers "staked their faith that liberty would prosper in the new nation not primarily upon declarations of individual rights but upon the kind of government the Union was to have." "No view of the Bill of Rights or interpretation of any of its provisions," the Justice concludes, "which fails to take due account of . . . [federalism and separation of powers] can be considered constitutionally sound."

For Justice Harlan, the decisions asserting judicial responsibility for the one man, one vote principle "cut deeply into the fabric of our Federalism," representing judicial entry into an area "profoundly ill-advised and constitutionally impermissible." Extending to accused persons in state courts the safeguards available to them in the federal courts is denounced as "historically and constitutionally unsound and incompatible with the maintenance of our federal system. . . ."

It is "the very essence of American federalism," Justice Harlan wrote in 1958, "that the States should have the widest latitude in the administration of their own system of criminal justice." Judicial censorship of obscene and indecent literature encroaches on the "prerogative of the states to differ on their ideas of morality," denying both nation and states the advantage of having fifty laboratories of experimentation for trying out "different attitudes toward the same work of literature."

Justice Harlan's wide-flung strictures revive the eighteenth-century debate between Federalists and Anti-Federalists as to whether a bill of rights was a necessary supplement to the protection afforded by federalism and separation of powers. Rejuvenated also is a variant of "dual federalism," the assertion that certain subject matter, notably the administration of criminal justice, is peculiarly within the domain of the states. Justice Harlan's indictment also recalls the charges dissenters Holmes and Stone hurled against the Court when, in deference to economic theory, the justices blocked government regulation of the economy. In 1905 Holmes affirmed that the Constitution does not enact any particular *economic* theory; in 1966 Justice Harlan insisted that the Constitution embodies no particular *political* theory. "One man, one vote" is, he insists, a judicial creation, a "political theory," "a piece of political ideology," reflecting "the Court's view of what is constitutionally permissible." Yet a political theory of federalism and separation of powers is strongly endorsed.

On April 5, 1965, shortly before he doffed judicial robes to become Ambassador to the United Nations, Justice Goldberg made a point-by-point reply to "Brother Harlan." The "incorporation" theory, Justice Goldberg argued, far from being discredited, had made notable progress. Now included among the Fourteenth Amendment's guarantees against infringement by the states are the liberties of the First, Fourth, Fifth, Sixth, and Eighth Amendments. Nor did Goldberg accept Justice Harlan's easy transition from Brandeis' claims for the advantages of federalism in the field of economics to the area of civil rights. "While I agree with Justice Brandeis," Goldberg observed tartly, "that it is one of the happy incidents of the federal system that . . . a state . . . may serve as a laboratory, and try novel social and economic experiments, . . . I do not believe that this included the power to experiment with the fundamental liberties of citizens safeguarded by the Bill of Rights."

Finally, Justice Goldberg did not believe that Harlan's restrictive view of judicial duty would advance any legitimate state interest. Said Goldberg: ". . . to deny to the states the power to impair a fundamental constitutional right is not to increase federal power, but, rather, to limit the power of both federal and state governments in favor of safeguarding the fundamental rights and liberties of the individual."

In the 1963 *Gideon* decision the Court held that guaranteeing a Florida indigent his constitutional right to counsel did not invade any legitimate state prerogative. Since *Gideon* v. *Wainright*, twenty-six states have instituted vital reforms in their criminal procedure. "I didn't start out," the triumphant Clarence Gideon observed "to do anything for anybody but myself, but this decision has done a helluva lot of good. . . ." More equitable representation, in response to judicial command, has not weakened the states, nor encouraged, as Justice Harlan anticipated, "inertia in efforts for political reform through the political process." In time, reapportionment, now in progress on a broad front, may better equip the states to meet twentieth-century needs, revitalizing rather than disabling these essential units of local government.

In June, 1965, Justice Harlan's campaign for judicial self-restraint won significant, though qualified, support from Justice Black, theretofore a fierce antagonist. Justice Douglas, speaking for the Court in *Griswold* v. *Connecticut*, invoked Amendments One, Three, Four, Five, Six, Nine, and Fourteen. In none, however, was there a specific bar against Connecticut's anti-contraceptive statute. Douglas found the constitutional killer in the right to privacy, in "penumbras, formed by emanations from those guarantees that give them life and substance." The right of privacy, the majority's spokesman declared, is "older than our political parties, older than our school system." This was too much for Justice Black. In dissent, he warned against the danger of falling into the judicial trap from which the Court had been narrowly extricated in 1937—the ever-seductive snare of judicial pre-eminence. "Subjective considerations of 'natural' justice," Black warned, are "no less dangerous when used to enforce this Court's views about personal rights than those about economic rights."

"I get nowhere in this case," the Justice went on, "by talk about a constitutional 'right of privacy' as an emanation of one or more constitutional provisions." "I like my privacy as well as the next one," the eighty-year-old Justice commented feelingly, "but I am nevertheless compelled to admit that government has a right to invade it unless prohibited by some specific constitutional provision." Black cautioned against reinstating *Lochner* "and other cases from which this Court recoiled after the 1930's. . . ." Apparently, the dissenting Justice noted, "my Brethren have less quarrel with economic regulations than former Justices of their persuasion had." For Justice Black the result is the same, whatever the orientation of penumbra written into the Constitution to enforce as law judicial predilections.

Justices Black and Harlan dissented again in the 6 to 3 decision, March 24, 1966, declaring unconstitutional the poll tax as a voting qualification. In protest against reading current political theory into the Constitution, Justice Harlan wrote:

> Property and poll-tax qualification, very simply, are not in accord with current egalitarian notions of how a modern democracy should be organized. It is of course entirely fitting that legislatures should modify the law to reflect changes in popular attitudes. However, it is all wrong, in my view, for the Court to adopt the political doctrines popularly accepted at a particular moment of our history and to declare all others to be irrational and invidious, barring them from the range of choice by reasonably minded people acting through the

political process. It was not too long ago that Mr. Justice Holmes felt impelled to remind the Court that the Due Process Clause of the Fourteenth Amendment does not enact the laissez-faire theory of society. . . . The times have changed, and perhaps it is appropriate to observe that neither does the Equal Protection Clause of the Amendment rigidly impose upon Americans an ideology of unrestrained egalitarianism." *(Harper* v. *Board of Education:* decided July 15, 1966.)

At issue broadly, within the Court and in the country, is the role of the Judiciary in a free society; rehearsed is the ages-old dichotomy concerning judicial restraint and judicial duty. The late Justice Frankfurter, an Anglophile much impressed with the virtues of the British system of free government, held that: "Judicial review is itself a limitation on popular government." Of course it is, and that is precisely what the framers intended it to be. But any implication that judicial review is, therefore, suspect as an alien intruder is mistaken. An informed student of the American political tradition might rewrite Frankfurter's statement: "Judicial review is but one among several auxiliary precautions the framers considered essential to the functioning of the American system of *free government*": or, in Corwin's pithy epigram: judicial review is "democracy's way of covering its bet." "Those who won our independence," Justice Brandeis noted in 1927, "recognizing the occasional tyrannies of governing majorities, . . . amended the Constitution so that free speech and assembly should be guaranteed."

The shift from constitutional limitations—featuring federalism and separation of powers, and applied, prior to 1937, to economic regulations—to constitutional limitations and affirmations grounded in the Bill of Rights, is reflected in a host of Warren Court rulings. Cases dealing with civil liberties now claim the lion's share of the Court's work load. In its 1935–36 term there were 160 decisions in which opinions were written. Of these only two were in the area of civil rights and liberties. In 1960–61, 54 of the 120 decisions in which opinions were prepared concerned civil rights and liberties. There were 28 such cases in 1961–62, 42 in 1962–63, and 39 in 1964–65. These figures afford a measure of the Warren Court's dynamic role in giving reality to the Bill of Rights. Fulfilled are Jefferson's and Madison's forecast of 1789 that enforcement of the Bill of Rights would become the special concern of the Judiciary.

The new interest of judicial guardianship, no more than that occupying the Court prior to 1937, has not won full support from the most liberal Justices, including Black. The cleavage, though not unprecedented, is more subtle. Underlying constitutional interpretation in the 1920's was Chief Justice Taft's conviction that as "the Constitution was intended, its very purpose was to prevent experimentation with the fundamental rights [property and contracts] of the individual." The dramatic change under Chief Justice Warren is reflected in his conception of law as a living process, responsive to human needs. For the present Chief Justice, "the issue . . . is not the individual against society; it is, rather, the wise accommodation of the necessities of physical survival with the requirements of spiritual survival." "Our system faces no theoretical dilemma but a single continuous problem: how to apply to ever changing conditions the never changing principles of freedom."

Prior to 1937, the Justices fashioned around the "due process" clauses and other provisions a penumbra of economic theory — laissez faire — to defeat government regulation of the economy. In recent years the Court has woven about the Constitution a cloak of political theory to protect and promote human dignity.

It is often said that the Supreme Court reflects the social conscience of the nation. In the desegregation decisions and others, including the rulings on reapportionment, the Warren Court has not only interpreted and enforced the social conscience, it has quickened it. In the face of delimiting precedents, the Court has taken the initiative in areas more appropriate, in the abstract, for the political organs of government. The failure of these organs to remedy recognized wrongs has driven the Court into untrod fields. Judge Cardozo, noting that *stare decisis* is not in the Constitution, expressed "willingness to put it there, ... if only it were true that legislation is a sufficient agency of growth."

American constitutionalism's continuing theme remains unchanged — the individual and his freedom are basic. But the content of these values is altered. Formerly the Court assumed special guardianship of property and contract rights. Now the Judiciary seems content to leave these to the mercy of political controls. Accorded more exacting scrutiny today are speech, press, and religion, the right to vote, the rights of the criminally accused, the rights of discrete and insular racial, religious, and national minorities, helpless in the face of a majority (or a determined minority) bent on curbing freedom. Just as the Court formerly claimed pre-eminence as protector of tangible rights, so today it asserts special responsibility toward intangible values that lie at the base of our culture. Judicial guardianship of human values was not present earlier.

Reflecting on the constitutional jurisprudence of the 1920's, the then Harvard law professor Frankfurter explained: "That a majority of the Court which frequently disallowed restraints on economic power should so consistently have sanctioned restraints of the mind is perhaps only a surface paradox. There is an underlying unity between fear of ample experimentation in economics and fear of expression of heretical ideas." Not least among the accomplishments of the Warren Court is its alertness to a subtlety to which Felix Frankfurter, as a Supreme Court Justice, sometimes seemed insensitive.

Thanks to judicial review, "revolution" has been domesticated, brought within the four corners of the Constitution. Professor Louis Lusky, who, as Justice Stone's law clerk, helped to write the *Carolene Products* footnote, stresses the close connection between the discharge of judicial duty and the right of revolution. He considers the second and third paragraphs of the footnote as "frank recognition" of the important part the Court performs "in the maintenance of the basic conditions of just legislation. By preserving the hope that bad laws can and will be changed, the Court preserves the basis for the technique of political obligation, minimizing extra-legal opposition to government by making it unnecessary."

In Supreme Court opinion, as nowhere else, it is recognized that, though freedom may be a dangerous way of life, it is ours. Despite the Communist threat, Supreme Court Justices still proclaim Jefferson's bold declaration of 1801: "If there be any among us who would wish to dissolve this Union or to change its republican form, let them stand undisturbed as monuments of the safety with which error of opinion may be tolerated where reason is left free to combat it." A remarkable irony: The Supreme Court, in structure and organization the most oligarchical branch of our government, is bringing us closer to the ideals embodied in the Declaration of Independence.

The story, of course, does not end on this note. In some of the most crucial civil liberties decisions the Warren Court's majority has been only 5 to 4 or 6 to 3, and replacements of judicial personnel are certain to occur in the near future. A living organism, the Supreme Court is always subject to change. Neither its membership nor the attitudes of its individual judges is fixed for all time. If, as Justice Harlan and some others contend, the Warren Court has gone too far in its reinterpretation of the Bill of Rights, one can take comfort in the knowledge that our system affords many ways of correcting judicial usurpation.

SELECTED BIBLIOGRAPHY

GENERAL WORKS

Cahn, Edmond, ed., *Supreme Court and Supreme Law*. Bloomington, Ind.: Indiana University Press, 1954

Carr, Robert K., *The Supreme Court and Judicial Review*. New York: Rinehart, 1942

Corwin, Edward S., *The Constitution and What it Means Today*, 12th ed. Princeton: Princeton University Press, 1958

———, ed., *Constitution of the United States of America*, revised and annotated. Washington: Government Printing Office, 1953

———, *The Twilight of the Supreme Court*. New Haven: Yale University Press, 1934

Crosskey, William W., *Politics and the Constitution in the History of the United States*. Chicago: University of Chicago Press, 1953, 2 vols.

Curtis, Charles R., Jr., *Lions Under the Throne*. Boston: Houghton Mifflin, 1947

Douglas, William O., *We the Judges: Studies in American and Indian Constitutional Law from Marshall to Mukherjea*. Garden City, N.Y.: Doubleday, 1956

Haines, Charles Grove, *The Role of the Supreme Court in American Government and Politics, 1789-1935*. Berkeley and Los Angeles: University of California Press, 1944

Kelley, Alfred, and Winfred A. Harbison, *The American Constitution*. New York: Norton, 1948, rev. ed. 1955.

McCloskey, Robert G., ed., *Essays in Constitutional Law*. New York: Knopf, 1957

Pekelis, A. H., *Law and Social Action*. Ithaca and New York: Cornell University Press, 1950

Peltason, Jack W., *Federal Courts in the Political Process*. New York: Doubleday, 1955

Pritchett, Herman, *The Roosevelt Court*. New York: Macmillan, 1948

———, *The American Constitution*. New York: McGraw-Hill, 1959

Read, Conyers, ed., *The Constitution Reconsidered*. New York: Columbia University Press, 1938

Rottschaefer, Henry, *The Constitution and Socio-Economic Change*. Ann Arbor: University of Michigan Law School, 1948

Schwartz, Bernard, *American Constitutional Law*. Cambridge, England: Cambridge University Press, 1955

———, *The Supreme Court: Constitutional Revolution in Retrospect*. New York: Ronald, 1957

Selected Essays on Constitutional Law, published under the auspices of the Association of American Law Societies. Brooklyn: The Foundation Press, Inc., 1938, 4 vols.

Sutherland, Arthur E., ed., *Government Under Law*. Cambridge: Harvard University Press, 1956

Swisher, Carl B., *American Constitutional Development*, 2d ed. Boston: Houghton Mifflin, 1954

Warren, Charles, *The Supreme Court in United States History*, rev. ed. Boston: Little, Brown, 1928

Wright, Benjamin F., *The Growth of American Constitutional Law*. New York: Holt, 1942

SELECTED BIOGRAPHIES

Beveridge, Albert J., *The Life of John Marshall*. Boston and New York: Houghton Mifflin, 1916, 4 vols.

Corwin, Edward S., *John Marshall and the Constitution*. New Haven: Yale University Press, 1919

Fairman, Charles, *Mr. Justice Miller and the Supreme Court, 1862-1890*. Cambridge: Harvard University Press, 1939

Frank, John P., *Mr. Justice Black*. New York: Knopf, 1940

Frankfurter, Felix, *Mr. Justice Holmes and the Constitution*. Cambridge: Harvard University Press, 1938

Hendel, Samuel, *Charles Evans Hughes and the Supreme Court*. New York: Columbia University Press, 1951

Jones, William M., *Chief Justice John Marshall: A Reappraisal*. Ithaca: Cornell University Press, 1956

King, Willard L., *Melville Weston Fuller*. New York: Macmillan, 1950

Konefsky, Samuel J., *Chief Justice Stone and the Supreme Court*. New York: Macmillan, 1946

————, *Legacy of Holmes and Brandeis*. New York: Macmillan, 1956

Lerner, Max, *The Mind and Faith of Mr. Justice Holmes*. Garden City, N.Y.: Halcyon House Reprint, 1948

Mason, Alpheus Thomas, *Brandeis—A Free Man's Life*. New York: Viking, 1946

————, *Harlan Fiske Stone: Pillar of the Law*. New York: Viking, 1956

Morgan, Donald G., *Justice William Johnson, the First Dissenter*. Columbia: University of South Carolina Press, 1954

Paschal, J. Francis, *Mr. Justice Sutherland*. Princeton: Princeton University Press, 1951

Pusey, Merlo J., *Charles Evans Hughes*. New York: Macmillan, 1951

Swisher, Carl B., *Stephen J. Field: Craftsman of the Law*. Washington: Brookings, 1930

————, *Roger B. Taney*. Washington: Brookings, 1935

CHAPTER ONE

Barnett, Vincent M., Jr., "Constitutional Interpretation and Judicial Self-Restraint," 39 *Michigan Law Review* 213 (1940)

Bernard, Burton C., "Avoidance of Constitutional Issues in the United States Supreme Court: Liberties of the First Amendment," 50 *Michigan Law Review* 261 (1951)

Burton, Harold H., "The Cornerstone of Constitutional Law: The Extraordinary Case of Marbury v. Madison, 36 *American Bar Association Journal* 805 (1950)

Cardozo, Benjamin N., *Nature of the Judicial Process*. New Haven: Yale University Press, 1932

Clark, Charles E., "The Dilemma of American Judges" 35 *American Bar Association Journal* 8 (1949)

Clark, Justice John H., "Reminiscences of Courts and the Law," *Proceedings of 5th Annual Meeting of State Bar of California*, 1932, vol. 5, p. 20.

Corwin, Edward S., *The Doctrine of Judicial Review*. Princeton: Princeton University Press, 1914

Douglas, William O., "Stare Decisis," Benjamin N. Cardozo Lecture, before the Association of the Bar of the City of New York, April 12, 1949. *The Record of the Bar Association of the City of New York*, vol. 4, p. 152 (1949)

Finkelstein, Maurice, "Judicial Self-Limitation," 37 *Harvard Law Review* 338 (1924)

Harlan, John M., Address delivered at Phoenix Club, Cincinnati. Oct. 3, 1896, published in the *Weekly Bulletin* (Ohio) vol. 35-6, p. 196

Harris, Robert Jennings, *The Judicial Power of the United States*. Baton Rouge, Louisiana: Louisiana University Press, 1940

Jackson, Robert H., *The Struggle for Judicial Supremacy*. New York: Knopf, 1941

———, *The Supreme Court in the American System of Government*. Cambridge: Harvard University Press, 1955

Latham, Earl, "The Supreme Court as a Political Institution," 31 *Minnesota Law Review* 205 (1947)

Morgan, Donald G., "The Origin of Supreme Court Dissent," *William and Mary Quarterly*, vol. x, no. 3, July 1953

Post, Charles G., *The Supreme Court and Political Questions*. Baltimore: Johns Hopkins, 1936

Ribble, Frederick D. G., "Some Aspects of Judicial Self-Restraint," 26 *Virginia Law Review* 981 (1940)

Stern, Robert L., and Eugene Gressman, *Supreme Court Practice*. Washington: Bureau of National Affairs, Inc., 1950

Symposium, "Policymaking in a Democracy: The Role of the United States Supreme Court," 6 *Journal of Public Law*, no. 2, Fall 1957

Thayer, J. B., "Origin and Scope of American Doctrine of Constitutional Law," 7 *Harvard Law Review* 129 (1893)

U.S. Library of Congress, Legislative Reference Service, *Provisions of the Federal Law Held Unconstitutional by the Supreme Court of the United States*, pp. 146-67. Washington: Government Printing Office, 1936

Warren, Charles, "Legislative and Judicial Attacks on the Supreme Court of the United States," 47 *American Law Review* 1 (1913)

Wendell, Mitchell, *Relations Between the Federal and State Courts*. New York: Columbia University Press, 1949

Weston, Melville F., "Political Questions," 38 *Harvard Law Review* 296 (1925)

Wilson, Woodrow, *Constitutional Government in the United States*, ch. vi. New York: Columbia University Press, 1917

CHAPTERS TWO AND THREE

Anthony, J. Garner, *Hawaii Under Army Rule*. Stanford: Stanford University Press, 1955

Binkley, Wilfred E., *President and Congress*. New York: Knopf, 1947

"Congressional Investigations, a Symposium," 18 *University of Chicago Law Review* 421, Spring 1951

Corwin, Edward S., *The President, Office and Powers*, rev. ed. New York: New York University Press, 1957

———, *Total War and the Constitution*. New York: Knopf, 1947

Davis, Kenneth C., *Administrative Law*. St. Paul, West Publishing Co.: 1951

Kauper, Paul G., "The Steel Seizure Case: Congress, the President and the Supreme Court," 51 *Michigan Law Review* 141, Dec. 1952

Landis, James M., "Constitutional Limitations on the Congressional Power of Investigation," 40 *Harvard Law Review* 153 (1926)

McClure, Wallace, *International Executive Agreements*. New York: Columbia University Press, 1941

Parker, Reginald, "Separation of Powers Revisited," 49 *Michigan Law Review* 1009 (1951)

Randall, J. G., *Constitutional Problems Under Lincoln*, rev. ed. Urbana: University of Illinois Press, 1951

Rich, Bennett M., *The President and Civil Disorder*. Washington: Brookings, 1941

Rossiter, Clinton, *The Supreme Court and the Commander-in-Chief*. Ithaca: Cornell University Press, 1951

——, *Constitutional Dictatorship*. Princeton: Princeton University Press, 1948

Schubert, Glendon A. Jr., *The Presidency in the Courts*. Minneapolis: University of Minnesota Press, 1957

Spindler, John F., "Executive Agreements and the Proposed Constitutional Amendments to the Treaty Power," 51 *Michigan Law Review* 1202 (1953)

Symposium, "Statutory Construction," 3 *Vanderbilt Law Review*, April, 1950

Taft, William H., *Our Chief Magistrate and His Powers*. New York: Columbia University Press, 1916

Ten Broek, Jacobus, Edward N. Barnhart, and Floyd W. Matson, *Prejudice, War and the Constitution*. Berkeley: University of California Press, 1954

Wilson, Woodrow, *Congressional Government*. Boston: Houghton Mifflin, 1885.

CHAPTER FOUR

Anderson, William, *The Nation and the States, Rivals or Partners*. Minneapolis: University of Minnesota Press, 1955

Anonymous, "Judge Spencer Roane of Virginia: Champion of States' Rights—Foe of John Marshall," 66 *Harvard Law Review* 1242 (1953)

Clark, Jane P., *The Rise of a New Federalism*. New York: Columbia University Press, 1938.

Corwin, Edward S., *Constitutional Revolution*, Ltd. Claremont, Calif.: Associated College, 1941

Kallenbach, Joseph E., *Federal Cooperation with the States under the Commerce Clause.* Ann Arbor: University of Michigan Press, 1942

Mason, Alpheus T., "Our Federal Union Reconsidered," 65 *Political Science Quarterly*, 502, Dec. 1950

Pound, Roscoe, Charles H. McIlwain, and Roy F. Nichols, *Federalism as a Democratic Process.* New Brunswick, N.J.: Rutgers University Press, 1942

Ranney, John C., "The Basis of American Federalism," *William and Mary Quarterly*, vol. 3, no. 1, Jan. 1946

Rottschaefer, Henry, *The Constitution and Socio-Economic Change.* Ann Arbor: University of Michigan Law School, 1948

Schaefer, Walter V., "Courts and the common places of Federalism," Lecture of February 10, 1959. *University of Illinois Bulletin*, vol. 56, no. 69, May, 1959

Schmidhauser, John R., *The Supreme Court as Final Arbiter in Federal-State Relations, 1789-1957.* Chapel Hill: University of North Carolina Press, 1958

Swisher, Carl B., *The Growth of Constitutional Power in the United States*, ch. ii. Chicago: University of Chicago Press, 1946.

Wendell, Mitchell, *Relations Between the Federal and State Courts.* New York: Columbia University Press, 1949.

CHAPTER FIVE

Abel, Albert, essays (with various titles) on the commerce clause, 25 *Minnesota Law Review* 432 (1941); 25 *North Carolina Law Review* 121 (1946); 18 *Mississippi Law Review* 335 (1947); 14 *Brooklyn Law Review* 38 (1948); 35 *Iowa Law Review* 625 (1950); 25 *Indiana Law Journal* 498 (1950)

Barrett, Edward L., Jr., "State Taxation of Interstate Commerce: 'Direct Burdens,' 'Multiple Burdens,' or What Have You," in a Symposium on Current Constitutional Problems, 4 *Vanderbilt Law Review* 446 (1951)

Corwin, Edward S., *The Commerce Power Versus States Rights.* Princeton: Princeton University Press, 1936

———, "The Schechter Case—Landmark or What?," XIII *New York University Law Quarterly Review* 151 (1936)

Dowling, Noel T., "Interstate Commerce and the State Power," 27 *Virginia Law Review* 1 (1940)

———, "Interstate Commerce and State Power," revised version, 47 *Columbia Law Review* 547 (1947)

Frankfurter, Felix, *The Commerce Clause under Marshall, Taney and Waite.* Chapel Hill: University of North Carolina Press, 1937

Kallenbach, Joseph E., *Federal Cooperation with the States under the Commerce Clause*. Ann Arbor: University of Michigan Press, 1942

MacMahon, Arthur W., *Federalism, Mature and Emergent*. New York: Doubleday, 1955

Powell, Thomas Reed, "Commerce, Pensions, and Codes," 49 *Harvard Law Review* 1, 193, Nov., Dec. 1935

————, *Vagaries and Varieties in Constitutional Interpretation*. New York: Columbia University Press, 1956

Stern, Robert L., "That Commerce Which Concerns More States Than One," 47 *Harvard Law Review* 1375 (1934)

————, "The Problems of Yesteryear—Commerce and Due Process," in a Symposium on Current Constitutional Problems, 4 *Vanderbilt Law Review* 446 (1951)

Wechsler, Herbert, "Stone and the Constitution," 46 *Columbia Law Review* 764 (1946)

CHAPTER SIX

Annotations, "Power of Congress to exercise its taxing power to restrict or suppress the thing taxed, or to accomplish some ulterior purpose," 81 *U.S. Supreme Court Reports, Lawyer's Edition* 776-789; and 91 *Lawyer's Edition* 50

Brant, Irving, *Storm over the Constitution*. New York: Bobbs-Merrill, 1936

Corwin, Edward S., "The Spending Power of Congress," 36 *Harvard Law Review* 548 (1923)

————, *Court over Constitution*. Princeton: Princeton University Press, 1938

Cushman, Robert E., "Social and Economic Control Through Federal Taxation," 18 *Minnesota Law Review* 757 (1934)

Fellman, David, "Ten Years of the Supreme Court: 1937-1947; I. Federalism," XLI *American Political Science Review* 1142, Dec. 1947

Lawson, J. F., *The General Welfare Clause*. Washington: Privately printed, 1926

Lowndes, Charles L. B., "Current Constitutional Problems in Federal Taxation," in a Symposium on Current Constitutional Problems, 4 *Vanderbilt Law Review* 469 (1951)

Roberts, Owen J., *The Court and the Constitution*, ch. 1. Cambridge: Harvard University Press, 1951

CHAPTER SEVEN

Annotation, "Federal Police Power," 81 *Lawyers' Edition, United States Supreme Court Report* 938 (1937)

Corwin, Edward S., *Constitutional Revolution, Ltd*. California: Clare-mont Colleges, 1941

Cushman, Robert E., "National Police Power under the Commerce Clause," 3 *Selected Essays on Constitutional Law*, pp. 62-79. Chicago: Foundation Press, 1938

Hamilton, Walton H., and Douglass Adair, *The Power to Govern*. New York: Norton, 1937

Powell, Thomas Reed, "Insurance as Commerce in Constitution and Statutes" LVII *Harvard Law Review* 937 (1944)

Pusey, Merlo J., *Charles Evans Hughes*, vol. 2, chs. 69 and 70. New York: The Macmillan Co., 1951

Rottschaefer, Henry, *The Constitution and Socio-Economic Change*, ch. II. Ann Arbor: University of Michigan Law School, 1948

Stern, Robert L., "The Commerce Clause and the National Economy, 1933-1946," LIX *Harvard Law Review* 645, 883 (May, July, 1946)

CHAPTER EIGHT

Clark, Jane Perry, "Emergencies and the Law," XLIX *Political Science Quarterly* 268, June 1934

Corwin, Edward S., *John Marshall and the Constitution*, ch. vi. New Haven: Yale University Press, 1921

———, *Liberty Against Government*. Baton Rouge: Louisiana State University Press, 1951

———, *The Twilight of the Supreme Court*, ch. ii. New Haven: Yale University Press, 1934

Jackson, Robert H., *The Struggle for Judicial Supremacy*. New York: Knopf, 1941

Mason, Alpheus T., *The Supreme Court: Instrument of Power or of Revealed Truth, 1930-1937*. Boston: Boston University Press, 1953

———, "Harlan Fiske Stone and FDR's Court Plan," LXI *Yale Law Journal* 791 (June-July, 1952)

———, "Charles Evans Hughes: An Appeal to the Bar of History," VI *Vanderbilt Law Review* 1, Dec. 1952

———, *Harlan Fiske Stone: Pillar of the Law*. New York: Viking, 1956

CHAPTER NINE

Cooley, Thomas M., *Constitutional Limitations*, 1st ed. Boston: Little, Brown, 1868

———, "Limits to State Control of Private Business," *Princeton Review*, March 1878, p. 233

Corwin, Edward S., "The Basic Doctrine of American Constitutional Law," 12 *Michigan Law Review* 247 (1914)

————, *Liberty Against Government*. Baton Rouge, Louisiana: Louisiana State University Press, 1948

Fairman, Charles, *Mr. Justice Miller and the Supreme Court, 1862-1890*. Cambridge: Harvard University Press, 1939

Flack, Horace, *The Adoption of the Fourteenth Amendment*, Baltimore: Johns Hopkins, 1908

Graham, Howard Jay, "The 'Conspiracy' Theory of the Fourteenth Amendment," 47 *Yale Law Journal* 371 (1938)

————, "The Early Anti-Slavery Backgrounds of the Fourteenth Amendment," 1950 *Wisconsin Law Review* 610 (1950)

————, "Procedure to Substance—Extra-Judicial Rise of Due Process, 1830-1860," 40 *California Law Review* 483 (Winter, 1952-53)

Hough, Charles, "Due Process of Law Today," 32 *Harvard Law Review* 218 (1919)

Jackson, Robert H., Address Before the American Bar Association, San Francisco, Calif., July 10, 1939. *The Legal Intelligencer*, July 25, 1939

Marshall, Charles C., "A New Constitutional Amendment," 24 *American Law Review* 908 (1890)

Mason, Alpheus T., "The Conservative World of Mr. Justice Sutherland," 32 *American Political Science Review* 443 (1938)

Ten Broek, Jacobus, *The Anti-Slavery Origins of the Fourteenth Amendment*. Berkeley: University of California Press, 1951

Twiss, Benjamin R., *Lawyers and the Constitution: How Laissez-Faire Came to the Supreme Court*. Princeton: Princeton University Press, 1942

Wood, Virginia, *Due Process of Law (1932-1949)*. Baton Rouge, Louisiana: Louisiana State University Press, 1951

Wright, Benjamin F., *The Contract Clause of the Constitution*, Cambridge: Harvard University Press, 1938

CHAPTERS TEN AND ELEVEN

Anonymous, "The Security of Private Property," 1 *American Law Magazine* 318 (1843)

Brewer, David J., "The Nation's Safeguard," An Address Before the New York State Bar Association, Jan. 17, 1893. *Report of the New York State Bar Association*, vol. 16, pp. 37-47

Brown, Henry B., "The Distribution of Property," 16 *Report of the American Bar Association*, 1893, p. 225

Brown, Ray A., "Due Process of Law, Police Power, and the Supreme Court," 40 *Harvard Law Review* 943 (1927)

Corwin, Edward S., "The Basic Doctrine of American Constitutional Law," 12 *Michigan Law Review* 247 (1914)

———, "The Doctrine of Due Process of Law before the Civil War," 24 *Harvard Law Review* 366 (1911)

———, *Liberty Against Government*. Baton Rouge, Louisiana: Louisiana State University Press, 1948

Graham, Howard Jay, "Procedure to Substance—Extra-Judicial Rise of Due Process, 1830-1860" 40 *California Law Review* 483-500 (Winter 1952-53)

Grant, J. A. C., "Natural Law Background of Due Process," 31 *Columbia Law Review* 56 (1931)

Hough, Charles, "Due Process of Law Today," 32 *Harvard Law Review* 218 (1919)

Howe, Lowell J., "The Meaning of Due Process Prior to the Adoption of the Fourteenth Amendment," 18 *California Law Review* 583 (1930)

McCloskey, Robert G., *American Conservatism in the Age of Enterprise*, chs. i, iv, v. Cambridge: Harvard University Press, 1951.

McLaughlin, Andrew C., "The Court, the Corporation, and Conkling," 46 *American History Review* 45 (1940)

Mason, Alpheus T., *Brandeis: Lawyer and Judge in the Modern State*, ch. vi, "The Brandeis Brief." Princeton: Princeton University Press, 1933

Mott, Rodney L., *Due Process of Law*. Indianapolis: Bobbs-Merrill, 1926

Twiss, Benjamin R., *Lawyers and the Constitution: How Laissez-Faire Came to the Supreme Court*. Princeton: Princeton University Press, 1942

Wood, Virginia, *Due process of Law, 1932-1949*. Baton Rouge, Louisiana: Louisiana State University Press, 1951

Wright, Benjamin F., *American Interpretation of Natural Law*. Cambridge: Harvard University Press, 1931.

CHAPTER TWELVE

Blaustein, Albert P. and Clarence C. Ferguson, Jr., *Desegregation and the Law*. New Brunswick: Rutgers University Press, 1957

Carr, Robert K., *Federal Protection of Civil Rights*. Ithaca: Cornell University Press, 1947

"Civil Rights in America," *The Annals of the American Academy of Political and Social Science*, vol. 275, May 1951

Frank, John P., and Robert F. Munro, "The Original Understanding of Equal Protection of the Laws," L *Columbia Law Review* 131, Feb. 1950

Harris, R. J., "The Constitution Education, and Segregation," 29 *Temple Law Quarterly* 409, 1956

Hyman, J. D., "Segregation and the Fourteenth Amendment," 4 *Vanderbilt Law Review* 555, April 1951

Konvitz, Milton R., *The Constitution and Civil Rights*. New York: Columbia University Press, 1947

——, *The Alien and the Asiatic in American Law*. Ithaca: Cornell University Press, 1946

President's Committee on Civil Rights, *To Secure These Rights*. Washington: Government Printing Office, 1947

Race Relation Law Reporter, published six times a year by Vanderbilt University School of Law

Ransmeier, Joseph S., "The Fourteenth Amendment and the 'Separate but Equal' Doctrine," 50 *Michigan Law Review* 203 (1951)

Reppy, Alison, *Civil Rights in the United States*. New York: Central Book, 1951

Roche, John P., "Education, Segregation and the Supreme Court—A Political Analysis," 99 *University of Pennsylvania Law Review* 949, April 1951

Sutherland, A. E., Jr., "The American Judiciary and Racial Segregation," 20 *Modern Law Review*, 201, May, 1957

Tussman, Joseph, and Jacobus Ten Broek, "The Equal Protection of Laws," 37 *California Law Review* 341 (1949)

Ziegler, Benjamin M., ed., *Desegregation and the Supreme Court*. Boston: Heath & Co., 1958

CHAPTERS THIRTEEN AND FOURTEEN

Beaney, William M., *The Right to Counsel in American Courts*. Ann Arbor: University of Michigan Press, 1955

Becker, Carl, and others, *Safeguarding Civil Liberties Today*. Ithaca: Cornell University Press, 1945

Bernard, Burton C., "Avoidance of Constitutional Issues in the United States Supreme Court: Liberties of the First Amendment," 50 *Michigan Law Review* 261 (1951)

Butts, R. Freeman, *The American Tradition in Religion and Education*. Boston: Beacon, 1950

Chafee, Zechariah, Jr., *Free Speech in the United States*. Cambridge: Harvard University Press, 1942

Commager, Henry Steele, *Majority Rule and Minority Rights*. New York: Oxford University Press, 1943

Corwin, Edward S., "Bowing Out 'Clear and Present Danger,'" 27 *Notre Dame Lawyer* 325 (1952)

——, *Liberty Against Government*, ch. iv. Baton Rouge, Louisiana: Louisiana State University Press, 1948

——, *Total War and the Constitution*, ch. iii. New York: Knopf, 1947

362

Dumbould, Edward, *The Bill of Rights and What it Means Today*. Norman: University of Oklahoma, 1957

Emerson, Thomas I., and David Haber, *Political and Civil Rights in the United States*. Buffalo: Dennis, 1950 (An outstanding collection of legal and related materials)

Fairman, Charles, "Does the Fourteenth Amendment Incorporate the Bill of Rights: The Original Understanding," II *Stanford Law Review* 5, Dec. 1949

Fellman, David, *The Defendent's Rights*. New York: Rinehart, 1958

Fraenkel, Osmond K., *Our Civil Liberties*. New York: Viking, 1944

Frank, John P., "Review and Basic Liberties," in Edmond Cahn, ed., *Supreme Court and Supreme Law*. Bloomington, Ind.: Indiana University Press, 1954

Freund, Paul A., *On Understanding the Supreme Court*. Boston: Little, Brown, 1949

——, "The Supreme Court and Civil Liberties," 4 *Vanderbilt Law Review* 533 (1951)

Gerald, Edward, *The Press and the Constitution, 1931-37*. Minneapolis: University of Minnesota Press, 1948

Green, John Raeburn, "The Bill of Rights, the Fourteenth Amendment and the Supreme Court," 46 *Michigan Law Review* 869 (1948)

——, "The Supreme Court, the Bill of Rights and the States," 97 *University of Pennsylvania Law Review* 608 (1949)

Hand, Learned, *The Bill of Rights*. Cambridge: Harvard University Press, 1958

Konvitz, Milton R., *Fundamental Liberties of a Free People*. Ithaca: Cornell University Press, 1957

McCloskey, Robert G., "Free Speech, Sedition and the Constitution," XLV *American Political Science Review* 662, Sept. 1951

Mendelson, Wallace, "Clear and Present Danger—From Schenck to Dennis," 52 *Columbia Law Review* 313 (1952)

Morrison, Stanley, "Does the Fourteenth Amendment Incorporate the Bill of Rights: The Judicial Interpretation," II *Stanford Law Review* 140, Dec. 1949

Pfeffer, Leo, *Church, State, and Freedom*. Boston: Beacon, 1953

Pritchett, C. Herman, *The Roosevelt Court*, ch. v. New York: Macmillan, 1948

——, *Civil Liberties and the Vinson Court*. Chicago: University of Chicago Press, 1954

——, *The Political Offender and the Warren Court*. Boston: Boston University Press, 1958

Rutland, Robert Allen, *Birth of the Bill of Rights, 1776-1791*. Chapel Hill: University of North Carolina Press, 1955

CHAPTER FIFTEEN

Christman, Henry M., *The Public Papers of Chief Justice Earl Warren.*
New York: Simon and Schuster, 1959

Conference of Chief Justices. Report of the Committee on Federal-State
Relationships as Affected by Judicial Decisions. Aug. 1958, Chicago
For the statements in opposition, see Proceedings, Tenth Annual
Meeting of the Conference Chief Justices, 1958. Chicago: The Coun-
cil of State Governments

Countryman, Vern, ed., *Douglas of the Supreme Court: A Selection of
his Opinions.* Garden City: Doubleday, 1959

Douglas, William O., "On Misconception of the Judicial Function and
Responsibility of the Bar," 59 *Columbia Law Review*, 227, Feb.
1959

Harlan, John M., "Some Fiftieth Anniversary Remarks," The New York
County Lawyers' Association, November 25, 1958

Latham, Earl, "Perspectives on the Warren Court," *The Nation*, Jan.
18, 1958

Limitation of Appellate Jurisdiction of the United States Supreme Court.
Hearings before the Subcommittee to Investigate the Administra-
tion of the Internal Security and other Internal Security Laws.
Committee on the Judiciary. U.S. Senate 85th Cong., 2nd Sess. on
S. 2646, Feb. 19-21, March 4 and 5, 1958

Lewis, Anthony, "Supreme Court Plays Vital Role: Deserves Respect
and Support," *Harvard Law Record*, Dec. 4, 1958

Mason, Alpheus Thomas, *The Supreme Court from Taft to Warren.*
Baton Rouge: Louisiana State University Press, 1958

————, "The Supreme Court: Temple and Forum," *The Yale Review*,
Summer, 1959

McCloskey, Robert G., "The Supreme Court Finds its Role: Civil Liberties in the 1955 Term," 42 *Virginia Law Review* 736, Oct. 1956

————, "Tools, Stumbling Blocks and Stepping Stones," 44 *Virginia
Law Review* 1034, Nov. 1958

McWhinney, Edward, "The Supreme Court and the Dilemma of Judicial Policy Making," 39 *Minnesota Law Review* 837, June 1958

Meiklejohn, Alexander, *Free Speech in its Relation to Self-Government.*
New York: Harper, 1948

Pekelis, Alexander, *Law and Social Action.* Ithaca: Cornell University
Press, 1950

Pritchett, Herman, *The Political Offender and the Warren Court.*
Boston: Boston University Press, 1958

Proceedings of the House of Delegates: Mid-year Meeting, Feb. 23-24.
Committee Report on Communist Tactics, Strategy and Objectives.

45 *American Bar Association Journal*, 365, 367, 400, April 1959. See also Ross L. Malone, "The Communist Resolutions: What the House of Delegates Really Did." *Ibid*., pp. 343-47

Swisher, Carl, *The Supreme Court in Modern Role*. New York: New York University Press, 1958

"The Role of the Supreme Court in the American Constitutional System," 33 *Notre Dame Lawyer*, 521-616, Aug. 1956

INDEX

TABLE OF CASES

For cases in last chapter see page 376

TABLE OF CASES FOR CHAPTER XVI